Performing New Media, 1890–1915

Funds for the publication of this volume were generously provided by Northwestern University in Qatar.

Cover image: Two Clowns (Dir. G.A. Smith, c1906).
[Photograph courtesy of the British Film Institute/Screen Archive South East, London and Brighton, U.K.]
Cover design: Monty George of Digitalworx, Evanston, Illinois, U.S.A.

Performing New Media, 1890–1915

Edited by
Kaveh Askari, Scott Curtis, Frank Gray,
Louis Pelletier, Tami Williams and Joshua Yumibe

British Library Cataloguing in Publication Data

Performing New Media, 1890–1915

A catalogue entry for this book is available from the British Library

ISBN: 9780 86196 714 8 (Paperback)

Published by
John Libbey Publishing Ltd, 3 Leicester Road, New Barnet, Herts EN5 5EW,
United Kingdom
e-mail: john.libbey@orange.fr; web site: www.johnlibbey.com
Direct orders (UK and Europe): direct.orders@marston.co.uk

Distributed in Asia and North America by **Indiana University Press**,
601 North Morton St, Bloomington, IN 47404, USA. www.iupress.indiana.edu

© 2014 Copyright John Libbey Publishing Ltd. All rights reserved.
Unauthorized duplication contravenes applicable laws.

Printed and bound in China by 1010 Printing International Ltd.

Contents

	Introduction Kaveh Askari, Scott Curtis, Frank Gray, Louis Pelletier, Tami Williams, Joshua Yumibe	1
PART I	**Performing on the Screen: Actors and Personalities**	
Chapter 1	Lois Weber at Rex: Performing Femininity Across Media Shelley Stamp	13
Chapter 2	Diva Intermedial: Lyda Borelli between Art, Photography, Theatre and Cinema Ivo Blom	22
Chapter 3	Why Sue 'Little Mary?': How Independent Moving Pictures Company of America v Gladys Smith and Owen Moore (1911) Defined Celebrity and Professionalism for Film Actors Leslie Midkiff DeBauche	34
Chapter 4	Camera Distance and Acting in Griffith Biographs Charles O'Brien	41
Chapter 5	Performance Times: The Lightning Cartoon and the Emergence of Animation Malcolm Cook	48
Chapter 6	La transparence du Fregoligraph en question Frédéric Tabet	57
Chapter 7	In the Flesh: Personal Appearances and the Picture Personality in Britain Chris O'Rourke	67
Chapter 8	Performers – Now Synchronised on Screen Ian Christie	76
PART II	**Performing Beside the Screen: Narrators, Showmen, and Musicians**	
Chapter 9	Missing Believed Lost: The Film Narrator, Then and Now Martin Loiperdinger	87
Chapter 10	Standards of Practice in Transition: The Showmanship of Jasper Redfern as It Emerged Peter Walsh	95
Chapter 11	Showmanship Skills and the Changing Role of the Exhibitor in 1910s Scotland María Antonia Vélez-Serna	104

PERFORMING NEW MEDIA, 1890–1915

Chapter 12	Showing Film in Winter (1904–1906): Albert Frères' Film Galas in Dutch Multipurpose Buildings *Ansje van Beusekom*	115
Chapter 13	Performing New Media and the Creation of National Identity: Kräusslich and Köpke in Norway before 1910 *Gunnar Iversen*	124
Chapter 14	Music Programming and the Formation of Swedish Cinema Culture *Christopher Natzén*	131
Chapter 15	'Marvelous and Fascinating': L. Frank Baum's Fairylogue and Radio-Plays (1908) *Artemis Willis*	141
Chapter 16	The Multiple-Media Lecture: *Racing with Death in Antarctic Blizzards* (1915) *Gregory A. Waller*	150

PART III	**Performing with the Screen: Audiences, Educators and Officials**	
Chapter 17	Kinoreformbewegung Revisited: Performing the Cinematograph as a Pedagogical Tool *Frank Kessler and Sabine Lenk*	163
Chapter 18	Health on Display: The Panama-Pacific International Exposition as Sanitary Venue *Marina Dahlquist*	174
Chapter 19	Lyrical Education: Music and Colour in Early Nonfiction Film *Jennifer Peterson*	186
Chapter 20	'Offensive and Riotous Behavious'? Performing the of Role of an Audience in Irish Cinema of the mid-1910s *Denis Condon*	193
Chapter 21	Tango Mad and Affected by Cinematographitis: Rhythmic 'Contagions' between Screens and Audiences in the 1910s *Kristina Köhler*	203

PART IV	**Intermedial Performance**	
Chapter 22	Screening Sensations and Live Performance: the Creative Blending of Traditional and New Projected Media at the Start of the Twentieth Century *Ludwig Maria Vogl-Bienek*	217
Chapter 23	Le spectacle de lanterne magique considéré sous l'angle de la conférence : quelques traces écrites d'une performance orale *Alain Boillat*	227
Chapter 24	Getting to Know the Dutch: Magic Lantern Slides as Traces of Intermedial Performance Practices *Sarah Dellmann*	236
Chapter 25	20 Minutes or Less: Short-Form Film-and-Theatre Hybrids – Skits, Sketches, Playlets, & Acts in Vaudeville, Variety, Revues, &c. *Gwendolyn Waltz*	245

Chapter 26	Between Karagöz and Cinema: Connectivity, Mobility, Collectivity, Collectivity *Canan Balan*	254
Chapter 27	Entre nouveauté et continuité : Le spectacle cinématographique serait-il une émergence des ombres françaises? *Thierry Lecointe*	263
Chapter 28	'Performed live and talking. No Kinematograph.' Amateur Performances of *Tableaux Vivants* and Local Film Exhibition in Germany around 1900 *Daniel Wiegand*	273
Chapter 29	Performing Painting: Projected Images as Living Pictures *Valentine Robert*	282
Chapter 30	Colour as Performance in Visual Music, Film Tinting and Digital Painting *Joshua Yumibe*	293

Coda

Chapter 31	Early Cinema Today and its 'Digital Performance': *The Re-discovery of The Soldier's Courtship* (1896) *Franziska Heller*	305
	Editors and Contributors	315
	Index of Films	319
	Index of Names	321

Introduction

Kaveh Askari, Scott Curtis, Frank Gray, Louis Pelletier, Tami Williams, Joshua Yumibe

Domitor, the international society for the study of early cinema, is a non-profit association for scholars interested in all aspects of early cinema from its beginnings to 1915. As its members know, Domitor is dedicated to exploring new methods of historical research; understanding and promoting the international exchange of information, documents and ideas; forging alliances with curators and film archivists; and nurturing the work of early career researchers. One of its most important activities is its biennial international conference. The first was held in Québec in 1990 and subsequent conferences were staged in Lausanne, New York, Paris, Washington, Udine, Montreal, Utrecht, Ann Arbor, Perpignan/Girona and Toronto. Brighton & Hove, England and the University of Brighton hosted Domitor in 2012 and this book is its proceedings.[1]

Domitor's members have been long involved in searching for and analysing the surviving primary evidence (such as films and documents related to production, retailing, distribution and exhibition), responding to the historiography of early cinema and engaging with the contemporary work of today's early film historians. Particularly apparent is the persistent fascination of these historians with the relationship between early cinema and its various historical and intellectual contexts. These myriad contexts are intertextual and intermedial, and connect early film to a wide range of cultural and commercial practices, technologies, networks, economies, geographies, cultures, identities and ideologies. Framing early film's production and exhibition practices within this wider terrain and determining the nature of these many relationships has defined much of Domitor's activity.

The City of Brighton & Hove provided Domitor in 2012 with an ideal location because of its distinctive screen history. At the end of the Victorian era, it was a modern conurbation on the south coast of England that hosted a vibrant tourist centre. These twin towns, approximately fifty miles south of London, had undergone a radical transformation in the nineteenth century. They began the century with a reputation as a genteel, fashionable royal resort but then, after the coming of the railway in the 1840s, exploded into a Victorian heterotopia of hotels, guest houses, theatres, music halls, piers, amusements, restaurants and shops. Over two miles of the seafront were developed to accommodate this 'pleasure world', known as 'London-by-the-Sea'. Millions each year visited this centre of amusement and spectacle.

As early as 1805 the Royal Pavilion staged a phantasmagoria; magic lanternists would continue to perform in public venues throughout the century. From the 1840s, photographers established studios and promoted this new vision technology. Pioneer filmmakers G.A. Smith and James Williamson (the major figures of the world-famous 'Brighton School') were both magic lanternists before they produced their first films. It was also here that both William Friese-Greene and Smith developed their respective additive colour film systems – Biocolor and Kinemacolor. The latter became the very first commercially viable colour system in the world. Screen work was exhibited everywhere – on the piers, in the theatres and at the aquarium. Purpose-built cinemas appeared from 1910, beginning with the Duke of York's. It still operates today and is the United Kingdom's oldest functioning cinema. Today this screen history is collected, preserved and displayed by the city's museum service (especially the Barnes collection of early English cinema) and by Screen Archive South East at the University of Brighton.

Building upon the society's mission, its past activities and inspired by the Brighton context, the theme chosen for the 2012 conference was 'Performing New Media, circa 1900'. From the 1890s to the start of the First World War, the arrival of film as a technology and as a cultural practice marked the emergence of a new medium. Performance was central to it. Through the use of the magic lantern and the cinematograph, events were staged that reflected the emerging social, cultural and commercial uses of these allied technologies. Given that these screen media were silent and the programmes were built from a selection of lantern slides and short films, these events were effectively always performances; each could combine the activities of a projectionist with the projections on screen and performers who could contribute live music, song, lectures, narration and sound effects.

The growth of these screen media and their performances precipitated the rise of the new film industry and gave birth to the concept of 'the cinema'. Around the world purpose-built cinemas opened for the first time, creating new and distinctive venues. However these screen practices were far from 'pure' (i.e., film only) as these first cinemas were also active participants in the exhibition of films within multi-media performances. Exploring the nature and uses of these hybrid and polymorphic media performances at this pivotal historical moment ('the invention of cinema') and analysing their social, cultural, economic and ideological meanings provided the Brighton conference with its subject and purpose.

Past and present: Brighton 1978 and the digital revolution

Two special events at the conference set Domitor's work in historical relief. The first was dedicated to a discussion on the legacy of the symposium, *Early Cinema 1900–1906*, that was held as part of the FIAF Congress in Brighton in 1978. It was introduced by three members of Domitor who were all at this past event: David Francis (who was the Curator of the British Film Institute's National Film Archive at the time and the organiser of the symposium), Paul Spehr (then at the Library of Congress) and André Gaudreault (then at the University of Laval in Québec). They pointed out that the symposium was a unique event because it drew together, for the very first time, a group of scholars and archivists to view and discuss 550 prints of fiction films originally produced from 1900 to 1906. The ensuing discussion at the 2012 conference acknowledged that the 1978 event launched an approach to early cinema that was rooted in the study of the evidence (i.e., films that could be seen), its historical meaning and an archival impulse to find and restore early work. It therefore very consciously steered away from the generalised, unsystematic and unscientific methods that had characterised a great deal of the earlier approaches to the study of early cinema. This Brighton event was instrumental in the development of a new community of archivists and scholars who were committed to the preservation and study of early cinema, recognising both the value and the necessity of the creation of a shared corpus of evidence and a shared corpus of related knowledge. It also generated a new respect for the preservation and exhibition of early work in areas such as colour (tinting, toning and hand-colouring), film speed, aspect ratio and print quality. The symposium's work contributed directly to the development of early cinema studies as an academic discipline and its spirit informed the subsequent launch of Le Giornate del Cinema Muto at Pordenone and Domitor in the 1980s. Gaudreault, reflecting on the meanings of the 1978 symposium, opined, 'Brighton was a moment of rupture!'[2]

The second special event considered the impact of the digital revolution on not only how we view early cinema (via laptops, tablets and mobile phones) but also how digitised and searchable primary resources are starting to open up research possibilities in dramatic and exciting ways. Two examples serve as powerful case studies. The Lucerna Database (http://www.slides.uni-trier.de) is an illustrated relational-field database that documents magic lantern slides and magic lantern material from a wide range of public and private collections. Based at the University of Trier, it brings disparate items together in a way that was never possible pre-digitisation. Conceived as an organic and developmental resource, it provides the user with free access to slides that capture the diversity of types and genres. The Media History Digital Library (http://mediahistoryproject.org) is a comparable project that is also 'liberating' resources – in this case, film periodicals from private and public collections. The MHDL's Early Cinema Collection (1903–1928) is already very impressive. It includes a run of *Moving Picture World* (1907–1919), the American film trade paper. (Domitor members donated funds to make this periodical available.) Both Lucerna and the Media History Digital Library are in effect democratising key resources, ensuring that scholars, no matter where they live and what institutional affiliations they have, can have instant and free access to this original material.

Domitor does not have a prescriptive research strategy; it celebrates a plurality of approaches to the subject. However it does use its biennial conference to present compelling questions in order to engender new enquiries and new debate. This process brings attention to not just an interdisciplinary curiosity but also to a shared investment in research practices that are rigorous, adventurous and tenacious. To do this well recognises the need to grapple with the historical specificity of early cinema and with the multitude of relationships it had with other forms and practices.

The chapters

Over one hundred papers were presented at the 2012 conference as well as two 'research performances'.[3] This volume represents approximately a third of those papers. The first part, *Performing on the Screen: Actors and Personalities*, considers screen performers, the public trade in their images, and the technologies that shaped their on-screen performances. Beginning with three chapters that focus on the careers of screen celebrities, the section gives particular attention to performers who worked to define artistic and professional quality in the early 1910s. Shelley Stamp's chapter on two of Lois Weber's early productions shows how Weber crafted allegories of female stardom that expanded commercial cinema's potential to confront gendered institutions. Ivo Blom offers an art-historical interpretation on the celebrity of Lyda Borelli on the eve of her screen debut. His chapter interlaces cinema, painting, and popular postcards through the iconography of a star performer in an artist's studio. Leslie Midkiff DeBauche finds another discussion of quality in the Independent Motion Pictures Company of America's 1911 lawsuit against Mary Pickford. These legal records provide Midkiff DeBauche with a case study in the shifting measures of professionalism and skill in the acting trade. Moving away from studies of individual performers, the chapters in the second half focus on how film techniques and technologies intervened between screen performer and audience. Charles O'Brien explores the causal links between acting style and framing in D.W. Griffith's Californian Biographs. His systematic analysis of Griffith's nine-foot staging reveals not only a chronology but also a geography of changing performance styles. Malcolm Cook, Frédéric Tabet and Chris O'Rourke offer connections between live and filmed performance. Cook suggests that the stage technique of the lightning sketch anticipates animation, while Tabet examines the use of the cinematograph by quick-change artist Leopoldo Fregoli; both authors reveal the relative complexity of these sophisticated multimedia performances. O'Rourke addresses the way live personal appearances created a sense of film characters as living personalities. Ian Christie closes this group of chapters on technological interventions in screen performance with a chapter on the spectre of recorded sound in films before 1914.

The second section of chapters, *Performing beside the Screen: Narrators, Showmen and Musicians*, covers a range of local and national cases and examines those showpeople, narrators, and musicians who drew from the period's rich intermedial environment to craft new forms of performance within the emerging medium of film. Martin Loiperdinger explores the role and legacy of the film lecturer through an investigation into how foreign films were localised, particularly in Germany, through the oral performances of lecturers – an ephemeral practice too often overlooked. Peter Walsh and Maria Antonia Vélez-Serna examine British showmen in northern England and Scotland respectively, tracking the impact of medial changes in the film industry upon performance practices. Walsh's chapter focuses on the work of Jasper Redfern in and around Yorkshire from 1896–1912, delineating Redfern's transformation from a studio photographer, to a filmmaker and showman, and eventually to a variety-format, cinema manager. Velez-Serna's chapter is grounded in historical newspaper research and it provides a detailed analysis of the transformation of the exhibitor and the decline of the cine-variety format in Scotland in the 1910s.

Another set of chapters looks at parallel exhibitor practices in the Netherlands, Norway and Sweden. Ansje van Beusekom investigates the itinerant exhibitor practices of the Dutch firm Albert Frères, which was known for its prestigious cine-variety shows in the early 1900s. Focusing on Paul Kräusslich and Carl Köpke, two German exhibitors working in Norway between 1900 and 1910, Gunnar Iversen examines how their itinerant performances deployed Norwegian scenics and actualitiés to help construct a national imaginary for the newly independent country. Shifting from exhibitors to musicians, Christopher Natzén draws on a recently digitised collection of cinema programmes at the National Library of Sweden to provide a detailed study of how the development of musical accompaniment helped shape the emerging Swedish cinema culture, from the early 1900s to the 1910s.

The final two chapters of the section, by Artemis Willis and Gregory A. Waller, look at two specific multimedia performances in the United States and beyond. Willis focuses on L. Frank Baum's 1908 Chicago-based stage extravaganza, the *Fairylogue and Radio-Plays*, which, guided by Baum's stage showmanship, combined live performance with music, lantern slides and coloured films in a two-hour 'intermodal' performance that portrayed episodes from Baum's Oz books. Turning to Sir Douglas Mawson's Antarctic expedition of 1911–1913, Waller's chapter carefully details the resulting non-theatrical, lantern slide and film lecture, *Racing with Death in Antarctic Blizzards*, that Mawson mounted in Great Britain, Canada, and the United States in 1914–1915.

The third section of the book, *Performing with the Screen: Audiences, Educators, and Officials*, examines the relationship between early cinema and the audiences, educators and officials who shaped a wide range of interactions with the screen. Looking at diverse local, national and international contexts in Europe and the United States, these chapters examine the dynamic permutations of cinema exhibition as an intermedial site for intellectual uplift (Kessler, Lenk), social reform (Dalquist), sensorial and lyrical instruction (Peterson), civic activism (Condon) and a rhythmically inspired mobilised spectatorship (Köhler).

Drawing upon contemporary discourses of learning and memory, Frank Kessler and Sabine Lenk's co-authored chapter examines how a heterogeneous group of educators, intellectuals and other professionals, using illustrated lectures and diverse multimedia and multisensory performance strategies, helped lay the groundwork for the early educational cinema *dispositif* in Germany. Moving from the auditorium as classroom to the exhibition hall and back, Marina Dalquist's chapter investigates the wide array of national and international visual media on display for the health and uplift campaigns of the 1915 Panama Pacific

Exposition in San Francisco, and how these modernising performative practices recast the 'sensual order' of progressive civic initiatives addressing sanitation, labour, childcare, education and recreation. Drawing our attention to the affective dimensions of early non-fiction cinema, Jennifer Peterson explores the lyrical and performative imperatives of early educational films, from the use of waltz music to the sensual expressivity of non-naturalistic colour and how these unexpected qualities transported early film pedagogy from the realm of the prosaic to the poetic.

The last two chapters in this section explore new cases in early film spectatorship. Examining early recurrences of 'riotous behavior' (or motion picture protest) by the Irish Catholic vigilance movement's film censorship campaign, Denis Condon gives us a rare glimpse into early audience behavior as 'a kind of spectacular performance' of national identity. Evoking variety theatre's aesthetics of astonishment and stimulation, Condon sheds light on the riotous regulation of audience responses to images on the screen, and provides evidence of the active and activist response of cinemagoers to the individuals and organisations that claimed to speak for them. Kristina Köhler looks at the tango craze of the 1910s and the two dance practices it inspired: dance instruction films and 'dance mania' film comedies. As an alternative to the idea of the 'disciplined, immobile spectator', Köhler makes a case for the early cinematic subject as a 'spectator-dancer' and for the early cinematic experience as a visual *and* corporeal one.

The final section, *Intermedial Performance: Histories & Practices*, looks at a range of hybrid practices in a number of countries. It begins with three chapters on the magic lantern. Ludwig Vogl-Bienek underlines the importance of the long history of performances with the magic (or optical) lantern and how it provided an important technological, economic, cultural and artistic context for the emergence of film as a new screen medium circa 1900. In particular, he emphasises not only the importance of the theatrical nature of a performance (the use of a linear dramaturgical narrative, narrators and musicians) but also how lantern slides and film were often combined within the same performance. Alain Boillat offers a more granular approach to screen performance through his investigation of period lantern manuals in order to recover the essential but largely undocumented verbal component of magic lantern shows. He demonstrates that the directives and pieces of advice relayed by different manuals frequently reveal diverging conceptions of the relationship between the verbal performance of the lecturer and the projected image. While some seemed to subordinate the commentary to the visual component of the show, others, especially in the educational field, strove to uphold the supremacy of the word.

Sarah Dellman's chapter explores how the performance of lantern slides in the Netherlands represented the Dutch, especially how performance both introduced and directed an audience to a particular interpretation of the screen image. As she argues, 'For scholars, to consider performativity in intermedial research is to engage with questions that address the production of cultural meaning.' This perspective leads her to deduce that screen imagery should not be defined as stable historical entities but as mutable cultural objects within a very dynamic context.

Gwendolyn Waltz's chapter focuses attention on the stage/screen relationship by examining the intriguing practice of incorporating motion pictures into vaudeville acts and playlets. Drawing upon extant scripts, films, and even court records, Waltz finds that these multimedia stage acts offer 'a glimpse of an innovative, medially interactive approach to presentation on stage'.

Two chapters consider the legacy of shadow play on early cinema in two countries. Canan Balan examines the early Turkish comedy film series *Bican Efendi* (1917–22) and its hybrid nature between early cinema and the Ottoman shadow play (*Karagöz*), Turkish and Western theatre and public storytelling. Thierry Lecointe draws our attention to the *ombres françaises*, a form of shadow play theatre popular in Paris in the last decades of the nineteenth century, one of the many cultural practices appropriated by early French filmmakers. Celebrated *ombres françaises* shows, such as Salis' *L'Épopée*, more particularly demonstrated that moving images accompanied by lecturers and musicians could be used to develop narratives over long performances made up of many successive tableaux.

The interaction of motion pictures and the *tableau vivant* is the focus of Daniel Wiegand's chapter, which investigates the use of *tableaux vivants* in the small Bavarian town of Nördlingen during the local fire brigade's fiftieth anniversary in 1905. Wiegand finds that the use of successive or sequential poses in the tableaux created a mini-narrative of the events that constituted another kind of performance of 'motion pictures'.

Valentine Robert's chapter explores another intermedial performance practice: using still or moving projections of paintings to enliven sermons, ceremonies, lectures, and catechism sessions within a religious context. These performances adapted famous iconography by projecting a reproduction, using films that had been based on famous paintings, or even incorporating lantern slides of life models posed, *tableau vivant* style, in scenes from well-known paintings, thereby 'transforming these *established* images into *performed* images'. Yumibe concludes this section by considering the palimpsistic nature of both the early coloured films and the digital image, drawing attention 'to colour's ability to add and superimpose meanings onto the moving image' and the performative nature of early experiments devoted to the combination of film, coloured light and music.

Franziska Heller's chapter serves as the volume's coda. In it she examines the performative character of early cinema when it is transferred to the present through digital restoration and the 'performance' of such restorations. Heller employs the valuable concept of the *dispositif* as introduced by Foucault and applied to early cinema studies by Frank Kessler (defined as the complex interrelationships between a film / text and the contexts of production, exhibition, institutions, discourses, society and technology at a particular historical moment) in order to explore the particular case of the discovery, restoration and public exhibition of Robert Paul's *The Soldier's Courtship* (1896) in 2011. This has created, Heller argues, a digital dispositif which is related to but different from the film's original analogue dispositif of 1896 and revolves around the film's 'firstness' in terms of being a first British fiction film and a first digital restoration.

The chapters in this volume reveal that the lens of performance displays particularly clearly early cinema's intimate relationships with a wide range of cultural practices. These include not only those related directly to performance histories (such as those associated with music, theatre, dramaturgy, acting, stars, personalities, lecturers, shadow play, and music hall) but also to exhibition practices (such as programming), venues and audiences, the relationship with allied audio-visual technologies (such as the magic lantern) and the communication of particular ideas and experiences (such as Antarctic expeditions). Studies such as these make apparent the very hybrid nature of early cinema as it emerged as a technology and a cultural form circa 1900. These practices and collaborations shaped the choice of textual strategies employed by early cinema. Performance, we would argue, serves therefore as a key that unlocks a vital aspect of early cinema's complex nature.

Acknowledgements: The editors wish to acknowledge the generosity and support of the University of Brighton for the 2012 conference and in particular Professor Anne Boddington, Dean of the Faculty of Arts, Professor Jonathan Woodham, Director of the Faculty's Centre for Research & Development and the staff of Screen Archive South East. We are also grateful to Dean Everette Dennis, of Northwestern University in Qatar, who dedicated funds for the publication of these proceedings. Thanks also to Monty George for his astute sense of design, and to John Libbey for his continued support of Domitor and its publications. Finally, Alicia Fletcher's expert editorial and organizational skills deserve more thanks than we can offer in these pages, but we offer them here nonetheless.

Notes

1. Domitor 2012 was co-directed by Scott Curtis (the President of Domitor) and Frank Gray (Director of Screen Archive South East at the University of Brighton). On the Conference Committee was Stephen Bottomore, Ian Christie, Martin Loiperdinger and Ludwig Vogl-Bienek. Debbie Hickmott (Screen Archive South East) served as the Conference's Administrator.
2. Roger Holman (ed.), *Cinema 1900–1906, Vol. 1: An Analytical Study* (Brussels: FIAF, 1982). This volume consists of introductions, transcripts of the proceedings and papers. André Gaudreault (ed.), *Cinema 1900–1906, Vol. 2: An Analytical Study* (Brussels: FIAF, 1982). This volume is dedicated to an analysis of 548 films by an international team under the direction of Gaudreault.
3. David Francis and Joss Marsh presented the first research performance: *Dickensian Light and Magic: Dickens, the Magic Lantern, and the History of Entertainment*, a research performance devised for the conference and Dickens' bicentenary. Using two hundred original slides, from early hand-painted to engraved, transfer, and late-nineteenth-century photographic 'life model' sets, and drawing on rare printed materials from the Francis Collection and contemporary sheet music from the Lilly Library at Indiana University (Bloomington) as well as the full range of Dickens's writings and letters, it celebrated and explored his relationship with the magic lantern, the lantern culture of his times, the adaptation of his works to the magic lantern screen and the long cultural trace of his impact on the history of story-telling. Woven into this lantern lecture-performance were the 'galantee' lantern of Dickens's childhood, the phantasmagoria of Pictures from Italy, Dickensian 'dissolving views', limelight and virtual travel, the nineteenth-century literary lantern, Victorian visual culture (pantomime, theatre, panorama, the photograph), London life and London types, Dickens and Cruikshank (through fairy tales and Temperance stories) and the visualisation of his work on screen by book illustrators. Francis and Marsh are co-curators of the Kent Museum of the Moving Image.

   Frank Gray presented the research performance *Brighton School Re-visited* at the Duke of York's Cinema. It was designed both to introduce and to re-consider the work of Smith and Williamson in relation to the work of the conference. Accompanied by Stephen Horne on piano, the first part introduced Brighton of the 1890s and 1900s through a selection of contemporary photographs and postcards and drew attention to the origins of the cinema in the city in 1910, especially the multi-media nature of its early programmes through the combination of film, music, lantern slides, variety acts and poetry. He then considered the relationship between a number of Brighton School films and music and concluded with SASE's digital re-creation of Smith's kinemacolor film, *Two Clowns*, circa 1906.

   On the next evening a reception took place at the Royal Pavilion, hosted by the Mayor of Brighton & Hove, Councillor Bill Randall.

PART I

Performing on the Screen: Actors and Personalities

Lois Weber at Rex: Performing Femininity Across Media

Shelley Stamp

Lois Weber's 1913 film *Suspense*, her extraordinary re-working of the well-worn last-minute rescue scenario, remains the best-known work from her early career at Rex. As Charlie Keil remarks, it is 'one of the most stylistically outré' films of the entire transitional period.[1] Re-making the most familiar of cinematic tropes, and playing the Griffith-esque heroine herself, Weber signals her interest in popular images of femininity circulating in commercial entertainment culture at the time. Two other, lesser-known Weber shorts released the previous year depict the production and circulation of female images in related media: *Fine Feathers* (1912) is set amidst the art market and in *A Japanese Idyll* (1912) commercial postcards feature prominently. Clearly allegorising cinema's own enterprise, both films were made as the star system solidified – with female stars at its heart – and as Weber was becoming a celebrity in her own right. Tracing Weber's career at Rex, we can read the filmmaker's evolving public persona against her own cinematic meditations on popular images of femininity, foregrounding her explicit interest in how feminine ideals were constructed across multiple media forms. Increasingly positioned as a celebrity herself, Weber was evidently keenly aware of cinema's role in producing and circulating commodified images of women, both onscreen and off.[2]

Weber established her professional reputation at Rex in the early 'teens. She and her husband, Phillips Smalley, joined in the company in the fall of 1910, shortly after it was formed by Edwin S. Porter. They began work on Rex's second production (ultimately its first release) *The Heroine of '76* (1911), in which Weber played a young woman who discovers a plot to assassinate George Washington and dies saving his life.[3] By February 1911 Rex had completed twenty films and began a weekly release schedule, issuing fifty-six titles that year, then moving to a twice-weekly schedule in 1912.[4] Weber began writing one scenario per week and continued this prodigious output for at least another three years.[5] She and Smalley acted together in most of their productions and shared work directing. Always careful to credit his wife, Smalley told an interviewer, 'she is as much the director and more the constructor of Rex pictures than I'.[6] Later recalling the time she spent at Rex with her husband, Weber remembered, 'we worked very, very hard'.[7]

As Porter's attention began to focus elsewhere – first on the amalgamation of independent producers like Rex under the umbrella of Universal Pictures and then on the formation on Famous Players – Weber and Smalley were increasingly left in charge of day-to-day operations at the company. When Porter formally severed his ties with Rex in the fall of 1912, the couple assumed leadership of the brand.[8] Early in 1913 the company relocated from New York to new facilities at Universal City in Los Angeles, where Weber, especially, began to assume a leadership role on the lot.

Rex films were immediately celebrated by trade commentators. They represented 'quality of the dependable, consistent variety', according to the *New York Dramatic Mirror*, which praised the company's well-written and carefully constructed narratives centered on a small number of well-developed characters, setting them against large-scale, action-oriented productions made at other outfits.[9] Critics praised the strong performances and sophisticated cinematography. Rex's 'characteristic style' was increasingly associated with the Smalleys, with Weber often given primary credit even in these early days, her 'feminine hand' recognisable in many releases. Early in 1913 *Moving Picture World's* George Blaisdell praised Weber's 'fertile brain', a comment echoed later that year when the same paper declared her 'famous through filmdom for her ability to inject psychological power into her writings'.[10] The following year another critic proclaimed, 'something substantial is always to be expected from the pen of Lois Weber'.[11] Characterising individual filmmakers as expressive artists aided the industry's larger bid to elevate cinema's stature during these years, as Keil reminds us, a fact all the more true with female artists.[12]

Though first marketed by Rex as an actress and 'picture personality', Weber quickly shifted the spotlight to her creative role as screenwriter and filmmaker.[13] The subject of interviews and profiles in trade publications like *Moving Picture World* and *Universal Weekly*, she was also written up in mass-circulation outlets like Gertrude Price's syndicated newspaper column and *Sunset* magazine's 'Interesting Westerners' feature.[14] As Eileen Bowser has pointed out, 'sending pictures of beautiful women to the press was a time-honored way for the newer production companies to get some publicity', and often female players carried the banner of their respective companies.[15] But Weber turned the tables on this practice, emphasizing her creative labor over glamour. She appeared particularly conscious of using her stature as a screenwriter to speak about her broader goals for the fledgling industry. In one of the earliest such profiles, a 1912 item entitled 'Lois Weber on Scripts', she bristled against formulaic plots that relied on happy endings and climatic sequences artificially engineered through murders, suicides, and elopements. 'Don't let us all cut out after the same pattern', she cautioned, resisting the trend toward standardisation.[16] A strong advocate for scenario writers, Weber's comments not only drew attention to this newly-identified craft, giving it weight and depth, they also articulated a forceful view of quality motion pictures. When a professional group of scenario writers began to form that same year, excluding women from its initial planning meetings, Weber protested and received a published apology from Epes Winthrop Sargent in his column 'The Photoplaywright'. 'We are sorry now that we barred the ladies', he wrote, declaring Weber 'a high degree playwright' who had 'written a lot of clever plays' and inviting her to subsequent meetings.[17]

Not only was Weber active in promoting the fledgling art of screenwriting during these years, she also fostered connections to the influential network of women's clubs. In the summer of 1913, for instance, she addressed the Woman's City Club of Los Angeles on 'The Making of Picture Plays That Will Have an Influence for Good on the Public Mind', sharing the podium with a female member of the local censorship board. Here Weber explicitly aligned her background in Christian social work with her filmmaking, noting the 'blessing' of working in 'a voiceless language', capable of speaking to so many on such a large scale.[18] Clearly she was aware not only of cinema's budding role in popular discourse, but also the importance of her own profile as activist bourgeois clubwoman working within the industry. Female filmmakers brought a unique vision to filmmaking and a unique mode of working in the industry, she suggested. She urged her audience to abandon 'the indifferent and often-condemning attitude held up by refined people toward motion pictures', embracing instead the 'artistic and educational potential' cinema held.[19]

By using her growing renown to promote her creative work as screenwriter and filmmaker and by using her public persona to convey a feminine presence behind the scenes in Hollywood, Weber showed herself to be keenly self-conscious about how female identity might be fashioned in movieland. She took an even bolder step when she ran for Mayor of Universal City on an all-female suffrage ticket in the fall of 1913, shortly after California granted women the right to vote, but well before women could vote in most other states, attracting national press attention and not a little ridicule.[20] Reports, predictably, lampooned the feminist ticket, with the *Los Angeles Examiner* noting that Universal City's 'scenic beauty' had been 'perturbed' by 'vociferous election speeches, soap box oratory and woman suffragist campaigning'.[21] Universal countered this rhetoric, suggesting that their newly elected roster of female officials were 'ladies of culture and high ideals … some of the brainiest as well as most beautiful women in America'.[22] As Mark Garrett Cooper has shown, a newly opened Universal City presented itself as a novel environment where work and play intermingled and where traditional gender roles might be reversed, a feature Weber clearly exploited in her campaign.[23]

As these examples demonstrate, Weber's evolving public persona pushed on familiar tropes of femininity – first to assert an image of craft and artistry against the notion of female stardom; next to interject a feminised social conscience into commercial cinema; and finally to connect her filmmaking to a more-or-less explicit feminist politics. Alongside this persona, two of Weber's films stand out for their reflexive examination of female representation: *Fine Feathers* and *Japanese Idyll* interrogate the reproduction, circulation and commercialization of female imagery in the art market and commercial postcards respectively, each plainly standing in for cinema itself.

In *Fine Feathers* Weber plays Mira, a young woman working as a maid for an artist, Vaughn (played by Smalley). Vaughn becomes famous after painting two images of Mira: the first created after he glimpses her cleaning his studio at night, dishevelled and sweaty from work; and a second created when Vaughn again catches her unaware, this time modeling an elegant robe he had left lying in the studio. Capturing and circulating to others scenes that only he has been fortunate to witness, Vaughn asserts his privileged, proprietary role over Mira, while at the same time turning her into an object of exchange. Enthralled by Vaughn's images of Mira, his patron falls in love with her, sight unseen.

Vaughn's exploitation of Mira's image is bound up in his subsequent sexual exploitation of her body, a point the film makes clear when he buys her a dress to celebrate the success of his art show. The dress, and its association with masquerade, lays bare the linked economic and sexual exploitation at the core of Vaughn's interest in Mira. It marks the shift in their relationship from employer/employee and artist/model to lovers, for in the next scene we see Mira wearing the dress as she entertains guests in his home, assuming the mantle of the bourgeois housewife even though the couple remains unmarried. Mira's movement through Vaughn's apartment also articulates the different stages of their relationship. As she evolves from maid to model to lover Mira penetrates deeper into his living quarters, moving from his public teaching studio to the smaller private painting studio adjacent, then from his front parlor to (we

Figure 1: Mira (Lois Weber) poses for a portrait by the artist Vaughn (Phillips Smalley) after he has discovered the maid cleaning his studio one evening in *Fine Feathers* (Lois Weber, United States, 1912).

presume) his bedroom, with the lateral trajectory of her movement mirroring the circulation of her portrait in the art world. The exchange of her image, in other words, is matched by the sexual effects on her body.

That this shift in the couple's relationship pivots on the dress is an ironic reversal of the earlier episode in which Mira had donned a costume in Vaughn's studio in order to fantasise a more glamourous self-image, the notorious 'fine feathers' of the film's title, an allusion to the ironic proverb 'fine feathers make fine birds'. If at first Mira was playing with class masquerade, fantasising how malleable social boundaries might be; here she is masquerading as married, a fact that outrages Vaughn's patron when he discovers she is not wearing a wedding band. Humiliated, Mira asks Vaughn to marry her and 'legitimate' their sexual liaison. When he refuses to do so, she leaves, casting off the dress, and in doing so rejecting the roles Vaughn has created for her as surrogate spouse and glamourous woman. Indeed, the 'fine feathers' Mira had longed for are false: one cannot simply pretend to be woman of privilege in order to transcend one's class background anymore than one can perform a semblance of marital propriety to mask a carnal relationship.

Though Vaughn does consent to marriage in the end, their liaison is forever compromised by its illegitimate performance. It is presented as nothing more than the evolution of Mira's role from cleaning obligations in the backroom to hostessing obligations in the front room and (unspoken) sexual obligations in the bedroom.

Released just six months later, *A Japanese Idyll* offers a similarly self-conscious meditation on the reproduction and commodification of the female image. In this case, the context is photography rather than painting, but again the story depicts a struggle for control over the circulation of a woman's portrait. Set in Japan, the story depicts Cherry Blossom's efforts to wrest herself from a marriage to a wealthy merchant. Without ever meeting or seeing her in person, the merchant has fallen in love with Cherry Blossom after glimpsing a portrait of her secretly taken by a western photographer and reproduced on a commercial postcard. He proposes the idea of marriage to her parents, who are delighted. Eager to get rid of the merchant, Cherry Blossom scares him away upon their first meeting by wearing western clothing borrowed from her American friend and making 'ugly' faces, thereby freeing herself to elope with her sweetheart.

Photography and desire are foregrounded from the outset. Scenes of the wealthy merchant gazing adoringly at Cherry Blossom's postcard are inter-cut with those of her secret liaisons with her lover in her back garden, a juxtaposition that clearly poses the merchant's idealisation of her image against the reality of her own desire. All three men – the western photographer, the infatuated merchant and Cherry Blossom's lover – are linked in their voyeuristic relation to her. Both the photographer and the suitor watch her, unseen, from identical vantage points, then the merchant falls in love with a photo taken from one of these same views. So even as the film ostensibly makes distinctions between each man's interest – purely commercial on the part of the photographer, blind passion on the merchant's part, and 'true' love on the suitor's part – in fact each man objectifies Cherry Blossom in a similar manner. By capturing, then marketing, her image, the photographer commodifies an experience both he and her lover have already had.

By setting the story in Japan, the film makes a further commentary on the racial dynamics of this situation.[24] The western photographer exoticises Cherry Blossom, ironically marketing this portrait of racial exoticism back to a Japanese man. It is not until the merchant sees her outside of her exoticised orientalism – when she dons western dress and makes unflattering faces – that he can shed his infatuation. Given that all Japanese characters, including Cherry Blossom, are played by white actors in 'yellow face', the film engages a further level of

Figure 2: Cherry Blossom's image circulates amongst male hands on a commercial postcard in *A Japanese Idyll* (Lois Weber, United States, 1912).

performativity. There is nothing 'real' at all about the eroticised, orientalised female image that circulates on the postcard.

In a film about secrecy, exhibitionism and voyeurism, both diegetic space and screen space become crucial vectors. There are three principal spaces at Cherry Blossom's home: the back garden when she meets her lover, the interior room where the family greets guests, and the rear porch that straddles these two spaces, separated from the house only by a shoji screen. Cherry Blossom is the only character who navigates all three realms, lending her a certain control and knowledge that other characters lack. The shoji screen, in particular, becomes a crucial prop that Cherry Blossom employs to control space: she uses it to conceal her trysts, at one point even canoodling with her sweetheart while the parents broker a deal with the merchant on the other side of the screen. Later she sneaks through the screen to meet her lover and elope.

Ultimately, *A Japanese Idyll* is about relative hierarchies of seeing and knowledge. Cherry Blossom is objectified, without her knowledge, by both the photographer who snaps her picture unaware and the merchant who falls madly in love with the image. In both cases, seeing without being seen oneself confers a certain amount of power onto the voyeur. But Cherry Blossom succeeds in reversing this dynamic, first by taking charge of her own representation in such a manner that she scares off her would-be husband; then by successfully concealing her love affair from her parents and allowing herself to elope. In both cases she is able to control who sees what, when. Although the ending does not produce as radical a critique of marriage and domesticity as Weber achieves in *Fine Feathers*, *A Japanese Idyll* pursues an even more self-conscious exploration of the particularly cinematic representations of femininity through its use of racialised performance, diegetic screens, and its elaborate play on seeing and being seen.

These two films, made during a time when Weber was herself the object of increasing public fascination, reveal her to be very self conscious about the production and circulation of images of women in the art market and mass-produced postcards, clear stand-ins for American movie culture. Weber also appears to have been very self conscious about her own image as a woman at work in early Hollywood, sidestepping her initial branding as an actress in favour of asserting her creative role as scenarist and filmmaker, using her association with feminine propriety to insist on films of social conscience and purpose, then finally claiming the legitimacy of female leadership in Hollywood. As Mayor of Universal City, Weber took on an increasingly prominent role not only at the studio, but as the face of feminine uplift in Hollywood. Her public comments on the industry, and on screenwriting in particular, suggest, however, that she was much more than the matronly do-gooder some thought her to be at the time. If we look again at the screenwriting methods Weber espoused in interviews, we see that when she disparaged simple happy endings in favour of more complicated plots, she was not just rejecting pat filmmaking formulas; she was calling for a wholesale re-thinking of the trope of heterosexual romance that, even then, governed cinematic narratives. When Weber advocated nuanced character development over action and spectacle, she was not just rejecting the trend towards sensationalism; she was demanding that we re-think roles typically assigned to men and women on screen.

The films Weber produced at Rex, while continually noted for their exceptional cinematography, well-crafted staging, nuanced performances and original storylines, were also advancing quite radical critiques of gender roles, patriarchal institutions, and mass culture itself. They are evidence of the commanding role that Weber envisioned for the medium just as it began to assume its status as the nation's premiere commercial entertainment – a capacity to reimagine feminine ideals both on- and off-screen.

Notes

1. Charlie Keil, *Early American Cinema in Transition: Story, Style, and Filmmaking, 1907–1913* (Madison: University of Wisconsin Press, 2001), 196.
2. In their essays for this volume, Leslie Midkiff DeBauche and Ivo Blom provide two other compelling examples. Whether Lois Weber, Mary Pickford or Lyda Borelli, complex negotiations surrounding female stardom during this era turned on the reproduction and circulation of women's images in commercial culture.
3. *New York Dramatic Mirror* (22 February 1911): 32; and *Moving Picture World* (25 February 1911): 373. *Moving Picture World* will hereafter be abbreviated as *MPW*.
4. George Blaisdell, "Phillips Smalley Talks", *MPW* (24 January 1914): 399; "Rex Company Success", *MPW* (27 January 1912): 269; H.F. Hoffman, "The Rex Director", *MPW* (24 February

1912): 674; "The First Birthday of Rex", *MPW* (24 February 1912): 671; and Charles Musser, *Before the Nickelodeon: Edwin S. Porter and the Edison Manufacturing Company* (Berkeley: University of California Press, 1991), 459–465.

5. "Miss Weber Has Record of One Script A Week for Three Years", *Universal Weekly* (14 February 1914): 17; and "Lois Weber's Remarkable Record", *MPW* (21 February 1914): 975.
6. Mabel Condon, "Sans Grease Paint and Wig", *Motography* (24 January 1914): 58.
7. L.H. Johnson, "A Lady General of the Picture Army", *Photoplay* (June 1915): 42.
8. "E.S. Porter Resigns from Universal", *MPW* (2 November 1912): 44; and Musser, *Before the Nickelodeon*, 463–465.
9. "Rex Company Success", *New York Dramatic Mirror* (23 August 1911): 20.
10. George Blaisdell, "At the Sign of the Flaming Arcs", *MPW* (5 April 1913): 59; and "Shadows of Life", *MPW* (4 October 1913): 51.
11. *MPW* (13 June 1914): 1541.
12. Keil, *Early American Cinema*, 126.
13. *MPW* (22 April 1911): 916; *MPW* (29 April 1911): 940; and "Players' Personalities", *Photoplay* (October 1912): 86.
14. See for example: Gertrude M. Price, "Should All Plays End Happily? Woman Movie Director Says 'No'. 'Yes' is Dictum of Managers", *New Orleans Statesman* (26 September 1913): n.p., env. 2518, Robinson Locke Collection, New York Public Library for the Performing Arts (hereafter RLC); "Lois Weber – Mrs. Phillips Smalley", *Universal Weekly* (4 October 1913): 8; and Bertha H. Smith, "A Perpetual Leading Lady", *Sunset* 32, no. 3 (March 1914): 634–636.
15. Eileen Bowser, *The Transformation of Cinema, 1907–1915* (New York: Scribner, 1990), 117.
16. "Lois Weber on Scripts", *MPW* (19 October 1912): 241.
17. Epes Winthrop Sargent, "The Photoplaywright", *MPW* (7 September 1912): 972. For more on this episode, see Torey Liepa, "Figures of Silent Speech: Silent Film Dialogue and the American Vernacular, 1909–16" (Ph.D. Dissertation, New York University, 2008), 194–195.
18. "High Standard of Pictures is Urged", *Exhibitors' Times* (9 August 1913): 7, 19–20, 22; and George Blaisdell, "At the Sign of the Flaming Arcs", *MPW* (9 August 1913): 640.
19. "High Standard of Pictures is Urged", 19.
20. "'Movie' Actress Runs for Mayor of Infant Town", *Los Angeles Examiner* (12 May 1913), n.p., Los Angeles Examiner Clipping Files, Special Collections, University of Southern California; "Miss Weber Heads Slate of Movie Actresses That Oppose Men at Election", n.d., n.p., env. 2518, RLC; "In Woman's Realm", *New York Telegraph* (10 June 1913), n.p., env. 2518, RLC; and *Photoplay* (September 1913): 73. Weber initially lost the election to studio manager A.M. Kennedy, but was elected to replace him as Mayor when he resigned from the studio later that summer.
21. "'Movie' Actress Runs for Mayor of Infant Town", n.p.
22. "Where Work is Play and Play is Work", *Universal Weekly* (27 December 1913): 5.
23. Mark Garrett Cooper, *Universal Women: Filmmaking and Institutional Change in Early Hollywood* (Urbana: University of Illinois Press, 2010), 45–89.
24. As Gregory Waller demonstrates, a significant number of American-made films 'put Japan on view' during these years. See Waller, "Japan on American Screens, 1908–1915", in Richard Abel, Giorgio Bertellini and Rob King (eds), *Early Cinema and the 'National'* (New Barnet: John Libbey, 2008), 137–150.

2

Diva Intermedial: Lyda Borelli between Art, Photography, Theatre and Cinema

Ivo Blom

Introduction

Media critics are still taken with the modernist myth of medium specificity through their emphasis on medial differences. Starting from a digital visual media perspective, however, Jay Bolter and Richard Grusin argue that the cultural significance of visual media instead lies in their tributes and references to, and their remodelling of, previous media.[1] So as photography seeks to reinterpret painting, cinema does with painting, photography, and theatre. Studies into intermediality take this one step further. In her 2005 article, 'Intermediality, Intertextuality and Remediation: A Literary Perspective on Intermediality', Irina Rajewsky refers to Sybille Krämer's concept of media-recognition (Medienerkenntnis), to Jens Schröter's idea of ontological intermediality, and to André Gaudreault and Frances Marion's contention that 'it is through intermediality, through a concern with the intermedial, that a medium is understood'.[2] A case study showed me how much the image of the diva in the Italian cinema of the 1910s owes not only to theatre but also to painting and photography. Here, I thought, is a case of inter-mediality, or rather, of inter-visuality.[3] In this analysis of the representation of the Italian diva in painting, photography and cinema, we will have a 'cast of characters' whose protagonists are the painter Cesare Tallone, the photographer Emilio Sommariva, and the actress Lyda Borelli. I invite you to join me in tracing the pedigree of a particular iconography.

The key to my research and to these three protagonists is an April 1911 photograph entitled *Nello studio del pittore* (In the painter's studio) by the Milanese photographer Emilio Sommariva. A synthetic photograph, it unites painting and theatre, and foreshadows the cinema as well. It has also been chosen as the starting point of the excellent essay by Giovanna Ginex, 'Donne divine

Figure 1: *Nello studio del pittore* (Emilio Sommariva 1911).
[Courtesy Biblioteca Braidense di Brera, Milan.]

nei ritratti di Emilio Sommariva' (Divine Women in the Portraits of Emilio Sommariva) in her book *Divine. Emilio Sommariva fotografo. Opere scelte 1910–1930* (2004).[4] In the photo, you see Cesare Tallone's studio. On the right sits the Milanese painter himself, appearing to have just finished a portrait of a woman. To his left is his model, Lyda Borelli. Already famous as a theatre actress, Borelli would make her film debut two years later in 1913. She inspired her own cult of the diva called *borellismo*. In the photograph, she assumes the same pose as in the portrait. We can also see two other Tallone portraits of the Milanese editor Ettore Baldini and the actress Lina Cavalieri, considered the most beautiful woman in the world at the beginning of the twentieth century, on the picture's left.

We get a better view of Borelli in another Sommariva photo.?[5] She is standing on a podium in front of a false column; behind her, a carpet hangs from the

Figure 2: *Lyda Borelli* (Cesare Tallone 1911). Italian postcard, unknown editor. [Collection Ivo Blom, Amsterdam.]

wall. She wears a fancy dress, leaving her shoulders and arms bare. She has put one leg in front of the other and her hands are lifting the transparent top layer of the dress. Holding her head so that her neck is revealed, Borelli's half-blonde, undulating hair – one of her glories – falls luxuriantly down her back.

The oil portrait of Borelli photographed by Sommariva was painted by Cesare

Figure 3: *Lyda Borelli as Salomè*
(Emilio Sommariva 1911).
[Courtesy Biblioteca Braidense di Brera, Milan.]

Tallone in 1911. It is a larger than life painting of 248cm x 112cm. Notice that her hair is more blonde than in the photograph, a trait common in painted portraits of Borelli. Tallone painted her as a strawberry blonde in the manner of the Pre-Raphaelites. Other painters portrayed her with flaxen hair, which coincides with accounts of girls dying their hair to look more like their idol. The reputation of the blonde diva was at least partially due, then, to her representation in the visual arts.

In Tallone's portrait, Borelli wears a yellowish green dress from which black transparent veils hang down. She lifts the veils sideways with her hands, showing the folds. Only her front leg is revealed as is her chest, shoulders, arms, neck, and face. Her expression corresponds with that of the tragedienne, according to books on theatrical pose: the raised eyebrows indicate pain and suffering, her eyes are narrowed, her mouth half open. She is placed against a decorative background, and like it, the podium on which she stands displays floral motifs. Real flowers are lying at the feet of the diva as if they were just thrown there by an audience. Presumably this was the inspiration for this painting: Borelli bows in front of a theatre audience and lifts the folds of her dress. The dress refers to her greatest stage triumph: her interpretation of Salome in Oscar Wilde's eponymously titled play.

This painting, and Sommariva's photographic staging of the process of portraiture, raises intermedial questions about painting, photography and cinema. First, where do we situate Tallone's portrait within his oeuvre and, more generally within Italian portrait painting around 1900? Second, what is the theatrical context of the painting? Third, what is the relationship between Tallone, Borelli and Sommariva? And finally: How decisive was the pictorial representation of Borelli's theatrical career for the construction of her iconic image in her first feature, *Ma l'amor mio non muore* (1913)?

Beloved and esteemed portrait painter

In 1911, Cesare Tallone (1853–1919) was a senior artist, but also a highly respected and frequently decorated cultural authority. From 1899, he was professor of painting and nude drawing at the famous Accademia di Brera in Milan. Prior to that, he was a teacher and director of the Accademia Carrara in Bergamo. He taught a whole generation of young painters, including several symbolists and futurists such as Pellizza da Volpedo and Carrà. At the turn of the century, Tallone was also a beloved and esteemed portrait painter in Milan. From far and wide, the aristocracy and upper middle class came to have their portraits painted by him, including Queen Margherita, who he painted three times.[6]

Tallone was not a great innovator, but he was aware of the vanguard and kept a keen eye on the art shows in Venice, where the works of Klimt were displayed. He exhibited there himself at the 1909 Biennale. Referring to Tallone's Salome portrait of Borelli, his granddaughter Gigliola Tallone writes: 'Sometimes Tallone gives you a painting richer in execution, a luxuriously refined but never descriptive pictorial background – with boa feathers or textiles – as in the portraits of Clerici, Castelli and Borelli, charmer *par excellence*, who, dressed in

Figure 4: Lyda Borelli in the film *Ma l'amor mio non muore* (Mario Caserini, Gloria Film 1913). [Courtesy Cineteca di Bologna.]

a beautiful mermaid robe highlighted with profound dark reflections, seems to come out from the canvas with a sinuous attitude indicated by her head of auburn hair, bent backwards, and the languor of her arms holding the impalpable robe'.[7] Futurist painter Carlo Carrà, a student of Tallone, pointed instead to the value of the past in Tallone's work, a pictorial legacy that he promoted himself.[8] The warm colours, the feeling for textiles and the reflections of light in Velazquez, Titian, and Hals seem to return in Tallone, but also in Gordigiani to Boldini, or, from abroad, in Alfred Stevens to Carolus Duran as well.

Tallone's style was dynamic. His portrait of Queen Margherita is classic, realistic, almost photographic, while Lina Cavalieri's portrait is a sketch, except for the actress's face. The Cavalieri portrait is in Art Nouveau style, halfway between John Singer Sargent and Boldini and the early twentieth-century poster.[9] Completed five years after the Cavalieri portrait, the portrait of Borelli, however, expresses a whole new style, reminiscent of Klimt but also of the warmth of the Venetian style, especially Veronese to Fortuny. In addition to its richness of colour, the portrait expresses the character's psychology.

Although Monteverdi does not prefer Tallone's landscapes, he praises his portraits. He glimpses a trace of the Scapigliatura in some of them: 'She is, in any case, more recognizable in her swiftly and skilfully executed outline than in any attempt to render the depth of her character, that is to say through any fanciful effort to interpret her psychologically'.[10] Even Touttain's reading of Tallone appears to deal directly with the Borelli portrait: 'There [in his portraiture], he excels, his faces are always enlightened by the subtle plays of light which enliven them and make them literally come out of their frame and materialize them'.[11] The portrait, however, had not been reviewed much at the time and did not leave Tallone's study for years. Yet, Sommariva's photos and mass-produced postcards introduced Tallone's painting into the public imaginary.[12]

The apex of her theatrical career

In 1911, Lyda Borelli (1887–1959) was at the apex of her theatrical career. Performing in Italy's most famous theatres, such as the Teatro Valle in Rome and the Teatro Manzoni in Milan, she appeared in plays by Victorien Sardou, Henry Bataille, Georges Ohnet, the very repertory that would soon become the backbone of diva cinema.[13] In 1904, at the Teatro Lirico in Milan, she had her first important role in *La figlia di Jorio* by Gabriele D'Annunzio, starring Irma Gramatica. A year later, she starred alongside Eleonora Duse in Sardou's *Fernanda*. Her fame grew quickly. In 1908 readers of the magazine, *Illustrazione italiana*, chose Borelli as the most beautiful Italian actress. The following year, the Milanese dramatic weekly *La Scena di Prosa* enthused in 1909: 'Borelli brings you the combination of her authentic beauty, her extreme elegance and, what counts the most, her artistic integrity, not only … in her physical skills but, even more… for her skills as experienced actress, gifted with a successful and tenacious will in service of a passionate, sensitive and artistic temperament'.[14] That year, she founded her own company with the actor Ruggero Ruggeri. For months the Compagnia Teatrale Ruggero Ruggeri occupied the Teatro Valle in Rome, the theatre most associated with the actress.[15]

Borelli's most acclaimed performance was in Oscar Wilde's *Salome*, which had its Italian premiere at the Teatro Valle on 10 March 1909. Ruggeri played Herod Antipas, Romano Calò played Jokanaan, and Ida Carloni Talli was Herodias. The costumes were by Luigi Sapelli, alias Caramba, who would become famous as the Scala's set and costume designer.[16] Borelli's costume can be seen in the Tallone painting and the Sommariva photographs. *Salome* was her greatest theatrical success. During a Latin American tour in 1909–1910, she played the role in Rio de Janeiro, São Paulo, Montevideo, Buenos Aires, Havana and Mexico City. It stayed in her repertoire when she switched to the Gandusio-

Borelli-Piperno company in 1912.[17] Mario Praz, philologist *par excellence* of late Romantic literature and art, recalled in *The Romantic Agony*: 'In Italy it [Salome] became part of the repertory of Lyda Borelli, and I still remember with what enthusiasm the gentlemen's opera-glasses were levelled at the squinting *diva*, clothed in nothing but violet and absinthe-green shafts of limelight'.[18] Her semi-nude appearance can be discerned neither in the Sommariva photographs of Borelli in her *Salome* outfit nor from the original reviews. Praz's memory of Borelli's nudity seems to have been largely wishful thinking.

A decisive counterpoint

Emilio Sommariva (1883–1956) did more than just photograph Tallone and his famous model. He also produced a large number of full-sized portraits and close-ups of Borelli dressed as Salome in Tallone's studio. The photographic images of Borelli in theatrical poses within Tallone's portrait are very different from those in the painter's composition.[19] To quote Giovanna Ginex: 'Sommariva chooses formal and compositional solutions in decisive counterpoint to the measured spatial composition and dramatic set up in *Nello studio del pittore*'.[20] Instead of the actress bowing to her audience in Tallone's canvas, Sommariva focuses on the facial expressions and body language that earned Borelli so much popular success. In the spring of 1911, Sommariva presented *Nello studio del pittore* along with five photographic portraits of Borelli at the Art Exhibition and the International Competition of Photography in Turin. If you look closely, you will see the same dress, the same column and the same studio floor. Most of these photographs were destined for wealthy collectors, thus, authentic prints were sold to customers. Other photographs, such as the close-ups of her, were popularised as postcards.

Emilio Sommariva not only made pictures of Borelli in her Salome costume but also took some pictures of her in elegant modern costumes against a painted backdrop. This was a trademark of his style in 1912–1913. These photos must have been produced in the photographer's studio and most are dated to 1912 and 1913. Thus, Borelli returned to Sommariva for these fashionable portraits.[21] The Sommariva Archive at the Biblioteca Nazionale Braidense in Milan contains various close ups of the actress. Notable is the contrast between photographs that are brown or sepia-toned and those in different shades of gray. The latter are direct scans from the glass plates while the former are original prints. Sommariva was a typical studio photographer: in his various portraits, the backdrops of his studio are visible. For the series in the Tallone's studio, he must have made an exception.

Did Lyda Borelli purposefully travel to Milan to be painted by the old master Tallone? Did she want to raise herself to the level of such distinguished colleagues as Cavalieri, and even to that of the Milanese aristocracy? Sommariva 'happens' to register the action of portraying but, of course, this is a well-thought out *mise-en-scène*. The inclusion of Cavalieri's portrait in Sommariva's photo is an act of legitimisation. Sommariva's photos were thus a smart promotional stunt by Borelli. They disseminated her image as theatrical star and, especially, in her biggest success, Salome. As mentioned before, some of these photographs were later mass-produced as postcards, just like those of Borelli's painted portrait.

All three media – painting, photography and postcards – had their effects. After the photo series of Borelli, theatre and film actresses discovered Sommariva. During the 1910s and 1920s, they flocked to his Milan studio to have their portraits made. Sommariva photographed the Italian film divas Elena Makowska and Diana Karenne, and many theatre and variety actresses who were also in films.[22]

Not only Salome. Other painted portraits of Borelli

Lyda Borelli set an example for other actresses who wanted to be photo-portrayed, but the Tallone portrait also set an example in a way. In the following years, Borelli was painted by many other artists. Well-known in its day was the portrait painted by Giuseppe Amisani (1881–1941), a pupil of Tallone's at the Brera. In 1912 the painting, presented as *Ritratto di Lyda Borelli,* won the Premio Fumagalli for portrait painting at the Esposizione nazionale di Brera.[23] According to Giorgio Nicodemi:

> The plastic beauty of the blonde actress that marked the moods of her heroines, with their rhythmic moves and slow and precise pauses, is rendered in a static moment which reveals the passionate freshness of the face, the white flesh of the shoulders and neck, and the nervous tremor of the hands. The lithe elegance of the body hides in the abandon of the pinkish dressing gown hanging down, and stands out against the red tones of the carpet. The delicate harmony in pink which comprises the figure, and which is vivified by the gold of the hair, the red of the lips and the black of the eyes – barely visible beneath her slightly closed eyelids – gives the portrait of the woman a representative character of reality which attains a new perfection through the impression of the painter.[24]

Borelli is represented in her costume from the play *Zazà* by Pierre Samuel Berton and Charles Simon which, in addition to *Salome*, was one of her most successful stage performances. Just like the Tallone painting, the portrait went to a private collector but postcards of it were widely distributed. They fueled the public imagination and increased the reputation of both Borelli and Amisani.

2 Diva Intermedial: Lyda Borelli between Art, Photography, Theatre and Cinema

In 1912, Sommariva made several photo portraits of Borelli in the same dress from *Zazà*, photos that are now in the Braidense collection as well as at the Burcardo.[25] One of these photographs is almost identical to the Amisani picture: the actress in the same pose with her head raised towards the back, the same dress and the same jewels around her neck, only the difference being the arms. In the painting she keeps her arms together, in the photo she keeps one hand on her thigh, the other stretched out, perhaps leaning against a chair.[26]

From theatre, painting and photography to film

How did all of the preceding merge into cinema, or rather, in the terms of Michael Baxandall, how did cinema actively *appropriate* these earlier arts and media?[27] Two years after Tallone's portrait and Sommariva's photographic series, Borelli made her cinematic debut. She was launched as film diva with *Ma l'amor mio non muore* (Love Everlasting, 1913), produced by the Turin-based company Gloria Film and directed by Mario Caserini. The film was specifically written for her. While the plot deals with espionage and love, the second part of the film is set in a world very close to Borelli – the stage. Her two successful performances, *Zazà* and *Salome*, reappear here. In a scene set on stage, Borelli acts as though she is dying, but this, in effect, is a doubling since her character has actually poisoned herself. Her princely lover is her political rival, so she cannot have him. The prince runs on stage when he notices that this is no mere performance. She dies in his hands like Violetta dying in the hands of Armand in *La Traviata* or, more broadly, repeating the 'inimitable life and death' promoted by D'Annunzio. Although not entirely similar, the actress is again wearing the dressing gown from *Zazà*, as seen in Amisani's painting and Sommariva's photos. She also wears the gown in her earlier farewell scene in her dressing room, making this scene also a foreshadowing and doubling of what will follow on stage. This duplicity and ambiguity is even multiplied by the three-panelled life-size mirror in front of which Borelli emotes, not only saying goodbye to her lover but also to herself and to her beauty.

In contrast, earlier scenes show Borelli's character (Elsa Holbein, aka Diana Cadouleur) acting and singing on stage as a kind of *Carmen*, but also in an outfit which clearly refers to *Salome*. No doubt it must have rung a bell to 1913 audiences.[28] Once again she is filmed while the audience applauds her, but this time the applause is not just implied as in Tallone's painting or Sommariva's photos. The camera stands in the wings of the stage, filming both the actress performing and the audience applauding and throwing her flowers. The audience on screen functions as a stand-in for us, the film's spectators, who are supposed to applaud the newly christened film star. Either the scriptwriters or Borelli herself must have insisted on the references to *Salome* and *Zazà*, bridging the gap between stage and screen, by using the iconographic tradition in shared between these two media. And as we know, citation promotes recognition, not only of the performance but also of the image of the diva herself.

Ma l'amor mio non muore was an international success and turned Borelli into a film star. It also started a new phenomenon: the Italian diva film. But as we saw here, this phenomenon didn't come out of the blue; it incorporates the legacy of the pictorial, photographic and theatrical culture of the Italian early twentieth century. So the art of Cesare Tallone, the stage play of Oscar Wilde, the costume design of Caramba and the photography of Emilio Sommariva, and especially their visual multiplication, shaped the iconography of one of the first film stars, Lyda Borelli, at the start of her cinematic career. This confirms Jens Schröter's statement, then, that, in order to define medium specificity or ontology, intermedial comparison is indispensable.[29]

Acknowledgement: This article is a shortened and reworked version of: Ivo Blom, "Lyda Borelli e la nascita del glamour. Dal teatro, via pittura e fotografia, al cinema", in Silvia Sinisi, Isabella Innamorati & Marco Pistoia (eds), *Attraversamenti. L'attore nel Novecento e l'interazione fra le arti* (Roma: Bulzoni, 2010), 69–96. In 2013 the Cineteca di Bologna released a DVD of *Ma l'amor mio non muore*, for which Ivo Blom wrote a text. The DVD holds several picture galleries, including many postcards with Borelli, partly from the collection of Blom.

Notes

1. Jay David Bolter and Richard Grusin, *Remediation. Understanding New Media* (Cambridge: MIT Press, 1999).
2. Irina O. Rajewsky, "Intermediality, Intertextuality and Remediation: A Literary Perspective on Intermediality", *Intermédialités* 6 (2005): 43–64.
3. See Nicholas Mirzoeff, *An Introduction to Visual Culture* (New York: Routledge, 1999), 30.
4. Giovanna Ginex, "Donne divine nei ritratti di Emilio Sommariva", in Giovanna Ginex (ed.), *Divine. Emilio Sommariva fotografo. Opere scelte 1910–1930* (Busto Arsizio: Nomos, 2004), 13–42. The photo *Nello studio del pittore*: cat.no. 31, pp. 46, 226. See also Elena Mosconi, "Lyda Borelli as Liberty Icon", in Sofia Bull, Astrid Söderbergh Widding (eds), *Not so Silent: Women in Cinema before Sound* (Stockholm: Acta Universitatis Stockholmiensis, 2010), 137–147.
5. Ginex (2004), cat.no. 25, p. 226.
6. A.M. Comanducci, *I pittori italiani dell'Ottocento* (Milan: Casa Editrice Artisti d'Italia, 1934), 716.
7. Gigliola Tallone, *Cesare Tallone* (Milan, Electa, 2005), 71. All translations from either Italian or French to English in this article were done by the author.
8. C. Carrà & C. Caversazzi (eds), *Cesare Tallone*, exhibition catalogue (Bergamo: Conti, 1953), 314. See also Tallone (2005), 58–59.
9. See also Rossana Bossaglia, "La gioia del dipingere", in Roberto Forcella, Rossana Bossaglia, Fernando Rea, Gino Angelo Scalzi (eds), *Cesare Tallone. Ritratti e Paesaggi* (Lovere: Lago d'Iseo, 1996), 7.

10. Mario Monteverdi, *Storia della pittura italiana dell'Ottocento* (Milan: Bramante, 1975), vol. II, 42.
11. Pierre-André Touttain, "Cesare Tallone", in E. Bénézit (ed.), *Dictionnaire critique et documentaire des peintres, sculpteurs, dessinateurs et graveurs* (Paris: Gründ, 1999), 444.
12. It was probably publicly exposed for the first time in 1924 at the Villa Reale in Monza. *Mostra del ritratto femminile contemporaneo* (Monza: Villa Reale, 1924), 54. Cfr. catalogue *Studiolo 2004* (Milan: Galleria d'Arte Lo Studiolo, 2004), ill. 19. The portrait is now in a private collection. The postcards are still offered for sale.
13. Ginex (2004), 203–204. Cfr. *Lyda Borelli, diva ritrovata* (La Spezia: Comune della Spezia, Istituzione per i servizi culturali, 2001) and Ivo Blom, "Das gestische Repertoire. Zur Körpersprache von Lyda Borelli", *KINtop* 7 (1998): 69–83.
14. *La Scena di Prosa*, 8 (6 March 1909): 4.
15. Alessandro D'Amico, Mario Verdone, Andrea Zanella eds, *Il Teatro Valle* (Rome: Palombi, 1998), 85, 89–91, 94–97.
16. Vittoria Crespi Morbio, *Caramba, mago del costume* (Milan: Associazione Amici della Scala, 2008).
17. For the Latin American tour, cfr. *La Scena di Prosa* 12 February 1909 / 1 April 1910. For the various reprisals of *Salome*, see Ginex (2004), 203–204.
18. Mario Praz, *The Romantic Agony* (Oxford: Oxford University Press, 1970), 317.
19. Ginex (2004), cat.no. 18–20, 22–23, 27, 29, 32, 34–35, pp. 16–19, 47–50, 61, 226–227.
20. Ginex (2004), 15.
21. Ginex (2004), cat.no. 12–17, 21, 26, 28, pp. 51–59, 224–226.
22. Ginex (2004), cat.no. 150–151, pp. 74–75 and 213–214.
23. Pasquale De Luca, "L'esposizione nazionale di Brera", *Emporium* XXXVI, no. 214 (October 1912): 302–309. See also Comanducci (1934), 13.
24. Giorgio Nicodemi, *Giuseppe Amisani* (Milan/Rome: Pizzi & Pizio, c.1922–24), 19–20.
25. Ginex (2004), cat.no. 16, 24, 30, 33, pp. 18–19.
26. Ginex claims the photo portrait by Sommariva served as a model for Amisani's painting. Ginex (2004), 19.
27. Michael Baxandall, *Patterns of Intention. On the Historical Explanation of Pictures* (New Haven/London: Yale University Press, 1985).
28. The *Salome* outfit and Wilde's play remained a point of reference in Borelli's film career, as in *Rapsodia satanica* (Nino Oxilia 1915–1917) and *La falena* (Carmine Gallone 1916).
29. Jens Schröter, "Intermedialität. Facetten und Problemen eines aktuellen medienwissenschaftlichen, Begriffes", *Montage a/v* 7, no. 2 (1998): 129–154.

3

Why Sue 'Little Mary?':
How Independent Moving Pictures Company of America v Gladys Smith and Owen Moore (1911) Defined Celebrity and Professionalism for Film Actors

Leslie Midkiff DeBauche

In 1911 the Independent Moving Picture Company of America (IMP) had cause to be litigious. Its two very popular and best publicised assets had jumped ship. Early in the year, Florence Lawrence reneged on her one-year contract and Mary Pickford (Gladys Smith) followed her lead on 1 September. More egregiously, each actress also violated the exclusivity agreement she had signed with IMP to begin working for the Lubin Manufacturing Company and the Majestic Moving Picture Company respectively. IMP sued both actresses and the case against Lawrence and her husband actor H.L. Solter had not been resolved when the company took Mary Pickford and her husband Owen Moore to court.[1] Pickford's defection may have been most galling to the film producer; it surely revealed a range of problems in the IMP organization. Majestic had been established specifically to capitalize on 'Little Mary's' talent and fame. The new company was headed by Tom D. Cochrane, formerly IMP's vice president and general manager. While comedy, character assassination, and vitriol are larded into the nearly two hundred pages of court documents in this case, unpacking the legal arguments and technical language helps us to gauge the value of celebrity for picture personalities and the studios who employed them in the early days of motion pictures. In addition, implicit in the evidence that plaintiff and defendant presented, is a nascent understanding of what constituted quality in motion picture acting. Further, examination of the criteria used by the film industry to sort the exceptional actress from the merely competent,

3 Why Sue 'Little Mary?'

guides our measurement of professionalism in the film acting trade in 1910 and 1911. Finally, *Independent Moving Pictures Company of America v. Gladys Smith and Owen Moore* provides another angle from which to view the dynamic creation of a movie star via interactions among film producers, directors, actors, fans, and film reviewers.

IMP sought an injunction against Mary Pickford on 23 September 1911 even though her contract only had three more months to run:

> The above named Plaintiff having applied to one of the Justices of this Court for an Injunction in the above entitled action, restraining and enjoining the *defendant* GLADYS SMITH, from in any manner violating the agreement in writing between the plaintiff and her of DECEMBER 3RD, 1910, and particularly from acting or appearing in any moving picture productions of any other person, firm or corporation than plaintiff until DECEMBER 19TH 1911, and from making any public or private appearance in any way connected with the theatrical or moving picture business without the consent in writing of plaintiff until DECEMBER 19TH, 1911 and particularly from acting or appearing in any moving picture productions of the Majestic Moving Picture Company until DECEMBER 19TH, 1911.[2]

These words comprised a standard legal jargon necessary to argue that the contract IMP had signed with Pickford should stand but especially that she should be restrained from working for any other studio while it was in force. More pointedly, IMP claimed:

> Defendant Gladys Smith is now and since prior to December 3, 1910, has been a moving picture actress possessing peculiar, unique, unusual and extraordinary skill and ability as an actress in this special line of work, and is widely known as possessing peculiar, unique, special, unusual and extraordinary skill and artistic ability, and her services cannot be duplicated.[3]

Adjectives including: 'peculiar', 'unique', 'unusual', 'special', and 'extraordinary' peppered *Independent Moving Pictures Company of America v. Gladys Smith and Owen Moore* (*IMP v Smith*). Although these words were synonyms, the fine gradations among their connotations mapped a terrain in which Mary Pickford was salient. She stood out, conspicuous amid the 'trained corps of actors appearing before photographic apparatus' for what was described as her 'method' or 'manner of acting' and also for her 'individuality'.[4] When the plaintiff's attorney Nathaniel A. Elsberg deposed Carl Willat, the new General Manager at IMP, one of the questions he asked was, 'in what the special and peculiar abilities of Mary Pickford as a moving picture actress consist?' Willet replied, 'She has an individual way of portraying and expressing different emotions and actions, the things she tries to, in front of the camera'.[5] The

35

presence and technical features of the camera, he seemed to say, required a special acting technique. More specifically the IMP's lawyer argued:

> Moving picture acting is a new art of recent development differing from legitimate stage acting in its methods because of the varying surroundings. On the legitimate stage the actor is part of a living picture and is stimulated by the presence of a living audience, while on the moving picture stage the actor lacks this stimulation and appears only before a camera which produces without mercy every detail of movement and expression. This literal portrayal of every detail demands peculiar qualifications for a successful moving picture actor which are not essential on the legitimate stage.[6]

Acting, mise en scene, and cinematography – gesture and the timing of movements, properties of the camera lens, as well as framing of the shot which affected the audience's understanding of the relationship of figure to ground all were mustered in the service of distinguishing stage from screen acting and to assert that Pickford was in a league of her own.

The legal precedent IMP cited in its suit was *Metropolitan Exhibition v. Ward* (1890). The New York Giants had sued its short stop Monte Ward for breaking his contract. In that case, baseball players were paralleled with stage actors for whom this facet of contract law was settled. In that decision, Judge O'Brien had written:

> Between an actor of great histrionic ability and a professional base ball [sic] player, of peculiar fitness and skill to fill a particular position, no substantial distinction in applying the rule laid down in the cases cited can be made. Each is sought for his particular and peculiar fitness, each performs in public for compensation, and each possesses for the manager a means of attracting an audience. The refusal of either to perform according to contract must result in loss to the manager, which is increased in cases where such services are rendered to a rival.[7]

Like Monte Ward who played short stop better than anyone else, Mary Pickford's method of acting for the camera was technically excellent, and since she had left to work for Majestic, IMP had found no replacement for her, especially in the ingénue roles where she truly shone. Because she was talented, Pickford like Ward, was a draw at the box office. IMP had hired her believing that she brought fans as well as acting experience, that her skill when combined with IMP's national advertising would only increase audiences for IMP productions.

Mary Pickford's unique and recognised picture personality and her acting talent were valuable assets to the varied interests in this case. She herself had profited from them by negotiating a seventy-five percent increase in salary when she went to work at IMP earning $175.00 weekly in her new job.[8] Although it was not written into the contract, Pickford also claimed that she had been guaranteed national publicity: 'Mr. Cochrane promised me that the plaintiff company would feature me, that is to say would advertise pictures, and that my name would appear in the advertisements so that I could become better known'.[9] 'Featuring' was industry jargon for advertising. IMP banked that it would also benefit from the investment in Pickford's salary and publicity to differentiate the company's brand from the competition. Advertising became one of the bones of contention in this court case and it may have also been one of a range of reasons why Pickford left Biograph in the first place.

Until 1913, Biograph held firm to the principle that it would not identify its actors, much less 'feature' any member of the stock company. Charles O'Brien, in his essay on Griffith's Biograph films in this section, suggests how acting style and camera placement may have interacted with this policy. Biograph's business strategy was contested in the pages of the *New York Dramatic Mirror* where readers from all around the United States wrote weekly asking to know the names of actors and actresses playing in films. Week after week, 'The Spectator', Frank Wood, reminded his readers that Biograph would not divulge the identity of its employees. Finally, he resorted to sarcasm. 'The Spectator' he joked, 'is more or less reliably informed that Biograph players have no names. When the director speaks to them it is by number, so it is said'.[10] A few weeks later, he explained the company's position more patiently:

> Players with little or no reputation and others with big reputations have appeared in Biograph pictures, some of them becoming favorites, but none of them individually essential to the advancement of Biograph's reputation. Why, then, it is asked, should a player who has been made, we might say by the Biograph seek to use for the benefit of another company that reputation which belongs mostly to the Biograph and not to him? It must be confessed that there appears to be considerable sense in this view of the matter.[11]

IMP's legal brief concurred. When Pickford absconded, she deprived the company not only of her individuality, technique, and her fans, but also, Carl Willat contended, 'large sums of money which have been invested in advertising and establishing the celebrity of the dramatic ability of said defendant ...'.[12] Setting Mary Pickford above the rest of its stock company had bound IMP's distribution leverage and drawing power at the box office to her reputation, skill, and talent effectively linking their success to her tenure with them – inadvertently proving Biograph's case for not naming its actors.

While IMP's strategy was to argue that Mary Pickford's 'marked individuality', costly promotion, and extraordinary method of screen acting contributed to her celebrity and made her irreplaceable, the defense claimed she was only as good as her directors and fellow actors. For the record Pickford stated:

> Repeatedly during the term of my employment, I spoke to Mr. Laemmle, the President of the plaintiff company, with reference to the poor quality and directorship of the pictures in which I appeared. I called his attention to the fact that Mr. Clifford, Mr. Ince, Mr. Grandon and others who directed pictures in which I appeared had never directed moving pictures before, and that the result was that pictures of a poor quality were produced. Mr. Laemmle agreed with me that the pictures were not up to the highest standard and that the directorship should be improved, but nothing was done except to supplant one director with another, and no competent director was ever placed in charge.[13]

No surprise, in his affidavit, Owen Moore reiterated Pickford's claim.

> During the larger part of the time that my wife has been working for the plaintiff she has complained of the inefficient directorship of the productions. I have repeated these complaints to Mr. Laemmle, the President of the plaintiff company, and he has admitted to me that the productions of his company suffered from inefficient directorship, but nothing was ever done about this while my wife was in the company's employ.[14]

Among its supporting documents, the defense included two items from the *New York Dramatic Mirror*. The first was a review of the IMP film *Stampede* from 29 April and the second was a letter from a fan published in September as the litigants prepared their cases. Why, the review asked, were IMP's films not among the best of all being produced since 'the photography is generally very good, having good detail and is clean; in fact, showing intelligently directed care'.[15] The reviewer, presumably Frank Woods, also praised the ability of the stock company and spotlighted Moore and Pickford in particular. If the cinematography was blameless and the actors accomplished, what accounted for IMP's lackluster productions? Rhetorically Woods wondered, 'Is she [Pickford] being properly handled?'[16] He pinpointed direction: staging that placed Mary Pickford too far in the background of a shot, costuming which obscured her face, and setting. The company was shooting in Cuba, which dictated stories highlighting a locale so 'exotic' it upstaged her. When he wrote that 'Mary is not made enough of in the stories', he was talking mainly about the director's control over *mise en scene*.[17] Pickford's fan was less specific, but her evaluation was similar: 'I used to think Mary Pickford was fine, but she made a mistake in leaving the Biograph, for she had good people and scenarios, but the Imp doesn't help her that way. I saw her in *The Toss of the Coin*, and she wasn't near so good. It was silly ...'.[18] Pickford and her attorney Walter Seligsberg might have appended additional proof: Woods, who reviewed nearly all her work in the *New York Dramatic Mirror*, noted of her second film for IMP, 'Miss Pickford enacted her role of the wife artistically, but one regrets her departure from the more youthful roles with which she has been associated. The part was miscast'.[19] A few weeks later his critique of *The Mirror* opined, 'Miss Pickford becomes almost her old self in the climactic scene of this bright little comedy'.[20] Neither the choice of scenarios which would have fallen under the purview of the director, nor the staging of her films measured up to the standards set when Pickford worked with D. W. Griffith at Biograph; she noticed this, marked it, if you will, and so did her public and the journalists who wrote about film.

From Mary Pickford's point of view, poor and inefficient direction made it impossible for her to do her best work and this was damaging her reputation with her fans and her potential to earn even more money as her skills increased and her audiences expanded. IMP had also not lived up to its side of the bargain, she noted, when it fired her husband and sister in the summer of 1911, discontinued its national advertising highlighting her, and when the company refused to pay her for several weeks in the spring when she was sick. Her art, her earnings, and her family's economic well-being all were threatened. Anyway, she was only nineteen when she signed the contract, and as an 'infant', she could not be held to its requirements.

IMP's interpretation was quite different. Pickford 'coolly' held onto her old job, collecting $175.00 a week until her new job with Majestic was ready. At that point she 'trumped up excuses' why she needed to 'escape from one employer to another'.[21] Furthermore, she was using the fact of her age as a weapon against her employer.

> The plaintiff is merely asking the Court to invoke the rule so clearly stated by Judge Lowell [in a precedent case] and to say to Mary Pickford that she shall not profit by her wrongdoing, that she shall not use her infancy as a sword, and that she shall not while attempting to exercise the privileges of an infant and break her contract, use such privilege for the purpose of making money unrighteously.[22]

In the end, the infant wielded her sword mightily and Pickford won the legal battle. After a brief stint at Majestic, she returned to work for Biograph early in 1912. While she won the case IMP had brought against her on a technicality, her age, she was right: the company had put unseasoned directors in charge of her pictures and teamed her up with inexperienced actors. She apparently also read her press and took notice that her fans and at least one influential film critic had noticed the quality of her work had slipped. *Independent Moving Pictures Company of America against Gladys Smith and Owen Moore* demonstrates how, from early in her movie career, Mary Pickford was self-aware and ambitious. While salary mattered to her, the evidence she and her lawyer presented shows that she was also concerned with the quality of her work and with her own professional development. She understood that to be a star, she needed the support of her audience and an infrastructure including national advertising and film reviewing. She was a pro and shrewd enough to understand the dynamics of this new story-telling industry.

Notes

1. Owen Moore was made a party to the suit by virtue of being married to Gladys Smith/Mary Pickford.
2. Undertaking on Injunction, *Independent Moving Pictures Company of American v. Gladys Smith and Owen Moore* (*IMP v Smith*), No. 21423 (N.Y. Sup. Court, New York County, 1911). This court file is located in the Division of Old Records, Room 703, 31 Chambers Street, New York, New York. I would like to thank James Peterson, attorney at Godfrey and Kahn, Madison, WI, for his help translating the *Legal Blue Book* and helping me to write the citations for this article.
3. Complaint, Fol.5, *IMP v Smith*.
4. For instance, see the set of Affidavits of Carl A. Willat, Julius Stern, Thomas Ince, Frank J. Grandon, William E. Shay, Edward J. LeSaint, Farrell MacDonald, William Robert Daly, Hayward S. Mack, and King Baggot, *IMP v Smith*.
5. Deposition of Carl A. Willat by Walter N. Seligsberg, Esq., for the Defendant and Nathan A. Ellsberg, Esq., and Francis Woodbridge, Esq. for the Plaintiffs, *IMP v Smith*.
6. Memorandum in Support of Motion to Continue Injunction, p.2, *IMP v Smith*.
7. *Met. Ex. Co. v. Ward*, 9 N.Y. Supp. 799 .
8. Affidavit of Carl A. Willat, Exhibit A, Contract between Gladys Smith and Ton D. Cochrane, Vice-President and General Manager, Independent Moving Picture Company of America, Dec. 3, 1910, *IMP v Smith*.
9. Affidavit of Gladys Smith Moore, Fol.7, *IMP v Smith*.
10. The Spectator, "Letters to 'The Spectator'", *New York Dramatic Mirror*, 1 February 1911, 30.
11. The Spectator, "Motion Pictures", *New York Dramatic Mirror*, 22 February 1911, 28.
12. Complaint, Fol.14, *IMP v Smith*.
13. Affidavit of Gladys Smith Moore, Fol. 26, *IMP v Smith*.
14. Affidavit of Owen Moore, Fol.6, *IMP v Smith*.
15. Deposition of Walter N. Seligsberg, Review of *The Stampede*, Fol. 2, *IMP v Smith*.
16. Deposition of Walter N. Seligsberg, Review of *The Stampede*, Fol. 4, *IMP v Smith*.
17. Ibid.
18. Deposition of Walter N. Seligsberg, "Letters and Questions, Answered by 'The Spectator'", Fol. 6, *IMP v Smith*.
19. *The Dream,* "Reviews of Independent Films", *New York Dramatic Mirror*, 1 February,1911, 33.
20. *The Mirror*, "Reviews of Independent Films", *New York Dramatic Mirror*, 15 February 1911, 31.
21. Memorandum in Support of Motion to Continue Injunction, p. 6, *IMP v Smith*.
22. Memorandum in Support of Motion to Continue Injunction, p. 15, *IMP v Smith*.

4

Camera Distance and Acting in the Griffith Biographs

Charles O'Brien

This paper examines how the naturalism that critics attributed to actors' performances in the films Griffith had directed for American Biograph stemmed from the director's innovations in camera placement and staging. A major stimulus for these innovations, I will argue, was Griffith's practice beginning in 1910 of shooting films in California as well as New York. The research presented in the following pages refers to seventy Griffith Biographs, divided into two broad categories: the films made in New York and those made in California. For each film, all shots featuring actors were classified by the distance between actor and camera, while all intertitles, inserts, and actor-less cutaways excluded from the count. The key issue circa 1910 concerned the reduction of the distance from twelve feet to nine, which allowed for performances that impressed critics as less conventionalised, more psychologically attuned and hence 'realistic' than what filmgoers were accustomed to. I will conclude by proposing that the nine-foot/twelve-foot metric – which refers to staging methods in not only the United States but France and other countries – might prove useful in the study of not just Griffith but early cinema as a transnational phenomenon.

Actors' performances have provided a central focus for assessing the style of the Biograph films since so much acclaim for Griffith's work as director concerned acting specifically. Moreover, the naturalism that Griffith's actors became known for required a close camera, which raises an important methodological issue for the study of early cinema: because camera distance is quantifiable in ways that acting ordinarily is not, an attention to camera placement provides a way of assessing changes in acting across Griffith's body of work as a whole, as well as other large samples of films.

The practice of permitting the actors to position themselves nine feet away from the camera rather than the customary twelve feet brought a big gain in expressive power for certain actors. Tom Gunning characterises the effect of the reduced distance as anthropocentric, whereby '[t]he frame became an actor's space rather than a proscenium arch, determined by the actor's height and position rather than the extent of the set'.[1] This actor-oriented framing distinguished Griffith from illustrious predecessors like Edwin Porter and Georges Méliès just as it brought him close to practices at the Vitagraph company, whose founder, J. Stuart Blackton, in his unpublished memoires, attributed the improved acting in Vitagraph films to the new nine-foot rule. Observing that Vitagraph player Maurice Costello 'brought something to the screen that it had lacked', Blackton stressed the actor's ability 'to convey a mood by the process of thought instead of facial contortion and pantomime': 'It was in the scenes nearest the camera that Costello's personality was most evident. At the time the front line was twelve feet from the lens. We changed it to nine feet'.[2] Like Griffith, Blackton sought the new, psychological acting style that came from reducing the camera distance.[3]

The acting in the Griffith Biographs was unimaginable without the change in camera position; but the causality, Roberta Pearson proposes, was complex, making it difficult to say whether the close camera had led to the naturalistic acting or the new acting had necessitated the close camera.[4] Similar developments in motion picture staging occurred in the United States and Europe at roughly the same time. Practices of camera placement drew notice in the motion picture trade press because they entailed a material infrastructure that anyone involved in filmmaking had to contend with. In the United States, France, and elsewhere, the actors' mobility was constrained by the act of literally staking out the ground of the playing space at the beginning of the work day, with nails, clothesline, wooden planks, chalk marks, and other physical barriers.[5]

By around 1909 the norm in both the United States and Europe was to stage the action on the twelve-foot line, which yielded shots that captured most of the actor, from the ankles up to the top of the head.[6]

In this opening shot of *A Corner in Wheat* (1909), the tall man in the foreground (James Kirkwood) implies a twelve-foot camera position: the body visible from the ankles up with an extra foot of space above the head.[7] In contrast, the nine-foot framing, Barry Salt observes, produced 'what would now be referred to as a medium shot, with the actors only visible from the hips up'.[8] In the Griffith Biographs the distance seems to vary somewhat from film to film, with the films of 1908–1909 sometimes showing far more headroom above the actors than the later films.[9] In any case, the effect of a change in camera placement will depend on the size of the actor, with short actors requiring less distance for their

4 Camera Distance and Acting in the Griffith Biographs

Figure 1: The opening shot of *A Corner in Wheat*, staged on the 12-foot line.

full figures to register. More important than the actual distance from actor to camera is the relative difference between a medium-shot position in the frame and a long-shot position, where so much of the action in the Biographs plays out.

Shots with the action staged at twelve feet began appearing in Griffith's films several months after he began directing, and such shots played a major role throughout his tenure at Biograph. My research into shot length reveals that shots whose main action is staged at twelve feet comprise more than fifty percent of the screen time for the New York Biographs, on average, as is indicated below in Figure 2.

The California Biographs, however, give less screen time to shots staged at twelve feet, and they contain many more shots with nine-feet or less-than-nine-feet

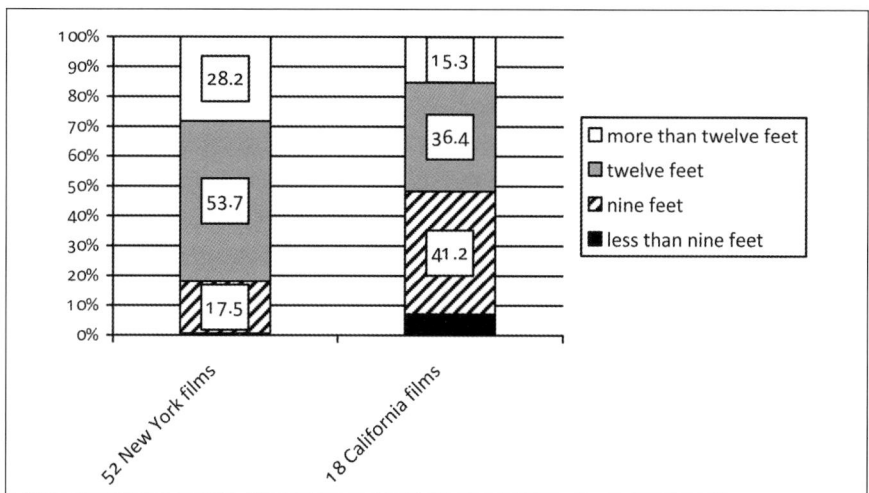

Figure 2: The percentage of screen time given to four shot types for seventy Griffith Biographs.[10]

43

placements than do the New York Biographs. The chart in Figure 2 shows that the combined percentages for the twelve-foot and nine-foot shots are roughly the same for the California films as for the New York, but the balance tips decidedly toward the nine-foot shots in the California productions, with much more of the running time of those films devoted to the close framings.

A pattern extremely common in Griffith's staging involves the actors starting at the twelve foot line at the beginning of the shot, then moving into the nine-foot foreground for the principal action, and then finally exiting the shot by walking past the nine-foot line and a bit further toward the camera. The opening shot of *The Unchanging Sea* (1910), one of the first Biographs shot in California, is an example. The young couple (Arthur Johnson and Linda Arvidson) exits the house and becomes visible on the footpath at twelve feet or thereabouts. They then continue to approach the camera until they reach nine feet, where they stop and interact prior to exiting on the left side of the frame. The second shot from *The Unchanging Sea* was taken in a different, wider location – on the beach with the sea in the background – but it amplifies the same basic pattern. The shot begins with the two actors entering the background on the right and then crossing all the way to the far left of the frame, and then back to the right, all the while moving continually closer to the camera. By the shot's end, the actors have covered the entirety of the deep space before coming to rest in the right foreground on the nine foot line, where the main, face-to-face interaction between them plays out. Finally, once again, the actors exit the frame by continuing slightly past the frontline.

Thanks to the staked-out location, the actors were able to stay within the limits of the visual field throughout the twenty-five seconds of the shot's duration. This shot, despite its deep space, counts in my calculations as a nine-foot shot since the main dramatic action – the face-to-face interaction and embrace of the couple – happens there. In counting shots for this analysis, the priority was to identify where the principle dramatic action is staged. Griffith's penchant for shallow staging usually made it easy to identify a single frontline per shot. In any case, I didn't let the deepness of the shot's space affect the labeling of the shot. If the main dramatic action happens on the nine-foot line, then I count it as a nine-foot shot, regardless of how deep the space is or whether the actors get closer while exiting the frame. This decision acknowledges a peculiar feature of the California films: the unusual depth of the represented space in both interiors and exteriors combined with the tendency for the actors to come up ever closer to the camera while performing. The preference for nine-foot staging holds even for the California films featuring impressive landscapes, such as *Ramona* (1910),

Figure 3: A frame from *The Musketeers of Pig Alley* (1912).

where Allessandro (Henry Walthall) rages close to the camera while his village is shown burning in the distant valley below.

A variation of the practice whereby the action shifts from one frontline to the other is the final tableau of *The Musketeers of Pig Alley* (1912), which features the reconciliation of the Snapper Kid (Elmer Booth) with the young couple (Lillian Gish and Walter Miller). The shot begins with the actors all on the nine-foot line but concludes with the action opening out to a somewhat larger space when the Kid, just before exiting the frame, steps back to the twelve-foot line to flash a gesture of solidarity to his new friends (see Figure 3).

The slight expansion in the playing space works as a closure cue, initiating the *dénouement* that will conclude the film. When critics cite the shallow staging in the Griffith Biographs, the many shots like this, where the action oscillates between nine and twelve feet, are perhaps what they have in mind. In any case, Griffith, unlike many European directors at the time, avoids staging a scene in depth so that character interaction plays out between the foreground and background of the shot. Instead, Griffith tends to keep the shot's main action on a single plane of the set.

Why study actors' performances in cinema circa 1910 relative to the nine-foot and twelve-foot rules rather than, say, the traditional categories of close-up, medium shot, and so forth? The answer is that the nine foot/twelve foot distinction reflects how the filmmakers themselves understood their work, and thus more closely corresponds to what we are studying than do the ordinary shot categories, which emerged at a later moment in film history, the late 1910s, when certain of the style conventions characteristic of the Griffith Biographs had become marginal to Hollywood practice. In conducting the research for this paper, I found it relatively easy to distinguish between nine-foot and twelve-foot framings because, I expect, such a distinction had been made by Griffith himself.

As Salt, Pearson, and Gunning have noted, the reduced frontline was by no means unique to Griffith but amounted to a transnational trend involving, for instance, the major French companies, where, as documented by Jean-Pierre Sirois Trahan, similar techniques of staging were practiced, whereby the playing space was marked off with chalk lines, ropes, and other barriers.[11] The transnational nature of the frontline-based staging in the Griffith Biographs thus raises the possibility that the nine-foot/twelve-foot metric might prove useful for comparative research into transnational cinema circa 1910, when in both the United States and Europe improvements in motion picture acting entailed reduced distance between actor and camera.

One possibility for pursuing this project further entails factoring in an important contemporaneous development examined by other contributors to this volume: the emergence of motion picture stars and other celebrity performers, which occurred simultaneously with the reduction in the frontline. Leslie Midkiff DeBauche, for example, in her chapter within this volume, contrasts Griffith's relatively anonymous actors to the stars promoted contemporaneously by Carl Laemmle of Independent Moving Pictures. In light of DeBauche's research into the emergence of movie stardom, acting in the Griffith Biographs begins to look like a special case, a divergence from what was becoming ordinary practice. In any event, the move in 1909 toward the reduced frontline was likely conditioned not only by the ambition of achieving psychologically expressive film performances but by a related but distinct development: the new prominence of film stars and personalities. Intriguing in this regard is Max Linder, whose films assigned more running time to shots staged at nine feet, on average, than did Griffith's; and they did so a year earlier, in 1907, with Linder's first appearances in lead roles in films.[12] The practices of close staging in Linder's oeuvre – such as the 'emblematic close-ups' that conclude so many of his films – seem informed more by the personality-driven comedy Linder had helped pioneer than by the interest in character psychology evinced in the Griffith Biographs.

Notes

1. Tom Gunning, *D. W. Griffith and the Origins of the American Narrative Film: The Early Years at Biograph* (Urbana and Chicago: University of Illinois, 1991), 207
2. Quoted in R. Pearson, *Eloquent Gestures: the Transformation of Performance Style in the Griffith Biograph Films* (Berkeley and Los Angeles: University of California Press, 1992), 162n. For more on the importance of the reduced frontline to acting in the Vitagraph films, see B. Salt, *Moving into Pictures: More on Film History, Style, and Analysis* (London: Starword, 2006), 111–113.

3. Salt states that the 'usual European forward limit' was four metres, or slightly over thirteen feet. B. Salt, *Moving into Pictures*, 111.
4. R. Pearson, *Elegant Gestures*, 94.
5. See the valuable survey of reports on staging practices in early cinema in Jean-Pierre Sirois-Trahan, "Le passage de la barre: transformation de la mise en scène dans le cinéma des premiers temps", in Laura Vichi (ed.), *L'uomo visibile/The Visible Man* (Udine: Forum, 2002), 33–40.
6. An important caveat regarding the analysis performed for this paper: I worked with digital copies of the films, which raises potential complications regarding the authenticity of the framings. Were the films cropped somehow when transferred digitally? A definitive analysis will require comparison of the digital versions to original 35mm prints.
7. Roberta Pearson's reference to the nine-foot line suggests a more distanced framing, whereby shots are framed to show 'the actors [...] from the ankles to the top of the head', R. Pearson, *Elegant Gestures*, 162n. From my standpoint, Pearson's description fits the twelve-foot rule more than the nine-foot.
8. B. Salt, *Moving into Pictures*, 26.
9. Ibid.
10. An independent t-test performed with SPSS software revealed a significant statistical difference for the percentage of running time devoted to the nine-foot shots in the California films (M= 36.4, SD= 28.5) versus those in the New York films (M= 18.5, SD= 30.5); $t(68)$= –2.18, p = .033. The running-time percentage for the nine-foot shots in the California versus the New York films thus appears due to an actual difference between the two samples rather than to chance. For the twelve-foot shots, however, the difference between the California (M= 41.2, SD= 31.4) and New York films (M= 54.2, SD= 31.4); $t(68)$= 1.52, p = .134 does not meet the same standard of significance. I am sure why. My guess is that achieving statistically significant results for the twelve-foot shots will require increasing the number of films in my sample.
11. See Jean-Pierre Sirois-Trahan, "Le passage de la barre: transformation de la mise en scène dans le cinéma des premiers temps", 33–40.
12. I refer here to my research on staging in Linder and Griffith, which will appear in an article forthcoming in the journal *Cinema et cie*.

5

Performance Times: The Lightning Cartoon and the Emergence of Animation

Malcolm Cook

Introduction

The lightning cartoon act is an important example of a music hall performance which transferred into early moving images.[1] It played a critical role in the formation of what would become known as animation not only in Britain, the primary focus of this chapter, but also worldwide. Key figures in the early history of animation are known to have performed this act, including J. Stuart Blackton and Winsor McCay in the United States, George Méliès in France and Walter Booth in the United Kingdom. This centrality of performance to animation has been highlighted in recent work by Donald Crafton; examining the lightning cartoon in both its stage and moving image guises allows an opportunity to understand how performance was central not only in the period Crafton focuses on but began at the inception of animation.[2] Furthermore, this chapter will show how the stage performance, which at first may appear an exemplar of 'live' performance, anticipated the complexity and multiplicity of 'performance times' present in early animated cartoons.

The lightning cartoon: A music hall genre

Making a performance out of the act of drawing, or the emphasis of an artist's skill through the speed and accuracy with which they could produce that drawing, have probably been in existence since humans learnt to draw. In Britain, however, it was only in the 1870s and early 1880s that a variety of practices coalesced into the widely recognised 'lightning cartoon' music hall act. Through the 1880s and 1890s there were approaching one hundred unique performers within this music hall genre in Britain, and while some of these performers may have been short lived, others such as Edgar Austin, Professor Thornbury, and Tom Merry had long periods of popularity, performing not only in Britain but on many international tours.³ The lightning cartoon act continued into the period following the appearance of moving images, with lightning cartoonists appearing alongside moving image presentations in music hall venues.⁴

In considering the performative aspects of the lightning cartoon, it would initially appear to be a clear example of a 'live' stage performance. This is indicated by a number of qualities. It was dependent upon the temporal and spatial coincidence of performer and audience, with trade press reviews drawing attention to the vocal interaction between performer and audience, as the cartoonist provided humorous patter or gave clues on what he was drawing with spectators shouting out their guesses or cheering or booing political figures depicted. Edgar Austin's act is described, wherein:

> "Lord Salisbury" was received in chilling silence, while no sooner was the "Grand Old Man" displayed than a most cordial round of applause went up. This latest reading of the political barometer is but a straw, but sufficiently indicates whence the wind blows.⁵

Tom Merry's act also provoked strong audience reactions:

> the partisans of Mr Gladstone cheered when Mr Tom Merry sketched his portrait, and his opponents of the Jingo tribe howled. They changed their howlings to applause when the late Earl Beaconsfield's visage was drawn; some applauded Bradlaugh's countenance, and some raved over Salisbury and that rash young man Lord Randolph Churchill.⁶

Child cartoonist Little Erskine made particular effort to get photographs of local figures, in one typical instance the Mayor of Portsmouth, in advance of a visit to allow him to draw a figure of local significance as part of his act, and his drawings would be handed to audience members at the end of the act, both practices further increasing the sense of intimacy and immediacy between performer and audience.⁷

In common with other music hall acts, the temporal and spatial coincidence of performer and audience required an institutionalisation of scheduled performances, with cartoonists appearing twice or thrice nightly at different halls in the same cities at rigorously precise times. In 1878 Tom Merry listed appearances in his personal advertisements as 'Oxford .... 8:50 Moore and Burgess Minstrels .... 9:50'.⁸ Similarly Hal Verdo performed thrice nightly, listing his times as 'Seebright Lounge .... 7:10, Royal Albert .... 9:10, Belmont's Palace .... 10:45'.⁹ Achieving these performance times depended upon the industrialisation of this entertainment form: fixed and published performance schedules, accurate timekeeping, rapid transport, and the syndication of acts. Thus, while the on-stage performance may not have been mechanically produced, the structure allowing it most certainly was.

Philip Auslander has argued 'liveness is not an ontologically defined condition but a historically variable effect of mediatization. It was the development of recording technologies that made it both possible and necessary to perceive existing representations as "live".'[10] The lightning cartoon act appeared alongside moving image presentations in music halls, as well as appearing on film in moving image presentations as a 'turn' in music halls; as such it certainly contributed to the formation of the notion of the 'live', even if that term was not commonly used until later.[11] As the industrialised scheduling already described suggests, even before mediatised performances created this distinction between live and non-live, the lightning cartoon exhibited qualities that make reading the act as 'live' problematic.

As its name suggests, the lightning cartoon act was predicated upon the rapidity with which the cartoon was drawn and the skill of the artist. Its appeal resided as much in the process of its production as in the finished result, which would be discarded or handed to the audience. The ease with which the image was produced and the sense of immediacy it created between performer and audience belied the effort performed beforehand to rehearse its production. Equally cartoonists worked hard to conceal other tricks used to prepare images before use, such as fine guidelines that would be invisible to the audience,[12] or acts in which the whole image was prepared and then covered in a whitewash which was then gradually removed during the act.[13] The outrage shown in the exposés of these tricks indicates the extent to which the audience was convinced by the immediacy of the performance, despite it in fact being heavily rehearsed and constructed.

To this construction might be added the performance of the stage persona. While lightning cartoonists were presented as appearing under their own names, as distinct from the performance of roles in legitimate theatre, many of them took stage names, indicating the extent to which their persona was itself an aspect of the performance. Edgar Austin's real name was William Edgar Piercey, Tom Merry's real name was William Mecham, and there is no evidence that Professor Thornbury's title was anything but self-attributed.[14] We may add to this a number of exotically named lightning cartoonists, including Azig Babalo ('Oriental marvel' and 'lightning cartoonist'), Kalulu, Ko-Ko ('the Japanese cartoonist'), Marishio, and Mefoto, whose acts undoubtedly contained a performance of 'otherness' whether they were genuinely from overseas or not.[15]

5 Performance Times: The Lightning Cartoon and the Emergence of Animation

The most startling example of this is Miss Lydia Dreams, the stage name of Walter Lambert.[16] Her act was described in *The Era* thus:

> "the lady" is no other than a young gentleman very cleverly made up to represent one of the fair sex; and the element of surprise comes in when the artist, who works a ventriloquial performance, gives utterance to some unmistakably manly tones supposed to proceed from one of the [lightning cartooned] figures.[17]

Not only does the use of ventriloquism anticipate animation in giving voice, and thus life, to drawn images, but it also adds further to the complex performance of gender. Ventriloquism was a common feature in other lightning cartoonist's acts and provides a further instance of the performance moving away from any simplistic notion of immediacy or authenticity, as it sees a dislocation between the mechanism of the production of the performance and its apparent source as perceived by the audience.

The lightning cartoon act can thus already be seen to have multiple performance times: the rehearsal or preparation time alongside the stage performance, which is perhaps better considered a re-performance, and can be seen to contain multiple levels, including the use of stage personas and ventriloquism that belie a simple monstration. In addition there is a further vital temporal period at stake in the act: the perceptual time of the audience watching the act. In the lightning cartoon the temporal relationship between the performance of the work of art and its consumption is intentionally played upon and exploited. As well as enacting the event of the production of a cartoon, the lightning cartoon also enacts the reading or decoding of a cartoon. While the act of producing the drawing is accelerated to 'lightning' speed, the act of perception is decelerated. Whether or not the viewer has been made aware, through a title, of what is being drawn, as each line appears the viewer must interpret it and understand its relation to those already drawn, sometimes reassessing their interpretation as conflicting elements appear. In doing so this performance extends and explores the 'narrative of perception' which normally occurs in milliseconds whenever a line drawing is viewed. This process provides an insight into the way the mind resolves the ambiguity present in a simple line drawing. There is simply not enough information to be sure what is seen, yet the mind makes a best endeavour assumption. The slow motion enactment of perception was a central part of the pleasures of the lightning cartoon act, a narrative of perception that would have been further emphasised by the withholding or revelation of contextual information, or by perceptual tricks, such as drawing inverted images. In emphasising, rather than eliding, the temporal disjunction between construction, presentation, and perception in its performance, the lightning cartoon anticipated the temporal dislocation of cinematic performance.[18]

Tom Merry: Early lightning cartoon films

Given these qualities of the lightning cartoon act, it is apt that it should have made the move into the new medium of moving images from their inception. In fact, the films of Tom Merry performing lightning cartoons produced by Robert Paul and Birt Acres predate the projection of moving images, as they were produced in 1895 for display in Edison's Kinetoscope. These films were included in Paul's first public projections at the Alhambra music hall in London's Leicester Square in March 1896.[19] Merry had been one of the most popular music hall lightning cartoonists from the late 1870s, performing twice nightly in London, and was known as a print cartoonist at the time of his film work.[20] While these lightning cartoons were performed for the camera apparently unchanged, the very act of filming shifted the terms of the performance times previously identified.

As with all films of music hall acts, the immediacy of 'live' performance, made salient by interaction between performer and spectator, was no longer possible. Instead during these early presentations it was Paul and his Animatographe machine that were physically present, emphasising the prepared nature of the entertainment, which had always been an implicit aspect of the music hall act. One short fragment of the Paul/Acres films of Merry, in which Merry is seen bowing towards the camera/audience, is still extant. This might be understood as an attempt to simulate the temporal immediacy of 'live' music hall performance, and as such indicate a failure of the filmmakers to recognise the nature of mediatised presentation involved in mechanical moving images. Yet as described above, the lightning cartoon performance was already a complex site of temporal disjunction and as such may have been considered a re-performance already. In light of this, Merry's bow in the film is simply a continuation of the stage practice in a more complex manner. Such a reading is bolstered by a later film *Peinture a l'envers [Painting Upside Down]*, thought to be an 1898 French film of Merry performing, which shows not only the performer but also his audience onscreen. This onscreen audience demonstrates the narrative of perception guessing game described in the music hall act, as they become visibly excited in trying to guess what Merry is drawing, gesticulating and discussing with their neighbours, before Merry unveils the drawing by inverting it, revealing it to be a woman's head drawn upside down. By including an onscreen audience, the film emphasises the performative nature of the lightning cartoon act, as well as visibly depicting the temporal dislocation between the performance and the audience as they experience the narrative of perception described earlier. Furthermore, the extra-filmic audience experience both Merry's act as a performance and the performance of the onscreen audience, adding another temporal level to the viewing of Merry's act.

There is one further important temporal shift in the production of these early lightning cartoon films: the role filming and projection speeds would have played. Originally made for display in kinetoscopes, Robert Paul's early films, including those of Merry, would have been shot at the forty frames per second that was used for those individual devices. When the films were reused by Paul in his early film performances they would have been projected at half that speed, around sixteen to twenty frames per second, resulting in a slow motion effect. As John Barnes argued, this undoubtedly added to the appeal of some subjects.[21] The film most often commented upon and praised in reviews of this period, *Rough Sea at Dover* would be given an ethereal, picturesque quality that would enhance the natural subject matter. In contrast the Merry films would be adversely affected, the 'lightning' speed damaged by doubling the screen time.[22] Furthermore, human performers' movements would be identified as unnatural more readily than phenomena such as waves, and the change in projection speed would have contributed to the flicker which caused one reviewer to remark 'it would not be safe for a man addicted to drink to look at that for more than a minute'.[23] While this mismatch between exposure and projection added to the appeal of some subjects, it would have damaged Merry's films by doubling the screen time thus degrading the lightning speed of the performance. In Tom Merry's case the mechanical intervention in the temporal basis of performance undoubtedly contributed to his films going out of circulation and becoming largely forgotten. In contrast, Walter Booth's utilisation of the same mechanical manipulation of performance time resulted in the creation of what would later be called animation.

Walter Booth: The emergence of animation

In 1906, Walter Booth took the lightning cartoon act and applied trick film techniques to produce what are generally credited as the first British animated films. Booth had performed as both a magician and lightning cartoonist at London's Egyptian Hall and on tour from 1897.[24] He appeared in between cinematograph performances presented by David Devant, a magician who had been an early adopter of Paul's Theatrograph, purchasing one of Paul's projectors and presenting films at the Egyptian Hall, operated by Maskelyne & Cook, from March 1896. It is presumably through this connection that Booth joined Robert Paul's film company after advertising for work in 1899.[25] As well as appearing on stage performing lightning cartoons between film performances by Paul,[26] Booth was responsible, with Paul, for a series of trick films which utilised in-camera manipulation to produce magical effects. In 1906, Booth moved to Charles Urban's film company where he combined these trick techniques with the lightning cartoon to produce a number of films, including *The Hand of the Artist* in 1906, *Comedy Cartoons* in 1907 and *Animated Cotton* in 1909. These saw a progression from the straight lightning cartoon to the drawn images taking on independent agency, and the gradual elimination of the outward symbols of the lightning cartoon, such as the artist, their hand, the drawing board or easel.

Comedy Cartoons (1907) provides a model for of the development of animated cartoons from the lightning cartoon. As the film progresses there is a stylistic narrative as the iconography of the lightning cartoon performance is replaced by a technologically propelled animation while retaining the aesthetic mode of the narrative of perception. The opening sequence provides a straight presentation of Booth performing the lightning cartoon act as he would have done in music halls in the 1890s including a direct address to the audience, the only adjustment from the stage performance being those seen in the films of Tom Merry. Equally the second sequence, while more closely framed, features Booth's hand drawing in more-or-less realtime, The opening of this second sequence provides a good example of the narrative of perception as it would have been seen in music halls, as the most pertinent features of the old lady's face are left to last to extend the perception of what is being drawn at lightning speed.

The end of this sequence, however, sees the elimination of the outward symbols of the lightning cartoon, as the image is erased apparently without human agency. It retains, however, the concern with temporal perception identified as central to the lightning cartoon act. Whereas in the opening of the sequence perception is delayed and decelerated by the slow unveiling of details, here the spectator is made aware of how long they are able to perceive a face even with the rapidly diminishing number of lines, right up to the very end when the eyes of the face are erased leaving a blank screen. Importantly, the temporal distinction seen in the music hall is further accentuated, as the effort and time to produce the films increased with the introduction of frame-by-frame construction. The accelerated 'lightning' speed of the performance serves to elide the tremendous time and effort required to create it; conversely the unveiling of the image serves to reveal the complex process, normally hidden, by which a line drawing is perceived by the spectator.

These relationships, between a lightning performance dependent upon a slow and laborious production time allied with a heightened viewing experience which plays upon normally instantaneous perceptual reflexes, may be seen as fundamental to what would become described as animation. While behind the scenes articles and effort saving patents attest to the laborious production process behind animation, the experience of watching such films is one of ease, to the extent that we attribute the performance we see not to the artist, but to the onscreen character. Equally animation may be considered to draw attention to the viewer's role in constructing the moving image world in contrast to the suppression of such spectatorial awareness in other modes of filmmaking.

Conclusion

The lightning cartoon may thus be seen to have anticipated the temporal dislocation of moving image performances, and consequently played a role in the exploitation of it in the early development of animation. As has been shown, and contrary to immediate expectations, the music hall act was not a simple 'live' stage performance dependent upon the temporal and spatial coincidence of performer and audience, with an attendant immediacy and authenticity based on the inherent skills of the performer. Some performers may have presented their act in this way, with Edgar Austin proclaiming his honesty in drawing without aids and child stars' inherent ability being emphasised in interviews.[27] Equally audiences' vocal responses indicate a naive acceptance of that immediacy and interaction. Yet, as we have seen, the act was carefully constructed, through the use of stage names and personas, rehearsals, rigorous schedules, and drawing tricks. Most importantly, the performance involved a dislocation between the time it took to produce the drawing and the spectator's cognition of it, termed here the narrative of perception. When the lightning cartoon was translated into early moving images, these various performance times were exacerbated, with their construction more readily apparent, and they were added to by the nature of the mechanical reproduction of the performance. While the earliest films of Tom Merry were inadvertently damaged by the mismatch between production time and projection time, Walter Booth exploited the difference to further extend the temporal dislocation between performer and audience, a quality that may be seen as typical of animation.

Notes

1. More details of this stage performance and its move into moving images can be found in Malcolm Cook, "The Lightning Cartoon: Animation from Music Hall to Cinema", *Early Popular Visual Culture* 11, no. 3 (2013).
2. Donald Crafton, *Shadow of a Mouse: Performance, Belief, and World-Making in Animation* (Berkeley: University of California Press, 2013).
3. *The Era*, 8 August 1891, 23; *The Era*, 4 February 1877, 10; *The Era*, 4 March 1893, 17; *The Era*, 8 August 1885, 23; *The Era* 7 December 1879, 20; *The Era*, 17 August 1879, 16.
4. *The Belfast News-Letter*, 1 November 1897, 4; *The Era*, 25 December 1897, 21.
5. *The Pall Mall Gazette* 23 April 1889, 6.
6. *The Era*, 12 November 1881, 4.
7. Diary of Little Erskine in collection of his daughter, Daphne Jones.
8. *The Era* 7 July 1878, 20.
9. *The Era*, 18 September 1886, 23.
10. Philip Auslander, "Digital Liveness: A Historico-Philosophical Perspective", *PAJ: A Journal of Performance and Art* 34, no. 3 (2012).
11. *The Belfast News-Letter*, 1 November 1897, 4; *The Era*, 25 December 1897, 21; *The Era*, 28 March 1896, 18.
12. Edgar Austin advertised 'my sketches are done off hand, without the aid of any tracing', his need to do so indicating that this was common practice. *The Era*, 24 December 1881, 21.
13. *The Era*, 22 September 1883, 20; *Northern Echo* 14 April 1893, 2; *Daily News* 10 October 1893, 5.
14. *The Illustrated Police News etc*, 11 March 1893, 4; *The Era*, 7 December 1895, 17.
15. *The Era*, 21 December 1895, 18; *The Era*, 13 June 1896, 19; *The Derby Mercury*, 9 June 1875, 4; *The Era*, 3 October 1891, 8; *The Era*, 5 September 1891, 15; *The Era*, 8 September 1900, 19.
16. *Northern Echo*, 5 January 1893, 1.
17. *The Era*, 24 November 1894, 16.
18. Such complexities foreshadow Crafton's notion of performance *in* and *of* animation: Crafton, *Shadow of a Mouse*, 15–57.
19. *The Era*, 28 March 1896, 18.
20. *The Pall Mall Gazette*, 4 July 1885, 16; *Jackson's Oxford Journal*, 31 March 1883, 5.
21. John Barnes, *The Beginnings of the Cinema in England, 1894–1901*, ed. Richard Maltby, Rev. and enl. ed., 5 vols., vol. 1 (Exeter: University of Exeter Press, 1998), 217.
22. The film of Merry sketching Bismarck is considered simply 'successful' by *The Era* reviewer, but the review does specifically comment on a film of two men boxing 'whose sparring seemed to us a little slow', as a result of a mismatch between the shooting speed intended for the Kinetoscope and projection speed. *The Era*, 28 March 1896, 18.
23. *The Pall Mall Gazette*, 26 March 1896, 2.
24. *Trewman's Exeter Flying Post or Plymouth and Cornish Advertiser*, 3 June 1897, 3.
25. *The Era*, 15 April 1899, 26.
26. *The Essex County Standard West Suffolk Gazette, and Eastern Counties Advertiser*, 10 November 1900, 7.
27. *The Era*, 24 December 1881, 21; *The Pall Mall Gazette*, 31 May 1890, 3; *Chums*, 9 May 1894, 587.

6

La transparence du Fregoligraph en question

Frédéric Tabet

Leopoldo Fregoli est un des nombreux artistes qui, au tournant du XXe siècle, se saisissent du cinématographe. Début 1900, à Paris, ce transformiste italien propose une formule qui a déjà fait sa renommée à l'étranger: changer de costumes plus d'une centaine de fois pendant sa représentation. Ce spectacle séduit les Parisiens et en quelques semaines sa performance connaît un succès important. Cette réussite semble liée à la structure de ses soirées: d'une part, il s'empare de l'ensemble des pratiques spectaculaires de son temps (il est tour à tour chanteur, danseur, musicien, mime, ventriloque, magicien), et, d'autre part, il propose un spectacle mixte, tirant un trait d'union entre les parodies ludiques des transformistes et les performances virtuoses des 'Hommes Protée'. Les projections cinématographiques souvent programmées dans les music-halls poussent toutefois Fregoli à modifier sa formule. Dès 1898, il incorpore en fin de spectacle des projections d'images animées, ce qui donne lieu au 'Fregoligraph'.[1]

Le spectacle de Fregoli a été souvent mentionné dans des histoires du cinéma, dont celle publiée par Georges Sadoul au milieu du XXe siècle.[2] Les travaux de Riccardo Redi[3] et Aldo Bernardini[4] ont plus récemment documenté l'évolution de la carrière italienne de Fregoli, tandis que Luiggi Colagreco,[5] Matthew Solomon,[6] Augusto Sainati[7] ont étudié la spécificité et l'influence esthétique de son spectacle. Cet article interroge l'intégration du cinématographe dans les soirées de l'Italien. Il vise à compléter ces approches en se penchant sur son spectacle parisien de 1900.

Pour approfondir ces études, nous adoptons un point de vue centré non pas sur l'évolution des films produits par Fregoli, mais sur les variations des performances de l'artiste au moment de l'émergence du cinématographe. Nous emprunterons donc ce que Jacob Smith,[8] à la suite de Rick Altman,[9] a nommé une approche 'axée performance' (*performance-oriented*). En effet, un des traits fondamentaux des premières projections cinématographiques est leur aspect performatif: aucune projection n'est sensiblement la même lors de la période dite muette du cinéma. Ces séances se rapprochent davantage du spectacle vivant. Ce ne sera qu'à la suite de lents glissements dans la forme qu'elles seront vécues sur le modèle des projections d'aujourd'hui. En prenant comme centre de gravité la performance, le chercheur est conduit à décloisonner la vision que les approches centrées sur les films ont eu tendance à entretenir. Pour concevoir ce qui a pu se jouer sur la scène, les sources provenant de différents médias doivent être considérées ensemble. Cette recherche s'appuie ainsi sur le dépouillement de nouvelles sources: articles de presse, affiches, disques tirés de collections privées,[10] etc. Ces sources variées nous permettront de nous attarder sur un cas particulier de résonance entre enregistrement médiatique et performance, soit l'intégration du Fregoligraph au sein des soirées de l'Italien. Nous chercherons plus particulièrement à démontrer que cette intégration a généré des effets de *transparence*, dans toute la polysémie que ce terme admet, entre évidence et invisibilité.

Le Fregoligraph et la transparence de l'écran

En 1935, Fregoli rédige une série d'articles pour la revue italienne *Scenario*.[11] Ces articles sont repris en 1936 dans ses mémoires *Fregoli raccontato da Fregoli*.[12] Dans l'un de ces textes, il décrit une supposée rencontre avec Louis Lumière en 1895, alors qu'il se produisait au théâtre des Célestins de Lyon. Fregoli aurait été invité à passer une semaine dans l'usine des Lumière pour '[s']instruire des secrets de reproduction, de développement, de tirage et de projection de leurs petits films'.[13] Ailleurs il décrit des performances *in vivo*: caché derrière l'écran, il 'double' les personnages, passe les bandes à rebours, les aboute pour les projeter sans interruption.

Ce passage souvent cité a attisé l'intérêt d'historiens qui ont attribué à Fregoli le titre de précurseur du cinéma sonore.[14] Les faits rapportés par l'Italien semblent toutefois contredits par un entrefilet de 1906: 'Samedi 6 janvier, représentation de M. Fregoli qui vient pour la première fois à Lyon'.[15] Ni les archives du Théâtre des Célestins ni la correspondance des frères Lumière ne permettent de confirmer le passage de Fregoli à Lyon avant 1906. Nous supposons seulement que c'est vraisemblablement en 1897 que l'artiste se procure un Cinématographe Lumière afin de proposer, dès janvier 1898, des projections de vues animées dans ses spectacles en Italie.[16] Le Fregoligraph – renommé pour l'occasion 'Fregoliograph' – est introduit à Londres six mois plus tard. Le 30 juillet 1898 on peut lire dans la presse:

At the Alhambra that clever actor and mimic, M. Frégoli, has introduced an amusing novelty into his entertainment. At the conclusion of his impersonations of famous composers we now have an animatograph show in which the active Italian is shown now before the curtain entertaining the audience and now behind effecting those lightning changes of costume and make-up, which are so amazing in their swiftness.[17]

D'autres articles de presse nous fournissent de plus amples détails.[18] Son dispositif scénique est composé d'un écran blanc de quatre mètres sur trois, posé au centre de la scène et fermé par un cadre garni de 200 lampes à incandescence. Celles-ci s'allument lorsque la bande cinématographique touche à sa fin afin de '[rompre] avec la monotonie de l'attente' pendant les changements de bobines. Une lampe à arc de 40 ampères permet l'agrandissement nécessaire, tandis que sept autres lampes à arc complètent le dispositif d'éclairage. Cet appareillage électrique assez complexe contraint les directeurs de l'Alhambra à s'alimenter en courant auprès d'une société extérieure. Le projecteur se trouvant à l'arrière de l'écran, l'image est perçue à travers l'écran[19] : nous avons un premier effet de transparence.

Fregoli se concentre cependant dans ses mémoires, non pas sur ce dispositif technique élaboré, mais sur la performance de la projection cinématographique : l'accompagnement musical, ses propres interactions avec l'image… Ces exemples de manipulation du cinématographe *in vivo* montrent que Fregoli transforme une simple exhibition mécanique en une véritable performance. Toujours d'après ses mémoires, il n'accompagne pas les images projetées, comme le ferait un bonimenteur, mais prête sa voix aux personnages représentés. Les spectateurs reconnaissent ainsi la voix qu'ils ont admirée au cours des parties précédentes de la soirée. Cette tentative de synchronisation image / son trouve sa place dans la lignée des attractions sonores déployées par Fregoli : ventriloquie, chants, imitations… En prêtant sa voix aux personnages de ses vues animées, Fregoli ne cherche ni à anticiper un certain réalisme cinématographique, ni à créer une illusion parfaite. Sa performance ne s'efface pas, le 'doublage' des vues n'a pas pour but de compléter l'appareil de projection, ni de faire du 'cinématographe perfectionné' en suppléant aux manques qu'une vision téléologique attribuerait au cinéma muet. Fregoli n'est pas le créateur du 'premier 'appareil' de projection sonore',[20] ou même un précurseur dans ce domaine. Il ne fait que poursuivre sa pratique avec un nouvel outil, le cinématographe. Ces interventions et manipulations lors de la projection affirment en filigrane, la présence de l'artiste. Et comme dans l'ensemble de son spectacle, Fregoli transparaît, au sens étymologique du terme, à travers ses costumes et ses interprétations comme à travers l'écran. La toile ne coupe pas le regard du spectateur, elle ne fait que le voiler; la performance affleure derrière l'écran.

La presse londonienne de 1898 décrit le Fregoligraph comme un dispositif singulier: à la fois mécanique, électrique, lumineux et sonore. Ces caractéristiques sont celles associées par les historiens du cinéma à la 'période de nouveauté', 'où les spectateurs se rendent aux séances pour assister à des démonstrations de machines'.[21] Cependant, comme pour de nombreuses autres formes spectaculaires, Fregoli reconfigure cette démonstration. La machine lui sert de prétexte, et permet de poursuivre son inscription sur la scène par la combinaison et l'appropriation de systèmes de représentation. Il y a d'ailleurs fort à parier qu'une fois l'écran retiré, c'est bien Fregoli et non sa machine que le public applaudit encore une fois. Nous n'avons toutefois que peu d'informations sur la réception des vues animées de Fregoli. Un des auteurs de la revue *The Electrical Engineer* nous apprend – presque accessoirement – que les vues du Fregoligraph sont 'exceedingly funny' – excessivement drôles ... .[22] Mais qu'en est-il au juste?

Le Fregoligraph et la transparence des décors

Des dix-sept bandes récupérées dans la demeure de Fregoli et conservées,[23] les plus singulières sont ses 'vues de coulisses'.[24] Dans celles-ci, l'artiste entre par la porte d'un décor, se change – aidé ou non d'habilleurs – puis sort par une autre porte et ainsi de suite jusqu'à ce que la bande touche à sa fin. Ces vues animées offrent au spectateur un regard nouveau sur la performance de l'artiste. Le point de vue adopté par la caméra lors des prises de vues – frontal sur l'arrière d'une feuille de décor – semble compléter la vision de l'espace scénique, dans une sorte de contre-champ radical. En donnant l'impression de voir à travers les décors des parties précédentes, la présentation en fin de soirée des projections du Fregoligraph permet de comprendre comment les changements de costumes ont été réalisés. On assiste à une nouvelle déclinaison de la transparence du Fregoligraph.

Le cas du Fregoligraph n'est certes pas isolé. Comme pour de nombreuses compagnies proposant des formes qui alternent entre des spectacles d'écran et des performances, les films ont pu créer des effets d'annonce, d'amplification (en relayant simultanément le spectacle dans différentes salles de spectacle) ou de rémanence (en prolongeant virtuellement leur présence par des projections). De même, le rôle des bandes de la série Fregoli est très différent selon le contexte. Aldo Bernardini a montré que ces vues animées ont effectivement eu une carrière autonome en Italie.[25] Ajoutons que dans le cas particulier des vues de coulisses, si on annonce dans les programmes et dans la presse londonienne de 1898 'The Exposure of Fregoli, by the Fregoliograph'[26] juste après son départ, c'est vraisemblablement pour stopper ses nombreux plagiaires.

Quoi qu'il en soit, on est surpris de la décision de Fregoli de retirer le Fregoligraph de son répertoire, ponctuellement à partir de 1905, puis définitivement en 1907. Pour comprendre ce retrait nous proposons un premier élément de réponse concernant sa performance parisienne de 1900.

La transparence du Fregoligraph et sa réception critique parisienne

La première représentation publique de Fregoli au Trianon-Théâtre de Paris a lieu le 20 janvier 1900. Un mois plus tard, un incendie détruit totalement l'intérieur du théâtre et une partie de son matériel. Fregoli renouvelle ses décors et costumes, et déplace son spectacle dans la salle de l'Olympia. L'incendie – qu'il met en scène lors de son retour – lui fournit par ailleurs une couverture de presse importante, sa mésaventure ayant touché les Parisiens. Dès lors, les guichets de réservation sont 'littéralement assiégés'.[27] Porté par la vogue de l'exposition universelle, Fregoli reste sur scène jusqu'au 7 octobre 1900, et jusqu'en 1916 revient régulièrement à Paris. L'épisode de l'incendie du théâtre est emblématique de son sens des relations publiques. Durant son premier séjour parisien, le nom de Fregoli est omniprésent dans la presse. L'artiste utilise de nombreux moyens pour entretenir la curiosité des chroniqueurs, notamment en jouant sur l'évolution de sa programmation. Les deux pièces présentées en alternance au cours des premiers soirs sont ainsi remplacées après une semaine par les premières représentations de la comédie *Garçon éclair*, à son tour remplacée la semaine suivante par une scène de ventriloquie. Fregoli, qui établit lui-même son programme hebdomadaire, propose à partir du 18 juin 1900 une première partie différente à chaque représentation.

Nous avons dénombré plus de soixante-dix comptes-rendus des spectacles présentés à Paris par Fregoli dans les pages du *Figaro* entre le 21 janvier et le 7 octobre 1900. Les chroniqueurs y détaillent les changements de programme, énumèrent les costumes, les voix utilisées, le type de public, les bénéfices de l'artiste… Ces comptes-rendus révèlent que six jours après la première de son spectacle au Trianon Fregoli introduit son Fregoligraph sur la scène parisienne. Or, on ne relève en 1900 que deux références à ces projections dans la presse parisienne:

> À Trianon-Théâtre, à partir d'aujourd'hui samedi, en dehors de son spectacle habituel, Fregoli présentera au public le Fregoligraph. Qu'est-ce que le Fregoligraph? Fregoli vu dans les coulisses effectuant des transformations.[28]

Le Fregoligraph donne ensuite au public un aperçu des coulisses de Trianon pendant que Fregoli effectue ses transformations.[29]

La situation se répète lors du retour de l'artiste en 1904: le *Figaro* annonce des 'tableaux Fregoliens'[30] sans autres commentaires. Les projections ne seront plus annoncées en 1905. Pourquoi un tel silence?

En 1900, le cinématographe n'est certes plus une nouveauté pour les Parisiens. Les frères Isola qui dirigent alors la salle de l'Olympia ont été parmi les premiers à proposer des vues animées, début avril 1896, dans leur théâtre Isola. Les spectateurs de cette salle ont d'autre part pu assister à des projections Lumière organisées au premier étage du bâtiment dès mars 1896,[31] puis au Musée Oller, situé au sous-sol de cette même salle, en juillet 1896. À l'époque des débuts parisiens de Fregoli, janvier 1900, des projections du Biograph sont intégrées à la programmation de nombreuses salles de spectacle.[32] D'autres projections à 'grand spectacle' ne manquent également pas de faire ombrage au Fregoligraph, un peu plus tard, lors de l'ouverture de l'exposition universelle le 15 avril 1900, tels le *Cinéorama*, le *Cinéma théâtre*, le *Phonorama*, le *Thépatroscope* ou le *Cinématographe-géant* des frères Lumière. Le manque d'intérêt de la critique pour les projections de Fregoli tend à faire penser que cette partie du spectacle n'est pas digne d'intérêt. La période de nouveauté est passée et la presse n'est plus intéressée par ce dispositif technique. Le Fregoligraph serait une pratique presque désuète, passée de mode et greffée de manière artificielle sur le spectacle. Cependant, ces projections qui pourraient paraître anachroniques,[33] resteront au programme de l'Italien jusqu'en 1905. Elles disparaîtront finalement de son répertoire en 1907.

Pour mieux saisir la réception timide réservée par la presse au Fregoligraph, nous pouvons la comparer à la promotion du spectacle par l'artiste. Ce qui frappe dans ses affiches, affichettes, ou cartes postales c'est la rareté des mentions concernant le cinématographe; par exemple, il n'est pas annoncé sur les affiches de l'année 1900. Fregoli semble réservé quant à son introduction. Ce n'est qu'en 1904 que les programmes mentionnent succinctement 'Fregoligraph Tableaux Fregoliens', en fin de seconde partie. En 1905, il n'y a plus aucune précision: Fregoli, en représentation au Barathford's Alhambra Théâtre de Paris, n'utilise plus les projections cinématographiques. Le Fregoligraph a été remplacé par des vues cinématographiques de la Maison Pathé.[34]

En 1900, le Fregoligraph aurait pu être adjoint *in extremis* à son spectacle Parisien, alors que le matériel promotionnel était déjà imprimé, d'où le sentiment d'un regain de publicité en 1904. Cette hypothèse ne tient cependant pas la confrontation avec l'article autobiographique rédigé en 1900 par Fregoli pour le journal *Le Gaulois*. Alors inconnu en France, l'Italien se présente aux Parisiens. Il décrit son parcours et ses succès dans les capitales du monde, mais ne mentionne pas les projections.[35] De même en 1904, il tente de justifier son absence de la scène parisienne dans un numéro auto-promotionnel du *Théâtre illustré*.[36] Là non plus il ne mentionne ni ses vues animées ni sa rencontre avec les frères Lumière. Il est donc difficile de concevoir ce qu'ont pu être ces projections parisiennes. L'étude détaillée de cette période ne permet à aucun moment de confirmer les affirmations faites par Fregoli en 1935 et mentionnant le doublage des personnages derrière l'écran, les projections à rebours, les opérations d'aboutage … Pour Augusto Sainati, ce passage des mémoires '[…] dénonce l'importance que Fregoli accorde encore … à son ancienne expérience cinématographique'.[37] Cette valorisation semble toutefois rétrospective, car aucun document du début du XXe siècle ne la laisse transparaître.

L'étude d'enregistrements sonores permet par ailleurs de formuler de nouvelles hypothèses sur les relations entre la scène et l'écran dans les spectacles de Fregoli. Ce dernier produit en effet au moins trois séries d'enregistrements distribués sur disque à l'époque où ses spectacles incluent les projections du Fregoligraph. La première série, éditée en 1898 pour la Société des Micro-Phonographes Bettini,[38] semble issue d'enregistrements réalisés alors que Fregoli se produit à New York en 1896.[39] En 1903, le catalogue du label Gramophone à Milan propose des monologues et des chansons comiques de l'artiste, dont certains en dialecte milanais et romain.[40] Finalement, en 1906, la Société italienne Fonotipia[41] enregistre sept titres pour sa série 'les grands chanteurs comiques Italiens'.[42]

Si les performances vocales de l'artiste ont souvent été relevées, peu d'auteurs se sont attardés sur ces enregistrements qui permettent d'éclairer autrement sa conception de la scène. Une première écoute fait ressortir un manque de clarté des voix. Fregoli brouille la bande sonore et ses paroles, souvent incompréhensibles, sont entremêlées d'onomatopées. Lorsqu'il chante, il change de registre, d'octave, enchaîne rapidement des bribes d'opéra et des couplets de chansons populaires dans des pots-pourris effrénés. Ailleurs, il accélère le rythme et le débit, bredouille, parle en dialecte, ou passe de l'italien à l'espagnol … À aucun moment, les commentaires de presse ne mentionnent ces disques, ce qui tend à démontrer que ces enregistrements étaient, à l'instar de ceux des vues du Fregoligraph, considérés comme de 'mauvais' objets. Or les spectacles de transformisme reposent sur la vitesse des changements, auxquels Fregoli apporte énergie et justesse d'interprétation. Si les enregistrements sont brouillés, à la limite de l'audible, ils illustrent parfaitement les prouesses vocales de l'artiste et la vive alternance des registres et des gammes.

Ainsi, qu'elles soient sonores ou cinématographiques, les projections médiatiques de Fregoli renforcent son aura. Bien qu'elles semblent disparaître dans les comptes-rendus critiques, elles les sous-tendent en filigrane. Dès 1900, le Fregoligraph aurait été ainsi sciemment présenté aux Parisiens, non pas comme une nouveauté (comme il semble l'avoir été à Londres), mais comme de simples vues prises sur le vif, auxquelles la presse est peu sensible.

Au final, le dispositif de réception des films est transparent: il disparaît pour ne laisser voir que la performance et non la projection, d'où la quasi absence de description de ces séances et la platitude des comptes-rendus de presse. C'est pourquoi les critiques décrivent un Fregoli toujours seul en scène ...

Historiographie de la transparence du Fregoligraph

Les évolutions du spectacle de Fregoli englobent des assemblages performatifs très divers, recomposés au fil du temps et selon les pays dans lesquels l'artiste se produit. Ces assemblages s'appuient sur des formes variées qui interagissent et créent un effet choral. Concernant les vues animées, le Fregoligraph illustre une relation intime entre enregistrement mécanique et performance, Fregoli modulant son spectacle lors de son interprétation pour l'œil unique de la caméra, puis re-modulant l'enregistrement mécanique lors de la projection. Les choix de Fregoli avant et pendant la prise de vues, puis au moment de la programmation et de la projection de ces bandes permettent de comprendre les fonctions qu'il attribue au Cinématographe Lumière et, par là, donnent des indices sur la réception des vues. Saisir et étudier la modulation des performances de l'Italien, les adaptations et ajustements de son spectacle, permet à la fois d'effectuer une étude comparée des spécificités nationales des pays qu'il visite et des choix effectués lors de différents enregistrements. Ces études *performance-oriented* mettent en évidence les spécificités attribuées à la presse, aux images animées, ainsi qu'aux enregistrements sonores.

Si pour la période parisienne les projections en marche arrière, l'aboutage des vues, et les tentatives de doublage de Fregoli lors de ses projections restent à démontrer, force est de constater que Fregoli a su jouer de l'ambivalence des vues animées, à la fois témoignages objectifs pris sur le vif et constructions trompeuses. Le Fregoligraph a permis de brouiller le souvenir du spectateur, lui donnant la sensation d'un rythme plus soutenu et d'un nombre plus important de transformations. Son spectacle montre une certaine sensibilité aux assemblages d'éléments appartenant à des séries culturelles voisines, et non une recherche de pureté formelle. Tous ces éléments hétérogènes concourent pourtant à prolonger son image. Fregoli s'est ainsi inscrit de plain-pied dans la culture du XXe siècle, à la recherche de la vitesse et du sensationnalisme.

Il faut aussi lui reconnaître son sens de la mise en spectacle. Fregoli a acquis une place importante dans les premières histoires du cinéma grâce à ses mémoires de 1935, dans lesquelles il livre une description améliorée des projections incorporées à son spectacle. Contrairement à ses contemporains ayant également mis à contribution les moyens du cinéma, Fregoli a réussi à marquer l'histoire du cinéma. S'il a produit des mémoires qualifiés de 'mirobolants',[43] il a pourtant réussi à intéresser les premiers historiens à des pratiques de projection hétérogènes alors sous-estimées. Le cas du Fregoligraph dépasse largement la seule question du couplage de la scène et de l'écran, il ouvre de nouvelles perspectives quant à l'inscription de la projection de vues animées dans le contexte culturel du music-hall, qui interagit sur ses usages et qui, en retour, est modifié par celui-ci.

Remerciements: Cette communication a été possible grâce aux travaux réalisés dans le cadre de l'UMR ACTE 8218 et du laboratoire Littérature savoirs et Arts (LISAA, EA 4120).

Notes

1. Nous adoptons l'orthographe la plus communément utilisée par l'artiste.
2. Georges Sadoul, *Histoire générale du cinéma, les pionniers du cinéma de Méliès à Pathé, 1897–1909* (Paris: Denoël, 1947), 46.
3. Riccardo Redi, *Cinema muto italiano: 1896–1930* (Turin: Fondazione scuola nazionale di cinema, 1999), 22.
4. Aldo Bernardini, *Cinema muto italiano*, volume 1, *Ambiente spettacoli e spettator 1896–1904* (Bari: Editori Laterza, 1980), 84; Aldo Bernardini, "Leopoldo Fregoli 'cinematografista'", *A nuova luce. Cinema muto italiano. I: Atti del convegno internazionale, Bologna, 12–13 Novembre 1999* (Bologne: Clueb, 2000), 181–185.
5. Luigi Colagreco, "Il cinéma negli spettacoli di Leopoldo Fregoli", *Bianco & Nero – Bimestrale della Scuola Nazionale del Cinema* nos 3–4 (2002): 40–59.
6. Matthew Solomon, "Twenty-Five Heads Under One Hat: Quick-Change in the 1890s", *Meta-Morphing: Visual Transformation and the Culture of Quick-Change* (Minneapolis: University of Minnesota Press, 2000), 6–9.
7. Augusto Sainati, "La personnalisation du Cinématographe: Fregoli et son 'Fregoligraph'", *L'aventure du Cinématographe, actes du Congrès mondial Lumière* (Lyon: Aléas, 1999), 181–185.
8. Jacob Smith, "Kissing as Telling: Some Thoughts on the Cultural History of Media Performance", *Cinema Journal* 51, no 3 (2012): 123.
9. Rick Altman, "From Lecturer's Prop to Industrial Product: The Early History of Travel Films", dans *Virtual Voyages: Cinema and Travel*, sous la direction de Jeffrey Ruoff (Durham, NC: Duke University Press, 2006), 61.
10. Nous tenons à remercier le collectionneur Jack Cooper pour sa disponibilité.
11. Leopoldo Fregoli, "Memorie della mia vita", *Scenario* (Rome) nos 6–12 (1934); nos 1–5 (1935).

12. Leopoldo Fregoli, *Fregoli raccontato da Fregoli* (Milan: Rizzoli, 1936), 217.
13. Leopoldo Fregoli, "Memorie della mia vita", *Scenario* no 3 (mars 1935).
14. Mario Corsi, "Fregoli pioniere del muto e precursore del sonoro", *Cinema* (Rome) no 11 (10 décembre 1936): 416–417.
15. "Théâtre des Célestins", *Le Passe-temps* (7 janvier 1906): 3.
16. Aldo Bernardini, *Cinema italiano delle origini. Gli ambulanti* (Gemona: La Cineteca del Friuli, 2001), 27.
17. F. Moy.Thomas, "The Theatres", *The Graphic London* (30 juillet 1898): 403.
18. "Electricity in Entertainments", *The Electrical Engineer* (7 octobre 1898): 451.
19. Corsi, "Fregoli pioniere del muto".
20. Glauco Pellegrini, "Fregoli ou Le Premier Appareil de projection sonore", *La Revue du cinéma* no 14 (juin 1948): 48–51.
21. Tom Gunning, "Le cinéma d'attraction: le film des premiers temps, son spectateur, et l'avant-garde", *1895* no 50 (décembre 2006).
22. "Electricity in Entertainments", *The Electrical Engineer* (7 octobre 1898): 451.
23. Adriano Aprà, "Filmografia", *Bianco & Nero* nos 3–4 (mai–juin 2002): 62–67.
24. Films de la série Fregoli, conservés à la la Cineteca Nazionale de Rome: no 18 *Fregoli transformista*, no 25 *Segreto per vestirsi (con aiuto)*, no 26 *Fregoli 2 retroscena*.
25. Bernardini, *Cinema italiano delle origini*, 27.
26. *Alhambra Theater* [programme] (22 août 1898): 2.
27. Abel Mercklein, "Spectacles et concerts", *Le Figaro* (6 mars 1900): 5.
28. Albert Deville, "Courrier des théâtres", *Le Figaro* (27 janvier 1900): 4.
29. Abel Mercklein, "Spectacles et concerts", *Le Figaro* (3 février 1900): 5.
30. Albert Deville, "Spectacles et concerts", *Le Figaro* (30 janvier 1904): 4.
31. Jacques Rittaud-Hutinet, *Dictionnaire des cinématographes* (Paris: Éditions Champion, 1999), 360.
32. Jean-Jacques Meusy, *Paris-palaces, ou le temps des cinémas, 1894–1918* (Paris: CNRS, 1995), 76–77.
33. Giusy Pisano, "Les spectacles mixtes: tradition ou anachronisme?", *Le muet a la parole* (Paris: AFRHC, 2005), 131.
34. Barathford's Alhambra Théâtre [programme] (1905): 13. Collection Jacques Cooper (Bruxelles).
35. Léopoldo Fregoli, "Fregoli raconté par lui même", *Le Gaulois* (17 mars 1900): 1–2.
36. *Théâtre illustré et les feux de la Rampe* (Paris: Marcel Simon, 1904).
37. Sainati, "La personnalisation du cinématographe", 182.
38. *Bettini Micro-Phonograph and Records* (New York: Bettini Phonograph Laboratory, 1898): 14.
39. Richard Spottswood, *Ethnic Music on Record*, volume 6 (Urbana: University of Illinois Press, 1990).
40. Alan Kelly, *His Master's Voice/La voce del Padrone* (New York: Greenwood Press, 1988).
41. Anita Pesce, *La sirena nel solco* (Milan: Guida Editori, 2005), 46–47.
42. Alex Rusconi, *Fregoli la biografia* (Rome: Viterbo Stampa alternative, 2011), 158.
43. Patrick Rambaud, *Les mirobolantes aventures de Fregoli* (Paris: Bourin, 1994).

In the Flesh: Personal Appearances and the Picture Personality in Britain

Chris O'Rourke

It is a truism that, in the cinema as opposed to the theatre, the performer and the audience are never in the same place at the same time. However engaging we deem them to be, film performances are characterised by being mediated, rather than immediate; recorded, rather than live. Historical investigations into the period of early cinema have complicated this distinction between theatrical and cinematic forms of address. Various studies have drawn attention to the ongoing importance of accompanying or interpolated performances at the level of film exhibition, as well as revealing the multiple ways in which film technology intersected with (otherwise) live performance traditions. For instance, in an essay that explores turn-of-the-century entertainments including the music hall sketch and the waxwork show, David Mayer spotlights the 'rare and awkward hybrids', which, he writes, 'emerge from the dark interstices between the stage and motion pictures'.[1] Such hybrids appear less rare (if no less awkward) as film and theatre scholarship becomes more attuned to their presence in the historical record. Gwendolyn Waltz's work on the multi-media genres that populated late-nineteenth and early-twentieth century American performance culture[2] and Greg Giesekam's work on the use of moving-picture technology in avant-garde theatre practice both attest to the variety and longevity of attempts to blur the boundary between live and filmic performance modes.[3]

In this essay, I want to discuss the 'personal appearance', in which film performers made orchestrated visits to moving-picture venues, as another kind of awkward hybrid. From about 1910, personal appearances became one of a number of promotional strategies available to producers, distributors, and exhibitors in order to exploit the marketing value of the relatively new figure of the film celebrity, or 'picture personality'. In their various guises, personal appearances could also be occasions to reflect upon the difference that film technology made to the conventional relationship between performers and audiences.

Richard deCordova has traced the emergence of the picture personality in the United States to the years 1909–1910, during which time major production companies began to advertise the names of their hitherto anonymous stock companies.[4] Research by Jon Burrows and Andrew Shail suggests that a concept of film celebrity emerged in Britain at around the same time.[5] A survey of the British trade press confirms that, throughout 1910, the names of American moving-picture actors, including Florence Lawrence, Ethel Clayton and Pearl White, began to filter into British film discourse,[6] and in 1911 a number of British and European companies began to publicise the identities of their own leading players.[7] The launch of Britain's first dedicated popular film magazine, *The Pictures*, in October 1911 accelerated this process of disclosure, quickly evolving what Jane Bryan describes as 'a generic format based around a proliferation of film stars and their lives'.[8]

Personal appearances were a formative component of American picture personality promotion, occurring throughout 1910, particularly in places with ties to local production companies. Vitagraph's Florence Turner was the star guest of a special 'Vitagraph Girl Night' in Saratoga Park, New York, in April 1910, and again at a theatre in Jersey City the following December.[9] Such events were taken at the time (and have been interpreted since) as indicators of the growing importance of picture personalities within an emerging popular film culture and in American society at large. Reporting on the 'Vitagraph Girl Night' in Jersey City for the *Moving Picture World*, F.H. Richardson argued that the 'small riot' that was said to have broken out upon Turner's arrival at the unnamed venue was evidence that 'those who pose for the Silent Drama' were beginning to 'gain a tangible hold on their audiences'.[10]

When Turner relocated to the United Kingdom in 1913, she continued to make personal appearances in between her film work and her performances on the British variety stage.[11] Turner's presence in moving-picture venues confirmed her acceptance among local audiences and lent a touch of transatlantic prestige to the places she visited. Along with her former Vitagraph co-worker Tom Powers, she was invited to be star guest at the Second International Cinematograph Exhibition held in Glasgow in February 1914, where the pair performed a sketch, which was filmed and later shown to visitors, and helped to judge the finalists in a contest for would-be film actors.[12] Film celebrities had also been a feature of the First International Cinematograph Exhibition held in March 1913 in London's Olympia. A writer for the trade paper *The Cinema* reported that many producers 'had their actors and actresses "on view" at their stall', including the French firm Eclair, who brought over the comic picture personalities

Funnicus, Jane, and Softy, so that they might 'make a closer acquaintance' with 'moving picture devotees' attending the exhibition.[13] Funnicus and Jane had in fact been in the country for over a month, making personal appearances at several London picture theatres.[14]

However, while the presence of foreign picture personalities in British venues attracted the attention of trade journalists, who were eager to project an image of the native film business as a hub for international activity, the earliest series of personal appearances in Britain seems to have involved an actor with a British firm: the Irish actor Percy Moran, who was a member of the British and Colonial Kinematograph Company (known as B&C). B&C were one of the more enterprising British firms during the 1910s, producing films across a variety of popular genres, and responding to the vogue for location shooting by sending crews as far as the West Indies in search of scenic spectacle.[15] As Burrows notes, B&C were also pioneers of the personal appearance format in Britain, using these events as part of a broader bid to promote players including Moran across a range of media.[16]

In some respects, Moran's picture personality persona was particularly well developed. An article in the young person's magazine *Pearson's Weekly* told how he had spent his early years as a boy boxer under his father's tutelage before finding work as a 'rough-rider' in Barnum and Bailey's Wild West show and later as a singer and actor in a 'travelling penny gaff' with the music hall star Kate Carney.[17] However, Moran was most familiar to the film-going public not by his own name but as Lieutenant Daring, the hero of a series of one- and two-reel adventure films produced by B&C between 1911 and 1914. Although he was neither the first nor the last person to play the character, having replaced the original Daring, Clifford Marle, when Marle failed to show up for work, Moran was nevertheless the most heavily publicised of Daring's various screen incarnations.[18] As the name suggests, Daring's on- and off-screen identity was based on his ability to outface danger. The stories that circulated around Daring tended to centre on hardships undergone in pursuit of effective cinematic spectacle, and this was certainly something that B&C were keen to foster as part of their brand identity. 'We now hear almost daily', a trade journalist commented wryly in 1913, 'of [a B&C actor] being nearly drowned, or hanging from a balloon, or risking his or her life over cliffs'.[19]

Moran's public appearances, the majority of which seem to have been undertaken in character as Daring, began at the end of 1911, when B&C sent him on an extensive tour of London picture theatres to promote the latest *Lieutenant Daring* release.[20] In an article supposedly written by Daring for the *Kinema-*

tograph and Lantern Weekly, it was claimed that the performer had visited no less than 160 picture halls, accompanied by people acting as his midshipman and personal orderly. An illustration in the same article showed Daring posing outside B&C's London offices in a specially decorated motorcar, in which he was transported between venues.[21] The staff at B&C's Publicity Department were hard taskmasters. On a single day (the last of his London tour), Daring made two appearances at the Poplar and Bromley Tabernacle in London's East End, once to an eight hundred-strong audience of children and again to an audience of adults, before setting off to visit another venue in the north of the city.[22]

Moran continued to visit picture theatres, still in character as Daring, into 1912. An incident in the spring of that year suggests how personal appearances could work in tandem with other publicity stunts to construct a coherent picture personality persona. In March 1912, the actor was reportedly involved in one of B&C's trademark life-threatening accidents, while filming on the Sussex coast near Brighton. An article in *The Bioscope* told how Daring – 'that famous English bioscope actor' – had slipped and fallen ninety feet from a cliff into the water below, being rescued with the help of the local coastguard and escaping the ordeal with nothing worse than a sprained wrist.[23] Interviewed by the same paper some weeks later, 'Daring' recounted how, shortly after 'the Brighton episode', he had visited the Theatre de Luxe in Brighton's North Street, where he gave a speech entitled 'The Life of a Cinematograph Actor'. Although the content of the speech was not relayed, it seems to have concerned the actor's recent brush with death, as Daring told his interviewer that the talk had been 'received with applause, and congratulation on [his] narrow escape'.[24] For Moran and his employers at B&C, then, a personal visit was one way to capitalise on, or manufacture, a news story. It also provided an opportunity to reinforce the image of Daring as a resolute and resilient performer, both in his personal address to picture theatre audiences and through subsequent media coverage.

While B&C were pioneering in their use of personal appearances as a marketing tool, they were not alone among British firms in trying to harness the drawing power of the picture personality in this way. Nor were personal appearances instigated solely by producers. Exhibitors, too, set out to integrate live appearances from film celebrities into their promotional practices. In January 1913 the management of the Royal County Theatre in Kingston-on-Thames, led by the managing director A.C. Massay, organised what was advertised as an 'All-British Week'. The British theme was reflected in special decorations, and was built around an all-British programme of films, including selections from

Alfred West, Cricks and Martin, B&C, the Clarendon Film Company, and Barker Motion Photography. The Hepworth Manufacturing Company, as one of the oldest British firms, were represented both in the theatre's programming and by the personal appearance of two of the company's leading female performers, Gladys Sylvani and Chrissie White.[25] Both actresses were then being featured in a number of Hepworth releases, and had received substantial publicity in the trade and popular press over the past year. Indeed, Sylvani has been cited by Rachael Low (perhaps erroneously, given the publicity surrounding B&C's Lieutenant Daring) as 'the first English star to receive treatment similar to that given the Americans'.[26] Sylvani was the subject of an extensive article in the trade press in February 1912,[27] while a covert publicity paragraph in May of that year claimed not only that she was 'the most popular English picture actress', but also that her image was the most heavily circulated of any British film celebrity. 'Her portrait is everywhere, in town and country, city or village, either upon the screen or in the papers', the article stated. 'Within the last two or three weeks, for instance, she has "appeared" in *The Bystander*, *Woman's Life*, and *The Penny Magazine*, to name only three out of a multitude'.[28] In contrast to Moran, Sylvani was promoted under her own name in such magazine 'appearances'. In *The Bystander*, she was given a full-page portrait (an honour usually reserved for stage stars and members of the aristocracy) above a caption that proclaimed her popularity among 'all patrons of the Cinematograph shows'.[29]

As Hepworth's statements at the time and in his subsequent memoirs make clear, he was a staunch advocate of British (or, sometimes, 'English') filmmaking, so it makes sense that two of his leading actors should be recruited as embodiments of the British cinema.[30] In this respect, it is worth noting that a decade later, during the first of the British National Film Weeks in 1924, Hepworth once again used personal appearances from his actors to underscore his commitment to British production, casting the star Alma Taylor and other performers in a live 'prelude' to the film *Comin' Thro' the Rye*.[31] Trade press coverage of the Royal County Theatre's 'All-British Week' in 1913 mentioned that Sylvani and White were 'greeted with rounds of applause from the enthusiastic audience', although we are left to imagine exactly how their visit was choreographed as part of the management's promotional efforts, or how successful it was in the theatre's attempts to inculcate patriotic viewing habits among local film-goers.[32]

One further example, involving a more international cast of picture personalities, provides a richer account of an audience's response to personal appearances within the context of a larger moving-picture programme, as well as allowing us to speculate about how these events sat alongside other hybrid performance practices. The Australian-born actor Marc McDermott and the American actress Miriam Nesbitt came to the United Kingdom in 1913 with other members of the Edison Manufacturing Company. The couple travelled to locations in southwest England and Wales, as well as visiting the Hepworth studio in Walton-on-Thames, in order to make a series of Edison dramas.[33] In July of that year, McDermott and Nesbitt made a personal appearance at the Marble Arch Electric Palace on London's Oxford Street. This was a fashionable, six hundred-seat establishment, with a sizeable orchestra and a managing director (Seymour Hodges) whose background as an actor and manager in West End theatres lent the venue a reputation for artistic presentation methods.[34]

The staging of McDermott and Nesbitt's personal appearance certainly displayed a flair for the theatrical. Reports of the event in the trade press described how, during an evening show, 'a neat little surprise was given to the crowded audience'. In the middle of the programme, Hodges announced the inclusion of an extra picture, 'the fine Edison release "The Gauntlets of Washington"', which was accompanied with special orchestral effects. Then, after a round of applause at the end of the film, 'it was seen that something was astir'. Hodges reappeared and explained that they were to be joined by 'two of the greatest photoplayers who had very often appeared upon their screen', and who had recently 'appeared' together at the Palace in the Edison film *The Two Portraits* (McDermott would have also 'appeared' just moments earlier in *The Gauntlets of Washington*). 'Amid loud applause', the article continued, 'Mr. McDermott, a fine bronzed athletic fellow ("just like the picture", as one lady remarked), stepped before the screen'.[35] McDermott proceeded to share jokes and anecdotes about his life as a film actor, and to compliment British exhibitors on the quality of London's picture palaces. He introduced Nesbitt, who made a brief speech and accepted a bouquet of flowers, and the couple left the auditorium 'amid loud applause'.[36]

McDermott and Nesbitt had both been stage actors before signing with Edison, and they seem to have been comfortable interacting with picture theatre patrons. But they also acknowledged the novelty of the situation, and the multiple forms of address initiated by their projection on the moving-picture screen and their material presence in the Palace. Introducing himself, McDermott quipped: 'I have, I daresay, appeared here a good many times "in the spirit", but I can assure you that it affords me much pleasure to appear before you in the flesh'. Nesbitt likewise reflected that she was not quite a stranger, despite never having been there in person. 'I have appeared before you on the screen', she was quoted as saying. 'I only hope that I may be spared to appear before you for many summers to come'.[37] Like other hybrid performances, then, the Edison actors' personal appearance played on the border between the virtual space of the moving-picture screen and the shared, physical space of the picture theatre auditorium. In the form practised at the Marble Arch Electric Palace, at least, it resembled what Waltz calls the 'film to life' effects of some multi-media vaudeville sketches, in which performers seemed to step out of, or into, the screen.[38]

Paying close attention to the responses generated by personal appearances also serves as a reminder that, as Philip Auslander has argued, the idea of 'live' performance is a relatively recent category. For Auslander, 'liveness' should be understood not as an ontological constant, but as a historically contingent 'moving target' related to changes in technology, and specifically to the advent of devices capable of recording and reproduction, including the phonograph and the cinematograph. In order for performance to be thought of as 'live' or immediate, Auslander contends, there has to be a mediated, 'canned' alternative.[39] Although the term 'liveness' does not figure in the turn-of-the-century English lexicon, early responses to moving-picture technology are full of examples of witnesses using similar vocabulary in an attempt to pin down the moving (or 'living') picture's curiously present-but-absent effect. The multiple meanings of the verb 'to appear' at work in Nesbitt's speech and in the trade press descriptions of the event, along with McDermott's appeal to the opposition between 'spirit' and 'flesh', show how everyday language was stretched to accommodate reflections on the relative status of what we would now call 'live' and 'cinematic' performances.

By bringing film actors and audiences together 'in the flesh', personal appearances seem to have made commentators particularly sensitive to the different modes of presence made possible by the moving-picture camera. It may be that other hybrid performance genres appealed to a similarly dizzying or enlightening experience. In closing, though, it is worth noting one more instance of the actor's presence in early picture theatres, besides films, which provides another context for thinking about the effect of personal appearances on contemporary audiences, and which might help to historicise the concept of 'liveness' further. While personal appearances were rare and special occasions, the use of picture personality portraits was a much easier and more economical way of presenting film celebrities to audiences between film screenings. In the United Kingdom, most producers and distributors were able to offer publicity posters and picture personality lantern slides, among a variety of other 'stock pictorials', for sale to exhibitors by 1912.[40] By 1914 the trade paper editor Low Warren could claim that a vestibule adorned with 'framed photographs [...] of leading picture artistes' was as essential a feature of an attractive picture theatre as well-scrubbed steps.[41] An article in the theatrical trade paper *The Era* advertising an early set of cabinet photographs of Hepworth players suggested the effect that such a souvenir would have on film-goers, describing it as 'a means of reminding them of the living personalities who they see only in pictures'.[42] If a book of photographs could serve as a reminder of the 'living personalities' behind the moving images projected on screen, then perhaps the poster displays of leading picture players that began to greet audiences on their entrance into film venues could be thought of in the same spirit as 'live' personal appearances: that is, as another iteration of the film actor's presence for the benefit of patrons, available for film-goers to encounter, if not quite 'in the flesh', then at least face to face.

Notes

1. David Mayer, "Learning to See in the Dark", *Nineteenth Century Theatre* 25, no. 2 (Winter 1997): 111.

2. Gwendolyn Waltz, "Embracing Technology: A Primer of Early Multi-Media Performance", in Leonardo Quaresima and Laura Vichi (eds), *La decima musa: Il cinema e le altre arti/The Tenth Muse: Cinema and the Other Arts* (Udine: Forum, 2001): 543–553, and "'Half Real-Half Reel': Alternation Format Stage-and-Screen Hybrids", in André Gaudreault, Nicolas Dulac, and Santiago Hildalgo (eds), *A Companion to Early Cinema* (Oxford: Wiley Blackwell, 2012): 360–380.

3. Greg Giesekam, *Staging the Screen: The Use of Film and Video in Theatre* (Basingstoke: Palgrave Macmillan, 2007).

4. Richard deCordova, *Picture Personalities: The Emergence of the Star System in America* (Urbana: University of Illinois Press, 1990), 52–53.

5. Jon Burrows, "She Had So Many Appearances: Alphonse Courlander and the Birth of the 'Moving Picture Girl'", in Andrew Shail (ed.), *Reading the Cinematograph: The Cinema in British Short Fiction, 1896–1912* (Exeter: University of Exeter Press, 2010), 161; Andrew Shail, 'The Invention of Cinematic Celebrity in the United Kingdon', in Gaudreault, et al., *Companion to Early Cinema*: 460–486.

6. See, for instance, "News from America", *The Bioscope* (21 April 1910): 19; "An Ideal Moving Picture Actress", *The Bioscope* (18 August 1910): 55, both about Florence Lawrence; "News from America", *The Bioscope* (25 August 1910): 52–53, about Ethel Clayton; and, "The Powers Girl", *The Bioscope* (22 December 1910): 55, about Pearl White.

7. As Burrows notes, a number of British and European companies published details of their regular actors for the first time in a special 1911 issue of the *Kinematograph and Lantern Weekly* (30 March 1911).

8. Jane Bryan, "From Film Stories to Film Stars: The Beginnings of the Fan Magazine in Britain, 1911–16", in Alan Burton and Laraine Porter (eds), *Scene Stealing: Sources for British Cinema Before 1930* (Trowbridge: Flick Books, 2003), 69.

9. "Vitagraph Girl Feted", *Moving Picture World* (23 April 1910): 644; F.H. Richardson, "A Vitagraph Girl Night", *Moving Picture World* (31 December 1910): 1521.

10. Richardson, "A Vitagraph Girl Night", 1521. See also Richard Abel, *Americanizing the Movies and 'Movie Mad' Audiences, 1910–1914* (Berkeley: University of California Press, 2006), 233.
11. See, for instance, "Personalities", *The Bioscope* (15 October 1914): 253–254, about Turner's appearance at a London trade show.
12. "The Exhibition", *The Bioscope* (19 February 1914): 772.
13. "England Wakes Up", *The Cinema* (26 March 1913): 3.
14. "Round the Trade", *The Cinema* (5 February 1913): 6.
15. Valentia Steer, *The Romance of the Cinema* (London: Pearson, 1913), 24.
16. Burrows, "She Had So Many Appearances", 163.
17. "'Lieut. Daring, R.N.' by Himself", *Pearson's Weekly* (27 August 1912): 229.
18. This is how Dave Aylott, one of the directors of the *Lieutenant Daring* films, remembered the casting process in an interview with Dennis Gifford, BFI Audio Collection. Moran was succeeded as Daring by the actors Harry Lorraine and James Russell.
19. "Cinema Acting on Alpine Crags", *The Bioscope* (11 September 1913): 865.
20. "Stroller's Notes", *Kinematograph and Lantern Weekly* (7 December 1911): 261.
21. "My Tour of London", *Kinematograph and Lantern Weekly* (21 December 1911): 375.
22. "Lieut. Daring's Tour", *Kinematograph and Lantern Weekly* (18 January 1912): 647.
23. "Lieut. Daring Nearly Killed at Brighton", *The Bioscope* (7 March 1912): 655.
24. "Interview with Lieut. Daring, R.N.", *The Bioscope* (28 March 1912): 929.
25. "An All-British Week at Kingston", *The Bioscope* (9 January 1913): 89.
26. Rachael Low, *The History of the British Film, 1906–1914* (London: Allen & Unwin, 1950), 126.
27. "A Famous English Picture Actress", *The Bioscope* (8 February 1912): 359.
28. "Items of Interest", *The Bioscope* (2 May 1912): 321.
29. "A Picture Palace Star", *The Bystander* (3 April 1912): 31.
30. See Cecil Hepworth, *Came the Dawn: Memoirs of a Film Pioneer* (London: Phoenix House, 1951), 144.
31. "Betty Balfour's Million Audience", *The Bioscope* (31 January 1924): 34b.
32. "An All-British Week at Kingston", 89.
33. "Edison Players in England", *The Bioscope* (26 June 1913): 929, 931.
34. "Popular Picture Palaces and Their Managers", *The Cinema* (February 1912): 6.
35. "Popular Edison Players in London", *The Bioscope* (10 July 1913): 137, 139.
36. "Edison Players in London", *Kinematograph and Lantern Weekly* (10 July 1913): 1203.
37. "Popular Edison Players in London", 139.
38. Waltz, "Embracing Technology", 147.
39. Philip Auslander, *Liveness: Performance in a Mediatized Culture*, second edition (London: Routledge, 2008), xiii, 52–53.
40. See, for example, "Popular Photos", *The Bioscope* (22 February 1912): 501, about Vitagraph's new line of 'high-class' cabinet photographs. Similar notices from the same year advertised picture personality portraits from Edison, Hepworth, Pathé, Dansk-Kino, and others.
41. Low Warren, *The Showman's Advertising Book: Containing Hundreds of Money-Making Tips and Wrinkles* (London: Kinematograph Weekly, 1914), 67.
42. "Film Gossip", *The Era* (2 March 1912): 26.

Performers – Now Synchronised on Screen

Ian Christie

There is a spectre still haunting the study of early film – the spectre of sound. Ever since the 1998 Domitor conference in Washington, entitled 'The Sounds of Silence', we have known that early film-shows were frequently accompanied by live music and other sounds. But more broadly, it is clear that film was born, so to speak, with the expectation that sound recording, an already-accomplished technology, would now be supplemented by movement recording. Every Domitorian surely knows the famous Edison sound-bite, predicting 'an instrument which does for the eye what the phonograph does for the ear', but how many have taken to heart the order of priority implicit in this?

Certainly there is now a level of routine acknowledgement of early sound accompaniment. In Washington, we witnessed the 'premiere' of Dickson's 'Experimental Sound film' deftly restored by Walter Murch, so that it could be experienced as conceived, if not actually experienced, in 1894 (and this is now available online).[1] Most accounts of early film technology and presentation are at least illustrated by the florid art nouveau poster for Clement Maurice's Phono-Cinéma-Théâtre, as presented at the 1900 Paris Exposition Universelle; although it was not until the Pordenone Giornate del Cinema Muto of 2012 that elements of this programme were heard as well as seen.[2] However, the Maurice presentation was only one of at least three rival talking films exhibits at the Paris expo – others were the Theatrescope and the Phonorama – which points to a high degree of interest in presenting synchronous performance, rather than an isolated experiment.[3]

More significantly, the two major systems of synchronised performances, Gaumont's Chronophone and Messter's Biophon, both of which lasted for over a decade, have been marginalised, if not wholly omitted from most synoptic film histories.[4] Yet as Alison McMahon argues in her biography of Alice Guy, 'the real extent of the relationship between Guy's *chronophone* production and Guy's career has not been understood'.[5] Guy not only directed over one hundred of the 150 *phonoscènes* produced for the Chronophone system during 1905–06, but, according to McMahon, it was these sound films that occasioned her partnership and marriage to Herbert Blaché, and took the pair to the United States, to launch the Chronophone there, before forming their independent Solax Company in New Jersey in 1910.[6]

The absence of any reference to Messter's Biophon and the 450 *tonbilder* he produced for showing at up to three hundred cinemas is to some extent symptomatic of a larger failure in Anglo-American historiography to explore early German cinema 'before *Caligari*'. It was not until a cluster of articles and references about Messter appeared in 1994–96 that his central role in establishing an early sound-cinema network was recognised.[7] In 1996, Frank Kessler and Sabine Lenk revealed negotiations between Messter and Gaumont to try to 'stabilise the market situation' for sound films as early as 1903, by making an agreement to distribute the other's films.[8]

While the Gaumont Chronophone (of which more later) and Messter's Biophon established substantial exhibition networks devoted to sound films, a second wave of synchronising systems appeared in 1907–09 which were aimed at occasional use, rather than requiring dedicated cinemas. In Britain, Hepworth's Vivaphone and Walturdaw's Cinematophone both appeared in 1907, while Barker and Jeapes' Cinephone was said to have been already installed in one thousand British cinemas before its transatlantic launch in 1909, with the prefix 'American'.[9] Another British system, the Animatophone, reported by Rachael Low to have been 'greeted in some quarters as the first really successful [synchronisation] system', came after onto the market in 1910.[10]

A more recent historian of film music has written about the 'meteor shower of sound-film devices' in this period, listing their 'colourful' names:

> the Animatophone; the Biographon; Biophon, the Biophonograph; the Chronophotgraphoscope; the Cinemacrophonograph; the Cinematophone, and Cineograph; the Graphophonoscope; the Kinematophone and Kosmograph; the Phoneidograph, Phone-Cinéma-Théâtre, and Phonoscope; the Photophone, Foto-Fone, and Photokinema; the Picturephone; the Synchrophone and Synchroscope; the Talkaphone and the Vivaphone.[11]

Such a list of elaborate variations on the basic sound-image concept can only make these devices sound like so many outdated contraptions; and indeed Wierzbicki concludes that, at least in the United States, Edison's 'improved'

Kinetophone effectively swept aside all competition in 1913. But he does not deny that this was 'an obviously crowded field'.

In view of all this accumulated and undisputed empirical evidence, we might wonder why successive generations of historians of early cinema have never really taken on board the fact that *recorded* sound was an integral, even if not a universal, component of the moving picture experience in the 1900s. In fact, Ben Brewster noted in a review of the Washington conference that 'the role of the synchronised film was perhaps a gap in the conference's coverage'. Subsequently Rick Altman's *Silent Film Sound* provided a systematic and exhaustive survey of sound accompaniment practices.[12] But I contend that the *performative* aspect of recorded accompanying sound has still not been acknowledged. A key to this may lie in the attitude of one of the early historians, Rachael Low, who included an appendix on 'Sound' in volume two of her influential *History of the British Film*. Low duly listed some of the bizarre apparatus names (including the Replicaphone and Appollogramophone) and provided details of their cost – which was a mere £5 5s in the case of the Vivaphone, compared with £72 for the Cinematophone. But in dismissing 'films with disc accompaniment' as 'little more than novelties, increasingly isolated from the advance of film technique',[13] Low not only ignored the sheer volume of such 'novelties', but betrayed a teleological prejudice from the 1940s, when she was writing, in favour of what was currently considered the 'truly filmic' fiction film.[14] Viewed from a later standpoint, the argument could be reversed: that such early performance-centred films anticipated not only a dominant trend in cinema since the 1930s, but also modern music-video culture. And it is indeed from a new generation of historians and collectors focused on early sound recording, such as Thomas Schmitt, that the impetus has come to reverse the condescension of film historians.[15]

Low's assumption was driven by the need to separate 'film' from its formative phase in music halls and vaudeville theatres, when it had been one among many 'acts'. A high proportion of early film subjects by both Edison and Paul (though not by Lumière) were indeed dancers, magicians and 'eccentrics' – such as Chirgwin, 'the White-Eyed Kaffir' – who usually performed novelty songs, but frustratingly could not be *heard* until the appearance of the first synchronisation systems. From this perspective, the desire to make audible popular performers, preferably by means of their already-recorded songs, is entirely understandable. Rather than see such devices as 'adding' sound, they might be better understood as *restoring* sound to the new regime of audiovisual representation.

Leon Gaumont's belief in synchronised film was fully equal to that of Edison, and the success of his Chronophone system occupied the period between Edison's first Kinetophonoscope venture and the Kinetophone of 1913. After his early demonstrations in 1902, Gaumont built a Paris studio for sound film production in 1905, and in 1908 the American studio that Guy-Blaché managed. 1907 was the year that Gaumont made a determined effort in the British market, gaining valuable publicity for the phonoscène programme already running at the Hippodrome Theatre with a special presentation at Buckingham Palace on 4 April, attended by Princess Alexandra of Denmark, the Prince and Princess of Wales and their children and a bevy of courtiers.[16] According to another report of the programme of five operatic 'singing pictures', 'the Queen showed her pleasure by commanding the putting on of extra pictures after the ordinary programme had been completed'.[17]

What the early synchronised film could offer was precisely what cinema and television have continued to provide: a visible performance synched most often to an optimised, pre-recorded soundtrack. When Leon Gaumont began issuing *phonescènes* for the Chronophone, an important consideration was how 'universal' in appeal these would be, hence an early bias towards popular classical music. The Buckingham Palace programme consisted of scenes from Verdi's *Il Trovatore*, Gounod's *Faust*, a song and dance from André Messager's operetta *The Little Michus* (*Les p'tites Michu*, 1897), which had recently enjoyed great success on the London stage, and two Gilbert and Sullivan numbers. The fourteen comic 'Savoy operas' written by W. S. Gilbert and Arthur Sullivan between 1871 and 1896 were by this time a cult attraction in Britain, and more widely across the Empire and English-speaking world, attracting a relatively wide class spectrum, and the ninth of these, *The Mikado*, became by far the most popular. Perhaps unsurprisingly, this became a focus of competition between rival sound-film systems. Gaumont produced the first series of *Highlights from The Mikado* in 1906, which Walturdaw then followed with another series using its Cinematophone system in July 1907, starring the baritone George Thorne, who had created the role of Ko-Ko on Broadway in 1885.[18]

Contemporary star performers offered the potential of attracting wide audience interest, and hence increased sales to exhibitors, even if there were issues of language and locality. Gilbert and Sullivan had at least guaranteed British and American appeal, while French singers were unlikely to appeal outside France, however popular they might be domestically.[19] In 1907, with the Chronophone business apparently prospering, Gaumont's British branch signed an exclusive deal with Harry Lauder (1870–1950), the Scottish ex-miner who had become a British and eventually international variety star, with a career that lasted until the 1940s. Lauder wore Highland dress and sported a distinctive twisted walking stick, while singing his own compositions, such as 'Roamin' in the Gloamin', 'I Love a Lassie', 'A Wee Deoch-an-Doris', and 'Keep Right on to the End of the Road', mostly about courtship, marriage and the stereotypical Scottish themes of drink and parsimony.

Lauder was reported to be the highest paid variety entertainer in the world between 1906–12, and his fee from Gaumont was rumoured to be 'four figures' for the seven songs which appear among the seventy-five Gaumont titles listed on Carl Bennett's 'Silent Era' website.[20] Gaumont's *Kine Weekly* advertisement of 16 July 1907 sheds some light on how the Lauder 'singing pictures' fitted into the evolving entertainment economy of the era, with 'pre-recorded' material gaining ground. These were clearly a major attraction at Gaumont's flagship London theatre, The Hippodrome, where they were fast approaching the 400th consecutive performance – playing, in fact, as if Lauder were appearing there in person. They are also advertised as being 'open to offers … in districts not affected by the Moss-Stoll circuits', which were presumably the music halls in which Lauder *was* actually appearing. The Chronophone titles were therefore envisaged as a kind of supplement to Lauder's main career as a performer, able to take him to an even wider range of venues. We do not, of course, have any idea of the scale of exhibitors' response to this offer, except for occasional mentions in *Kine Weekly*'s impressionistic survey of exhibitors around the country.[21] But far away in Reno, Nevada, the Chronophone was billed as a major attraction in 1910, for the re-opening of the Grand Theatre, where 'the perfected talking picture apparatus… will present such artists as Harry Lauder, Victoria Monks, Blanche Ring, Dan Michaels and other celebrated stars in their best sketches'.[22] This advertisement explains that:

> the Chronophone is an electrically synchronized machine for the purpose of reproducing in sound and motion picture sketches by the greatest vaudeville artists in the world has been added to the equipment of the Isis company and will take the place of the illustrated songs, which have always been a part of the program heretofore.

The Grand's proposed programme of 'three reels of the high class motion pictures and two reels of talking pictures' sounds like an unusually high ratio of synchronised to unsynchronised pictures, but unfortunately there is no information to hand about its progress or success.

1913 seems to have marked the climax of aspiration, and perhaps also of exploitation of sound-film systems. In March, *Moving Picture World* offered a survey of 'talking picture' systems which concluded that Edison's Kinetophone had been 'instrumental in gaining recognition for the "talking pictures"'.²³ A report in the following month from Louisville indicated that, while the response was not universally enthusiastic, it was enough to support plans for a dedicated theatre:

> The Edison kinetophone has made its appearance in Louisville, B. F. Keith's vaudeville house presenting the latest device of the inventor to the public. Largely speaking, it may be said that the Louisville patrons of the theater enjoyed the talking pictures, even though some expressions of disappointment were heard. Devotees of the animated pictures, perhaps, had been led to expect too much, and the performance therefore fell a bit beneath anticipations. One of Louisville's amusement companies is now negotiating for the local rights of the kinetophone, and one of its houses will shortly be devoted to the talking pictures.²⁴

Such plans did not come to fruition. Although confidence in the Kinetophone and other systems was at its height – Harry Lauder entering a new partnership with Selig Polyscope to make seventeen sound-films, to coincide with his latest American tour – Altman notes that 'as suddenly as they appeared, the ads for synch-sound systems disappeared'.²⁵ Why did this happen? Altman points to 'two devastating events' which affected the market. One was the outbreak of the Great War in Europe, which 'jeopord[ized] the Kinetophone's export income' – and would also affect drastically the fortunes of both Gaumont's multi-national business empire and Messter's immediate market in German-speaking countries. The other was a major fire at Edison's West Orange plant in December which 'destroyed every Kinetophone record and film master'.²⁶

While these factors were clearly significant, especially for Edison, other explanations have been offered for the rapid decline of sound-films in 1913–14. The most common is an assumption that the systems were inherently fragile or unreliable, since they depended on operators' skills and on systems of signalling, or mechanical coupling between projectors and turntables. This can certainly be challenged by pointing to the considerable technical advances made by, especially, Gaumont and Messter in developing their systems. During the entire era of short-duration recorded discs, skills in moving between turntables were well-developed; and such equipment continues to be used in modern disc-based performance by DJs. Martin Loiperdinger has challenged this account of inherent technical and practical problems, as articulated by Thomas Elsaesser in several accounts of early German cinema, insisting that '*tonbilder* did not disappear due to technical problems… but because their production was no longer profitable'.²⁷ Messter's sound-films, according to this view, were the victim of their own success, with over-production leading to price-decline, making them ultimately unprofitable to produce, since they represented an 'advanced technology [requiring] an increased investment by producers, on which they could then expect a higher return'.

Loiperdinger's argument provides a valuable counterbalance to the familiar assumption that these were in some sense 'primitive', compared with later sound-on-film systems. But it needs to be supplemented by noting the parallel trends towards longer films (which would erode the market for all short films, including the more expensive synch-sound ones), and larger cinemas of two thousand seats and more, which must have challenged sound amplification technology in 1913–14. The very low rate of survival of early sound-films and our inability to play any of those that do – other than through digital restoration – have undoubtedly contributed to making this once-substantial and 'advanced' sector of early film experience largely unknown.[28] Both Gaumont and Messter operated sound-film successfully for most of a decade; and by 1912–13, the idea of pre-recorded music and film was beginning to interest artists, notably Paul Klee and Arnold Schoenberg.[29] The most successful international variety performer of the era, Harry Lauder, continued to involve himself in sound-film ventures, making a demonstration for Orlando Kellum's Photokinema system in 1921.[30]

Low, as we have seen, set the tone for commenting on early synchronised sound, dismissing it as 'quite outside the general stream of artistic development';[31] and more recent historians, including Altman, Elsaesser and Wierzbicki, have tended to adopt a similar position, albeit for different reasons. I want to argue that it is unjustified to write off what was a very substantial and persistent part of early film presentation – one which required 'performance' (which was undoubtedly both a problem and a challenge), but also offered cinemas 'the means to distinguish themselves from the competition'.[32] Very few participants or observers of the pre-1915 period seem to have thought it was undesirable or misguided. And many leading performers of the period were happy to participate, lending sound film their prestige. We know very little about how many such performances were in circulation, and how they interacted with live and 'normal' recorded performances of the same songs. No doubt they were, in effect, the 'music videos' and proto-YouTube clips of the era; and we can no longer regard them as 'outside' audiovisual culture. Now we know what part they played in developing the popularity of cinemagoing by making the new moving-picture venues seem more like variety theatres – an important link in the long-suppressed history of cinema as a hybrid form of entertainment, and one which is once again topical, with the rise of live performance being transmitted directing into cinema theatres.

Notes

1. See filmsound.org, http://filmsound.org/murch/dickson.htm (accessed 19 June 2013)
2. See the presentation of 'Phono-Cínéma-Théâtre' (1900), Catalogue of the Giornate del Cinema Muto, Pordenone, 2012, 24–28.
3. See Emmanuelle Toulet, 'Cinema at the Universal Exposition Paris 1900', in *Persistence of Vision*, the Journal of the Film Faculty of the City University of New York, 9 (1991): 10–36.
4. David Robinson dated Messter's 'experiments' with sound film to 'around 1908', in his *World Cinema: A Short History* (London: Eyre Methuen, 1973), 87. Most single-volume histories made no mention of Messter's Biophon system.
5. Alison McMahon, *Alice Guy Blaché: Lost Visionary of the Cinema* (New York: Continuum, 2002), 64.
6. Ibid.
7. These included: Martin Loiperdinger (ed.), *Oskar Messter: Filmpionier der Kaiserzeit* (Basel and Frankfurt: Stromfeld/Roter Steren, 1994); Ian Christie, *The Last Machine: Early Cinema and the Birth of the Modern World* (London: BBC/British Film Institute, 1994); Jan-Christopher Horak, 'Oskar Messter: Forgotten Pioneer of German Cinema', Historical journal of Film, Radio and Television, 15, no.4 (October 1995).
8. Frank Kessler and Sabine Lenk, 'The French Connection', in Thomas Elsaesser (ed.), *A Second Life: German Cinema's First Decades* (Amsterdam: Amsterdam University Press, 1996), 67–68.
9. Cinephone claim recorded by Rick Altman, *Silent Film Sound* (New York: Columbia University Press, 2007), 164.
10. Rachael Low, *The History of the British Film 1906–1914* (London: George Allen & Unwin, 1948), 266.
11. James Wierzbicki, *Film Music: A History* (New York: Routledge, 2009), 76.
12. Rick Altman, *Silent Film Sound* (New York: Columbia University Press, 2007).
13. Low, *History of the British Film*, vol. 2, 266
14. The aesthetics of the period are laid out in Ernest Lindgren, *The Art of the Film* (London: George Allen & Unwin, 1948), exactly contemporary with Low's history, in which the Cinephone, Chronophone and Vivaphone are described as 'a fashionable novelty' (97–98).
15. See, for instance, Thomas Schmitt, "The Genealogy of Clip Culture", in Henry Keazor and Thorsten Wübbena, (eds), *Rewind, Play, Fast Forward: The Past, Present and Future of the Music Video* (Bielefeld: Transcript Verlag, 2010).
16. 'An afternoon entertainment of "Singing Pictures" at Buckingham Palace afforded much enjoyment. The Queen's command was received at the Hippodrome yesterday morning, instructing a private exhibition ... to be given in the Palace, commencing at three o'clock. ...[T]he instrument, placed in the [throne room], cast the pictures through the folding-doors [into the Green Drawing Room] upon a screen hung behind a bank of palms.' *Daily Telegraph*, 5 April 1907.
17. *Daily Mail*, 5 April 1907.
18. Another case of Walturdaw duplicating a previous Gaumont release is their rival version of the 1906 song 'Beside the Zuyder Zee' for the Cinematophone. There is no information to hand about the kinds of legal agreements that might have underpinned the early sound-film releases, which are likely have been regarded as experimental – especially at a time when the whole issue of film-related copyright was unclear. See my contribution to the previous Domitor proceedings, "'What is a picture?' Film as defined in British law before 1910", in Marta Braun et al., (eds), *Beyond the Screen: Institutions, Networks and Publics of Early Cinema* (New Barnet: John Libbey, 2012), 78–84.

19. Gaumont made nearly forty phonoscènes starring three popular French singers, Polin, Mayol and Dranem, according to McMahon, *Alice Guy*, 322–323. But these were unlikely to have been released outside France and Belgium.
20. If the fee was at least £1000, this would be the equivalent of $114,000 USD today.
21. The *Kinematograph and Lantern Weekly* (usually known as *Kine Weekly*) ran a regular column, 'Around the Shows', which reported impressionistically on various United Kingdom exhibitors' programmes – clearly depending on those who sent in information most assiduously.
22. *Reno Evening Gazette*, Reno, Nevada, Tuesday, 5 April 1910, .4c. Reported *at Footlight Notes*, http://footlightnotes.tripod.com/ArchivePressText2008/20080510.html (accessed 19 June 2013).
23. "Talking Picture Devices", *Moving Picture World*, 29 March 1913.
24. G.D. Crain, Jr., 'Correspondence: Louisville', *Moving Picture World*, 12 April 1913.
25. Altman, *Silent Film Sound*, 177.
26. Ibid., 178.
27. Martin Loiperdinger, "German *Tonbilder* of the 1900s", in Annemone Ligensa and Klaus Kreimeir (eds), *Film 1900: Technology, Perception, Culture* (New Barnet: John Libbey, 2009), 194.
28. Thomas Schmitt notes that of the 774 phonoscènes produced by Gaumont between 1902 and 1917, only about twenty are currently accessible. For details of these, see http://www.le-forum.dutempsdescerisesauxfeuillesmortes.net/viewtopic.php?f=14&t=44 (accessed 20 June 2013).
29. See Ian Christie, "*Before the Avant-Gardes: Artists and Film*, 1910–1914", in Leonardo Quaresima and Laura Vichi (eds), *The Tenth Muse* (Udini, 2001), 368–370.
30. As did D.W. Griffith, who made a sound version of *Dream Street* for Photokinema.
31. Low, *History of the British Film*, vol. 2, 267.
32. Loiperdinger, "German *Tonbilder*", 195.

PART II

Performing Beside the Screen: Narrators, Showmen, and Musicians

9

Missing Believed Lost: The Film Narrator, Then and Now

Martin Loiperdinger

From the turn of the century up to the First World War, audiences of cinematograph shows did not only expect films on the screen and musical live accompaniment. They also were used to hearing the voice of a film narrator. Though an essential figure of live performance in early cinema, the film narrator was an ephemeral being, which did not leave many traces behind. Contrary to the silent film piano player, the profession of commenting on films live during screenings has not been reanimated in the cultural heritage business of film archives and silent film festivals, apart from very few remarkable exceptions.

The institution of the film narrator was deeply rooted in the tradition of the lantern lecturer whose spoken words usually accompanied the projection of slides already long before the cinematograph was introduced into the entertainment business. When it was introduced, cinematograph shows and lantern shows shared the screen, (Only recently, the notions 'screen history' and 'screen culture' have been established to analyse and understand the close connections between the art of projection and early cinema).[1] Furthermore, lantern and cinematograph shows shared sound: live music, imitation of noises, and comments spoken by the lecturer or film narrator. Most lantern shows in the last decades of the nineteenth century were offered as 'illustrated lectures' with a lecturer or showman explaining the pictures[2] – and most cinematograph shows up to the early 1910s saw the film narrator as mediator between audience and screen.

Illustrated lectures offered by charities, educational associations and the labour movement contained the projection of slide sets and an oral commentary. The large charity organisations in Great Britain had professional lecturers with their own repertories of 'illustrated lecture' performances. For example, Luther Hinton, a traveling Sunday School Union lecturer, performed his commentary on the set *Martin Luther, his Life and Times* at least sixty-four times. Reports state that, with his entertaining lecturing style, he knew how to secure the attention of the audience.[3] Experts in lantern performance were also busy in the educational sector, as for example Jens Lützen, who is said to have performed around 2,500 illustrated lectures from 1890 to 1908 on behalf of the Berlin-based *Gesellschaft zur Verbreitung von Volksbildung* (Society for the Promotion of Public Education).[4]

The text spoken by the lecturer was indispensable for the lantern show *dispositif*. This is evidenced by the readings which the producer or distributor always delivered alongside the slide set. The readings offered wordings of the text to be spoken for each slide of the set. With the advent of cinematograph shows the close connection between the images on the screen and the spoken text started to dissolve: Usually there were no readings available anymore to comment on films. Film narrators had to improvise and were free to adapt their words to any audience and situation in the auditorium. In the absence of the written and printed text, the spoken word in cinematograph shows became the most evanescent element of the performance.

Of all European countries, most information about film narrators seems to be known in the Netherlands – as instructive articles by Ansje van Beusekom, Ivo Blom, Ine van Dooren, Bert Hogenkamp and others demonstrate.[5] The film narrator played an essential part in early Dutch film exhibition. Cinema adverts in local newspapers often announce film narrators by their name. Thus the *Cinema Context* database which covers film exhibition in the Netherlands lists as many as sixty-six so-called 'explicateurs'.[6] These film narrators were well-known and highly respected persons in Dutch cities and towns – and had leading positions in the trade union of cinema and theatre employees.[7]

Although there are not even a dozen German film narrators known by their names, in the early 1910s, numerous adverts in the trade press, paid by film narrators looking for employment or by cinema owners looking for a trained film narrator, widely evidence the significance of this profession also in Germany's film exhibition business. The adverts clearly reveal the prominent position of the film narrator in the everyday business of fixed-site cinemas, not only as far as live performance is concerned. Film narrators also regularly offer their services in the cinema's advertising, and even propose to act as manager of the entire cinema enterprise. Multi-tasking is a common feature of the profession sometimes including not only the jobs of film narrator, calligrapher and advertising manager, but also the pianist's and foley artist's jobs as well. Such a multi-talented applicant claimed sixty marks a week, and ten marks for his wife who might sit at the cashier.[8] Another couple looked for an employment as duet to perform dramatic and humoristic dialogues during the screenings of respective films.[9] As film programmes usually were composed of comedies and dramas, most adverts in the trade press emphasise the lecturer's experience in commenting on both genres. Some trained and experienced theatre actors only advertised their qualification to comment dramas: they tried to present themselves as sounding artists of orator.

In the film exhibition business, the position of the film narrator worked as an interface between the film trade and the audience. While the film operator was cranking reel after reel in the projection cabin, and the musicians were playing the accompanying live music sitting aside or in a pit, it was the lecturer who addressed the audience face-to-face with his voice and words. He (or she) was responsible for the emotional atmosphere during the screenings, and, after all, for the reputation of the cinema enterprise among the patrons. His performances were a crucial factor in local competition, at least between neighbouring cinemas, which were often located close to each other in the same street. The educated lecturer, in many cases a trained actor who called himself *Rezitator* (reciter), commented in standard German for an educated audience – or an audience to be educated. Entrepreneurs of cinemas located in working class quarters of the big cities, in middle-size and small towns and in rural areas usually employed film narrators who performed their comments in the local or regional dialect, on eye level with the audience.

Of the locals who worked as film narrators in German film exhibition before the First World War, we have sufficient information only about Peter Marzen from Trier. First, he had served as impresario for the stand-alone film shows of his father's town hall travelling cinema. When the Marzen family took over a fixed-site cinema in Trier, in March 1909, the local newspaper published a long article titled 'In a "Trierish" cinematograph show' which portrays Peter Marzen's local vernacular as outstanding live performance:

> It is only the proprietor – in explaining the moving pictures – who makes the cinema 'truly Trierish'. The voice is sobbing, weeping, howling, wailing, laughing, cursing, whispering, rumbling – and this often within five minutes, depending on the situation. Best standard German alternates with the most beautiful Trier dialect.[10]

Thanks to the narration in local vernacular, many characters of foreign films 'spoke' the same dialect as the audience did. French, Italian, or American films were 'localised' through oral performance during screening. Like Peter Marzen, seemingly many film narrators assisted the audience in appropriating films from abroad by entertaining comments in the local dialect.

Most film narrators were male, but there are also a few adverts by women who were looking for an employment. The trade press welcomed female narrators expecting them, though, to perform their comments without vulgar and risqué jokes. As film narrators usually improvised the oral performance, their spoken words were beyond control. Censorship procedures aimed to work on the films, but not on the film narrators' comments during screenings. Trade journals as well as daily newspapers from time to time complained about film narrators who catered to the 'low taste' of audiences, instead of using their desire for entertainment as a chance to educate them. Film narrators felt free to change the original plot of a film drama completely in order to adapt the film to the local audience, e.g. to entertain and to approve the moral feelings of local patrons – in other words to make them feel like at home in the cinema. When popular 'social dramas' were shown in cheap store-front cinemas in the proletarian quarters of big cities, the film narrator would even turn the moral message upside down: "The film narrator sobbed, the viewers clenched their fists, and a tragedy raced past before their eyes, which was totally different to the one envisaged by the film producer".[11] The writer of these lines had observed the procedures of film censorship in the headquarters of the Berlin police, and then he entered some of the store-front cinemas close to Alexanderplatz, in the Scheunenviertel, a notorious proletarian quarter in the middle of Berlin. He was much surprised to experience film narrators who squeezed unexpected lessons for the poor out of boring films which had passed censorship of the Prussian police. He watched a 'social drama' of a working class girl engaged to a distinguished young gentleman who leaves her on news of her depravity. She returns to her past lover, a worker, who by now repudiates her. The observer describes the film narrator at work:

> [He] fumed with pure moral indignation. He uttered the words of the scum of big cities, slowly, as if they were delicacies, laying it on thick. He described the inner emotions of those people, and he took even me, or at least all my thoughts, captive, and all of a sudden I realised: the heartless woman, a victim of posh society, the poor worker who they [the bourgeois lovers in the film] thought good enough to raise her up from the filth of the gutter, the poor worker, the cornerstone of proud respectability, who flings this woman back to the murderers up there. This is the *social tragedy* of the entire audience, although the ladies present have not taken the detour via becoming a high official's mistress but have rather stayed in the gutter from the beginning.[12]

The article was published in the last 1912 issue of the liberal daily newspaper *Frankfurter Zeitung*. According to the writer who slightly exaggerates, the film narrator must not be underestimated with regard to the potential impact of 'social dramas' on cinema audiences:

> Alas Mirabeau, Danton, Marat! We have the Kintop [Berlin dialect for store-front cinema] and the Kintop lecturer who knows to construct a completely new basis for the plot which enrols on the screen, who knows to invent and to develop leitmotifs which the audience wants to hear. Every word spoken by him is underlined by the action to be seen on the screen: his impact on the audience means more than Mirabeau, Danton, Marat.[13]

From 1911 onward, film narrators focused on explaining the plots of the long-feature films, a new format which was often too complicated for audiences to follow. On the other hand, the rise of the feature-length format meant the beginning of the film narrator's end as a leading contributor to the cinematograph show: Growing audiences of 'better people' visiting cinemas in the city centres preferred live music without any spoken comments, thus growing numbers of intertitles made the film narrator disappear from cinema history. Among cinema palaces and cinema theatres in big city centres seemingly were the first venues to fire the film narrator.

The profession of the film narrator has not been reanimated yet; on the contrary, the silent film piano player has become the only remaining live performer regularly used when films from the early period are programmed at film museums and archives and film festivals devoted to the history of cinema. In that cultural heritage context, these film screenings are attended by 'culturally-astute audiences' of today: well-educated cinéphiles and early cinema scholars evidence the gentrification of early cinema showings. Before 1914, audiences of cinematograph shows came from all social strata, while academics had the lowest ratio of all groups of the population, as Emilie Altenloh found out in her survey on audiences of cinema theatres in the city of Mannheim.[14] Today's educated audiences of early film screenings in film museums obviously do not miss the film narrator at all. They feel pleased to view the moving pictures on the screen and to listen to the tunes played by a piano player who is an expert in accompanying silent films with live music. Even the highly professional film screenings and performances at the festivals *Il Cinema Ritrovato* in Bologna and *Le Giornate del Cinema Muto* at Pordenone only use piano players or small orchestras to accompany films from the period prior to the First World War – and there seems to be not one film scholar who misses the sounding voice of a film narrator as it was usual when those films were shown in the old days. To my knowledge there were only two exceptions in today's re-animation of early cinema which were in need of the film narrator as the essential figure of the show. Remarkably enough, they presented early cinema to ordinary people who come from all social strata.

The first exemption were the many successful local film shows for local people which were organised by Vanessa Toulmin for the British Film Institute to make today's Brits familiar with moving local views of their towns and cities a hundred years ago, from the now world-famous Mitchell & Kenyon Collection. The film production company of the same name was based in Blackburn, Lancashire, and catered local films to travelling cinemas in the northwest of England. In over 130 carefully programmed local shows which oftentimes must be repeated to accommodate all viewers, for local audiences in cities and towns all over Britain, Vanessa Toulmin herself, along with members of her team, performed the film narrator's part to explain local spots and sights, and the locals of Edwardian times, to the locals of today who attended these local film shows:

> The audience expected the narrator to know the essential parts of their history and street names, important historical and architectural landmarks had to be noticed and explained but with enough left out to allow the audience to be part of the proceedings. For example, the Blackpool show contained an eight minute tram ride from Blackpool to Lytham from 1903 on the newly opened tram line which is still used today. The audience were invited to shout out and name the landmarks shown on screen and it was decided to only correct the audience if they were wrong.[15]

The second exemption was *Crazy Cinématographe*, the fairground tent which the Cinémathèque de la Ville de Luxembourg ran three weeks a year, from 2007 to 2011, at the *Schueberfouer*, the fairground of the city of Luxembourg. *Crazy Cinématographe* was curated by Nicole Dahlen and Claude Bertemes (with Vanessa Toulmin in 2007).[16] Projecting 35mm short film programmes of twenty minutes maximum in a fairground tent on the Luxemburg funfair was not possible without barkers and film narrators: The fairground is a most demanding environment which absolutely requires fighting for the attention of the fairground visitors. To attract the passers-by, staged front-shows had to precede the film screenings inside the tent. The latter offered the opportunity to observe and to experience the resurrection of the film narrator who had almost disappeared, nearly a century ago:

> [...] two actors performing both as barkers and lecturers play an important role as mediators between the audience and the images. They appear as reminiscences of the historical presenters of fairground shows and at the same time as their modern variant, their interventions being of course of a rather different nature as they include filmographic and other historical background information.[17]

While bridging the gap of a century which extends between silent short films of the 1900s and today's fairground audiences, the film narrators who act and perform within the '*Crazy Cinématographe* apparatus', as Claude Bertemes and Nicole Dahlen call it, emerge from the historical fairground cinema *dispositif* as well as from the modern 'archival and museological *dispositif*'.[18]

> The two film narrators introduce themselves to the audience as the siblings Vincent and Marie Minestrone. They say that they appeared in New York the day before in front of 100,000 people, when the women enthusiastically threw their brassieres, and the men their wives, onto the stage in Vincent's direction. They therefore see themselves as being entitled to demand thunderous applause, which the audience then provides – but not without a hint of expectant reticence. In a ping-pong exchange, Vincent and Marie recount the baffling distant years of the films' production, from 1897 to 1909, the various countries in which they were produced, from France to Poland, and the genres to be anticipated, from the animated film to the documentary scene.[19]

Being mediators between the late nineteenth century and the first decade of the twenty-first century, their performance oscillates between circus and fairground on the one hand, and a guided film museum tour on the other hand, as their introduction before the start of the film screening clearly shows. Contrary to this observation, at least one film of the 2011 programmes marked an exemption from the hybrid character which the film narrators had to play and stage within the '*Crazy Cinématographe* apparatus': Winsor McCay's animation film *Gertie* (United States, 1914) shows Gertie, the dinosaur, walking on the banks of a big lake. Gertie is accompanied by her creator, who cannot be seen on the screen. Winsor McKay performed the live act of Gertie's tamer in vaudeville theatres, standing beside the screen, cracking a whip and throwing sweets into Gertie's mouth as reward for good behaviour. The film narrator in the *Crazy Cinématographe* fairground tent performed the role of Gertie's tamer just in the same way, thus copying Winsor McKay's performance of a hundred years ago.

After a century of film exhibition without oral live performance, it seems most difficult to reanimate the art of the film narrator. Live performance projects like the Mitchell & Kenyon screenings in Britain or the fairground cinema *Crazy Cinématographe* in Luxembourg need considerable budgets and particular environments which make the film narrator an essential aspect of the film shows. Thus, unlike the silent film piano player, the film narrator certainly will not become a regular performer in screenings of early films at festivals or in film museums. On the other hand, thanks to DVD, YouTube and video streaming, access to early films in adequate quality is not a serious problem anymore: Oral live performances of film narrators here and there in the context of film festivals and film archives might be incentive for theatre groups and teachers at schools, high schools and universities to re-invent the film narrator.

Notes

1. See Charles Musser, *The Emergence of Cinema: The American Screen to 1907* (Berkeley, Los Angeles, London: Scribners 1990); Ludwig Vogl-Bienek, Richard Crangle (eds), *Screen Culture and the Social Question, KINtop Studies in Early Cinema 3* (New Barnet: John Libbey, 2013).
2. Joe Kember, *Marketing Modernity. Victorian Popular Shows and Early Cinema* (Exeter: University of Exeter Press, 2009), 44–68.
3. Torsten Gärtner, *The Sunday School Chronicle* – eine Quelle zur Nutzung der Laterna magica in englischen Sonntagsschulen", *KINtop* 14/15 (2006): 25–35.
4. Jens Ruchatz, *Licht und Wahrheit: Eine Mediumgeschichte der fotografischen Projektion* (Munich: Wilhelm Fink, 2003), 257.
5. Ivo Blom and Ine van Dooren, "Ladies and Gentlemen, Hats Off, Please! Dutch Film Lecturing and the Case of Cor Schuring", *iris* 22 (1996): 81–102; Ansje van Beusekom, "The Rise and Fall of the Lecturer as Entertainer in the Netherlands. Exhibition-Practices in Transition Related to Local Circumstances", *iris* 22 (1996): 131–144; Bert Hogenkamp, "The Impact of Audiovisual Media in the Town of Utrecht. A Research Project at the University of Utrecht", *KINtop* 9 (2000): 117–129.
6. See www.cinemacontext.nl, advanced search, people.
7. Hogenkamp, "The Impact of Audiovisual Media", 124–125.
8. Pianist advert, *Der Kinematograph*, 311 (11 December, 1912).
9. Advert "Rezitations-Duett", *Der Kinematograph*, no. 371 (28 January 1914).
10. Martin Loiperdinger, "'The Audience Feels rather at Home ...' Peter Marzen's 'Localisation' of Film Exhibition in Trier", in Frank Kessler and Nanna Verhoeff (eds), *Networks of Entertainment: Early Film Distribution 1895–1915* (New Barnet: John Libbey, 2007), 123–130, esp.124–125.
11. Ulrich Rauscher, "Die Welt im Kino", *Frankfurter Zeitung* (31 December, 1912), repr. in Jörg Schweinitz (ed.), *Prolog vor dem Film. Nachdenken über ein neues Medium 1909–1914* (Leipzig: Reclam, 1992), 195–201; here 199.
12. Rauscher, "Die Welt im Kino", 198–199, English translation quoted from Caroline Henkes: "Asta Nielsen and Her Destitute Female Characters", in Martin Loiperdinger and Uli Jung (eds), *Importing Asta Nielsen. The International Film Star in the Making 1910–1914, KINtop Studies in Early Cinema*, vol. 2 (New Barnet: John Libbey, 2013), 338–339.
13. Rauscher, "Die Welt im Kino", 198.
14. Emilie Altenloh, *Zur Soziologie des Kino. Die Kino-Unternehmung und die sozialen Schichten ihrer Besucher* [1914], Andrea Haller, Martin Loiperdinger and Heide Schlüpmann (eds), *KINtop Schriften* 9 (Frankfurt and Basel: Stroemfeld, 2012).
15. Vanessa Toulmin, "Programming the Local: Mitchell & Kenyon and the Local Film Show", in Martin Loiperdinger (ed.), *Early Cinema Today. The Art of Programming and Live Performance, KINtop Studies in Early Cinema*, vol. 1 (New Barnet: John Libbey, 2011), 71–72.
16. Claude Bertemes and Nicole Dahlen, "The Art of Crazy Programming. Documentation of *Crazy Cinématographe* Programmes, 2007 to 2010", and Claude Bertemes, Nicole Dahlen, "Back to the Future: Early Cinema and Late Economy of Attention. An interim report about *Crazy Cinématographe*", both in Loiperdinger, *Early Cinema Today*, 115–134 and 79–105 respectively. See also Claude Bertemes, "Cinématographe Reloaded: Notes on the Fairground Cinema Project *Crazy Cinématographe*", in Martin Loiperdinger (ed.), *Travelling Cinema in Europe. Sources and Perspectives*, *KINtop Schriften* 10, 191–218.
17. Frank Kessler, "Programming and Performing Early Cinema Today: Strategies and Dispositifs", in Loiperdinger, *Early Cinema Today*, 144.
18. Ibid.
19. Bertemes and Dahlen, "Back to the Future", 89.

Standards of Practice in Transition: The Showmanship of Jasper Redfern as It Emerged

Peter Walsh

Our perspective on showmanship and the nature of performance in early cinema is informed by a range of widely adopted terms, and by the common language we use in categorising patterns of practice and behaviour. Some are contemporary to the period, taken directly from the parlance of those who appropriated and adapted these labels to promote new hybrids of cinematic and live performance. Other terms are modern, following more general trends observed in the period, and by necessity they are marked by our knowledge of the film industry that followed. While concessions might be made to specific cultural, linguistic, or hyper-local peculiarities in the application of this shared vocabulary, the position of outliers who seemingly defy any immediate categorisation offers a valuable insight into how these labels map onto the hierarchies of exhibition practice which emerged in the new market of early cinema.

When considering the early British market of itinerant exhibition the practices of Jasper Redfern, a Northern English filmmaker, exhibitor, and eventual cinema manager, offers a pertinent example of a showman who struggles to fit the more obvious categories into which he might be placed. Having previously been overlooked as a relatively unexceptional showman, my reappraisal of his enterprises has as its basis the materials of the Fred Holmes Collection, an archival holdings of photographic plates, correspondence and ephemera which all pertain to Redfern's operations between 1899 and 1912.[1] Originally held by descendants of a projectionist and later manager in Redfern's employ, the varied materials of the Collection has shed valuable light on the practices of an idiosyncratic exhibitor who found success touring in and around the English county of Yorkshire.[2] Approaching Redfern within the context of a broader study into early film enterprise in the region, my attempts to chart his progress through the emerging British film market consistently struggled to align either his practice or his own promotional labels with either those of his contemporaries, or with some of the more consistent categories we employ today. In attempting to reconcile this difference, Redfern's behaviour resists being justified either by means of a new schemata, or by settling on the facile observation that at one time or another he had operated as a 'Jack of All Trades'. Instead it should be noted that for the decade that Redfern was active in the industry, the terms of his engagement were in regular re-negotiation, expanding and adapting to meet the changing demand for varied and updated motion picture entertainments. His behaviour does not easily map onto some of the trends already observed and labelled in the early British film industry, and his divergence from these recognisable lines of development offers a starting point for a discussion on the economic viability of those showmen and managers who sought to follow their own path through the expanding market of motion picture exhibition.

The starting point for any examination of this nomenclature within the British market must by certain necessity begin with the categories outlined by Colonel A.C. Bromhead, who in a 1933 address to the British division of Gaumont sought to pinpoint the broadest trends in the performance and presentation of early cinema.[3] Speaking as a veteran of the industry, Bromhead reflected that there were three distinct types of cinematographic showmen evident in the early British market. Namely:

(1) The fairground showman;
(2) The town or public hall showman;
(3) The music hall or variety theatre showman.

Bromhead's categories took as their basis the site of a show's performance, and by extension incorporated the three fields of popular entertainment into which the new technology had been successfully integrated. However, in focusing on what was already extant in the field of popular entertainment, these categories are limited in their application to discussions of both market entry and the development of practices across fields. The assumption inherent in this categorisation was that each form was defined by its difference, and that on some level each must remain discreet from the others. Defined by their widespread occurrence in the market of the time, these categories reflect the most successful and prominent modes of practice and performance. This makes the case for understanding the position of outsiders and outliers within this field even more vital.

A more recent and valuable framework of categorisation has been put forward by Deac Rossell who in analysing the uptake and trade in motion picture projection equipment was able to determine the background of many showmen drawn into the market of itinerant exhibition.[4] By looking at the dissemination of new technology, the categories Rossell put forth hinge on understanding the barriers to entry into the market of this period, and by extension adds greater nuance to Bromhead's three types of showmen. In particular Rossell stresses the difference between an experienced and a wholly novice public hall showman, and how the nature of performance for someone working a pre-established circuit would contrast with that of an exhibitor going from show-to-show, without any long term scheduling to rely on. His final catch-all category encompasses the ephemeral get-rich-quick opportunists who had neither the skill nor the ability to establish themselves as showmen, and it is their withdrawal which is seen in the many individual advertisements for 'as-new' and 'barely used' projection equipment in the trade presses of the period. Rossell's analysis of records as fleeting as the notice of an agent leaving the market demonstrates the value of reading around conventional public records to find the traces of the less conventional outliers in this market.

Considering these frameworks, my attempts to map any of their criteria onto Jasper Redfern sat awkwardly with what is known about his entry and development within the field of motion picture exhibition. A newly qualified and recently established studio photographer, Redfern brought his technical education to bear during his first demonstrations of the Kineopticon and Röntgen's 'X' Rays, which opened at the YMCA in Sheffield in September 1896. The competition Redfern faced was considerable and direct, as his show opened the same week as Birt Acres' very own Kineopticon show, and came only a week before a well advertised return of the Lumières' touring show to the city. Redfern's presentation distinguished itself by being more immediate and interactive in a way that the high profile cinematograph turns could not be. This was in part inherent from the scale of the venue, being a small lecture theatre with a raised platform and non-fixed seating for scarcely over one hundred patrons.[5] The central presence and technical performance of the projector was of course an important element in many film screenings, yet where audiences at Sheffield's Albert Hall, or at the rival Empire Theatre would have the Cinematograph or Kineopticon introduced at a distance, audiences at the YMCA sat immediately next to the projector itself. This combined with a public invitation in the local press to 'see by the New Light your own bones, and other things invisible to the naked eye' demonstrates that Redfern's unique selling point was the immediacy and presence his technical demonstrations offered audiences.[6] Recognising the limitations and value of this exclusivity he also charged a premium ticket price relative to the city's other popular entertainments. A short tour followed his successful run at the YMCA, and Redfern's scientific double-bill visited the satellite towns of Chesterfield, Doncaster and Rotherham, all passed over by the national tours of Acres and the *Lumières*, and all within a short commute of Redfern's base of operations in Sheffield.

By Bromhead's definition, Redfern was quite distinctly a public or town hall showman, a lecturer and technical demonstrator and a markedly novice one at that. Having started from this point, Redfern was by January 1897 accepting bookings as the interval's entertainment for a traditional winter pantomime in Sheffield. While in practical terms it was a small step to upscale his show to suit a larger crowd, this turn could also be read as the first performance in Redfern's prolific career as a variety hall showman. While this direct transition from one form into another is not at odds with the categories themselves, the weakness of such a perspective is the assumption that it might be an absolute change. The definitive shift from one field into another can easily be ratified within a given narrative of a showman's developmental arc, and while an initial overview of Redfern leant itself to such a position, the discovery of the Fred Holmes Collection upended such an assumption. The ephemera of the Collection shows that alongside his growing profile in the musical halls, Redfern maintained an active career as a public hall showman, yet in so doing he developed a form of performance which became wholly malleable to the demands of his employers. While the immediacy of Redfern's shows at the YMCA appeared to have been superseded by his more outwardly prominent position in the music halls, Redfern's public hall show continued to be offered to anyone interested in booking him for their event. While his availability for such shows was noted in local advertisements for his photo-studios, the impact of these private shows garnered little or no attention from the local press, and the artefacts of the Fred Holmes Collection now stand as the sole record of these performances.

The bookings Redfern received for these private engagements came from religious groups, political organisations, social groups and sports clubs, as well as from schools and children's clubs. While in outward appearance the form of these shows recall those Redfern gave in public halls, they operated under a set of demands separate from those faced by the lecturer/showman. The favour of repeat audiences did not have to be courted and the programming and form of the show could instead focus on the novelty of bringing this technology to a limited gathering. As wider audiences were growing tired of topical productions only a week or two after their release, Redfern found new life for outdated material in these private shows. Commenting on a presentation given by Redfern to an assembly of pupils at Sheffield's Central Grammar School in 1898, a candid student reporter noted that footage of Queen Victoria's visit to

Sheffield, an event at that point over a year old, kept the rapt attention of an audience of young schoolboys. In this instance, the film of the monarch's visit was set alongside demonstrations of 'Natural Colour Photography', and while the show was intended as educationally uplifting, the unnamed reporter noted that it was the films of Sheffield United that were the most warmly received, with cheers from his peers upon sight of the large bellied goal-keeper William 'Fatty' Foalkes.

The materials of the Fred Holmes Collection also give us a greater understanding of the range of entertainments Redfern offered for private commission, combining technical demonstrations, films of local and topical interest, and culturally uplifting material in a manner directly tailored to meet the expectations of the event and its organiser. With these shows, Redfern developed a set terminology with which to encapsulate and brand the form, and in particular the Italianate 'Conversazione' appears across a number of these events. Taken in isolation these shows might easily appear coincidental, yet when taken as a whole we can begin to understand how Redfern developed a wider performative persona which made him equally at home introducing cinematograph demonstrations at society balls and presenting a whole evening's entertainment at a large inner-city musical hall. A prime example of this parity is found when contrasting the programme presented by Redfern at a lucrative show for the Albert Hall in Leeds over the Christmas holidays in 1901 with the show he presented five days later at the Abbeydale Primitive Methodist Church in Sheffield. With venues differing in structure, purpose, and intended audience, both shows still shared an almost identical programme of films, centred primarily around a series drawn from the German Oberammergau passion plays. While not topical films in their own right, their religious focus made them apt for such a seasonal performance, and while the films were still new to Redfern, it appears he saw no reason to keep such 'fresh' titles away from the smaller and less lucrative Methodist audience.

Reconciling such a spread of performative modes, Bromhead's categories could at best label the Redfern of 1902 as a concurrent music and town hall showman. The limitation of such a perspective is that it fails to accommodate Redfern's status as a showman in transition. By the second half of 1902, records in the Fred Holmes Collection show that Redfern was making his first overtures to co-ordinate a complete show of travelling variety, all billed under the rubric of 'Redfern's No 1. Vaudeville Company'. Bringing together soloists from his intimate film and music recitals, with comedians and performers sourced from his time touring the variety theatres, Redfern presented a show which interwove these artistes with motion pictures, colour photographic slides, and 'turns' from an Edison concert Phonograph. Interplay between the live and the mechanical acts was a central part of the show, and in particular footage of the strongman George Dinnie was enlivened with personal appearances from the man himself, happy to demonstrate his strength and to take on anyone willing to challenge him in the wrestling ring. While the roster of this troupe lost and gained members across a number of short tours across the North of England, the length of these runs gradually grew in size, and a core of central performers coalesced around this emerging format. The growing length and regularity of these shows suggests that they were increasingly lucrative and sustainable, and as Redfern increased his involvement, it becomes clear that he had crossed the gap from novice to established itinerant exhibitor. As the self-styled manager of his own travelling show, Redfern had grown a side interest into the dominant focus of his enterprises.

While the tours of these 'complete' variety shows grew, a turning point came when he made a concerted push into greater permanency in the spring of 1904, during a run of public halls around the Thames estuary. Culminating in a high profile booking at the Empire theatre in Southend-on-Sea, Redfern's now established troupe of performers were joined by the 'champion trick cyclist of the world' – W. Salmon. Capitalising on this prestige, Redfern staged a media event around his star guest, and the opening night of the show was promoted with a high profile unicycle tour by Salmon up, down and around Southend's main streets. Photographs were taken and Redfern personally filmed the event from a raised platform, recording both the trick cyclists and the gathered crowds. The combination of a star performer, the prominent filming of the event and the screening of the films the very same evening were all part of a promotional drive to give both the showman and his show a distinct and recognisable profile in the market of entertainments at this popular seaside destination.

Successful as this drive was reported to be, Redfern's run at the Empire was a limited booking, and his ties to W. Salmon and the venue lasted only a week. Seeing the potential market in the rotating audience of holidaymakers that flocked to Southend-on-Sea over the summer months, Redfern took steps to set up a semi-permanent home for his complete show of variety entertainments. With the Empire already booked with other acts from the nationwide Moss circuit of variety theatres, Redfern took a cue from the practices of the fairground showman and erected a temporary beach-side stage as a new home for his troupe. With its back to the sea and a stage facing inland, a fenced off section of stalls comprising benches and deckchairs was reached through a box-office set up at the rear of the site. With the exception of Salmon, the beachside show remained much the same as the one presented at the Empire, with a programme of prominently billed 'name' film titles supported by a regular cast of musicians, comedians, acrobats and of course the strongman Dinnie. While it remains unclear how successful this venture was in terms of box-office returns, the nature of the structure left it open to both the elements and the wiles of local planning officers. This outdoor enterprise only lasted until the end of that summer.

While this temporary enterprise was a quick response to an opportunity as it arose, the beach-side venture proved to be a valuable proof-of-concept for the possibilities open to Redfern's now established format. While he continued to bill this show as his 'No. 1 Grand Vaudeville Combination', the general definition of the term vaudeville, with the familiar set of discrete acts, does not adequately define his work. Instead the term cine-variety lends itself to the form of show Redfern had settled on as it was a complete programme of varied entertainments in which the motion picture element was not an isolated but an integral part, with individual titles consistently named and promoted, and established in such a manner that all other live acts were positioned in relation to it. The case against using this term is that it is neither one he himself used nor one that has any notable contemporary precedent, instead being more prominently used after 1930 to describe a cinema show which included live events, notably at a point in time when this had become a clear exception and not the rule. While the term applied in relation to early cinema is more widely used as an informal referent rather than as a definite category, its direct usage has begun to increase in recent studies devoted to this field. A notable example is to be found in Joe Kember's *Marketing Modernity* in which his analysis of a series of articles from *The Bioscope* in 1908 delineates a discussion related to the value of combined variety and motion picture shows and the risks of not suitably balancing the two.[7] Redfern's work serves as a valuable precursor to this debate as his cine-varieties marked the shift which occurred when the cinematograph was elevated from being one turn in many to becoming the central and rotating core of a 'complete' film-driven variety show.

The concentration of Redfern's efforts around the cine-variety format came at the point of his transition from travelling shows to greater permanency. His success at settling into fixed venue exhibitions fuelled a rapid expansion in the years that followed. The range of materials in the Collection relating to the smaller private shows dwindle after Redfern's season at Southend-on-Sea, and it becomes apparent that he had dedicated most of his resources towards supporting his touring show, eventually expanding his operations to include another troupe working with the same rubric under his direct management. The Grand in Manchester became his new base of operations, and having managed a successful residency at the venue, the organisation of Jasper Redfern & Company bought the hall outright in 1907. While the exposure of this large investment would eventually lead to the company's bankruptcy in 1912, in the years prior to this Redfern's cine-variety format continued to grow and draw new audiences and this particular combination distinguished his show from the rash of film-only venues which were emerging at the time.

In his gradual departure from itinerant film exhibition we can reflect that Redfern drew on the many forms of exhibition practice previously touched on by Bromhead and Rossell, and having entered the field as a novice, he had by 1907 managed to grow his then incorporated company into a position where it could acquire a sizeable piece of real-estate for a flagship venue and a permanent base of operations. In contrast, his earliest years as an itinerant exhibitor were marked by the fact that cinematographic exhibition always remained a side-interest to his primary concern in the running of his photo-studio in Sheffield, and it can be noted that Redfern's earliest ventures all remained within a short commute of Sheffield. Understanding this shift in enterprise is key to understanding why Redfern is such a poor fit with the categories of cine-showmanship already noted. Unlike other early film exhibitors who were more set in their approach to touring and exhibition, Redfern was not dependent on this enterprise as his only source of income, and he retained the luxury of choice over any opportunity that presented itself to him. Public lecturing led to variety theatre, and while his profile as a cinematic turn grew he was still able to accept commissions for private shows as and when they were offered. Working across this range of audiences and performative styles, Redfern was able to draw together a format which brought a 'complete' yet film-focused entertainment show to both public halls and variety theatres. The point at which Redfern turned his attention wholly to the touring of this cine-variety show marks his re-launch into a market which was witnessing the gradual subsidence of the itinerant forms of cinematic performance. The match of working a circuit he had already established, with a format that stood out from many of his peers, gave him a competitive edge in the years after 1904.

Understanding why this form fell so quickly out of favour with the new emerging cinema audiences is less clear, although Vanessa Toulmin's article 'Cuckoo in the Nest' offers a balanced evaluation of the precedents set by itinerant film exhibitors for the permanent forms of cinema that followed.[8] By establishing that the music hall could only function as a temporary home for motion picture shows, Toulmin focusses on the practices of the public hall showmen and their contributions to the development of purpose-built cinemas after 1909. With examples drawn from the many commissioners tied to the work of Mitchell & Kenyon, Toulmin pinpoints that it was the showmen's use of extensive advertising and localised and specialised programming which helped them launch new shows at public halls, and that combined with a consistently renewed programme of films, this approach cemented the longer residencies that many of these showmen were able to enjoy. This analysis underscores why Redfern's consistently renewed cine-variety format enjoyed some success with audiences eager for a regular source of new films. However while it was also the case that as the field grew to prioritise even greater renewal of programmes at an ever shrinking cost of admission, Redfern's chosen format would eventually get priced out of the market. His rapid expansion matched with his precarious financial exposure left him vulnerable as audiences drawn to the cine-variety format began to dwindle. While the detachment Redfern had as an outlier gave him the ability to explore formats and to modify his own approach to showmanship, the show which he put together as his 'No. 1 Grand Vaudeville Combination' was the one that could best address the gaps in the market he had observed between 1902 and 1904. While his initial success on some levels confirms that his observations were astute, the changing expectations of the emerging cinema-going audience of 1912 left Redfern with a format that was ultimately stuck between categories, and, that sadly, became untenable.

Notes

1. For further details of the discover and restoration of this collection see Vanessa Toulmin and Peter Walsh, "Archive Article: The Fred Holmes Collection", *Early Popular Visual Culture* 10, no. 3 (2012): 299–311.
2. My analysis here, and my work more generally into early cinema in Yorkshire is borne out of the research conducted towards my doctoral thesis, "Pictures by the Mile: The Development of the Cinematograph in Yorkshire, 1900–1910" (PhD dissertation, The University of Sheffield, 2012).
3. "Alfred Claude Bromhead", on *The Who's Who of Victorian Cinema*, accessed 4 May 2013, http://www.victorian-cinema.net/bromhead
4. Deac Rossell, "A Slippery Job: Travelling Exhibitors in Early Cinema", Simon Popple and Vanessa Toulmin (eds), *Visual Delights* (Trowbridge: Flicks Books, 2000), 50–60.
5. Details regarding the inside of the lecture hall discerned from contemporary photographs held by Sheffield's Local Studies Library.
6. *The Sheffield & Rotherham Independent*, 5 September 1896.
7. Joe Kember, *Marketing Modernity: Victorian Popular Shows and Early Cinema* (Exeter: University of Exeter Press, 2009), 124–126.
8. Vanessa Toulmin, "Cuckoo in the Nest: Edwardian Itinerant Exhibition Practices and the Transition to Cinema in the United Kingdom from 1901 to 1906", *The Moving Image* 10, no.1 (2010): 51–79.

Showmanship Skills and the Changing Role of the Exhibitor in 1910s Scotland

María Antonia Vélez-Serna

At the core of many of the transformations that make the 1910s so interesting is a struggle over the definition of commodity relations: who owned films, who controlled their exhibition contexts, and how this peculiar good should be traded. This effort to grapple with the complex materiality of cinema was in part about the emergence of large business interests in the international film industry, but it was also intensely localised. This paper will use a sample of cinema adverts from Scottish newspapers to analyse how they both reflect and perform a shift in the role of the exhibitor on a local level.[1] I will argue that, while the transition to renting and towards longer narrative films shifted the balance of power away from local exhibitors and their traditional showmanship skills in favour of the manufacturing sector, this process rewarded new managerial and advertising skills, thus redefining showmanship rather than making it redundant. Although this shift entailed the loss of the means of production, it also tended to recast the exhibitor's labour along the lines of the professional middle class, and was framed by a discourse of legitimation.

Property relations in early exhibition

The reshaping of the film trade between the American nickelodeon boom and the end of the First World War can be understood as a redefinition of the commodity nature of film, or rather, as a change in the role of film as a commodity within the broader phenomenon of cinema. To throw this transformation into relief, it is useful to return to Charles Musser's formulation of the three practices that constitute cinema's mode of production, where exhibition is defined as one.[2] In the first stage, the film print is produced as a material object (bearing intellectual content) with a use value and exchange value – a commodity, but not an ordinary one. This object is then used in the production of a show, in such a way that the film is neither depleted nor removed from the market. Access to the show is then sold to the public. In a more technical way, Gerben Bakker has discussed films as an *intermediate good* – an input for the production of something else. So while films were indeed traded as a commodity, the audience was paying for the 'spectator-hour' – the economic unit that was produced using the films amongst other things.[3] For simplicity, throughout this article I will refer to this as *the show*: the localised event of exhibition and reception embracing both live and filmed entertainment. Showmanship, for the purposes of this paper, can be thought of as the additional labour and skill required to transform films into spectator-hours.

As Musser puts it, over the first few years of the nickelodeon boom, 'the reel of film became the basic industry commodity', and the development of more self-contained forms of narrative entailed a relative loss of editorial control by exhibitors, as compared to the highly performative role they had within itinerant practices.[4] The first Scottish exhibitors, with their diverse backstories of fairground, lantern lecturing, and music hall entertainment, certainly had plenty of performative showmanship skills.[5] Between 1909 and 1913, the boom years for cinema opening in Scotland, the new kind of cinema entrepreneur that came into the exhibition business was, in contrast, a skilled manager and programmer rather than a performer. Furthermore, he or she tended to no longer own the apparatus or the venue (as fairground exhibitors had), and the films were also rented rather than bought outright. These films were in turn increasingly standardised and self-sufficient, transferring the weight of textual production to the manufacturers and diminishing the value added by showmanship.[6] In other industries, this loss of control over the means of production and devaluation of artisan skills brought about by more standardised processes is a hallmark of proletarianisation. This is not, however, how this change was perceived by a film trade engaged in a process of expansion. Furthermore, the shift of attention from 'show' to 'film' was neither sudden nor uniform. The Scottish programme samples provide a suitable illustration of the tensions around mixed programming and the role of live performance in cinemas.

Live performance and cine-variety

The contrast between the 1913 and 1918 situation as represented in the two samples of cinema adverts shows how the exhibitor's labour became increasingly obscured as the live elements of the show were marginalised. A first instance of this process involves the decline of the mixed show combining live variety and films. In the United States, as Bakker notes, 'small-time vaudeville' was on the way out by 1910, having been 'automated away' by moving pictures.[7] This was not the case in Scotland where, according to Paul Maloney, the working-class culture of live entertainment survived in industrial districts in the form of cine-variety (a programme format akin to the 'small-time vaudeville' described by Robert C. Allen, incorporating a few simple variety turns in alternation with single- or double-reel films).[8] In 1913, a mixed programme was offered in forty-four per cent of the adverts in the Scottish sample. Two years later the *Bioscope Annual* still described thirty-six per cent of the 399 Scottish cinemas in its list as presenting 'pictures and varieties'. As Figure 1 shows, the geographical pattern of this mode of exhibition was uneven, with a higher concentration in Glasgow, Dundee, Ayr, and the mining towns of North Lanarkshire and Linlithgowshire (in other words, in the densely populated, industrial central belt of Scotland, between Glasgow and Edinburgh). The proportion of mixed programming in the 1918 sample had dropped to twenty-six per cent – which was nonetheless still a significant presence.

The links between cine-variety and earlier forms of working-class entertainment help explain the disdain expressed by some sectors of the trade. Even when the live element involved something as respectable as the engagement of vocalists by several Glasgow cinemas, exhibitors lamented it 'as it is but a step from this to a full variety programme'.[9] A separate performing tradition existed, however, as practised by lecturers and elocutionists. There are only three instances of 'speaking to pictures' in the newspaper sample for 1913. At the Bannockburn Picture House, a Mr. J. Newby would recite Tennyson's poem before 'The Charge of the Light Brigade' was shown, and describe the film.[10] Meanwhile, in Aberdeen, Dove Paterson was presenting his trademark act at the Gaiety and the Music Hall. The history and peculiarities of Aberdeen elocution have been discussed by Trevor Griffiths in a recent article, which also traces the influence of local regulations, economic pressures and taste cultures on the vocal and musical accompaniment of silent cinema in Scottish venues.[11]

The local nuances of these intermedial presentation contexts played an important role in popularising film with Scottish audiences. The desire to define film as a self-sufficient form of entertainment, however, was a common topic amongst contributors to the trade press, and it demanded a new style of management. The generation of city cinema managers that took up the job during the cinema building boom privileged a rhetoric of efficiency and standardisation, through which a stable patronage could be secured amongst the desirable classes. They frowned upon the old forms of showmanship that some

11 Showmanship Skills and the Changing Role of the Exhibitor in 1910s Scotland

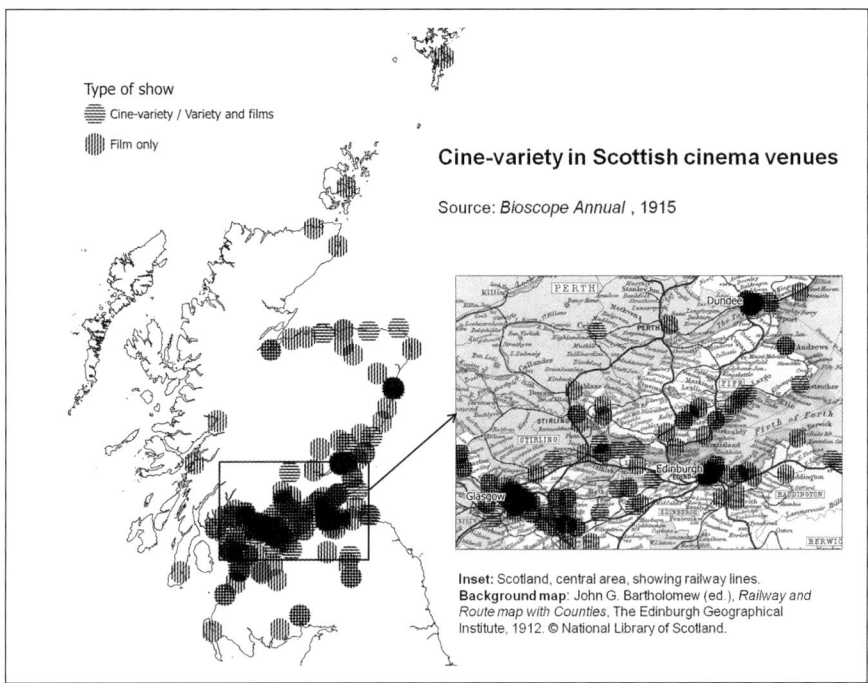

Figure 1: Main type of show given at permanent exhibition venues in Scotland, as listed in the 1915 *Bioscope Annual*. Venues only used occasionally, as well as those that do not include this information, have been excluded, for a total of 366 listings.

exhibitors had inherited from the fairground. In a particularly ungracious article published when the transformation was irreversible, W.A. Williamson wrote that 'the old showman does not understand the cinematograph trade, a trade requiring not showmanship but sympathy'.[12] This 'sympathy' suggests a relationship with the audience that is somewhat different from the outsider appeal of fairground performers. It will be noted that, as early as 1911, the author of the *Handbook of Kinematography*, Colin Bennett, did not mention any performing abilities as desirable for the picture house manager. His or her 'showmanship' was to be expressed in 'the comfort, cleanliness and beauty of his [sic] hall', in 'judicious advertising', and in 'catering for the continual education and amusement of regular and chance patrons'.[13]

Such advice is indicative of the aspirational tone that permeated the trade press, in which the professionalisation of cinema management was a constant topic. Although the companies registered to control cinema venues in Scotland tended to be small and local, their legal configuration as limited liability companies signalled a shift towards more corporate business models. The redefinition of the exhibitor's job mainly in terms of house-management and programming reflected his or her increasingly subordinate and accountable position in the new pattern of venue ownership. Within these confines, however, the cinema manager had the task of addressing and bringing in a growing audience. This is where newspaper advertising proves to be a rich, if complicated source. Because they are enmeshed in the same web of transformations as the phenomena they refer to, advertisements must be understood as having a performative function: they are acts of showmanship, part of the labour to produce the show. Analysis of a systematic collection of adverts provides a way to observe how the function of cinema was negotiated and constructed in response to local contexts and through the changing nature of the exhibitor's role.

Creating the habit

After the building boom, once it became clear that cinema was not a passing fad, the challenge was to convert the audience that had first come in for the technical novelty and the attractions, into a regular patronage that would provide a solid foundation for further investment. There were potentially several ways of achieving this. Michael Hammond has observed that, up to the beginning of the war, the advertising rhetoric used by Southampton cinemas emphasised 'the social utility of the space as part of the cinema-going experience', so that working-class, peripheral venues were presented as 'warm and cosy', while city-centre cinemas provided facilities such as tea rooms and ran a continuous show to enhance the sense of convenience and respite for urban strollers.[14] The same emphasis can be seen in the Scottish context.

While more than thirty per cent of the 1913 Scottish adverts surveyed omit the mention of specific films, most of them include show times and prices of admission. Furthermore, there are numerous references to the permanent characteristics of the venue, rather than the specific show. Thus, for instance, the Scenic, in the South side of Glasgow, claimed to have 'comfortable seats and every convenience'; Slora's Electric Theatre in Cowdenbeath (perhaps unwisely) advertised the fact that the auditorium was disinfected with Jeyes fluid; and the Whitburn Picture Theatre promised 'Beautiful Pictures! Appreciative Audience!'.[15] A few city-centre venues that opened through the afternoon offered free tea, and the resident orchestras were mentioned in ten cases. Finally, the music-hall background of many managers came in handy when it came to judging local talent competitions; at the Airdrie Hippodrome, for instance, an aspiring artist could win a week's engagement for 'not less than 30s'. On another day of the week, the theatre would be the starting point for a marathon race. This direct appeal to the local audience points to an active engagement that sought to foster repeated custom, which is why the mention of the week's films is sometimes cursory, giving only titles and sometimes genres. Not much else was needed to convey the appeal of a mixed programme of short films, or a cine-variety bill.

Putting together such a programme was arguably the most trade-specific skill a manager had to master during the transitional era. This task involved negotiating with distributors, viewing and selecting films, and arranging the transport. While in the United States some of these functions had been outsourced to the film exchanges who put together a film package delivered to each cinema daily, in the United Kingdom the attachment to free-market renting meant that exhibitors resisted some forms of programme standardisation. This resistance to relinquish control over the show can be found well into the 1920s in the debates around block-booking, but it was already present from the introduction of single-reel features and packaged 'service' programmes before the War. The growing length of films and the development of more restrictive rental practices (such as exclusive and territorial rights) focused opposition from the trade, at least discursively. In practice, however, feature programming had taken over by 1918.

The skills required to market a programme of short films are different from those required for a long film, and the rhetorical strategies used in the advertising reflect this. While 1913 adverts contain more information about the venue and exhibition practice, 1918 publicity yields more film titles, but it can be more laconic in terms of presentation strategies. This elision of showmanship from advertisement does not necessarily signify its disappearance from actual practice. It is however apparent that the personal appeal and direct address that, as Joe Kember's work has showed, helped tame the unsettling modernity of the moving image, were receding from view. As Kember has also suggested, a different form of personalisation was taking hold, connected to the emergence of the star system and new ways of marketing the film product.[16] Understanding and managing audience expectations for particular films became much more important, and a new style of advertising reflected this changing relationship.

Luring the transient audience

The 1913 sample, taken at the height of the Scottish cinema boom, reflects a trade that is becoming embedded in everyday life. 'Usual times – usual prices' is a phrase often seen in the collection, but most of the venues list specific show times and prices. This is much less prevalent in 1918, when a third of the adverts do not list times, partly because half of the venues are running a continuous show. Although this mode of operation is mostly associated with high-street venues, many suburban and small-town cinemas had stopped advertising two shows a night (or even one), and instead offered a continuous show throughout the evening, with only enough time to run the films twice. The informality of the continuous show no doubt contributed to the embedding of cinemagoing into everyday routines for many Scots, and not only the deprived inhabitants of inner-city slums who might go to the cinema just to escape their overcrowded tenement rooms and to sit in the warmth for a couple of hours in the winter.[17] In a tendentious but interesting editorial, the Scottish trade journal, *The Entertainer*, tried to explain 'the rise of the picturehouse' with arguments that seem to contradict some standard assumptions about early audiences:

> In the aristocratic quarters the audience is interested, and it is a kind of club rather than a place of entertainment, while in the industrial neighbourhoods the people who enter the picturehouses do so to learn the ways of the world, to see how others live, how others die.[18]

This is a curious inversion of the more established idea of bourgeois spectatorship as more attentive to the film text, and popular cinemagoing as a social rather than intellectual activity. In its optimism about the self-improving aims of working-class spectators, it might be filed together with earlier discourses of uplift or regarded as wishful thinking on the part of the trade. However, the mention of high-class cinemas as 'a kind of club' is in line with developments in exhibition that were taking place around the time the article was published. As Michael Quinn has pointed out, the trade's idea of the 'transient audience' did not define it as lower-class.[19] Many of the new, luxurious cinemas that had appeared on the central commercial streets of the main Scottish towns had entrance prices starting at six pence – three times as much as most neighbourhood halls. Their appeal to a more affluent audience was founded on convenience and atmosphere; the addition of tea-rooms, smoking rooms and foyers to many of the larger picture houses further created club-like social spaces which were only loosely connected to film viewing. Exhibitors imagined that these spaces would attract the businessman with some time to spare between appointments, or the respectable lady who needed a break from her shopping. The preferred strategy to cater for these desirable customers was the continuous show, and it was from this quarter that opposition to the feature-length film often came.

As Ben Singer has found for the American context, 'the feature craze was not a tidal-wave phenomenon that instantly wiped out the short film' or the variety programme.[20] Feature programming, furthermore, did not become dominant

11 Showmanship Skills and the Changing Role of the Exhibitor in 1910s Scotland

at the same time everywhere, and its patterns of expansion are surprising in the Scottish case. The twice-a-night show was initially thought better suited to longer films than the continuous city-centre programme, and thus a consistent programming policy based on longer films (rather than the occasional 'big' exclusive) was adopted by peripheral cinemas before central ones. By 1918, however, all of the cinemas in the Glasgow city centre represented in the sample were showing a feature programme, even though the shows were continuous. The apparent contradiction between feature films and the continuous show was resolved through the reformulation of the concept of the transient audience, which required city-centre cinemas to reinvent their address to the individual, discriminating customer rather than the curious passerby. The assumption of mobility (transience) as a characteristic of city-centre audiences was reinterpreted as meaning that spectators could be drawn in to particular films, enticed by the advertising columns that lay out the urban environment as a seductive menu for the middle class.[21] Their choice was increasingly a choice of film, and the manager's role was to sell each title. The new style of advertising reflected this shift, and the emergence of the star system was deeply intertwined with it. One of the most radical changes observable in the sample of adverts has to do with the prominence of star performers in the promotional rhetoric for particular films. While in 1913 only 3.5 percent of the adverts mentioned an actor, the proportion is over sixty percent in 1918. The manufacturer's brand and the length of the film were also used widely in advertisements: while fewer than one in ten of the 1913 adverts contain information on either manufacturer or length of the film, over thirty-eight percent of the 1918 sample mentions a brand, and forty-four percent the length.

Although the turn towards promotion of the individual film is visible in most of the cases in the collection, the Glasgow Picture House can be cited as a particularly striking example. The 1913 advert starts by listing opening times and prices, and goes on to mention 'The Palm Court Smoke Room, Wedgewood Lounge and Palm Court Balcony. The Finest Tea Rooms in Glasgow'. There is no mention of titles for the films being shown on that day, but rather of two 'special' films – longer European exclusives – that will be shown during the following two weeks. This then captures a moment of transformation, when features were not yet a regular part of the programme; instead, they disrupted routine, because longer films were not produced or marketed in a systematic way.[22] Five years later, in contrast, this cinema advertises using a large block print depicting the protagonists in a film titled *His Golden Hour*. The copy praises the performance of French actress Suzanne Grandais, inviting the audience to enjoy 'a wonderful piece of work', an 'artistic triumph' inscribed within theatrical discourse through the use of the term 'in Five Acts' (rather than the more prosaic '5-reel').[23] This rhetoric is a sharp departure from the continued use of adjectives such as 'thrilling' and 'strong' that were more common in adverts for popular venues, but it is also very different from the previous idea of a more casual and briefer engagement with the film. The shift in emphasis from practice to product, mediated by the rise of the star system and feature programming, contributed to a transference of power back to manufacturers. The process through which the film industry reined in the diversity and localism of early cinema exhibition, while still relying on skilled individuals to market the films to audiences, is illustrative of the contradictory field of forces in which cinema exists: between local and global, reality and fantasy, and, in the words of Robert Allen, 'poised between the ordinary and the extraordinary'.[24] The dual nature of cinema as a live event that depends on mechanically reproduced inputs redefined showmanship, but still needed it to mediate between films and viewers.

Conclusion

This paper started as an attempt to map the transformation of the showman's role in Scotland during the transitional era, using newspaper advertising as evidence. However, it became evident during the research process that advertising is a very opaque source, because it does not simply record or reflect historical phenomena but contributed to shape it. Insofar as advertising on the local press was locally organised, it was one of the exhibitor's roles and was indicative of the changes in that profession. The foregrounding of film titles, brands and stars over a more direct and personal address is a consequence of the shift in the balance of forces between the show-product to the film-product, or, in other words, between film as text and cinema as practice. This is not, however, a tension that was resolved one way or the other, but one that structured a matrix of diverse practices that continues to be remade in every encounter between films and audiences.

Acknowledgements: This paper is based on my doctoral research on early film distribution in Scotland, funded by an Overseas Research Award/College of Arts scholarship and under the supervision of Prof. John Caughie. My current research is part of the AHRC-funded project, 'Early Cinema in Scotland, 1896–1927', also led by Prof. Caughie, for whose support and guidance I am grateful. I would also like to thank Dr. Joshua Yumibe for his comments.

Notes

1. The main dataset consists of two collections of cinema adverts taken manually from over a hundred local newspapers around Scotland for two particular dates: the second Thursday of January in 1913 and in 1918. With a total of 129 and 143 programmes collected for 1913 and 1918 respectively, these samples represent about a third of the exhibition venues that were active in Scotland for those dates. These collections constitute an attempt to build a source that is systematic enough to allow for some degree of quantitative exploration, in the spirit of larger projects such as Cinema Context (http://cinemacontext.nl/), the German Early Cinema Database (http://www.earlycinema.uni-koeln.de/) and the CAARP database (http://caarp.flinders.edu.au/), but on a more modest scale. The information was transcribed into a PostgreSQL relational database and analysed using the open-source geographical information software Quantum GIS (www.qgis.org/). Please contact the researcher for access to the dataset. (All websites viewed on 5 April 2013).
2. Charles Musser, "'The Nickelodeon Era Begins: Establishing the Framework for Hollywood's Mode of Representation", *Framework* no. 22/23 (1983): 4.
3. Gerben Bakker, *Entertainment Industrialised: the Emergence of the International Film Industry, 1890–1940* (New York: Cambridge University Press, 2008), 320.
4. Musser, "The Nickelodeon Era Begins", 4; Musser, *Before the Nickelodeon: Edwin S. Porter and the Edison Manufacturing Company*, 158. [e-book http://ark.cdlib.org/ark:/13030/ft3q2nb2gw/ accessed 23 December 2011].
5. See María A. Vélez-Serna, "Mapping film exhibition in Scotland before permanent cinemas", *Post Script* 30, no. 3 (2011); Adrienne Scullion, "Geggies, Empires, Cinemas: The Scottish Experience of Early Film", *Picture House* no. 21 (1996): 13–19; and Trevor Griffiths, *The Cinema and Cinemagoing in Scotland, 1896–c.1950* (Edinburgh: Edinburgh University Press, 2012).
6. As Pierre Chemartin and André Gaudreault have argued, the loss of ownership of the film print also meant that exhibitors were not free to cut up and re-assemble the views. With this withdrawal of their editing role, they became excluded from production, so that the *exhibiteur* of early cinema becomes the *exploitant de salle* in institutional cinema, Chemartin and Gaudreault, "Les consignes de l'éditeur pour l'assemblage des vues dans les catalogues de distribution", in Frank Kessler and Nanna Verhoeff (eds), *Networks of Entertainment* (Eastleigh: John Libbey, 2007), 195.
7. Bakker, *Entertainment Industrialised*, 143–147.
8. Paul Maloney, *Scotland and the music hall 1850–1914* (Manchester: Manchester University Press, 2003), 16–17; Robert C. Allen, *Vaudeville and Film, 1895–1915: A Study in Media Interaction* (New York: Arno, 1980), 111–113.
9. "Scottish News and Notes", *Bioscope*, 15 October 1914, 245.
10. Advert, *Stirling Sentinel*, 7 January 1913.
11. Trevor Griffiths, "Sounding Scottish: Sound Practices and Silent Cinema in Scotland", in Julie Brown and Annette Davison (eds), *The Sounds of the Silents in Britain* (Oxford: Oxford University Press, 2012), 72–91.
12. "The Passing of the Old Showman", *Bioscope*, 26 August 1917, 360–361.
13. Colin N. Bennett, *The Handbook of Kinematography* (London: Kinematograph Weekly, 1911): 250.
14. Michael Hammond, *The Big Show: British Cinema Culture in the Great War, 1914–1918* (Exeter: University of Exeter Press, 2006), 16–21.
15. Adverts: *Evening Times* (Glasgow), 9 January 1913; *Cowdenbeath Mail*, 11 January 1913; *West Lothian Courier*, 3 January 1913.
16. Joe Kember, *Marketing modernity* (Exeter: University of Exeter Press, 2009), 5, 44–83.

17. Nicholas Hiley, "'At the picture palace': The British cinema audience, 1895–1920", in John Fullerton (ed.), *Celebrating 1895: The Centenary of cinema* (Sydney: John Libbey, 1998), 100.
18. "The rise of the Picturehouse", *The Entertainer* (Glasgow), 13 June 1914, 1.
19. Michael Quinn, "Distribution, the Transient Audience, and the Transition to the Feature Film", *Cinema Journal* 40, no. 2 (2001): 42.
20. Ben Singer, "Feature Films, Variety Programs, and the Crisis of the Small Exhibitor", in Charlie Keil and Shelly Stamp (eds), *American Cinema's Transitional Era: Audiences, Institutions, Practices* (Berkeley: University of California Press, 2004), 79.
21. Paul S. Moore, *Now playing: Early Moviegoing and the Regulation of Fun* (Albany: SUNY Press, 2008), 161.
22. Michael J Quinn, "Paramount and early feature distribution: 1914–1921", *Film History* 11, no. 1 (1999): 99.
23. Regarding the role of a discursive association with legitimate theatre in the expansion of the cinema audience in the late 1910s, see Jon Burrows, *Legitimate cinema: Theatre stars in silent British films, 1908–1918*, Exeter Studies in Film History (Exeter: University of Exeter Press, 2003), 185.
24. Robert C. Allen, "Reimagining the history of the experience of cinema in a post-moviegoing age", in Richard Maltby, Daniel Biltereyst, and Philippe Meers (eds), *Explorations in new cinema history: Approaches and case studies* (Chichester: Blackwell, 2011), 51–52.

Showing Film in Winter (1904–1906): Alberts Frères' Film Galas in Dutch Multi-Purpose Buildings

Ansje van Beusekom

In this article I wish to investigate a well known phenomena: that of the itinerant cinema. From a more intrinsic perspective, concentrating on the art of performing film in a exclusive film programme consisting of two hours of films, the 'winter tours' of Dutch travelling showmen Alberts Frères will be addressed. First of all, I thank Rommy Albers from the EYE-Film Institute, who researched Alberts Frères thoroughly and was so kind to share his knowledge with me.[1]

Alberts Frères were really brothers: the brothers Mullens, Bernard Albert and Willem or Willy were born in 1878 and 1880 and named their company Alberts Frères in 1902.[2] They are not unknown to film historians in or outside the Netherlands. Quite the contrary: they have always been part of the historiography of Dutch film culture, first as the producers and directors of the first Dutch fiction film *The Adventures of a French Gentleman Without Trousers* (1905).[3] Later in the early 1980s Frank van der Maden described them as the most important travelling film showmen on the Dutch fairgrounds, 'les rois du bioscope', again with an emphasis on their own film productions.[4] Moreover, the activities of Willy Mullens as documentarist in the 1910s in Holland and in the 1920s in the Dutch Indies (Indonesia) were the object of research of Bert Hogenkamp.[5] What films they showed besides their own productions has not yet received much attention, nor did Willy Mullens' activities as cinema owner in the Hague, or Bernard's career as owner of the Amsterdam Grand Theatre in the 1910s to the 1930s. The latter are part of a larger research project and will not be discussed here.

Moreover, due to all the attention for the Desmet collection in the last twenty years, Alberts Frères have disappeared in a fragmented way to the margins of Dutch film historiography. Thanks to the Desmet archive, however, we know what we mean when we talk about films instead of film titles and because we have discovered so many early films since that famous Brighton conference in 1978, a closer look at the film programmes of Alberts Frères and their performances is justified. Their performances fit into the larger picture composed by Joseph Garncarz who analysed the development of cinema in Germany between 1895 and 1914. He claims that the itinerant cinema's that replaced itinerant theatre and variety around 1900 in a vast international infrastructure of fairs, festivals and markets, formed the bulk of the European film business before 1910.[6] Europe therefore has a very different early cinema history than the United States. Opposed to the emerging national cinemas of the 1910s, the Dutch itinerant early film programmes were fundamentally international.

The commercial business perspective has always been considered as the main drive of travelling cinema owners, but in my view it is not the only one. Without excluding the commercial interests, I wish to state that what made Alberts Frères so much better and longer lasting in the business of film exhibition, compared to their colleagues like Jean Desmet or Willem Hommerson, was their understanding of film and fascination with the new technology and especially of performing a film programme for a theatre audience outside the fairgrounds. At the base of this understanding lies their love for film.

So, I wish to reconsider the position of Albert Frères from 1904 to 1907 in the infrastructure of the itinerant cinema and see if distinction, in the sense of calling them 'the best' in their trade in the Netherlands, can be a useful concept for comparing their film programmes and practises with that of their contemporary competitors. Their skills in performing the new medium of film are at the core of their success and deserve a closer look. Whereof do those skills exist and where do they come from?

Alberts Frères

The Mullens brothers grew up travelling with their parents from fair to fair all over the Netherlands, areas of Belgium, and sometimes also in Germany. Their father exploited the 'Koninklijk Nederlandsch Cagliostro theatre Alber and Basch' with 'mysterious and pseudoscientific spectacles' until his death in 1890. His enterprises were promoted with the adjective 'Royal', a practise his sons continued with their itinerant cinema. While continuing the business with their mother after their fathers' death, they added acrobats and pantomime to the illusionist performance.[7] They fell in love with the new technology of the cinematograph at the end of the nineteenth century and persuaded their mother to buy one: first attempting to in Paris but without any luck. Travelling to Lyon, they were able to buy one at the Lumière factory. They started performing film shows in 1899 under their father's name and from 1902 on as Alberts Frères becoming one of the handfuls of families who travelled from fair to fair with an itinerant cinema in the Netherlands.

In 1902 they started to distinguish themselves with the performance of a 'talking bioscope' but this limited their freedom of selection and, more importantly, their ability to manipulate the film show in terms of speed and accompaniment by a lecture. They kept a few sound films on the programme, though, and were always keen to introduce new systems, like Gaumont's Chronophone in 1911. Likewise they watched the new film productions closely and travelled to Brussels and Paris to buy their stock, so they would not have to depend on the imports of Nöggerath, the first Dutch film distributor. Between 1904 and 1906 their business, that was not small to begin with, expanded importantly: touring the fairs from May to October with their own travelling bioscope and more and more venues in fixed multi-purpose buildings in winter.[8]

The Giant Winter Tour in 1904

In 1904 Alberts Frères toured the fairs in summer with a 'big tour'. They travelled all over the Netherlands to the fairs of provincial capitols and towns of middle size, excluding the largest cities Rotterdam and Amsterdam, the Protestant province of Zeeland and the north of Noord Holland and the islands. From October they toured from town to town to give performances in fixed multipurpose buildings, containing a big room with seats for between eight hundred and two thousand visitors, usually in or near the city centre. These buildings were mostly founded in the nineteenth century by cities and by private groups of well-to-do liberal citizens, to provide a venue for public gatherings and events in the heart of their city. Names like Stadsgehoorzaal, Harmonie, Musis Sacrum, De Vereeniging or Societeit underline their public functions. They were also rented to travelling companies like theatre groups, orchestras, variety ensembles, or public lectures. Film programmes fit also into this multi-purpose format, and many of those buildings still function today as a theatre or concert hall.

In December 1904 Alberts Frères called their tour 'A Giant Winter tour'. They advertised by naming the towns and buildings they had visited so far: the Royal Harmonie in Groningen (North), the Harmonie in Leeuwarden (North), the Vereeniging in Nijmegen (East), Stadsgehoorzaal in Leiden (West), Concordia in Bussum (Mid), Amicitiae in Amersfoort (Mid), Musis Sacrum in Arnhem (East), de Kunstkring in The Hague (West) and Concertgebouw 's Hertogenbosch (South). In the following years Deventer (East), Zwolle (East), Zutphen (East), Tilburg (South), Tiel (South), Maastricht (South), Breda (South), Zaandam (North), Haarlem (North) and Utrecht (Mid) could be added to their tour list. Also they went abroad to Belgium: Bruges and Leuven. Mostly they returned the following year in the same period. In their negotiations with the cities they tried to insist on exclusivity and aimed at an elite audience.[9]

During the fairground season, they stayed generally between three and eight days at the big fairs, depending on the license, but in the buildings this could be limited to one evening in Leiden, the next in Amersfoort and three days after that in Bussum. Because the capacity of the buildings was big, it still was worthwhile to travel to a city for a one-night performance. In The Hague, however, they stayed each year for several weeks in Christmas time and at the beginning of the new year, performing three days a week at the Haagsche Kunstkring with sometimes a show in another city. In July and August 1905 they spent most of their time at beach resort Zandvoort, near Amsterdam, where they rented the fixed venue Olympia Palace. Looking at the data from October 1904 to April 1907, we see a fully booked agenda. Alberts Frères were able to pay the increased prices for a place at a fairground. In 1907 they paid 2.200 guilder for fifteen days at the fair in Haarlem, but they attracted thirty thousand visitors: an average amount of two thousand visitors a day, who paid 30 to 75ct a ticket.[10]

Advertisement strategy

Although many travelling cinematographers advertised their shows in local newspapers with little announcements, the strategy that Alberts Frères adopted can be called a real campaign. Their shows were advertised weeks in advance by large advertisements in the local newspapers and often a recommending article that quoted from newspapers from the city they performed shortly before. These advertisements were much larger and grander than those of their colleagues. In them, they aimed at the reading public and promoted themselves as the 'grandest Dutch exhibitors in the cinematic field (bioscopisch gebied)', and they always mentioned the adjective 'royal' and advertised a Gala performance for their: 'Expositie van levende sprekende schilderijen in meesterlijke kleurenpracht / Exhibition of living, talking pictures in wonderful colours' in 1905. In 1906 this was changed into Koninklijk Nederlandsche Kunst-exploitatie van Gekleurde levende schilderijen / Royal Dutch Art-exploitation of coloured living paintings'. Also in 1906, they presented proudly their own production, the 'chase film': *Les avontures van een Fransch heertje zonder......pantalon op het strand te Zandvoort*.[11]

Alberts Frères typically gave one show in the evening, a children's matinee, and a Gala night as their last performance. Their shows lasted from 8:00 until 10:30 pm with a short break, and tickets cost 30 to 75ct. The admission for children was less, but not for their adult chaperones. The Gala-matinee was organised to accommodate people from outside town so that they could travel home in the evening. However, the brothers charged the same rates as in the evening.

Venues, programmes and films

The interior of their typical theatre, which usually seated around one thousand patrons, was decorated with electric illumination they brought with them and that was powered by their 'loco mobile', a portable electric generator powered by steam. If needed, they installed their own temporary red velvet chairs and decorated the room with flowers. The programme consisted of around twenty short films, accompanied by piano music and sometimes also a violin, a famous singer for some films and lectures of Willy Mullens accompanying others.

Old and new films were blended and the programme changed daily, but not entirely – the most successful films were kept on the programme. They always made sure they had an ample stock of films to choose from, so that even visitors who returned every night would not have to be disappointed by having to watch the same programme again. One of their strategies was that they invested in quality: quality of the venues and decoration, preparing the projection and composing the programmes or 'series' as they would call them themselves in 1908 with appropriate accompaniment, and last but not least, the quality of the films. They obtained coloured copies if possible and experimented with sound. In Brussels they purchased films from Pathé themselves, and they often managed to show new ones even before the catalogue was published. What is most striking however, in looking at their programmes, is the amount of Méliès films present, especially the 'grande féeries' in colour, such as *Cendrillon, Barbe-Bleue, La Légende de Rip van Winkle, Faust aux enfers, Le voyage dans la lune, Le voyage à l'imaginaire,* and *La voyage à travers l'impossible.*

More than seventy-five percent of the programme consisted of fiction and within that, more than half we can characterise as *féerique* and quite a substantial part is from Méliès. For Alberts Frères, it did not matter that there were older films among their offerings, as long as the audience loved them. They did not advertise these films heavily, but they often were mentioned in the articles. They blended these older films with new ones and with their own new productions and proudly announced *Ah Ah die Oscar* and *Les mesavontures van een Fransch heertje zonder pantalon* in 1905.

In the press the performances of Albert Frères were praised often because of the quiet projection, the variety of offerings in drama and comedy, their colour films and musical accompaniment, the explanations and lectures of Willy Mullens, and finally cosiness and atmosphere of their theatre spaces. Also specific genres of film such as the coloured spectacles, auto races, nature films and actualities like *The Zeppelin*, are mentioned. Alberts Frères thus offered a total experience, an event, with films at the heart of that event.

A balanced variety of genres was important according to Willy Mullens who explained Alberts Frères' commitment to a good show in the spring of 1905, at the end of their first Giant Winter Tour.[12] He distinguished three categories of films: actualities, local scenes and staged performances with 'deliberate acting'. The local scenes were filmed by Bernard Albert Mullens who was also the projectionist. Willy Mullens meticulously prepared his lecture because it came all down to timing and a good choice of words: 'a single word could do it'. They worked in tandem: Bernard Albert slowed down his cranking in a death scene and Willy lowered his voice. Moreover, Willy Mullens emphasised how much their own presentation added to the performance as a whole and that their competitors often neglected the importance of a good presentation.

Comparison with others

Of course, Alberts Frères were not the only travelling showmen with film programmes and they were certainly not the first with an itinerant cinema. Alberts Frères were not pioneers like the Lumière brothers or in Holland Franz Nöggerath or Christian Slieker, but they definitely saw more potential in the new medium than their peers. All the activities described above were also done by their competitors, but the difference in intensity is remarkable. Their advertisements are exemplary for the other practises: larger, richer, more frequent, more colourful, more enchanting and keen on expanding their success. No other company was so busy to keep their show on the road, covering almost the entire Netherlands with visits to Flanders and Germany from 1906 on. Their cinema tent was one and a half times as large as those of the other families and was shaped as a Greek temple. In the winter they had more engagements with important multi-purpose buildings in more towns spread over the Netherlands, than any other itinerant cinema. They made optimal use of the infrastructure of fairgrounds and of the multi-function buildings they and their family had worked in for decades through their former attraction, the Cagliostro theatre. Having grown up with the know-how of practises that went with the trade of travelling showmanship, they were well equipped to adapt quickly, and at a high level, to the performance requirements of the new medium. Moreover, their love for the films, watching them (and producing some) and seeing their potential, choosing them and presenting them with care in a well-balanced programme without being pennywise, like the many competitors that thought second-hand stock was good enough. They were able to keep their programmes attractive until the 1910s. Performing film, despite its own specific difficulties, was in many ways also cheaper and less troublesome than performing a travelling stage show with a variety of artists employed. Used to large investments, they could afford expensive stock and trusted its value. Other itinerant cinema's showed expensive Méliès and Pathé films as well, but not as frequently as Alberts Frères, 'les rois du bioscope' did. Their background was very different from cinema owners as Jean Desmet, who had exploited a Wheel of Fortune and a 'Canadian Toboggan' (a thrill ride) before he tried his luck with an itinerant cinema in 1907.[13] These attractions at the fair sold themselves: the customer saw in front of him what he could expect once he stepped in. The owner of the attraction did not have to perform, or at least, his performance was no part of the presentation as it was with the performance of a film or stage programme. Although successful in his distribution and exhibition practises for about ten years, the film business formed a transition from a travelling existence to a safe career in real estate.

Alberts Frères' success with performing film thus has much to do with their former attraction, the Cagliostro theatre: like Méliès they moved from performing staged visual tricks (with light, mirrors and mechanics) and hired other acts to performing miracles and actualities on film. Both practises were turned into a show for a large paying audience and both core acts were completed with music, illumination and explanation in order to create their remarkable atmosphere. They understood how to entertain an audience on all levels.

Conclusions

In a few years, Alberts Frères had built a name for themselves as 'kings of the cinema': the best in their profession in the Netherlands. According to the Dutch press they gave much more attention to their shows than their competitors. Combining a good selection of the best films made at the time with a careful and balanced programming strategy that included apt accompaniment tuned for the occasion in a tasteful decorated venue made them the best. Their experience in staging events, combined with their real interest and love for films, formed the heart of their success.

Cinephilia, apart from its anachronism, would not be a good term to explain this love. We would appropriate their dealing with film into our contemporary domain of film criticism. Instead, it was the qualities and skills developed in the context of their performances that made the Mullens brothers what they were. After all, although they were special, they also were not so different from their competitors. All travelling showmen showed car races or the Bullfights in Barcelona and many of them showed Méliès' films – but rarely four or five in one programme as Albert Frères did. They created an enchanted world of attractions within a well-established, itinerant entertainment circuit. With this world they were already familiar. Size was crucial for their events. The shows of two-and-a-half hours were aimed at audiences of a thousand or more. Such a large audience is comparable with that of a variety theatre or a concert hall, not with that of the first permanent cinemas that would soon appear in the cities. The film performances of Alberts Frères were not part of everyday life but special: to be experienced at most a few times a year. Their programmes were composed accordingly: although new films were added throughout the year, the programme did not change entirely every week as they would in permanent cinemas that started to emerge in the Dutch cities from 1907–1910 on. They would profit from the shift from buying films to renting films as introduced by Pathé in 1907 and commercially improved and expanded by the German Monopol system in 1911 – the second birth of cinema as André Gaudreault calls it – while the activities of Alberts Frères encountered a decline in supply of attractive spectacles that run parallel to the decline of Méliès. Already in 1908 there were complaints that the film programmes were no longer what they used to be. In the Netherlands, most permanent cinemas did not take over the lavish programme format of the itinerant cinemas: they could not afford it because they were too small, seating five hundred visitors or less. Moreover the big 'boom' in cinemas in Dutch cities only occurred after 1910. With the decline of the film activities of Alberts Frères on the fairgrounds and in the multi-purpose buildings, a grand form of cinema performance ended. Cinema transformed to other forms, as did the programmes and the institution. Therefore it would not be right to see these performances as the first of a new practise, but rather as one of the last in a long tradition of itinerant stage practises.

In 1911 the brothers split up. Bernard Albert bought the Grand Theatre in Amsterdam and turned it into a cinema and Willy started his own cinema in The Hague and pursued film production, specifically documentaries. Each in their own manner continued to do well in their new positions. Other family members took over the itinerant cinema and kept on travelling into the teens.

Notes

1. Rommy Albers et. al. (eds), *Film in Nederland* (Amsterdam/Gent: Filmmuseum Amsterdam/Ludion, 2004); See also: www.filminnederland.nl
2. See for the confusion about the names: Guido Convents, *Van kinetoscoop tot café-ciné. De eerste jaren van de film in België 1894–1908* (Leuven: Universitaire Pers Leuven, 2000), 186–187.
3. S. van Collem, *Uit de oude draaidoos* (Amsterdam: Uitgeverij De Bezige Bij, 1959); A. Briels, *Komst en plaats van de Levende Photographie op de kermis: een filmhistorische verkenning* (Assen, 1973); See for the first Dutch films G. Donaldson, *Of Joy and Sorrow. A Filmography of Dutch Silent Fiction* (Amsterdam: Filmmuseum, 1997).
4. F. van der Maden, *Mobiele film exploitatie in Nederland 1895–1913, voor zover het mogelijk is deze te beschrijven en analyseren aan de hand van de ontwikkelingen in Nijmegen* (Masters thesis, Katholieke Universiteit Nijmegen, 1981); Idem, "De komst van de film", in K. Dibbets en F. van der Maden (eds.) *Geschiedenis van de Nederlandse film en bioscoop tot 1940* (Weesp: Het wereldvenster, 1986): 11–52.
5. Bert Hogenkamp, *De Nederlandse Documentaire film 1920–1940* (Amsterdam: Van Gennip, 1988).
6. Joseph Garncarz, "The Fairground Cinema- A European Institution", in Martin Loiperdinger (ed.), *Travelling Cinema in Europe: Sources and Perspectives* (Frankfurt am Main and Basel: Stroemfeld, 2008), 79–90; Idem, "Perceptual Environments for Films: The development of Cinema in Germany, 1895–1914", in Annemone Ligensa and Klaus Kreimeier (eds), *Film 1900: Technology, Perception, Culture* (New Barnet UK: John Libbey Publishing Ltd., 2009): 141–150.
7. According to a review, "De Kermis" in the *Leeuwarder Courant*, 23 July 1897.
8. Information on dates found in advertisements in the KB database Historische kranten, Cinema-Context.nl and data collection from Rommy Albers, EYE film institute.
9. Convents, 192.
10. R. Albers, *Film in Nederland*: 379.
11. Advertisement Alberts Frères in *Nieuwe Tilburgsche Courant*, 10 February 1906.
12. Quoted in Van der Maden, "De komst van de film", 35.
13. Ivo Blom, *Jean Desmet and the Early Dutch Film Trade* (Amsterdam: Amsterdam University Press, 2003): 38.

13

Performing New Media and the Creation of National Identity: Kräusslich and Köpke in Norway Before 1910

Gunnar Iversen

Among the most significant pioneers in the earliest years of itinerant exhibition of film in Norway were two German exhibitors: Paul Kräusslich (1867–1919) and Carl Köpke (1855–1910). Both came to Norway before the year 1900, and they became important in the early years of travelling exhibition as well as in the years after permanent cinema theatres emerged in Norway between 1904 and 1908. Both also produced actualities, and Paul Kräusslich, in particular, was an important producer of local actualities. These local films, made in the middle and northern part of Norway, were very popular, especially in the years around 1905, when Norway became an independent nation after being a part of Sweden for nearly a hundred years.

In this short article, I will discuss the showmen and their performances with films, and how films *performed* in Norway in the earliest years of itinerant exhibition, through Kräusslich and Köpke. I will address the special role of actualities in their shows. The article will discuss how the actualities also acted, or performed, when the new country Norway was established, and how itinerant showmen not only took images of the world to Norway, but also helped create the identity of a new nation by disseminating images of Norway to local audiences. In this context performance means not only the actual performances where films were shown with different forms of musical accompaniments, but also the way the films acted or performed within the newly formed nation state, creating and sustaining the image of Norway.

Paul Kräusslich

One of the most important early exhibitors in Norway, Paul Kräusslich was born in Stettin, worked as a pharmacist in Germany, but started as an itinerant film exhibitor in Germany as early as 1896. In a recently published book, Trond E. Haugan writes that he was in Norway showing films as early as 1897 but without reference to primary sources, so this is highly uncertain.[1] After 1900 he only worked in Norway, but in June 1899, Kräusslich was in Göteborg in Sweden, and his American Biomatograph-show at Lorensberg's varieté at Folkteatern was so popular that Kräusslich returned in August, playing his programme of films the whole month.[2] One of the local newspapers, Göteborgs-Posten, wrote that the American Biomatograph was not the best cinematograph they had seen, but it had the funniest pictures (*'muntraste bilder'*) you could wish for.[3]

In the year 1900, Kräusslich settled in Trondheim, the third largest city in Norway, on the west coast, and travelled extensively in the middle and northern part of Norway with his programme of films. At first his Boer War films were the main attraction, but very early on, Kräusslich included material he had produced himself, and like so many other travelling exhibitors around the world he became well known for producing actualities in the areas he visited, so that people could see themselves or their own towns and landscapes in the shows.

However, his actualities were not only local films for local people. Kräusslich was the first travelling exhibitor to show films in many of the most northern towns in Norway, and the films he produced from the northern part of Norway became very popular in the middle and southern parts of Norway. For a differing and changing audience in the many localities he visited, his films from the middle and northern part of Norway were big successes.

Paul Kräusslich's itinerant film-show had many names. In the beginning, it was the American Biomatograph, and Kräusslich may have bought a Biomatograph from the German pioneer Hermann O. Foersterling in 1896.[4] Later, Kräusslich used either the names The Royal Bioscope or Kräusslich's Immortal Theater ('Udødelige Theater'). When Kräusslich visited the small northern mining town Rana in October 1902 – the town where the Norwegian National Library now stores all their films in an old mine – his advertisements indicate that his programme was a mix of actualities. One film did show the eruption of the volcano at Martinique early in 1902, but most of the films shown were Norwegian actualities. On his way to Rana, Kräusslich had made a film depicting a reindeer camp in Tromsdalen, but most of the actualities were from around the city of Trondheim.

Paul Kräusslich produced different types of actualities: views of landscapes and topography, as well as films about big events. His biggest success came in 1905, when he was one of a large number of cinematographers who captured the crowning ceremonies of the first king of the newly independent Norway. He filmed the crowning procession of King Haakon and Queen Maud on 14 June, and could show the film only three hours later in a rented locale.[5] Another type of event Kräusslich used to film was sports events. In particular, winter sport played an important role in the earliest history of actualities in Norway, and Kräusslich made many films showing speed skating and ski jump events. These actualities were also an important part of his programmes when he opened a permanent cinema in Trondheim in 1906. Later Kräusslich opened a number of other cinemas in the middle and northern parts of Norway, in Kristiansund (1909), Stjørdal (1910) and Vardø (1911). His actualities were not only shown in his own different cinemas, but he also rented and sold actualities to other itinerant showmen and cinema owners.

Paul Kräusslich became a very respected person in Trondheim, where he had his base and most important cinema. His production of actualities gave him a special position and legitimacy, due to his Norwegian actualities in these nationalist times. His special position was demonstrated when the cinemas were municipalized in Trondheim in 1918. As the only private cinema owner, Kräusslich was allowed to continue his business, while all other cinemas were bought by the municipality. Kräusslich died in 1919.

Carl Köpke

Another significant pioneer in the earliest period of itinerant film exhibition in Norway was Carl Köpke. In 1896, Köpke moved from the small German town Peine close to Hannover to Lista in southern Norway with his wife and their four children. Köpke was employed by the British company The Anglo-Norwegian Kieselguhr Company. He was involved with different businesses in minerals, but due to the fact that he could not raise capital for the ventures, he eventually found other jobs.[6]

Visiting Germany in 1901, Köpke saw his first film, a version of *The Passion Play of Oberammergau*, and he became so interested in film that he immediately bought a projector.[7] On 11 December 1901, Köpke started his work as an itinerant film exhibitor, and exhibited a copy of the Oberammergau-film in Norway's capital Kristiania (later named Oslo). He called his itinerant cinema show Cineographen 'Renaissance', and he travelled to the minor town Drammen close to the capital in 1902 where he had up to six daily shows.[8] The Oberammergau-film was also shown in cities like Trondheim, Bergen and Stavanger. On his very first tour, three of his children helped him. The projectionist was his daughter Gertrud, while his sons Curt and Erik sold tickets and assisted their father in booking and preparing the venues for the shows. At the very end of his first long tour, Köpke added an actuality of the volcano at Martinique as an extra, possibly a copy rented or bought from Kräusslich.[9]

From 1903, Köpke called his itinerant business Nordiske Biograf, and in the spring and summer this year, he visited Sweden, showing a Robinson Crusoe-film and Ferdinand Zecca's 1902-film *Les Victimes de l'alcoholisme*.[10] During the autumn of 1903 Köpke travelled in Norway, and from September he added his own actualities for the first time, taken around the southern town Kristiansand. At this point, Köpke's shows were a mixed programme of shorts, which included local scenes as well as Biophon-films. When he visited Stavanger in October 1903, the newspapers were very excited about his local films from the city.[11]

On 4 November 1906, Köpke opened a permanent cinema in Trondheim, one and a half months before Kräusslich opened his permanent cinema in the same city, but Köpke's business in Trondheim did not last as long as his rival. After a short, expansive period, when Köpke opened another cinema in Trondheim as well as opening cinemas on Iceland and the Faroe Islands, the Köpke family decided to leave Norway. In January 1908 the Köpke family sold their cinema in Trondheim, and moved to Kazan in Russia, where they continued to show films, until Carl died in 1910. Not much is known about why he left Norway, or his business in Russia. It has been suggested that the reason Köpke moved was his belief that the business opportunities were better in Russia, but the move has also been linked to his connections to Ole Olsen's Danish company Nordisk, and that moving was a part of Olsen's attempt to expand in Russia.[12]

Performing new media and the role and function of actualities

Tom Gunning has written: 'While recognizing that a historiographic project which attempts to fully reproduce the past "as it really was" is doomed to a naive historicism, nonetheless, a responsible historian must try to recreate the original horizon of expectation in which films were produced and received'.[13] Very few sources exist in the period before 1910 in Norway that could indicate the original horizon of expectation in which films were produced and received, and that could tell us in more detail *how* the films and the actualities of Kräusslich and Köpke were *used* by their audiences. However, their popularity is one indication that they were important. It also shows that they had different roles and functions in individual lives as well as in society.

The new medium of moving images was launched at a time when different aspects of public life and culture in Norway switched between a culture of attractions and a culture of education. The culture of education was both linked to a general sense of the good things about education and to the new nation. Educators often argued that the young and new nation needed the uplift through education. Cinema as well as old media like theatre did have value as educational experiences, but were also criticised for being too occupied with mere entertaining attractions. In the theatre it also became important that audiences be educated by plays as well as by the experience of going to the theatre itself. In the city of Trondheim, where both Kräusslich and Köpke opened their cinemas, the theatre went through major changes in repertoire as well as in audience behaviour in the last part of the nineteenth century. Being exposed to culture and getting *bildung* through theatre were regarded as important, especially since the city of Trondheim did not have a permanent theatre between 1865 and 1911, and the itinerant theatre companies that visited the town were judged by their educational as well as their artistic merits.[14]

The general reception of film between 1900 and 1910 mirrors this conflict between a culture of attractions and a culture of education. Even though many were sceptical or even hostile towards the new medium, even the concerned citizens, teachers and educators highlighted the educational value of actualities, and especially actualities from Norway.[15] When Kräusslich arranged a special show for children in December 1904, a local newspaper described the actualities displaying Kräusslich's scenes from the northernmost part of Norway, as 'a whole small course in the geography of northern Norway'.[16]

National topographies were very popular with audiences as well as educators, and one important function of these actualities was communicating the nation. The display of actualities from Norway to Norwegians helped create and reproduce the new nation-state, with a familiar geography. The display of actualities especially around the year 1905 in Norway, are examples of a process of projection and naturalising an imagined community and a new nation-state.

Following Benedict Anderson's *Imagined Communities*, many social scientists have privileged the role of language and print media, and especially newspapers, in the creation and spread of nation states and nationalism.[17] However, images, visual representation and visual media obviously have played and still play important roles in these processes.[18] Actualities celebrated the emerging new nation of Norway through everyday landscapes and views of everyday life as well as through big winter sports events or the crowning of the new king and queen. Especially the topographic and the sports films were important and popular.

Sociologist Michael Billig presented a major challenge to ordinary conceptions of nationalism in his book *Banal Nationalism* (1995). Instead of analysing or theorizing nationalism through extreme expressions, Billig focused on the everyday. He studied all the less visible forms of what he sometimes calls symbolic 'flag waving', unnoticed reminders that operate mindlessly, below the level of conscious awareness, to create and sustain nationalism. Sport is one of his examples of this 'flag waving'.[19] Considering the fact that public discourses were largely structured by a national logic before and after Norway became an independent nation in 1905, it is not surprising that the most important genres in the actualities produced by Kräusslich and Köpke were geographical views as well as sports films.

The winter sports films were especially important in early film production in Norway.[20] They were both news items, reports from local or national events, exciting new *moving* images, a novelty in the entertainment environment, and at the same time expressions of the privileged position of national sentiment and identity. The celebration of the Norwegian landscape in these films, local views as well as views from remote regions, gave the diverse audiences a new sense of the national topography, like the reviewer in Trondheim wrote: a whole small course in the geography of the new Norwegian nation.

Landscapes had been important in the creation of a national identity in Norway throughout the nineteenth century, through paintings and dioramas.[21] Topographical actualities continued a long tradition of creating a national identity, by creating a national topos through landscapes that was different from Sweden or Denmark, the countries that Norway had been part of prior to its independence. This was done through banal 'flag-waving', showing off the 'real' Norway, and declaring certain landscapes as closer to being Norwegian than others. In his book, Billig at one point uses weather reports as one small way the nation is constantly recreated in the minds of those who watch or listen.[22]

Scenics and actualities about local Norwegian customs functioned in the same way around 1905 in Norway. The privileged position of the nation and the national logic is an important part of the horizon of expectations of the early movie audiences in Norway. The actualities of Kräusslich and Köpke performed a continuous 'flag-waving', a nationalist performance that helped to create a national consciousness in the new nation before and after 1905.

Notes

1. Trond E. Haugan, *Byens magiske rom – Historien om Trondheim Kino* (Trondheim: Tapir Akademiske Forlag, 2008), 11–14.
2. Rune Waldekranz, *Levande fotografier – Film och biograf i Sverige 1896–1906* (Stockholm:

Unpublished Lic. Thesis, Department of Theatre- and Film Studies, University of Stockholm), 112.
3. Ibid.
4. Deac Rossell, "Beyond Messter: Aspects of early cinema in Berlin", *Film History* 10, no.1 (1998): 52–69.
5. Johan Jensen, *De levende bilder – Trondheim Kinematografer 1918–1968* (Trondheim: Trondheim Kinematografer, 1968), 12.
6. Sturle Holmen, *Köpke og filmen*, Unpublished manuscript from 2005, 1ff.
7. Ibid., 20–21.
8. Ibid., 23–24.
9. Ibid., 50.
10. Waldekranz, 118, 173, 359.
11. Holmen, 56, 63–67.
12. Ibid., 127.
13. Tom Gunning, "Before Documentary: Early nonfiction films and the 'view' aesthetic", in Daan Hertogs and Nico de Klerk (eds), *Uncharted territory – Essays on early nonfiction film* (Amsterdam: Nederlands Filmmuseum, 1997), 9–24.
14. Thoralf Berg, *Teater blir kunst – Om dannelsen av et moderne publikum og teater i Trondheim på 1800-tallet* (Trondheim: Tapir akademisk forlag, 2009).
15. Gunnar Iversen, "'And They Can See Half-Naked Dancers, Catching Young Men In Their Nets': Teachers and the Cinema in Norway, 1907–1913", Rob King et al. (eds), *Beyond the Screen: Institutions, Networks and Publics of Early Cinema* (New Barnet: John Libbey, 2012), 126–130.
16. Ibid., 128.
17. Benedict Anderson, *Imagined communities: Reflections on the origin and spread of nationalism*, revised edition (London: Verso, 2006).
18. Gunnar Iversen, "Inventing the nation: Diorama in Norway 1888–1894", *Early Popular Visual Culture* 9, no. 2 (2011): 123–129.
19. Michael Billig, *Banal Nationalism* (London: SAGE, 1995), 119–125.
20. Sigurd Evensmo, *Det store tivoli* (Oslo: Gyldendal, 1967), 20–23.
21. Iversen, "Inventing the nation", 123–129.
22. Billig, *Banal Nationalism*, 116–117.

Music Programming and the Formation of Swedish Cinema Culture

Christopher Natzén

Introduction

The film portal Filmarkivet.se was launched in 2011 as a joint venture between the Swedish Film Institute and the National Library of Sweden. The site contains unique archival moving image material that otherwise is rarely accessed; mainly shorts, non-fiction films, newsreels and commercials; in short, films that reflect the transformation of Swedish society over the last century. The site became an instant success both among researchers and the general public with five hundred thousand unique visitors during its first year and since then it has had between nine thousand to fifteen thousand unique visitors per week. A new project set to run from March 2013 to the end of February 2016 has the ambition to expand the current film project on the web which as of 2012 contains approximately eight hundred entries. So far the films shown on the site are showcases disconnected from viewing habits in the early 1900s. When selecting a film the viewer gets basic information regarding the production company, director, original format, etc. as well as a short description of the film. However, there is no information about the original viewing context and the role the film might have played in contemporary cinema programming. For a viewer looking at these films today through the window of the browser it is hard to get an understanding of the cinema culture that these films were a part of.

A focus in the new project, apart from adding more film content, is therefore to add other categories of material to give the user a better idea of both the original viewing context and the formation of Swedish cinema culture. One such category of material will be a collection of cinema programmes previously digitised but until now inaccessible for researchers and the general public. In 2005 the then State Archive for Sound and Image (SLBA) in Sweden, since 2009 a department of the National Library of Sweden, started to digitise two collections of cinema programmes from Lund and Uppsala respectively. The collections consist of 7,755 programme notes from across Sweden and the period 1905 to 1920. By presenting the search results through geo-mapping the programmes can be cross-referenced showing where initially a specific development started and later spread out around Sweden.

The programmes illustrate the mixture of actualities, journals, short films, and later feature films that were screened. Since most films from the early silent era have disappeared, researchers wanting to reconstruct their narratives have often done so with the help of programmes, reviews and adverts. All films were not reviewed in Sweden, however, and it was not always an obvious choice for exhibitors to advertise specific films in the press. Nor, are there many sources that give a glimpse into the day-to-day activities related to presenting the mixed programmes. Seen against this background, therefore, the surviving collection of cinema programmes is an indispensable resource for film researchers attempting to reconstruct early cinema culture in Sweden. In the programmes the films are listed, although it is impossible to be completely certain that the listed films also were shown or run in that particular order. But the programmes do not only list films, they also mention guest appearances, music accompaniment, information regarding the venue, and particular screenings. The programming was a way of presenting the films in a thought-through way to attract an audience. The scanned cinema programmes, their graphic design and their placement of films and other acts provide an illustration of contemporary cinema culture in Sweden that has so far been difficult to analyse.

In this article I will focus on the formation of the Swedish Cinema culture from a music perspective. My hypothesis is that live music accompaniment and music provided by different mechanical sound carriers played an important role in establishing these programmes and that this is visible in the programming. Music in any form was a way of presenting the mixed programmes, filling in 'dead spots' as the projector was reloaded, and as the programmes were developed so did the music accompaniment.

Little is known about this early period in Swedish film history concerning the use of music. Few contemporary resources exist that talk about the music accompaniment. If it is mentioned at all, it is because of special guest appearances as in this news item from 1904:

> The Cinematograph show at the theatre yesterday evening was visited by a large audience. The images on display were extremely successful. Signor Fusella's

masterful violin evoked thunderous applause and even Mister Protus Åslund's piano number was greeted with enthusiastic applause.[1]

Other early contemporary recollections are however rare. The articles, like this excerpt from a film magazine a few years later in 1909, are more commonly focused on the poor quality of music:

> No ideal cinema exists in Sweden. There are those who have some kind of proper music, but most are mediocre and bad. Hopefully improvements will come about with time. The music that accompanies the images, and that should be in perfect harmony with these, is usually not given enough attention. Piano and some sound equipment for the imitation of water noise, etc. are considered sufficient for several of the capital's major cinemas.[2]

This downplaying of the music is continued in texts written about the music several years afterwards:

> Is there not a touch of disdain in this specific word [film music]? Some people consider film music to be something vulgar and stereo-typed. Such music cannot be regarded as real or genuine art. Thoughts from the earliest days of cinema interfere with later experiences of a small cinema box, where a lonely hack pianist plays polkas and mazurkas every night for 2 to 3 crowns to keep the audience in mood.[3]

The predominantly negative reviews of music in cinemas might be one explanation as to why research on the early use of music accompaniment in Sweden has been deemed inessential. What is known, or more accurately, what is *believed* to have been the exhibition practice of early music accompaniment to moving images in Sweden, can actually be summarised in a few lines. Before the 1910s, the music accompaniment to moving images in Sweden was characterised by improvisation, performed on a single piano or another instrument, although there is evidence that there were some exceptions with better planned accompaniment. Some cinemas may for example have employed smaller ensembles to perform. However, more in-depth research has not yet been done and it is unknown how a Swedish cinema music practice was established as well as which role music played in the growing Swedish cinema culture.

The question I want to ask is what the collection of digitised early film programmes can tell us about the use of music in the organisation of the performances? How is music approached in the programmes? Is it a selling point used in competition between different cinema venues? Is it something worth mentioning or do the owners of the cinemas see the accompaniment as an evident fact not worth advertising? What do the programmes tell us about the emerging cinema culture in Sweden's various regions and towns and is music a part of this development? In short, can the cross-referencing of the cinema programmes, together with other sources, help to stretch out the all too many question marks regarding the formation of early Swedish cinema music? The digitised cinema programmes facilitate and speed up my research as the geo-mapping lets me visually examine year by year how presentation of music shifted in the programmes.

My aim is to approach the cinema programmes from six different perspectives, investigating respectively the use of technology; the use/non-use of music/musicians; the establishment of permanent exhibition venues; the formation of the Swedish Musician's Union; the length of the films shown/the length of the programmes; and the role of female musicians. In the following I will present some preliminary results from my research-in-progress in order to illustrate what the programmes have to say about a Swedish cinema music practice and its role in the formation of a Swedish cinema culture.

Music practice and cinema culture

The period preceding 1908–1909 in Sweden was the heyday of the itinerant exhibitors who to a large degree used technology as one means to attract audiences. Technology in itself became a selling point and several early programmes in the collection emphasise the use of technology both when it comes to the images and the music. Since film technology in itself prior to 1908–1909 still was much of a technical novelty it must have seemed natural to also include the almost equally new technology for music reproduction in an exhibition environment. Focus in the programmes typically lies on the sound technology of the phonograph and the gramophone rather than on the music or the musicians. Part of a 1906 programme, for instance, reads:

> The Light Cinema is a newly designed, high-quality machine that reproduces vivid images astonishingly lifelike/.../during the screening an instrumental and vocal concert by a giant gramophone will also take place.[4]

The experimentation with different sound carriers, together with the exhibition of moving images, started in Sweden from an early point in film history. The exhibitor Numa Peterson brought the sound to the country in 1901 after witnessing a screening at the Paris world exhibition of 1900. Peterson's impression of the sound resulted in him setting up the so-called 'Swedish Immortal Theatre' (Svenska Odödliga Teatern) which toured the country with song-films. These films consisted of well-known performers singing opera parts. Peterson's success encouraged others to experiment with sound and between 1905 and 1908 a diverse group of characters, trying to capitalise on the name 'Immortal Theatre', screened short sound films with song and dance numbers with varying success. However, in 1909, when Charles Magnusson became the new CEO of

Svenska Biografteatern, now Svensk filmindustri, he started to produce gramophone-based sound films with similar song and dance numbers at a more professional level. The bulk of the production took place between the years 1909–1910.[5] These song films show up in numerous cinema programmes. The numbers are also highlighted and are given a specific point in the programmes. At times even two numbers per programme are shown, intertwined with screenings of other films.

Apart from illustrating the experimental nature of film exhibition, the use of these different sound carriers and their placements within the programmes highlight the use and non-use of music and musicians. The question of non-use of music during silent film exhibition is an on-going discussion since at least Rick Altman's publication of the article 'The Silence of the Silents' in 1996.[6] Without delving too far into the American context, it is worth noting that Donald Crafton convincingly argued in 'Playing the Pictures: Intermediality and Early Cinema Patronage' in 1999 that 'it goes against common sense' for films to be shown in silence when an exhibitor had invested in musicians.[7] My aim here is not to take sides in this debate, but rather to note that there are advantages in taking into account both of these perspectives. This allows for an understanding of cinema culture that comprises both of conditions and changes between the film medium and other media and cultural expressions, as well as of various aspects within the film medium itself, for example between music, images and sounds, but also between different aspects of exhibition practices and other technological parts of the production apparatus. The use of different sound carriers thus plays, from this perspective, one role in establishing a music practice for the formation of a cinema culture.

The Swedish cinema programmes of the period prior to 1908 provide information about the music, where the utilisation of different technological sound carriers and the use and non-use of music/musicians seems to walk hand in hand. For example in the programme for the 'Stockholm Theatre' which toured the country 1906–1907 it is said that: 'During the screenings – Piano Concerto by music director H. Nilsson – if a useful instrument is available on the premises'.[8] Other programmes like one from Pariser-Cinema-Theatre in Gävle show the diversified use of music and other performances. This is shown in the programmes as music often has its own point in the programme and seems not always to accompany the actual images. The programme lists 'music' as a special point without describing it in closer detail, which opens up for questions if it was a gramophone or live musicians, and if music played throughout the programme or not. Furthermore, two points in one programme from the cinema are given to performances by Norrgårds-Petter AKA Einar Scherlund (the latter was his real name), a revue artist who was an early collaborator to Ernst Rolf, a more famous Swedish performer. However, these points can probably stand in for the 'breaks' allowing for the exhibitor to reload the projector which is also spelled out in some programmes from the same exhibitor.[9]

Apart for these reel breaks that could clearly involve some kind of performance or music, how was it with the actual screenings of images? Did they have a music accompaniment, and if so, was it technically reproduced by a gramophone or performed by musicians? As mentioned previously, it is hard to know exactly how these things worked in Sweden, since the daily press and other sources rarely mention the accompaniment. To further complicate matters other programmes also present 'music' before every point in a programme as in one from the Swedish itinerant exhibitor the brothers Gustaw and Anton Gooes who were famous for hiring well-known musicians.[10] Yet, other programmes write out in detail when there is music accompaniment and when it is not (even mentioning at which specific hours during the day music will be featured).[11]

My point is that all these programmes show diversified ways of including music – sometimes music was used together with the images, sometimes not; sometimes a reproduction technology was used to accompany the images, sometimes the accompaniment was provided by musicians – in short there is a palette of different options in which the use of musicians was one possibility. However, as both Altman and Crafton argue, even if they arrive at different conclusions, the music accompaniment also came to be influenced by other aspects of the exhibition environment. These features all tended to be part of the formation of cinema culture, which focused on a more controlled environment and music practice. That is, parallel to development of the programmes occurred the establishment of more permanent exhibition venues.

With the establishment of permanent venues after 1909 a shift in music practices happens and this is shown in the collection of cinema programmes. With the introduction of permanent venues and a more established cinema culture, other demands were raised, both concerning the content of the films and how they were presented. The skill of the accompanying musicians became in themselves an advantage in the competition with other cinemas. This put more demands on the actual musicians. If musicians during the heyday of the itinerant exhibitors played to the same film day after day on different locations the establishment of permanent venues for film screenings meant that it became harder to have a well-planned accompaniment following the constant rapid change of programmes; sometimes a venue would show several different programmes per week.

During 1908–1909, comments regarding the music accompaniment increasingly appeared in the daily press and periodicals, and many of these accounts emphasized the bad quality of the music, as previously exemplified. In the programmes this shift is shown in the use of general expressions concerning the use of music instead of listing 'music' as a specific point in the programme. However, the music is here described, if it is at all mentioned, as 'Good', 'of high-quality', 'with piano', etc. Unless there is a prominent musician giving a guest appearance, music is no longer given a specific emphasis in the programmes: it is presumed to be there throughout the programme but not advertised.

In parallel with the establishment of more permanent venues in Sweden the Swedish musician's union was formed. The union was inaugurated in December 1907, and clearly made an impact on music practice. The growing importance of music accompaniment for moving images is illustrated by an early tariff from the union in 1909 that as one possible employer lists 'Cinema' – a tariff that also illustrates the low position cinema musicians had vis-à-vis other musicians.[12] The newly founded Musicians' Union in Sweden worked in favour of establishing regulations concerning both working conditions for cinema musicians and to create a raison-d'être for film music trying to establish a better reputation than that reflected in the above quotes or in this anecdote from an autobiography:

> It was a film based on Anton Dvořák's "Humoresque" [about] a small chap who obtained a violin by force from his stingy father and after that became a great violinist. The film was good, but it was prescribed that we were only allowed to play "Humoresque" during the whole screening. It became damned tiresome, four hours per evening, and on Sunday eight with the matinee. ... But one night, the last Wednesday screening in the fifth week, there was a boozer in the theatre who suddenly screamed to me: - Don't you know any other piece, you bugger? Then the audience awoke! Then the audience was listening ... at last there was someone who had listened to the actual piece of music.[13]

As previously mentioned, with the establishment of permanent venues a shift in musical practice occurs, and with the formation of the Musician's union, a standardisation of the musical content can also be seen in Sweden during 1908–1909. This process reaches a certain standard in the late 1910s and the most common way to set music to film became the compilation of already existing compositions. In Sweden, it soon became customary to use compositions from the classical romantic period of the eighteenth and nineteenth centuries as well as to use popular melodies from the melodramatic theatre.¹⁴ This music seems to begin in an autonomous state vis-à-vis the image and could be rather unrelated to image content although familiar pieces from other contexts were used. However, an improvising single piano player or small ensemble could function for the benefit of the film as it made it easier to change direction and mood of the music to follow the anticipated action on screen. The establishment of permanent venues and the formation of a musician's union meant that all music started to share the same aim of absorbing the audience into the diegesis. Evidenced by the numerous film music catalogues that started to be produced at this time, a continuous accompaniment, a correspondence between the music and the overall theme of the film, and the use of musical motifs for structural coherence became increasingly standardised as film form gradually transformed into more complicated and longer narratives.

The preserved correspondence and minutes from the Swedish Musicians' Union are an important source for exploring the role music played in cinema culture. However, these documents are more concerned with the working conditions than focused on how, when and where the music should be used when scoring a film. The cinema programmes on the other hand describes a day-to-day activity where exhibitors tries to attract an audience. Music is one aspect of this programming. However, another aspect also came to influence the accompaniment during these transitional years. The permanent venues facilitated the introduction of longer programmes and longer films which from 1911 are clearly presented in the programmes. It is also possible to see a development starting in Stockholm and spreading out from there to the south of the country and finally to the north.

From this point onwards there is a clear and constant development in Swedish film music practice where the compilation score becomes the norm, the musician's union gains greater and greater control and European romantic composers are favoured alongside Swedish popular melodies. However, a key to understanding the formation of a Swedish music practice and its continued development is the roles played by female musicians – a sadly under-researched subject in Sweden. If musicians' sons during the early 1900s became employed at more prominent orchestras, their daughters often took engagements at the cinemas. This is evident in the membership rolls of the union, which since its foundation counted many women among its members. Furthermore, all-women ensembles played in restaurants and cafés, and later when the cinema orchestras grew larger many included female musicians. Some women also reached the position of conductor. The early presence of female musicians is well illustrated by the programmes as several female pianists are mentioned. But perhaps the most important document as to the importance of the female musicians is a decision made by the Gothenburg branch of the musician's union in 1908 in relation to an employment question at the Concert Association. On 3 April 1908 the decision is made that 'On the lady question for the orchestra the board expresses that they should have equal salary as the male members',[15] indicating that women were well represented in this job.

The female musicians at the cinemas played a central role in the process of the establishing a Swedish cinema music practice and thereby an important part of the formation of a Swedish cinema culture. The music at the cinemas and the performing musicians in Sweden acted as intermediaries between producers, distributors and audiences. From itinerant exhibitors with their experimental way of including music both by means of technology and live accompaniment, to the increased standardisation with permanent venues, and finally through the formation of the Musician's Union, a uniform and nationwide musical accompaniment for film was established in Sweden. Musicians came to participate in the construction of the concept of 'the cinema'. The collection of the 7,755 cinema programmes from every corner in Sweden all contribute to the same story.

The cross-referencing of the cinema programmes shows a high degree of involvement of music in the formation of a Swedish cinema culture. Be it technically reproduced by a sound carrier or provided by accompanying musicians', or for that matter its absence, music was seen as an important part for the organisation of early film performances. When film form changed and moved into permanent exhibition venues, music accompaniment developed too, strengthening this transformation. The music accompaniment was highlighted, but during the 1910s a process began to assimilate these sounds and music into the diegesis of the film. In this manner, music played an important role in both the establishing of a cinema culture as well as in its transformation of integrating the audience into the diegesis – in fact equal to other aspects of the medium like camera angles, lighting and editing.

Notes

1. *Sundsvalls-Posten* (26 October 1904): 3.
2. "Musik å biograferna", *Nordisk Filmtidning* 1, no. 9 (August 1909): 1–2.
3. "Biografmusik", *Filmbladet* 2, no. 24 (18 February 1916): 349.
4. Cinema programme for Ljus-Biografen (Bollnäs, 1906).
5. Jan Olsson, *Från filmljud till ljudfilm: samtida experiment med Odödlig teater, sjungande bilder och Edisons Kinetophon 1903–1914* (Stockholm: Proprius Förlag, 1986), 20–28, 42–54, 77–84.

6. Rick Altman, "The Silence of the Silents", *The Musical Quarterly* 80, no. 4 (Winter 1996): 648–718.
7. Donald Crafton, "Playing the Pictures: Intermediality and Early Cinema Patronage", *Iris* 27 (Spring 1999): 152–162. Page 154 for the quote.
8. Cinema programme for Stockholms-Biografen (Orsa, 1906), 2.
9. Cinema programmes for Pariser-Biograf-Teatern (Örebro, 1906).
10. Cinema programme for Bröderna Gooes biografuppvisningar (Eskilstuna, 1905).
11. Cinema programme for Jönköpings Biografteater (Jönköping, 1906).
12. Tariff for Swedish Musician's Union, Malmö branch (Malmö, 1909).
13. Waldemar Hammenhög, *Det var en gång en musiker* (Stockholm: Wahlström & Widstrand, 1942), 92–93.
14. Ann-Kristin Wallengren, *En afton på Röda Kvarn: svensk stumfilm som musikdrama* (Lund: Lund University Press, 1998), 119–120.
15. Minutes from board meeting, Swedish Musician's Union, Gothenburg branch (3 April 1908), 3.

'Marvelous and Fascinating': L. Frank Baum's *Fairylogue and Radio-Plays* (1908)

Artemis Willis

What is a *fairylogue*? A discourse concerning the realm of the wee folk? And what is a *Radio-Play*? An audio broadcast of a performed drama? The very name of L. Frank Baum's 1908 multimedia spectacular, the *Fairylogue and Radio-Plays* connotes a wide range of past traditions and future possibilities. 'Fairylogue' combines two highly popular precedents: the *féerie*, a stage and screen genre that presented dazzling effects within fantastic universes; and the travelogue, the magic lantern and motion picture entertainment that illuminated wondrous views of the real world. If early cinema demonstrated strong affinities with fantasy and actuality, Baum's portmanteau describes a synthesis of these two tendencies.[1]

'Radio-plays' is a curious choice for the second term. In contrast with the one-way broadcast medium established in the 1920s, in 1908, anything occasionally called 'radio' was synonymous with wireless telegraphy, the two-way transmission of signals, voice or music, usually from shore to ship. Baum's use of 'radio-play', therefore, is most likely the first publicised use of the phraseme; a coinage prophesying an expressive mode yet to exist.[2] Another contemporary usage of radio was 'radio-activity', the emanations and transmutations of the luminous element, radium (from the Latin 'radius', meaning a beam of light or 'ray'). Radium's recent discovery engaged the popular imagination, which associated it with screen and stage entertainment. In 1907, for instance, a Nickelodeon called the Radium Theater opened in Des Moines.[3] Several years later, radium's pale emerald glow inspired Loïe Fuller to lecture on the element, and to develop a light-emitting dress that generated enough multi-colored brilliance to illuminate an entire theatre.[4]

Taken together, Baum's *Fairylogue and Radio-Plays* thus suggests the otherworldly energy behind developing technology, and conveys his entertainment's fundamental association with magic, modernity and mystery. Indeed, his title seems to operate in the mode of a Sphinx-like riddle, defamiliarising by maintaining multiple perspectives.

But what was the *Fairylogue and Radio-Plays*? It was a two-hour show that combined actors, magic lantern slides, coloured films and music within a series of episodes from Baum's Oz books. The fairylogue was a fictionalized travelogue to the Land of Oz, in which Baum himself performed as the lecturer. As such, it provided a frame story for the two radio-plays, or acts, which presented the adventures of his beloved characters on stage and screen. It was described the *Chicago Daily Tribune* as 'For the benefit of grownups, who always have to have fairyland explained to them':

> It may be stated that a fairylogue is a travelogue that takes you to Oz instead of China. A radio-play is a fairylogue with an orchestra at the left hand corner of the stage. Moreover, in a radio-play there is the added advantage of having a cast of characters before you and knowing just who impersonate the people on the stereopticon screen. *The idea is a new one* ...[5]

Although it is impossible to reconstruct the *Fairylogue* – ephemeral performances of over a century ago are unattainable, and few of the production's elements survive. I would like us all to ponder the reviewer's last sentence as we explore this extraordinary entertainment. What was it that made Baum's idea *new*? After all, as early cinema history has shown, the travel and fairy genres had been popular for at least a decade prior to Baum's production. Likewise, a full evening's entertainment combining slides, films and a lecturer around a single theme was an established mode of exhibition since the late 1890s. Given the rich and rapid innovations during the first decades of motion pictures, the *Fairylogue* does not readily suggest a new form of entertainment. Rather, as a production from early cinema's transitional era, it seems downright retrograde.

However, a close study of extant materials and related ephemera, (considered outside the *Fairylogue*'s historical moment) suggests the opposite. It suggests a prograde intention to sequence the production's diverse media within a single narrative, in which Baum and his Ozian characters made multiple crossings between stage and screen, (an example of which I shall discuss shortly). Baum was able to effect these passages by integrating lantern slides, films, and live actors, facilitating transitions between stillness and motion, black and white and color, and second and third dimensions. He evoked a kind of animation in the round, anticipating an entertainment years ahead of its time; a form not even technologically realized by *Oz the Great and Powerful*.[6] Could it be that Baum

15 'Marvelous and Fascinating': L. Frank Baum's *Fairylogue and Radio-Plays* (1908)

was holding the master key to a moving image practice that 'has not yet been invented' (as French critic André Bazin once famously suggested)?

I see the *Fairylogue* as a visionary early attempt to perform a sequenced combination of old and new media. In doing so, I posit the need for a new tool for conceptualising early cinema as performed new media. Following a brief description of the *Fairylogue*, I consider the show's intertextual and intermedial correspondences, to which I offer a third layer of inquiry, which I am calling an *intermodal* approach: a means of thinking about how media combine and interact within an early cinema performance. Just as intermodal transportation moves cargo containers across land and sea, from barge to railway or ship to shore, so too were Baum and his cast carried across formats as they traveled between Oz and Chicago. Significantly, an intermodal consideration of the *Fairylogue* looks to its way stations, transfer points or gaps between media, such as Baum's onstage presence as the showman, his interaction with the screen, and his canny integration of the still-to-moving attraction from slides to films within the *Fairylogue*'s transmedial narrative. For if the *Fairylogue* was a seamed enterprise (which it indeed was), its 'intermodes' helped to delineate a space between actuality and fantasy, which were given equal measure in Baum's entertainment. With Baum the showman's easy traversals of this space, the *Fairylogue and Radio-Plays* was able to reveal a gateway to a utopian modern fairyland that exists alongside the world we know, if we are young at heart enough to discover it.[7]

The *Fairylogue and Radio-Plays*

In the fall of 1908, audiences in Chicago's Orchestra Hall enjoyed a 'Marvelous and Fascinating' event, L. Frank Baum's multimedia spectacular, the *Fairylogue and Radio-Plays*, based on scenes from *The Wonderful Wizard of Oz* and its sequels, and presented by the author himself. A hybrid production of projection and performance, which appeared after the novel and stage versions of 1900 and 1902/03, and before the first exclusive screen version of *The Wonderful Wizard of Oz* in 1910, the *Fairylogue* consisted of one-hundred and fourteen magic lantern slides, twenty-three stencil and hand-coloured films, a full orchestra and twenty-two live performers.[8] Most unusually, Baum, 'The Wizard of Oz Man', cast himself as an illustrated travel lecturer, journeying with Dorothy, the Scarecrow and others between stage and screen. His *Fairylogue* was an innovative form of entertainment – a transmedial narrative depicting a fantastic virtual voyage to and from Oz.

The first radio-play, 'The Land of Oz' combined fourteen scenes from *The*

Wizard of Oz, *The Marvelous Land of Oz* and *Ozma of Oz*. The second radio-play, adapted Baum's 1907 fantasy, *John Dough and the Cherub* into six scenes. Some of the scenes featured projected lantern sequences, others the coloured films or a combination of the two media. A fifteen-minute intermission featured a 'Dissolving Scene' entitled 'The making of a book cover', promoted Baum's latest book, *Dorothy and the Wizard of Oz*. A 'Magical Dissolving Scene', 'Adieu!' ended the show. The lantern slides consisted of hand-coloured photographs of the players as well as adaptations of John Neill's illustrations. E. Pollack designed the sets. The films, which are no longer extant, were directed by Francis Boggs (*The Land of Oz*) and Otis Turner (*John Dough and the Cherub*), produced in Chicago at the Selig Polyscope Studios and coloured in Paris by Duval Frères.[9] Nathanial D. Mann, the composer for the 1902 stage musical, wrote the score.

The *Fairylogue* was critically acclaimed throughout its tour of thirteen venues in twelve cities. It appeared twice in Chicago, where its tickets cost between twenty-five cents and one dollar. But while reviews of Baum's performance as well as the production's overall novelty and entertainment value were superlative, the cost of mounting the *Fairylogue* devastated Baum's finances. Perhaps as a result, it has been considered an eccentric multimedia attempt to promote the Oz books, or even a failed first effort to produce a filmed adaptation of *The Wonderful Wizard of Oz*.

Intertextual and Intermedial Correspondences

Thirty-four years after the legendary thirty-fourth FIAF conference in Brighton, an exploration of the *Fairylogue and Radio-Plays* has much to contribute to current discussions of early cinema as performed new media. During the first phase of early cinema scholarship, with its emphasis on periods (novelty, early, transitional) and tendencies (display, storytelling) the *Fairylogue* would most likely be identified as an anachronism within the period of increasingly widespread production of narrative-dominated films. Although it was presented in 1908, Baum's boldly heterogeneous performance recalls the presentational mode of an earlier variety format; it is indeed gloriously out of step with the practices which were beginning to dominate production and exhibition, i.e., films circulating as self-contained narratives during the nickelodeon boom, which was itself a performance-dominated situation (as Rick Altman's Living Nickelodeon delightfully suggests). In this context, we can take Miriam Hansen's cue and read the *Fairylogue* alongside Edwin S. Porter's 1907 *The Teddy Bears* as another text that combined traditionally segregated genres (the fairytale,

15 'Marvelous and Fascinating': L. Frank Baum's *Fairylogue and Radio-Plays* (1908)

chase film, political cartoon) and their respective discourses (domesticity, imperialism) within an 'intertextual bricolage'.[10] Like Porter's film, the *Fairylogue and Radio-Plays* forged connections between several well-established genres and intertexts – *féeries*, travelogues and known moments from Oz, i.e., audience familiarity with the books and the stage musical. Thus, Baum, like Porter, was able to establish a unique zone of experience for the *Fairylogue's* spectators.

During the second and third decades after the 1978 symposium, as Tom Gunning has identified, the initial focus on narrative models and periodization of early cinema expanded to include a wider variety of diverse approaches, tendencies and correspondences, some considerably later in the pre-feature era.[11] Building on our intertextual model, we can constellate the *Fairylogue's* broader range of intermedial correspondences, including Baum's own works as well as other fictional and nonfictional practices from which he promiscuously borrowed. Baum's comic strip, *Queer Visitors from Oz* first transported his characters to the United States in 1904[12] and from his oeuvre beyond Oz, we can find numerous allusions to inanimate objects becoming animate, in fictional works such as his *American Fairy Tales* (1901) as well as nonfiction references in *The Art of Decorating Dry Goods Windows and Interiors* (1900).[13]

An intermedial exploration of the *Fairylogue* must, of course, also take into account Chicago's 1893 World Columbian Exposition. The White City, as many have suggested, is the probable inspiration for the Emerald City, and it is also where the Fairy of Electricity (as she was subsequently dubbed at the Paris Exposition in 1900) first announced her great powers of illumination. Electricity, as Michael Patrick Hearn has noted, is ubiquitous in Baum's stories, and is prominently featured in his electrical fairy tale, *The Master Key* (1901).[14] Moreover, Baum's early short story, 'Yesterday at the Exposition (from the *Times-Herald*, June 27, 2090)', an imagined report from a Chicago World's Fair two-hundred years in the future (written in 1896), describes large-scale audio-visual entertainments, long-distance communication via thought-transference and actual time-lapsed plant growth, evoking his long-standing faith in the marvelous.[15]

But Baum was also deeply inspired by the attractions of the Midway, where over two million guests were afforded a visit around the world. As he put it, 'Who can forget Chicago in 1893 and the people of all nations?'[16] At the center of the Midway were the fair's two top-grossing attractions, the Street of Cairo and the Ferris Wheel. The Cairo exhibit featured reproductions of old buildings, camel rides, and perhaps most famously, performances by the great Syrian-born dancer with a Greek name, Farida Mazar-Spyropoulos, who introduced American audiences to the *dance du vent*, or Belly Dance, (also known as the hoochie-coochie dance). Meanwhile, the Ferris Wheel animated spectators views with moving panoramas of this fantastic micro-cosmopolis, and the actual metropolis beyond it. Chicago, with its juxtapositions of immigrant cultures and modern urban development, was mirrored by the Midway as a topography in which foreignness, domestication, fantasy and authenticity intermingled. Thus the fair staged a kind of blurring of the side-by-side realms of fairyland and Chicago.

Intermodal Sequences in the *Fairylogue*

If the *Fairylogue* was intertextual and intermedial, it was also intermodal, in that it combined diverse modes of media and dramaturgy to transport Baum's inanimate characters and worlds to life, from page to screen to stage. To think through his intermodal strategy, we can examine the *Fairylogue*'s initial sequence, which animates its characters in the round. The sequence unfolded thusly: as Baum appeared onstage, a curtain was drawn to reveal a square, ten-foot screen framed in red velvet plush. Pointing to a lantern slide of a map, he addressed the audience with a short account of how he was transported by the fairies to Oz, where he became acquainted with the land and its customs. He then stepped to the wings, continuing his narration offstage. From an enclosed steel booth in the rafters, Baum's son, Frank Joslyn Baum, began projecting the first reel with a Selig Polyscope projector.

In the first film, the audience encountered the image of a large closed book. Fairies swung the cover open to reveal a black and white picture of Dorothy. Next, Baum appeared inside the film next to the book, gesturing to Dorothy. As he described it, 'I beckon, and she straightway steps out of its pages, becomes imbued with the colors of life and moves about. The fairies then close the book, which opens again and again till the Tin Man, the Scarecrow and all the others step out of the pages of the book and come, *colored, to life*'.[17] Baum then returned to the stage, where he was joined by his cast of characters in the third dimension.

I want to touch on Baum's use of colour within his sequence of media, for it seems central to his intermodal impulse to animate characters as they traverse worlds. As Gunning has emphasized (as has Joshua Yumibe), colour in early silent cinema was 'applied primarily for its sensuous, spectacular, and metaphorical effects, rather than for its indexical and realist associations'.[18] Baum's *Fairylogue* slides and films also employed colour to perform magical transitions, metaphorically linking color with processes of animation and transformation. This impulse is apparent even on the pages of Baum's first novel, in which Dorothy transitions to colour when she falls into Oz's atmosphere, and the

15 'Marvelous and Fascinating': L. Frank Baum's *Fairylogue and Radio-Plays* (1908)

strategy has continued from Ted Eshbaugh's 1933 animated film, to the 1939 MGM production to *Oz the Great and Powerful* (United States, 2013).

The Showman between Stage and Screen

Above all, it was Baum's dual role as celebrated author and showman that held the *Fairylogue* media together. His role as a kind of intermodal guide between Oz and Chicago was quite possibly the real master key to the show's magic. Baum's own characterization as 'Wizard of Oz Man' blended the approaches of two famous showmen – Georges Méliès and E. Burton Holmes. Méliès's persona of the stage/screen magician, who animates the inanimate (and vice versa) provided a clear model for Baum. Méliès, who noted that the *féerie* 'allows the supernatural, the imaginary, even the impossible to be rendered visually',[19] played a critical onscreen role as the magician performing transformations from inanimate to animate. Baum readily adapted Méliès's pioneering substitution, transformation and superimposition effects in the *Fairylogue* films. Baum's effect of pulling his characters out of the pages of a giant book, for instance, is identical to Méliès in *Le Livre Magique* (1900) and *Les Cartes Vivantes* (1905), itself a trope of nineteenth-century stage magicianship. Méliès also created films for stage productions, such as the 1905 stage *féerie*, *Les 400 coups de diable*, including a projected tableau featuring a cyclone.[20]

A second direct model for Baum's characterization, E. Burton Holmes, had recently appeared on the same stage at Orchestra Hall with his travelogue of 1907 (a multi-media performance with a 'modular structure', as Gregory Waller discussed during the conference), which featured views of Cairo and the Nile. In fact, it was Holmes who coined the word 'travelogue' to distinguish his performances from lectures (which he thought connoted the dull and impersonal), and was probably the first to combine films with slides, which he did as early as 1897 in Brooklyn.[21] Incidentally, Holmes was also a former stage magician.

Some final influences that might help us to think through Baum's inspiration for integrating media between stage and screen come from two very different contemporary showmen – Winsor McCay and Lincoln J. Carter. Baum's comic strip *Queer Visitors from Oz* ran during the same time as *Little Nemo*, but it was McCay's animated performances (the lightening sketches), and especially his persona as a modern technician who reflexively flaunts his means of production that suggests the emergence of a new, modern showman. Like Baum, McCay 'is the twentieth-century man ingenious enough to put the complex apparatus of animation cinematography at his service', as Donald Crafton describes.[22]

147

In an entirely different manner, Lincoln J. Carter provided another modern model for stage/screen showmanship. Carter achieved innumerable scenic marvels with lantern and film projections, many of which he (like Baum) described in the popular press. As the first person to include projected films on the legitimate stage in the United States (with *Chattanooga*, which opened in Chicago in 1898), Carter understood the importance of employing projections within theatrical tableaux. He created his sensation melodramas and their main dramatic situation around these effects.[23] These practices are potentially productive sites for exploring other intermodal sequences, particularly the 'film to life effects' Gwendolyn Waltz identifies.[24]

To return to the question posed at the outset, what about Baum's idea was new? Perhaps it was, as the *Chicago Tribune* suggested, a continuity of actors across discontinuous formats. For if the *Fairylogue* hovered between Wagner's illusionistic *Gesamtkunstwerk* and Kracauer's total artwork of effects, it did not attempt to amalgamate its media. Instead, it celebrated its discrete elements while it combined them. With its marvelous presentation of supernatural events in the real world, transmedial narrative sequences, and gaps between the intermodal seams, the *Fairylogue* holds a fascinating promise for new cinematic utopias of the future; a promise Baum fulfilled for his youthful audiences a century ago.

Notes

1. See Siegfried Kracauer, *Theory of Film: The Redemption of Physical Reality* (New York: Oxford University Press, 1960), especially 30–37.
2. Early use of the word 'radio' deserves further research. Both Lee De Forest and Reginald Fessenden appear to have attempted rudimentary shore-to-ship entertainment with voice and music in the early 1900s, and in his autobiography of 1950, *Father of Radio*, De Forest mentions forming his De Forest Radio Telephone Company in 1906. I am grateful to Neil Verma and A. David Wunsch for their valuable insights in this regard.
3. "The Radium", *Midwestern* (July 1907), 59–60; Richard Abel, "That Most American of Attractions, the Illustrated Song", in Richard Abel and Rick Altman (eds), *The Sounds of Early Cinema* (Bloomington: Indiana University Press, 2001), 146.
4. "New Luminous Dance", *New York Times*, 5 February 1911.
5. *Chicago Daily Tribune, 3* October 1908. Italics are mine.
6. Disney's 2013 production, which features a projection praxinoscope in the oddly anachronistic year of 1905, does reflect Baum's theme of technology's connection to wizardry, particularly in the magic shows at the beginning and end of the film.
7. For an early discussion of Oz as Utopia, see Edward Wagenknecht's chapbook, *Utopiana Americana* (Seattle: University of Washington Bookstore, 1929), 30–37.
8. For a comprehensive history of the *Fairylogue and Radio-Plays* as well as the 1902 stage musical and the 1910 Selig one-reeler, see Mark Evan Swartz, *Oz before the Rainbow: L. Frank Baum's the Wonderful Wizard of Oz on Stage and Screen to 1939* (Baltimore, Maryland: The Johns Hopkins University Press, 2000).

9. Baum attributed the colouring of the *Fairylogue*'s films to a Paris-based outfit called Duval Frères. However, it remains unclear as to whether such a firm ever existed. It appears most of the films were coloured by the Pathé stencil process, with the exception of the opening sequence, which probably adopted a hand-colouring strategy for each character as they became animated. For an excellent discussion of hand-colouring firms in Paris, including Selig's 1906 inquiry about the feasibility of colouring prints in Paris see Joshua Yumibe, *Moving Color: Early Film, Mass Culture, Modernism* (New Brunswick: Rutgers University Press, 2012), 35–75.

10. Miriam Hansen, "Adventures of Goldilocks: Spectatorship, Consumerism and Public Life", *Camera Obscura* 22 (1990): 59.

11. Tom Gunning, "Enigmas, Understanding, and Further Questions: Early Cinema Research in Its Second Decade Since Brighton", *Persistence of Vision* 9 (1991): 4–9.

12. *Queer Visitors* appeared in the *Philadelphia North American* and the *Chicago Record-Herald* from August 1904 – February 1905.

13. L. Frank Baum, *The Art of Decorating Dry Goods Windows and Interiors* (Chicago: Show Window Publishing Company, 1900), 87–111. In his article, "What Manikins Want: *The Wonderful Wizard of Oz* and *The Art of Decorating Dry Goods Windows*", *Representations* 21 (1988): 97–116, Stuart Culver reads Baum's two 1900 texts together to show commodity relations and capitalist exchange values reflected in *The Wonderful Wizard of Oz*. Unfortunately, his slight misquoting of Baum's treatise suggests subtle differences in meaning from those in *The Art of Decorating*.

14. Michael Patrick Hearn (ed.), *The Annotated Wizard of Oz* (New York and London: W. W. Norton and Company, 2000), 184.

15. L. Frank Baum, "Yesterday at Expo", *Chicago Times-Herald* (2 February 1896).

16. L. Frank Baum, *The Art of Decorating Dry Goods Windows and Interiors* (Chicago: Show Window Publishing Company, 1900), 166.

17. See Baum's description of how he achieved this and other metamorphoses in "In the Fairyland of Motion Pictures", *New York Herald*, 26 September 1909: Italics are mine. The stage version of this magic trick is described by Robert-Houdin in *The Secrets of Stage Conjuring* (London: George Routledge and Sons, 1881), 229–245. For a fascinating discussion of the Blow Book's relation to animation, see Colin Williamson, "Watching Closely with Turn-of-the-Century Eyes: Obscured Histories of Magic, Science, and Animation in the Cinema",(Ph.D. dissertation University of Chicago, 2013).

18. Tom Gunning, "Colorful Metaphors: The Attraction of Color in Early Silent Cinema", *Living Pictures: The Journal of the Popular and Projected Image before 1914* 2, no. 2 (2003): 5. For Baum's theory on colour harmony, see *The Art of Decorating*, 22–26.

19. Georges Méliès, "Cinematographic Views", in Richard Abel (ed.), *French Film Theory and Criticism*, Volume I: 1907–1939 (Princeton: Princeton University Press, 1993), 45.

20. Frank Kessler, "The *Féerie* between Stage and Screen", in André Gaudreault, Nicolas Dulac and Santiago Hidalgo (eds), *A Companion to Early Cinema* (Oxford, UK: Wiley-Blackwell, 2012), 73.

21. Charles Musser, *The Emergence of Cinema: The American Screen to 1907* (New York: Scribner, 1990), 221–223.

22. Donald Crafton, *Before Mickey: The Animated Film, 1898–1928* (Chicago: University of Chicago Press, 1993), 134. Crafton's discussion of McCay and metalepsis during the conference would be applicable to Baum's traversals between stage and screen in the *Fairylogue*.

23. See George C. Pratt, "Early Stage and Screen: A Two-way Street", *Cinema Journal* 14, no. 2 (1974–5): 16–19.

24. See, for instance, Gwendolyn Waltz, "Filmed Scenery on the Live Stage", *Theatre Journal* 58, no. 4 (2006): 547–573.

The Multiple-Media Lecture: *Racing with Death in Antarctic Blizzards* (1915)

Gregory A. Waller

While the lecturer had virtually disappeared as a regular attraction in American movie theatres after 1912, by the mid-1910s, the combination of spoken address, motion pictures, and (often) lantern slides was arguably the prime format in the burgeoning field of non-theatrical cinema in the United States.[1] Most visible of these multiple-media lectures – particularly in metropolitan areas – were regularly scheduled tours by Burton Holmes and other specialists in travelogues or travel talks booked as commercial offerings in large, multi-purpose halls and opera houses, culturally prominent sites that also often featured more directly topical presentations about the war and current geopolitics.[2] But lectures that incorporated still and moving images were in fact to be found in all manner of venues – including churches and YMCAs, universities and schools, fairs and expositions, factories and department stores. In these sites, illustrated lectures were presented to a targeted audience (almost always for free) under the auspices of a particular, readily identified sponsor, which could be, for instance, a religious group or a business enterprise, the National Association of Manufacturers or a state agency.[3]

Of the lectures incorporating moving pictures that were intended to turn a profit in the marketplace, among the most highly publicised and broadly circulated were performances that followed in the wake of the remarkable success of the feature-length moving picture, slide, and lecture programme usually billed as *Paul J. Rainey's African Hunt* (1912), which ran thirteen months in New York City, then toured across the United States through 1914 (even after a film version with intertitles designed to replace the lecturer became available). Subsequent film lectures detailing perilous quests undertaken in the name of high adventure, scientific knowledge, or national prestige included various newsworthy polar expeditions, like the Amundsen South Pole Expedition and the example I will focus on in this essay, the Australian Antarctic Expedition (hereafter AAE) of 1911–1913, led by Sir Douglas Mawson (1882–1958).[4] The illustrated lecture presented by Mawson himself on a North American tour in 1915 stands as a particularly well-documented and historically rich example of the full-length, for-profit, multiple-media performance. My reconstruction of this lecture is based on motion picture footage and slides shot during the expedition and on the extensive personal correspondence and business records housed in the Mawson Centre and the South Australian Library in Adelaide, Australia, supplemented by Mawson's U.S. copyright application and reviews from North American newspapers.

Planned and promoted as a largely scientific undertaking, yet clearly carried out in the name of Australia and the British Empire, the AAE departed from Tasmania in December 1911. Mawson established an outpost with a wireless transmitter at Macquarie Island, halfway to Antarctica, and a base camp at Cape Denison in the Antarctic territory called Adelie Land from where several small sledge parties explored the vast coastal territory. On 10 November 1912, Mawson along with two younger colleagues, Dr. Xavier Meertz and Lt. Belgrave Ninnis, embarked from the base camp on an arduous trek across dangerous glaciers, a journey that was to become one of the period's most remarkable narratives of survival against all odds.

On 14 December, more than three hundred miles from the base camp, Ninnis disappeared into a crevasse along with the sledge containing practically all of the group's food, supplies, and the most fit dogs. The two survivors immediately took the most direct route back to Cape Denison, with little protection against the unremitting cold and gale force winds. Facing starvation as their situation grew increasingly desperate, Meertz became incapacitated and delirious before dying on January 8. Alone, weakened, and frostbitten, Mawson continued his solitary trek and reached the base camp a month after Meertz's death, barely missing the departure of the expedition's ship, which was not able to return until December 1913 for Mawson and the handful of his colleagues who had remained behind. Through syndicated newspaper accounts based on wireless reports, Mawson's quite extraordinary story of survival received wide media attention well before the publication of his two-volume account of the AAE, *The Home of the Blizzard* (1915).[5]

Mawson's trek was the stuff of which legends are made – and, in the 1910s, of which lecture tours were mounted. In fact, the production of still photographs, lantern slides, and motion pictures documenting the journey and the landscapes and animals of the frozen South had been part of the larger AAE plan from the outset. Serving as the expedition's official photographer – and cinematographer – was Frank Hurley, who on this trip and later as a member of Ernest Shackleton's ill-fated 'Endurance' expedition, would take some of the era's most memorable and iconic photographs of Antarctica.[6] Before leaving Australia, in November 1911 Mawson had signed a contract with Gaumont, which agreed to provide a moving picture camera and lenses for use on the expedition and to cover the costs of developing the negative delivered by Mawson. In return, Gaumont would have the exclusive right to 'exhibit lease sell let or hire and generally exploit commercially' these films worldwide for two years with both parties splitting the net profits. Mawson was allowed to use the footage 'for the illustration of his own personal lectures and speeches', provided these did not conflict with any exhibition arranged by Gaumont. Significantly, Mawson also held the copyright to all film shot in connection with the expedition.[7]

Beginning with public screenings of the AAE footage in Australia as early as May 1912,[8] the moving pictures of the expedition circulated over the rest of the decade under various titles and lengths, at times with different intertitles and colour tints. In the United States, footage of the expedition was featured in both sponsored and unsponsored screenings across a range of theatrical and non-theatrical venues, sometimes even shifting generic identities to become programmed and marketed as animal film, thrilling adventure, penguin-filled comedy, or exotic scenic. For the purposes of this essay, however, I will focus on Mawson's well-documented 1915 North American tour, which provides a rich example of how motion pictures, lantern slides, and spoken words were combined for the purposes of a full-length multiple-media lecture designed to turn a profit outside of the movie theatre.

By June 1914, when Mawson gave his first public lecture in England (billed as being 'fully illustrated by Lantern Slides and Kinematograph Films'),[9] he was engaged in conversations with New York promoter Lee Keedick about a series of 'cinematograph lectures in the United States'.[10] Signing with Keedick made good sense. Head of his own lecture bureau since 1907 and experienced working with a range of venues, the thirty-five-year-old Keedick had made his name promoting lecture tours by prominent non-Americans, notably the polar explorers Ernest Shackleton in 1910 and Roald Amundsen in 1913.

Initially, Mawson and Keedick agreed to an American tour for a lecture entitled, *Racing with Death in Antarctic Blizzards*, beginning 15 January 1915 and lasting not less than two months, with net receipts shared 50/50.[11] The six-week itinerary Keedick arranged took Mawson into Canada and across the Eastern and Midwestern United States, with stops in most major metropolitan areas and a few smaller cities like Harrisburg, Pennsylvania. Virtually all these engagements were one-night-stands, sometimes with a matinee as well as an evening performance. None of the venues were movie theatres, yet in other respects they were quite varied, ranging from the world-class Carnegie Music Hall in Pittsburgh and Brooklyn's Academy of Music to various civic halls and auditoria and even to unexpected sites like the La Salle Hotel in Chicago and the gymnasium at the University of Wisconsin, Madison.

The tour opened on 15 January 1915 in Washington D.C. at the New Masonic Temple under the auspices of the National Geographic Society, though the more high-profile event came two days later in midtown Manhattan. Keedick planned the New York opening with an eye toward generating publicity for the rest of the tour, booking the 1,100-seat Aeolian Hall, one of the city's premiere musical venues, with ticket prices running from 50c to $1.50. In this refined setting, appearing under the auspices of the American Museum of Natural History and the American Geographical Society, Mawson was hailed as a scientist and explorer who had demonstrated 'incredible fortitude' and a 'magnificent endurance of suffering' while 'battling at the ends of the earth against the appalling forces of nature ... in pursuit of an ideal – a contribution to the world's fund of knowledge'.[12]

Generating $1100 at the box office, the Aeolian Hall event turned a $500 profit according to Keedick's itemized account. Equally important, at least for promotional purposes, the Australian Antarctic Expedition, Mawson as a lecturer, and the motion pictures he screened all received the highest praise from the city's newspapers, with particular kudos to footage of penguin antics and hurricane force winds. The *Bulletin of the American Geographical Society of New York* lauded the AAE film as superior in clarity and vividness to all earlier moving pictures of Antarctica, deeming the exhibition to be 'a revelation of the possibilities of such views in geographical education'. While the *Moving Picture World* – more attentive to theatrical box office prospects than pedagogical potential – found Mawson's lecture to offer 'a wonderful story of adventure, heroism, and endurance',[13] 'Arranged in logical sequence and properly sub-titled', the moving pictures used in the lecture 'would make an interesting subject in themselves', proposed the *New York Dramatic Mirror*.[14]

Francis Hubbard Flaherty, after viewing the AAE film in Canada later that January, was equally enthusiastic. Francis had in 1914 married Robert Flaherty, who had returned to Toronto from Hudson Bay with footage that he was attempting to shape into a marketable film, perhaps with intertitles substituting for a lecturer. His wife thought otherwise and saw in Mawson's lecture a successful model. In her diary entry for 1 February 1915, Francis reasoned:

> On the lecturer will depend the success or failure of the [Flaherty] pictures in so far as their appeal to the general public is concerned. The public demands some sort of thrill, either the thrill of sheer beauty or the thrill of battle. Sir Mawson's pictures of the Antarctic had both; his ice pictures were beautiful beyond words, those of the violence of Antarctic tempests were spectacular, and the animal pictures were unique.[15]

An equally enthusiastic American reviewer identified a different set of attractions, noting that *Racing with Death in Antarctic Blizzards* succeeded because it included 'a little of everything that goes to make up a heart-gripping recital, a contribution to popular science and a human document of the most searching value ... [all] delivered without a tinge of self-importance'.[16]

What specific details in the lecture prompted these claims for its manifold appeals? As Quentin Turnour has demonstrated, Australia's National Sound and Film Archive holds a considerable amount of footage from the AAE drawn from different prints, yet there is no extant copy of the complete lecture.[17] We can, however, piece together what I propose is a reasonably accurate version of Mawson's multiple-media performance, using the following surviving documents:

- a five-page outline of the film that Mawson submitted on 30 January 1915, in his application for a United States copyright for twenty photographs from the expedition and for a film entitled, *Racing with Death in Antarctic Blizzards*;[18]
- a typed forty-eight-page lecture dated 1915 that Mawson sent to Keedick, presumably to be used by other lecturers who might appear with the AAE film. This typescript indicates precisely when certain slides or moving pictures are to be projected and commented upon by the speaker;[19]
- a list of eighty-eight slides described as being 'as used in improved American lecture' that correspond closely to the order of images indicated in the typescript lecture;[20]
- newspaper reviews during the lecture tour.

The first half of the lecture introduced the audience to the working and living conditions of the expedition while also highlighting the harsh but geologically interesting and beautiful, even sublime, environment of Antarctica, in three main sections:

1. film sequences of the *Aurora*'s journey, the setting up of the camps, and panoramic vistas of the icescape
2. some fifty slides depicting 'artistic ice forms' and geological details of Antarctica; the base camp (with lengthy light-hearted spoken anecdotes about cooking and haircutting to give a sense of the men's day-to-day life); and a quick survey of the birds, penguins, and seals inhabiting this site
3. film sequences of the blizzard conditions, sledging methods, and the departure of Mawson, Meertz, and Ninnis on their trek.

16 The Multiple-Media Lecture: *Racing with Death in Antarctic Blizzards* (1915)

Then, at roughly the midpoint of the performance, the projection of images stopped, the house lights came on, and for fifteen to twenty minutes Mawson spoke of this trek:

> Mawson's first-person account of the 'tragic story' of death and survival. After concluding his tale of extraordinary physical suffering and 'supreme' individual effort, Mawson announced, 'we will now return to the pictures to finish off the story' and a slide appeared showing the memorial cross erected at Cape Denison for Meertz and Ninnis.

The remainder of *Racing with Death in Antarctic Blizzards* shifted to what the copyright outline called simply 'Animal Life' – focusing on the comic, exotic, and marvelous side of a more manageable Antarctica:

1. a series of thirteen slides pictured albatross, sea-elephants, and penguins;
2. the lecture's longest film sequence, including footage of Skua gulls and petrels; penguins 'surf bathing' and marching inland to a hilltop rookery; sea elephants sleeping, being tickled by one of the expedition, teased by a Spaniel, and serving as an unwilling steed for another of the expedition's pranksters; men making mischief with nesting penguin; penguins diving into the water to feed and leaping back ashore; and seals quarreling, sliding caterpillar-like on the ice in a 'distinctly humorous' manner, scratching themselves, and being ridden by a man, cowboy-style.

Racing with Death in Antarctic Blizzards, as I have reconstructed it here, was distinctly modular. 'The pictures taken by Sir Mawson's camera man comprised about four thousand feet of film', noted the *Motion Picture News* in its review of the Aeolian Hall performance: 'between each reel a series of slides were projected'.[21] Moving pictures and slides were grouped separately, with little if any rapid alternation between still and moving images (perhaps because of the technology of projection). While the lecturer spoke over both slides and moving pictures, in certain sequences the spoken word became the dominant or even the sole medium, for example, when the audience was treated to lengthy comic anecdotes about camp life, as a single slide held on screen. Of course, the spoken word was most dramatically foregrounded when the story of the deadly trek was told, with apparently no images at all being projected. At other points, moving pictures became the privileged medium for depicting 'animal life' and blizzard conditions. And lantern slides, in turn, proved to be the medium for most effectively capturing the pristine beauty of the frozen world. In this regard, *Racing with Death in Antarctic Blizzards* seems not so much an illustrated lecture or a motion picture supplemented by slides and commentary, as a multiple-media presentation.[22]

This modularity and multiple mediality allows for the variety so evident in *Racing with Death in Antarctic Blizzards*, which blended in different quotients what in the period would typically have been thought of as the distinct imperatives of entertainment and education. Following Francis Flaherty and the first reviewers we might label the lecture's modes and attractions as:

- narrative ('a heart-gripping recital'; 'a wonderful story of adventure, heroism, and endurance' filled with 'thrilling incidents'),
- spectacular ('the violence of Antarctic tempests' on land and sea),
- aesthetic ('the thrill of sheer beauty')
- expository or instructional ('a contribution to popular science' and 'geological instruction'; a display of creatures rarely or never seen)
- inspirational (Mawson as a contemporary model of heroic white manhood)
- comic ('Chaplinesque' penguins and mischievous men)

Embedded in the film lecture, these elements were rarely pure and discrete. For example, the 'tragic story' of Mawson's trek, filled with harrowing accidents, blinding blizzards, and extreme physical suffering, was thrilling and spectacular while also being instructional and inspirational about the limits of human endeavor. And by aiming its final spotlight not on Mawson but rather on the antics of penguins and seals and the men who tease and ride them for the camera's benefit, *Racing with Death in Antarctic Blizzards* belies its title, turning into something akin to slapstick comedy, much as it had veered earlier into generic territories associated with the travelogue or scientific lecture, the nature film or 'operational' documentary. While quite distinct from what might be seen as the increasingly prescriptive and causally driven narrative logic of Hollywood's emerging feature film, the modular presentational format *Racing with Death in Antarctic Blizzards* facilitated variety and genre shifting, but it did not represent a return to or continuation of early cinema's array of spectacular, astonishing, and momentary attractions.

In the hands of Mawson (and I have no reason to assume that he was particularly unique in this regard), the multiple-media lecture was flexible and inclusive, garnering uniformly positive reviews that highlighted its manifold pleasures, from laugh-provoking penguins and sea elephants to thrilling glimpses of polar blizzards and inspiring views of Antarctica's 'majestic splendor'.[23] Mawson's on-stage modesty and lack of affectation or bombast likewise came in for much praise. According to reviewers, audiences were spellbound by Mawson's account of the death of his two comrades and by his own remarkable and 'awe-inspiring' story of survival, recounted in the 'most unelaborated fashion' as a sort of 'heart-to-heart talk'.[24] 'There is nothing of the finished orator about Sir Douglas', declared the *Baltimore Sun*,

> but he has a story to tell that does not need oratory to enhance its interest. To see the tall, slender young chap with the clean-cut features, and somewhat drawing

voice, dressed in immaculate evening clothes of the latest cut, and to hear him tell of living on the meat of dogs that had starved to death, of heartbreaking tramps over snow and ice, of the death of two of his companions, and of his own miraculous escapes as if they were commonplace things, and then to see in a series of wonderful pictures the desolate land in which he had lived for more than two years was enough to make every one who heard him marvel at the stuff of which he was made.[25]

Clearly, Mawson's actual presence on stage was absolutely vital to the success of the lecture, and his embodiment of what was taken to be civilized, understated manliness was itself a powerful affective attraction. 'Here and there in the audience', observed the *Philadelphia Public Ledger*, 'women were dabbing at their eyes with their handkerchiefs. The men were shifting in their seats, feeling that, after all, they led stupid, humdrum existences'.[26]

Mawson's broader symbolic import for American and Canadian audiences as a model of the new Australian man, as a living testament to 'British reticence and modesty', or in his delivery style as somehow 'synonymous' with 'democracy' surely merits further investigation.[27] So, too, does the sublime, dangerous, pure whiteness of the Antarctica he conjured for his audiences, a territory – paradoxically – also filled with Chaplinesque penguins and other novel and frequently comic creatures that gave the hardy expedition members a chance to play like adolescent pranksters. These potential lines of inquiry point us back to what I have called the modularity, generic mélange, and varied pleasures of *Racing with Death in Antarctic Blizzards*. These characteristics – along with the essential role of the living speaker who at the very least presents and in some fashion sponsors the projected images – might well define the multiple-media lecture as a primary non-theatrical format in in this period. At the same time, Mawson's North American tour and the subsequent public life of the AAE footage – in ways I have only begun to suggest here – stands as a particularly revealing example of how moving pictures circulated outside the movie theatre in the 1910s.

Acknowledgements: Thanks to Richard Maltby and Ruth Vasey for their gracious hospitality; to Quentin Turnour and Katie Saarikko of the Australian National Film and Sound Archive and Mark Pharoah of the South Australian Museum's Mawson Center for invaluable assistance; and to Indiana University's Office of the Vice President for International Affairs for an Overseas Research Grant.

Notes

1. On the lecturer, see, for example, Charles Musser, *High-Class Moving Pictures: Lyman H. Howe and the Forgotten Era of Traveling Exhibition, 1880–1920* (Princeton: Princeton University Press, 1991); Rick Altman, *Silent Film Sound* (New York: Columbia Press, 2004), and André Gaudreault, *Film and Attraction: From Kinematography to Cinema* (Urbana: University of Illinois Press, 2011): 27–31.

2. See, for example, Richard Abel, "Charge and Countercharge: 'Documentary' War Pictures in the USA, 1914–1916", *Film History* 22, no. 4 (2010): 366–388; and Jeffrey Ruoff (ed.), *Virtual Voyages: Cinema and Travel* (Durham: Duke University Press, 2006).

3. For more on sponsorship and targeted audiences, see Gregory A. Waller, "Locating Early Non-Theatrical Audiences", in Ian Christie (ed.), *Audiences: Defining and Researching Screen Entertainment Reception* (Amsterdam: Amsterdam University Press, 2012): 81–95.

4. Jan Anders Diesen, *Roald Amundsen's South Pole Expedition, 1910–1912* (Oslo: Norwegian Film Institute, 2010).

5. See, for example, "Two Deaths Added to Antarctic Toll", *Richmond [Virginia] Times-Dispatch*, 26 February 1913, 1; "Mawson Reached in Time: Explorers Forced to Subsist on Hearts and Tongues of Sea Elephants", [Boise] *Idaho Statesman*, 28 August 1913, 1.

6. For more on Hurley, see Robert Dixon, "Travelling Mass-Media Circus: Frank Hurley's Synchronized Lecture Entertainments", *Nineteenth Century Theatre & Film* 33, no. 1 (2009): 9–29.

7. Memorandum of Agreement between Dr. Douglas Mawson of the Australian Antarctic Expedition and the Gaumont Company Limited (Mawson Centre [hereafter MC], file 169AAE).

8. On the various Australian screenings, see "With Mawson in the South", *Sydney Morning Herald*, 11 May 1912, 15; "Spenser's Antarctic Special", *Sydney Morning Herald*, 15 May 1912, 2; Lyceum ad, *Sydney Morning Herald*, 14 May 1912, 2.

9. Poster for *The Story of Our Expedition*, Queen's Hall, 20 June 1914 (MC scrapbook M462M).

10. Mawson letter to Keedick, 19 July 1914 (MC file, 171AAE).

11. Mawson's contract with Keedick (nd). MC file, 171AAE. Signed contract with Keedick, 21 May 1914 (South Australia Library, PRG 523, Series 11, envelope 1).

12. "Sir Douglas Mawson in New York", *Bulletin of the American Geographical Society of New York* 47, no. 1 (1915): 120–121.

13. "Sir Douglas Mawson in New York", 122; "Antarctic Pictures", *Moving Picture World* 23, no. 4 (23 January 1915): 494.

14. *New York Dramatic Mirror* 73 (17 March 1915): 24.

15. Robert J. Christopher, *Robert and Frances Flaherty: A Documentary Life, 1883–1922* (Montreal: McGill-Queen's University Press, 2005): 232.

16. "Mawson Exhibits Wonderful Views of Polar Scenes", *St Louis Democrat* (19 February 1915).

17. Quentin Turnour, "'A.K.A. *Home of the Blizzard*': Fact and Artefact in the Film on the Australian Antarctic Expedition, 1911–1914", *NFSA Journal* 2, no. 4 (2007): 1–12.

18. Mawson copyright application for twenty photographs (#4357-4376) 30 January 1915, 6 February 1915, *Library of Congress Catalogue of Copyright Entries* Part 4 New Series, Volume 10 (Washington: Government Printing Office, 1915), 84; Mawson copyright application for Racing with death in Antarctic blizzards (#7909). 15 March 1915, *Library of Congress Catalogue of Copyright Entries* Part 1 New Series, Volume 12 (Washington: Government Printing Office, 1915), 323.

19. MC file, 188AAE.

20. South Australia Library, PRG 523

21. "4,000 Feet of Antarctic Exploration", *Motion Picture News* 11, no. 4 (30 January 1915): 66.

22. See the detailed discussion of Frank Hurley's 'synchronized lecture entertainments' in the 1920s, in Dixon, "Travelling Mass-Media Circus".

23. *Brooklyn Citizen*, 27 February 1915; these points are underscored in "Mawson Antarctic Pictures", *Moving Picture World* 23, no.12 (20 March 1915): 1751.

24. "Mawson's Antarctic Pictures", *Billboard*, 30 January 1915, 46; *St. Louis Democrat*, 19 February 1915.

25. "Sir Douglas Thrills", *Baltimore Sun*, 9 February 1915, 3; A review of Mawson's lecture to an audience of three thousand at the University of Michigan praised his 'simple language with no attempt at oratory … sitting tight on the edge of their chairs, his audience found themselves awed at his gripping story one minute and convulsed with laughter in the next minute', "Polar Medal Given Mawson", *Ann Arbor [Michigan] Daily Times News*, 13 February 1915, 4.
26. "Audience Thrilled by Mawson's Tale of Antarctic Trip", *Philadelphia Public Ledger*, 21 January 1915.
27. "Audience Thrilled by Mawson's Tale of Antarctic Trip"; "British Explorer here to Lecture", *Philadelphia Press*, 17 January 1915.

PART III

Performing with the Screen: Audiences, Educators and Officials

Kinoreformbewegung Revisited: Performing the Cinematograph as a Pedagogical Tool

Frank Kessler and Sabine Lenk

'But what has become of pantomime drama today? In most cases it is having a brutalising effect on the audience through an accumulation of crimes and baseness in invented, realist dramas. Conradt inspected 250 dramas: "One could be generous and turn a blind eye on every single drama, thinking: that's what life is like, sometimes. But looking at this whole sort of pictures and taking into consideration that in 150 plays there were 97 murders, 51 adulteries, 19 seductions, 22 abductions and 45 suicides, that 176 thieves, 25 prostitutes, 35 drunkards, an army of policemen, detectives and bailiffs made their appearance, then one has to understand that things cannot go on like that, or all morality will be destroyed".'[1]

This is a rather characteristic quote from one of the many publications by teachers, educators and pedagogues, who participated in the first phase of the German *Kinoreformbewegung* (cinema reform movement) between 1907 and 1915, continuing an earlier battle against trash and pulp literature. However, those participating in the movement should not be seen simply as enemies of moving pictures, even though most studies on the *Kinoreformbewegung* foreground their sometimes very violent criticism of cinema. As the name under which they were organised indicates, they wanted to reform the cinema business, both by improving the aesthetic quality of the films and by stamping out everything that in their eyes was harmful or unwholesome about the new medium. Inspired by predecessors such as Wilhelm Börner, Ernst Schultze and especially Heinrich Wolgast, who protested against trash literature,[2] a group of teachers in Hamburg founded in 1907 a commission for the protection of the youth. They protested against the unhealthy conditions in cheap movies houses[3] and fought against 'horrible dramas', like the ones inspected by the protestant pastor Walther Conradt. The group wanted to have sensationalist stories replaced, in particular by non-fiction films, and started in

1912 to publish regularly lists of recommended films.[4] These contained travelogues, industrial pictures, educational films on biological, chemical and physical phenomena as well as technical demonstrations.

In spite of the seemingly common goals of the various initiatives that in Imperial Germany worked towards a *Kinoreform*, a closer look at their writings and activities reveals that what is often perceived as a movement was in fact a rather heterogeneous conglomerate of individuals or interest groups: teachers, pedagogues, educators (Hermann Lemke, Adolf Sellmann, Willy Warstatt), academics (librarian Ernst Schultze or art theorist Konrad Lange), journalists, intellectuals, but also medical doctors (psychologist Robert Gaupp), churchmen (the above-mentioned Walther Conradt), lawyers, politicians or other representatives of the state (magistrate Albert Hellwig, civil servant Berkermann or Berlin's main censor Karl Brunner), and even people that were part of the film business (such as editor Emil Perlmann and free-lance journalist and author Hermann Häfker, both writing for the Düsseldorf trade journal *Der Kinematograph*).[5] So there could be quite divergent views on how to achieve this reform.

In addition to efforts to improve and regulate cinema, in their reflections on the medium the reformers also developed interesting theoretical insights into the formal and aesthetic characteristics of film (as demonstrated in particular by Helmut H. Diederichs' pioneering work since the 1980s).[6] Another aspect of the cinema reform movement's activities, however, has drawn less attention: in order to demonstrate that it was indeed possible to create a different kind of cinema show, various local and regional groups organised screenings that were meant to uplift and educate the audience. Their final goal was to establish their brand of educational screening as a model also for commercial film theatres. From 1909 onward, there were several initiatives to open municipal cinemas with regular programmes, whose commercial viability, however, proved to be too precarious.

In the following we will concentrate on the *Kinoreformer*'s activities with regard to educational screenings. We will argue that the didactic principles according to which these were structured are firmly embedded in contemporary discourses on learning and memory, and that the German pedagogy reform movement provided arguments for the *Kinoreformer*'s efforts to establish film as a teaching tool.

We will first look at Hermann Häfker's ideas concerning educational programmes and their composition, which we will then relate to psychological conceptions of memory at that time. In the next step, we will discuss some of

17 *Kinoreformbewegung* Revisited: Performing the Cinematograph as a Pedagogical Tool

the pedagogical debates in turn-of-the century Germany, and how these could be used by the *Kinoreform* in their campaign for film screenings in schools. We will then return to the specific *dispositif* Häfker had conceived for his own presentations in order to see how these principles were translated into a concrete performance practice.

Programming: the Screening as a Multi-Media Event

In the very first issue of *Bild und Film. Zeitschrift für Lichtbilderei und Kinematographie*, the section '*Rundschau*' (panorama) opens with an item on model shows (*Mustervorstellungen*).[7] As the journal is published by the Lichtbilderei, a catholic institution created on 27 May 1909 by the editor Wilhelm Hahn[8] to promote and facilitate the use of media in schools, this presentation of exemplary screenings has to be considered a programmatic initiative. From this issue dated March 1912 up to its last in 1914, *Bild und Film* reproduced various programmes, such as, for example, one from the '*Kosmographia*' in Dresden plus several others organised by a Women's Association in Magdeburg in cooperation with the local Teachers' Commission.[9] All combine cinematographic projections with recitations and music or songs. Some of the titles listed may refer to slides rather than views, but this is not specified. The programmes were thematic ones: in Dresden the audience enjoyed a 'recitational-cinematographic evening' on 'Animals in Poetry and Life', the cinematograph being in charge of providing the latter. The Magdeburg performances presented programmes on geographic regions: Scandinavia and the polar North, or the 'Sunny South'.[10]

One year later, an article came to the conclusion that the *Kinoreformbewegung*'s efforts to establish educational screenings in commercial cinemas had failed, at least for the time being. Instead its author, the journalist Alfred Rosenthal, suggested they should rather turn to leagues, clubs and other associations. He listed seven different model programmes for specific organisations, which could be used as templates: one for a circle of aviation enthusiasts, one for a society for the protection of birds, one for medical doctors and staff, one for a women's association, one for a veterans' union, one for a colonial propaganda league and one programme for an evening dedicated to social issues. Again, these shows were to combine lectures, slides, films and music (maybe in some cases played from a gramophone), poems and songs, though not necessarily all of them in the same event.[11]

According to Hermann Häfker, a central figure of the Lichtbilderei group, a projection (*Vorführung*) had to become a performance (*Vorstellung*) in order to create a maximum effect on the audience.[12] In his reflections on the organisation of educational screenings, he particularly stressed the importance of pauses in order to give some rest to the spectators' eyes, and for the same reasons he suggested to introduce kaleidoscopic colour interludes or shadow plays.[13] Most of all, Häfker warned against any form of sensory overload: music was to be used sparingly, either to complement the image (when dances are shown, for instance) or in its 'melodramatic' function, to enhance the rhythm or the atmosphere of the pictures. The lecture, with or without projection slides, should precede the screening of the films, during which there should be no verbal explanations.[14]

Häfker describes '*Schauspiele der Erde*' (Wonders of the Earth), one of the performances he organised together with his association 'Bild und Wort' (Images and Word) that can be summed up as follows: the lecturer provides a short general introduction, then turns to the first slide and explains what the show will be about, in order to prepare the audience for what they may expect. Then films are projected, beginning with a phantom ride through the Alps accompanied by railway sounds, which fade away once they have created the atmosphere. There are short breaks between the views, and the first part of the programme ends with a slide. Then the lecturer reappears and comments on a series of slides to explain what the audience has seen in the first section of the programme and to prepare them for the second part. The lights fade, and the audience can hear sounds of water to introduce a film showing a waterfall, etc.[15]

Häfker explicitly conceived of the screening as a performance, but he meant a kind of performance that had nothing in common with the commercial forms of showmanship. Some of the principles evident in Häfker's description have their origins in reform pedagogy, which wanted to shape the learning process in accordance with children's learning capacity: the insistence on variation and pauses in order to make possible continuous attention and contemplation, the separation of verbal address and moving pictures as well as the selective use of music in order to avoid sensory overload and the overfeeding of the audience, and finally the thematic approach combining various forms of expression, thus creating connections between, for instance, poetry, factual knowledge, music and visual information.

Kinoreform – Screenings and Theories on Memory

One possible source for the pedagogic principles the *Kinoreform* set out to promote are contemporary theories on memory such as William James' treaty on memory in his *Principles of Psychology* (1890). According to Heike Klippel, James' concept is based on the idea that, in order to be retained in a human mind, an impression has to be of a certain duration and substance. The stimulus needs to be intense, therefore it has to be repeated several times, but neither too often, nor in a monotonous way. Furthermore, the person experiencing a phenomenon needs to believe, to a certain extent at least, in the truthfulness of the sensory impression, which, in addition, has to be received with a fresh mind allowing a high level of concentration so that it can be easily reproduced.[16] Häfker's programme in fact contains all these elements: the non-fictional moving images, both lifelike and spectacular, as a powerful, trustworthy and varied stimulus, accompanied by special sound effects enhancing their impact; the slides and comments providing the same information, but through different channels, and finally the pauses, to give rest to the spectators' eyes (and minds).

Whether Häfker actually read James' treaty or another author writing about the 'physiology and pathology of the mind' (Henry Maudsley)[17] is not known. It is striking, however, that the general principles that he outlined in his book are in line with the contemporary discourse on memory: his performances proposed a multi-sensory address through both moving and still images, verbal explanations and music, but were composed in such a way that they avoided sensory overload, provided the necessary periods of relaxation, and made use of documentary films as a guarantee for the authenticity of the material the audience was presented with.

Kinreform and the Principles of Pedagogy Reform

Even though in the *Kinoreformbewegung*'s texts we studied there are no direct references to contemporary initiatives of pedagogical reform (nor from the latter to the former), there clearly was ample common ground as well as shared values: a conservative critique of industrialisation and its consequences, in particular mass culture; the already mentioned fight against trash literature or films; anxieties about the decline of cultural values and institutions such as literature or theatre; and a generally nationalist attitude.

Reform pedagogy was directed against a tradition of learning built upon frontal lecturing, memorisation rather than understanding of subject matter, a strict separation of disciplines, abstract theory rather than practice, absolute authority of the teacher and physical punishment. In this context, again, contemporary theories on memory are relevant, but there is also another possible connection between pedagogy and *Kinoreform*: new tendencies in teaching art.[18]

Understanding, not Learning by Heart

One issue divides pedagogues in this period: on the one hand there are scientists such as Ernst Meumann (*Ökonomie und Theorie des Gedächtnisses. Experimentelle Untersuchungen über das Merken und Behalten*, Leipzig, 1912), Georg Elias Müller (*Zur Analyse der Gedächtnistätigkeit und des Vorstellungsverlaufes*, 3 vol., 1911–1917) or Müller's disciple Alfred von Sybel (*Über das Zusammenwirken verschiedener Sinnesgebiete bei Gedächtnisleistungen*, Leipzig, 1909), who insist that knowledge requires learning by heart and repetition. They advocate a relatively slow learning pace, optimisation of memory by disciplined attention and the elimination of all sources of distraction. But there are also critical voices: in her book *Die Vernichtung der Intelligenz durch Gedächtnisarbeit* (München, 1913) Mathilde Vaërting protests against learning by heart, which she sees as an obstacle to real understanding. The mechanical repetition that is involved consumes too much energy, which then is no longer available for the act of thinking. It dries up imagination and thus blocks the acquisition of new knowledge through an active understanding of things hitherto not learned. Memorising causes stupidity, she warns.

For most *Kinoreformers*, understanding trumps learning by heart. According to Sellmann, watching a film demands discipline, attention and concentration in order to observe and understand the film's subject.[19] Nevertheless the pace can be too fast, as the psychologist Robert Gaupp explained.[20] He feared that looking at film images entailed the same risks as reading a book: children are exposed to an avalanche of information they have to digest in a very short time. Gaupp warned against the strain on a child's soul caused by an overload of impressions that the mind is unable to process. All *Kinoreformers* were convinced that film is not detrimental to imagination, on the contrary: images inspire a child and may even lead to following examples seen on the screen. Therefore they demanded that films should be chosen carefully.

Evidently, scientists studying memory and pedagogues shared some common beliefs. Nevertheless, it would take more primary source material to prove that teachers in that period were aware of the scientific experiments in the field of memo-techniques. According to Klippel, these and other studies on memory were widely published in specialised journals.[21] Experiments to study the mind were popular at the end of the nineteenth century, and memo-techniques became more and more important. It is possible that teachers read these periodicals or learned from pedagogical journals, maybe even in the popular press, what happened in the field of memo-experiments. Dedicated teachers certainly would be interested in research on learning processes. Especially those working at the *Volksschule* (elementary school) were keen on reforming teaching methods. For them, a concept of memory such as Vaërting's provided arguments to abandon the traditional methods and look for new and more efficient ones. Johann Friedrich Herbart's concept of a *Lernschule*[22] (learning school) implied frontal lecturing and a strictly pre-choreographed programme for every lesson, organised around books, whose content had to be reproduced and repeated. Rather uninspiring for both pupils and teachers, it represented a humanistic ideal (studying classical languages, but no practical training) that fit the model of the lyceum. But in the eyes of many *Volksschule*-pedagogues this teaching style was inappropriate for the 'uncultured' children they were confronted with daily.

Kinoreform and Reform Pedagogy: Links, Contacts, Common Ground

'No faction within reform pedagogy embraced the new technical, optical and acoustic teaching tools'.[23] This observation by Rudolf Kipp, specialist in audiovisual teaching tools, referring to films, slides and the phonograph, suggests that teachers pioneering moving images in school could hardly count on being supported by their colleagues, let alone school authorities.

But even if school reformers were not openly in favour of the new medium (and sometimes even vehemently against it) at least one of the major new pedagogical concepts that existed around 1900 can be considered essential for the introduction of film in school: the *Kunsterziehungsbewegung* (art education movement) in literature and art. Two of its representatives participated also in the *Kinoreform* and may have functioned as links: Konrad Lange, devoted to the reforming of art education, and Ernst Schultze, director of the public reading hall in Hamburg, who contributed to Alfred Lichtwark's influential reform art journal *Der Kunstwart*. Here, too, we can only hint towards some conceptual parallels, as claiming a more fundamental relationship would ask for a more thorough study of primary sources.

Alfred Lichtwark, a former teacher and director of the Kunsthalle Hamburg, also founder-editor of *Der Kunstwart*, and Ferdinand Avenarius were two eminent leaders of the *Kunsterziehungsbewegung*. They preferred a classroom where pupils were trained to observe, understand and reflect on what they see and hear instead of being 'stuffed' with knowledge out of books as in the old 'Herbart school'.[24] This can be considered a first step towards an alternative educational program, which over time would embrace modern didactic tools such as the film projector.

Heinrich Wolgast advocated educating the young eye to make the children receptive and help them understand the world they live in.[25] This is in line with

Sellmann's conviction that film, if accompanied by a lecture, trains a child's intellect and sense for reality.[26] Film and photography were appreciated particularly for their capacity to reproduce the real, which, precisely, prompted the *Kinoreformers*' rejection of dramatised story films.

Teacher Carl Götze even rejected reading as an inadequate tool, providing but 'second hand knowledge'.[27] Similarly, some *Kinoreformers* denounced the teacher's lecture for producing confused ideas in the pupils' minds, praising the cinematograph as 'first hand' informant.

Konrad Lange warned against illustrations in children's books and classrooms, claiming that they presented wrong impressions of nature, which caused unrealistic 'memory images'. Instead, he advocated studying the objects themselves.[28] In turn, the *Kinoreformers* saw film as a perfect substitute supplying an excellent reproduction of the object, and even helping to discover how things work as it can reveal phenomena invisible to human eyes. Fiction film, on the contrary, was rejected for creating a fantasy-image of the world.

More parallels between *Kinoreform* and the different strands in reform pedagogy, such as the '*Arbeitsschule*' (working school), conceived by Georg Kerschensteiner and Hugo Gaudig, or Wilhelm Dilthey's '*Erlebnispädagogik*' could be mentioned. Also, Ellen Key's famous book *Barnets Århundrade* (1900), published in 1902 in Germany as *Das Jahrhundert des Kindes*, one of the most widely read educational texts before and after the War, may have had some influence on the *Kinoreform* movement.

The *Dispositif*

These examples from reform pedagogical theories suggest at least some links to *Kinoreform* practice. Reading *Bild und Film* and other sources,[29] there were at the minimum eight municipal reform cinemas and other reform oriented screening facilities: in 1909 the *Ernemann Reformkino* in Dresden; in 1910 the *Kosmographia* in Dresden and the *Reform-Kino* in Braunschweig; in 1911 the *Reformtheater* in Bremen; in 1912 the *Gemeindekino* in Eickel (today Wanne-Eickel), the *Germania Saal* in Hagen and the *Musterlichtbildbühne* in Altona and last, but not least in 1914 the *Urania* in Stettin. So how were the performances organised?

Häfker describes in some detail the specific set-up of the hall in Dresden where his screening took place.[30] When the performance started, the screen, framed by a proscenium arch covered in a dark red plush material, was hidden behind a red velvet curtain. Four bay trees were added for decoration. The lectern stood on one side of the screen, so that the lecturer could retreat behind the proscenium arch while the films were shown. The film projector and the lantern were situated behind the screen, as were the sound machine and the trio of musicians and their instruments consisting of a piano or harmonium, a cello and a violin. The lecturer and the technical section communicated through bell signals and an assistant signalled the projectionists when it was time to put up a new slide or start the screening of a film.

This set-up is most interesting, as it tries to maximise the effect of the moving images, which were projected without any verbal commentary, but were accompanied by sounds and occasionally by music. The whole set-up, including the musicians and during the film projection the lecturer, were all shielded from the audience's view in order not to cause any kind of distraction to the contemplative gaze of the spectators. The general principles formulated by Häfker thus find their counterpart in this particular *dispositif* of the screening.

Conclusion

The two reform movements evidently had much in common, but a thorough analysis of these parallels still remains to be done. It is certain that their ideas circulated in publications or during meetings such as the *Kunsterziehungstage* (Dresden 1901, Weimar 1903, Hamburg 1905) or congresses such as the one in Berlin in 1908 where '*Schulkinematographie*' was discussed. A first book – Georg V. Mendel's *Kinematographie und Schule* (1909) – provided theoretical reflections and practical guidelines. As a consequence, some teachers started to introduce film in the classroom or, more accurately, brought the classroom to moving picture houses. These initiatives were closely followed in books and periodicals for teachers and publications related to cinema (the series *Lichtbildbühnen-Bibliothek* and *Bild und Film*). The First World War put an end to these efforts. After the war, motivated teachers re-launched the idea of educational cinema – this time for good.

Notes

1. Lorenz Pieper, "Kino und Drama", *Bild und Film* 1, no. 1 (March 1912): 6. This and all subsequent translations are ours.
2. In 1891, Wolgast founded the 'Vereinigung deutscher Prüfungsausschüsse für Jugendschriften' (association for German juries examining literature for the youth), which prepared a list of appropriate readings for the young. His efforts led to the foundation in 1911 of the 'Zentralstelle zur Bekämpfung der Schundliteratur' (central office for the fight against trash literature) headed by Karl Brunner.
3. Teachers from Hamburg warned: 'Bad air can be noticed everywhere. The reason: insufficient ventilation, cigarettes and cigarette smoke. The bar service in the theatres during children's visits

have already been the object of several court cases', quoted by Paul Ferd. Siegert, *Bürgerliches Selbstverständnis, Kinoreform und früher Schulfilm. Eine kulturwissenschaftliche Analyse* (MA-thesis, Universität Lüneburg, 1997, http://dok.uni-lueneburg.de/texte/Kinoreform.pdf, 23.3.2013), 95 The commission's report *Bericht der Kommission für 'Lebende Photographien'. Erstattet am 17. April 1907 und im Auftrage des Vorstandes von C.H. Dannmeyer*, was published by Gesellschaft der Freunde des vaterländischen Schul- und Erziehungswesens zu Hamburg. See also Rudolf W. Kipp, *Bilddokumente zur Geschichte des Unterrichtsfilms* (Grünwald: Institut für Film und Bild in Wissenschaft und Unterricht, 1975), 59.

4. See the commission's lists in Herbert Birett, *Verzeichnis in Deutschland gelaufener Filme – Entscheidungen der Filmzensur 1911–1920 Berlin, Hamburg, München, Stuttgart* (München, New York, London, Paris: K.G. Saur, 1980), 641–677.

5. See also Thomas Schorr, *Die Film- und Kinoreformbewegung und die deutsche Filmwirtschaft. Eine Analyse des Fachblatts "Der Kinematograph" (1907–1935) unter pädagogischen und publizistischen Aspekten* (PhD-dissertation, Universität der Bundeswehr, München, 1990).

6. See Helmut H. Diederichs, *Frühgeschichte deutscher Filmtheorie* (Habilitation, J. W. Goethe Universität, Frankfurt am Main, 2001, download at http://publikationen.ub.uni-frankfurt.de/frontdoor/index/index/docId/4924)

7. "Mustervorstellungen", *Bild und Film* 1, no. 1 (March 1912): 19–22.

8. See Siegert, 124.

9. "Mustervorstellungen", *Bild und Film 1*, no. 1 (March 1912): 19–22.

10. Ibid.

11. Alfred Rosenthal, "Kinovorstellungen in Vereinen", *Bild und Film* 3, no. 8 (1913/13): 198–200.

12. Hermann Häfker, *Kino und Kunst* (M.Gladbach: Volksvereinsverlag, 1913), 52. See Helmut H. Diederichs, "Naturfilm als Gesamtkunstwerk. Herman Häfker und sein 'Kinetographie'-Konzept", *Augen-Blick. Marburger Hefte zur Medienwissenschaft*, 8 (1990): 37–60, for comments on Häfker's theoretical reflections on film.

13. Ibid., 53–63.

14. Ibid., 57.

15. Ibid., 60–61.

16. William James as summarised by Heike Klippel, *Gedächtnis und Kino* (Frankfurt/Main: Stroemfeld Verlag, 1997), 21–32.

17. According to Klippel, 32, Henry Maudsley in his book *Physiology and Pathology of the Mind* (London, 1867) is the first to suggest the 'concept of the organic memory'.

18. The following ideas on memory studies and experiments are based on Klippel, 50–53, 57–59.

19. See Adolf Sellmann, *Kino und Schule* (M. Gladbach: Volksverein-Verlag, 1914), 15.

20. Robert Gaupp, "Der Kinematograph vom medizinischen und psychologischen Standpunkt", in Robert Gaupp, and Konrad Lange (eds), *Der Kinematograph als Unterhaltungsmittel* (München: Callwey, 1912), 5–9.

21. See Klippel, 53.

22. See Johannes von den Driesch, Josef Esterhues, *Geschichte der Erziehung und Bildung* (Paderborn: Ferdinand Schöningh, 1925), 413.

23. Kipp, 12.

24. See Ludwig Praehauser, *Kunst und unerfüllte Pädagogik. Sieben Kapitel über Kunsterziehung und pädagogische Reformen* (Wien: Österreichischer Bundesverlag für Unterricht, Wissenschaft und Kunst, 1925), 13–17, 41.

25. See Heinrich Wolgast, "Die Bedeutung der Kunst für die Erziehung [1902]", in Hermann Lorenzen (ed.), *Die Kunsterziehungsbewegung* (Bad Heilbrunn: Julius Klinkhardt, 1966), 18–19.

26. See Sellmann, *Kino und Schule*.
27. See Carl Götze, "Zeichnen und Formen [1901]", in Lorenzen, 31.
28. See Konrad Lange, "Das Wesen der künstlerischen Erziehung (1901)", in Lorenzen, 23.
29. For instance Kipp.
30. See Häfker, 59.

Health on Display: The Panama-Pacific International Exposition as Sanitary Venue

Marina Dahlquist

> The Panama Canal is the most remarkable achievement of man, not only because of the great engineering ability and the vast financial outlay involved in its construction, but because humanity, man's consideration for his fellow man, has so progressed that now the deadly miasmas of the tropics are nullified and the battle lost to climatic and physical conditions is turned to victory by the science of hygienic sanitation.[1]

This triumphant belief in hygienic efforts is part of the discourse that promoted the upcoming Panama Pacific International Exposition in San Francisco in 1915 – and as this example, from 1913, makes evident – years in advance of the actual event. As it turned out, sanitation, health, reform and education became prominent themes at the Exposition together with industrial inventions and explorations of national and cultural diversities.

The early twentieth century teemed with initiatives aimed at improving and modernising American everyday life. These uplift campaigns, initiated in top-down fashion, zoomed in on sanitation, working conditions, childcare, education, and recreation. The strive for better health conditions brought together a cross-section of civic movements and organisations, which in turn inspired the implementation of governmental infrastructures at federal, state or municipal level.

Health exhibits were an important gateway for reaching out to the general public during the 1910s. And the Panama-Pacific International Exposition was *the* high-profiled venue, and a summation up a phalanx of visual health campaigns, placed adjacent to each other, as it were, within a much wider scope of exhibition practices.

The purpose of this article is to explore the health exhibits at the Exposition and their use of media within the multitude of national as well as international projects put on display in San Francisco. The roster of participants featured the Bureau of Public Health Education, the International Health Commission, the U.S. Sanitary Campaign in Panama, the Fly-Fighting Committee of the American Civic Association, the American Red Cross, the American Medical Association to mention only a select few. And for additional emphasis, 12 October 1915 was singled out as a Health Day at the exhibition. Due to the anthology of sanitary displays in place, the Panama Pacific Exposition became a key progressive hub by putting public health on the agenda and creating added social awareness for such issues.

In exhibition and campaign work, visual material was often used in order to catch the public's attention. Moving pictures' putative pedagogical might and potential for civic education underpinned the work to raise awareness about modern society and its social and sanitary shortcomings, or 'evils' in contemporary vernacular. From 1910 on, and in this spirit, moving pictures were regularly harnessed as a pedagogical tool for health campaigns in a multitude of contexts across the United States. These educational films were often produced in collaboration between organisations (municipal, medical, religious and other philanthropic institutions) and the film industry. Educational films were rarely commercially released, but had a circulation and exhibition outside the traditional movie theatre. There are of course exceptions. In the 1910s the Edison studio regularly produced social-interest films in cooperation with various welfare organisations and institutions, such as the American Red Cross and the Anti-Tuberculosis Association. Just to mention a couple examples: *Hope, a Red Cross Seal Story* (1912) was made in collaboration with the Society for the Study and Prevention of Tuberculosis, and social reform titles such as *The Public and Private Care of Infants* (1912) was produced in cooperation with the Department of Child-Helping at the Russell Sage Foundation, and *Charlie's Reform* (1912) was produced by Edison but devised by Clarence A. Perry in charge of the Division of Recreation at the Russell Sage Foundation.

Moving pictures were important vehicles for spreading the word of sanitation and health under the institutional design of the exposition at least in three ways: as part of the visual aid used at the location, to advertise the exposition, and, finally, as a way to reach audiences who did not have the opportunity to go to San Francisco themselves. The Publicity Department had enlisted the Miles Bros. to make film records of all the Exposition events. These films, accompanied by illustrated lectures, were put into the field to arouse interest in the exposition and promote State participation. But the footage was more widely circulated in newsreels distributed by Pathé, Gaumont, Hearst and others throughout the world. According to Frank Morton Todd's impressive five volumes *The Story of the Exposition*, moving pictures of exposition subjects did more to advertise the exposition than anything else.[2]

Even if moving pictures were perhaps the most important vessel for public health work, an array of visual media was brought together to create attention for the causes at hand: lantern slides, photographs, models, posters, pamphlets, cartoons, billboards, newspaper articles and ads. At the Panama-Pacific Exposition different visual media were mixed, in line with early twentieth century exhibition practices. In the pursuit of capturing the mass-audience's attention, well-established visual media such as wax models and lantern slides were used along with newer media such as moving pictures. And the organizers even encouraged the use of moving pictures and stereopticons whenever possible.[3] Models were recurrently used to demonstrate health work such as the overview model of an American Red Cross relief camp or a typical Infant Welfare Station showing a dispensing room, with ice-box, and dispensing table, as well as a consulting room with weighing equipment.[4] At times the models were even alive and in need of special care as the premature children put on display at the Infant Incubators Exhibit. Somewhat surprisingly, at least for us today, the exhibit was located at the midway-like amusement area of the exhibition named the Zone.

One of the main impetuses for sanitation and health efforts during the decades around 1900 was the high death rate among infants. Alvin E. Pope, the Chief of the Department of Education and Social Economy at the exposition had for many years been engaged in educational and corrective work and was one of the organisers of the first child welfare exhibit in the United States, which took place in Chicago. According to Pope: 'The death rate for hogs in the United States during the first year is five per cent, for sheep three, for calves one. For babies it is 12'.[5] To mitigate this condition and prevent illness amongst workers every conceivable sort of visual representation were used in multiple-media exhibits: lectures, moving pictures, transparencies, stereomotorgraphs (automatic lantern slide projector), charts, pamphlets, personal instruction, models, and topographical maps. Through this multi-medial demonstration the visitors got acquainted with the very latest modus operandi of progressive America in regards to child welfare, health conservation, hygiene, social relations and economic tendencies. According to a letter sent to the Rockefeller Foundation, Pope made an effort to make every exhibit educational. The aim was not to promote certain agencies, but to educate the visitors.[6]

Social Economy was a rather new area of exhibition. Both Social Economy and Education exhibits occupied the Palace of Education as their activities were intimately related across a vast number of subjects. The art of living was a recurrent theme within Social Economy striving to 'conserve the moral and the physical attributes of the citizen',[7] by hygiene, insurance, industrial-welfare work, banking, public parks, play grounds, swimming pools etcetera. Health was one of the leading topics.

Besides the United States, Argentina, China, Cuba, France, Japan, the Philippines, and Uruguay were represented in the Palace of Education. Japan had an exhibit of Red Cross work with life-size wax figures of surgeons, nurses, and patients, models of field telephones used to communicate with chief surgeons, hospital supply and base hospital.[8] The treatment of wounds was demonstrated, equipment such as surgical instruments, sterilising apparatus was exhibited, and army hygiene in the field was illustrated.

At several exhibitions methods of bodily conservation were clinically demonstrated as well as educational processes, but what was argued as perhaps even more important: the visitor could acquire education about domains not yet in the curricula of the schools. The Mouth-Hygiene Association of America had for example a free, open, dental clinic, where visitors were instructed in mouth hygiene. The California Association for the Study and Prevention of Tuberculosis offered illustrated lectures. At the Children's Bureau booth examinations of children were available daily. And the last week of June was their Child Welfare Week. In one of the eight moving picture theatres of the Palace of Education,[9] leading authorities on the subject of child welfare discussed the problem and hundreds of babies were examined and graded for points.

At the Race Betterment booth, Dr. A.J. Read lectured daily on eugenics and related, but equally contentious topics. Four live persons were on display representing the human race at its allegedly best.[10] The American Social Hygiene Association presented fifty wall charts, models, photographs and illustrations dealing with medical, educational, religious and legal phases of social hygiene, including a campaign about sex education. An issue brought to the social mind by Eugène Brieux's play *Les Avaries* (Damaged Goods), and with Tom Ricketts' film with the same name from 1914. According to Frank Morton Todd, the aim of the Department of Social Economy was that the exposition should usher in marked improvements in the habit of living – by national and international movements along all lines of social service.

In less than ten years, social issues had become not only a concern for philanthropic organisations, municipal and federal agencies, but educational cinema had become more or less institutionalised with several specialised production companies, and moving pictures were often a given component in exhibitions and campaigns on health issues. As Gregory A. Waller has shown, virtually all non-fiction films offered at the exposition were free, sponsored, regularly scheduled, organised into programmes and exhibited in makeshift theatres. The use of moving pictures as an instructive and educational tool was vast, but more mundane and in line with nickelodeons or educational cinema screenings than the new cinema palaces from the mid-1910s, and they were distinctly separated from the Midway's commercial theatres. The medium's importance was manifested on 15 July when Metro Moving Picture Day was celebrated in recognition of moving pictures and its stars' cachet.[11] This celebration of a single film company was according to the *Moving Picture World* an important acknowledgement besides a huge success. A dense crowd welcomed Francis X. Bushman and Marguerite Snow, two leading Metro stars, when they arrived at the exposition.[12]

Regarding social betterment and public uplift, the New York State exhibition set the tone. In 1913, New York enacted a public health law that soon became a model for some of the most progressive States in the Union. Under this law, the Public Health Council was given the power to formulate a statewide sanitary code and administrating sanitary matters. A wall-panel diagram with electric flashes presented the organisation, down to its smallest unit.

The New York State Hospital exhibit put the 'great humanitarian work' for treating the insane, together with information concerning cost, causes, extent, and diagnostic increase of insanity on display. A glass-covered model of a state hospital plant for two thousand insane patients dominated the exhibit and garnered most interest. The exhibit included ninety coloured lantern views and a motion picture reel showing the housing, occupation, and recreation of patients. According to New York State's own report the film depicting the Binghamton, St Lawrence and Manhattan State Hospitals was advertised as the first ever shown from inside institutions of the insane.[13]

The New York State Department of Health also had an exhibition showing the organisation and activities of the Department, including an electric flash-wall panel depicting the relations between the different divisions, supervisors and health officers within the Department. A moving model called 'The Path of Life' illustrated the proportions of a given population dying at different ages. The most important aspect of the public health movement was obviously to prevent premature death. Different kinds of media were used to illustrate the systematic life-saving work: to emphasise the danger from improper sewage disposal, a model showed three villages along a stream polluting the water. Cases

18 Health on Display: The Panama-Pacific International Exposition as Sanitary Venue

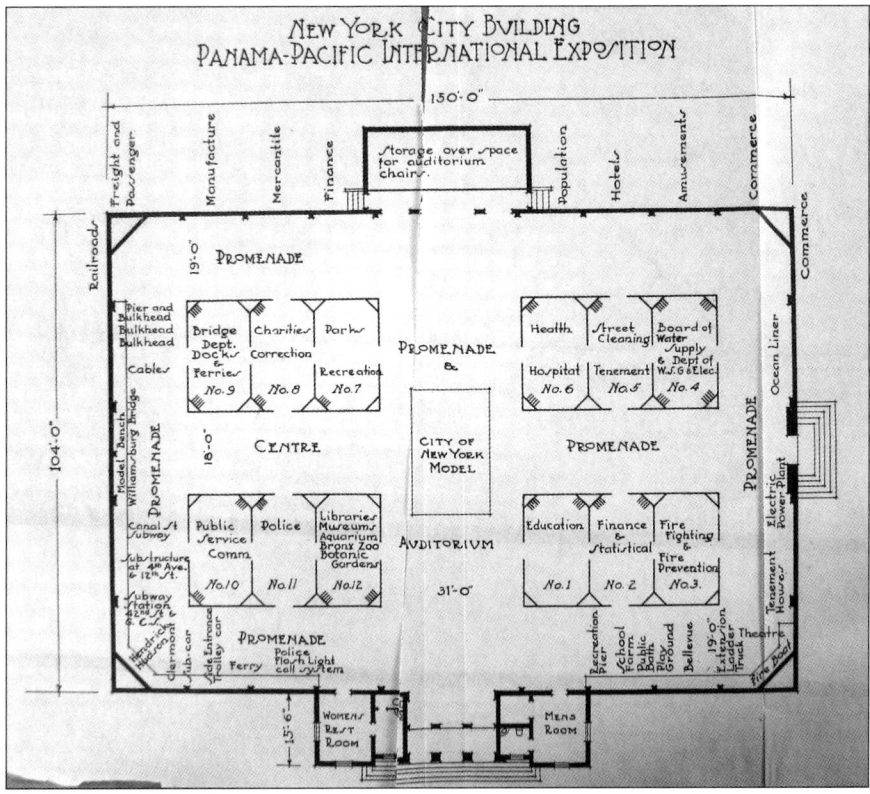

Figure 1: Interior plan of exhibitions in the New York City Building.

of typhoid fever were indicated by electric lights, a large relief map of the State illustrated its principal topographic features, various coloured flashing lights indicated location of water supply and sewage disposal plants, and a model illustrated an ideal life-size Infant Welfare Station.[14] And moving pictures were shown daily at the New York State Social Economy Pavilion (in the Palace of Education) portraying, among other topics, the inspection work performed by the Health Officer of the Port of New York.[15]

The Bureau of Public Health Education prepared an exhibit showing the activities of the entire Department, as part of the Municipal exhibit of New York City, the only municipality as such with an independent display at the Panama-Pacific Exposition. The City of New York gave a comprehensive display of municipal functions, according to Todd this was probably the most complete exhibit of a municipality ever brought together.[16] Henry Bruère, the chairman of the sub-committee in charge of New York City's exhibits, writes that an attempt had been made in preparing for the exhibit to give a picture of

179

Figure 2: The auditorium ready with 400 seats for moving picture screening at the New York City's Exhibit.

the progressive and efficient activities of the city, including the subway, police flashlight system, a typical playground, etcetera.[17]

New York State had a free standing 'Moving Picture Pavilion' in the Palace of Education showing a daily programme of different aspects of activities in the state, including the work of the State Departments concerning education, health, hospital and labor for free every afternoon.[18] Apart from representative business concerns of New York State, moving pictures of every city and business community in the State were on display in the State's Social Economy Pavilion.

In 1914, the Bureau of Public Health Education was established as a specialised branch within the New York Health Department. Among the responsibilities was to 'prepare and exhibit moving picture films dealing with public health work'.[19] The Bureau received a fully equipped moving picture machine as a gift and arrangements were made for the municipal exhibit of New York City by a moving picture show of twelve to fourteen reels at the Panama Pacific Exhibition. Together with the principal sights of the metropolis, the city's health work was shown.[20] To be able to use educational films in conjunction with the exhibits of municipal activities, the centre concourse of the building could be turned into an auditorium seating four hundred persons. The city model, usually occupying a central position could be revolved and in just twenty seconds turned into a passageway, curtains were then released enclosing the auditorium and chairs were rolled into place. Initially Pathé was about to enter a contract to

18 Health on Display: The Panama-Pacific International Exposition as Sanitary Venue

produce the pictures, but the company was prevented by the outbreak of the war. Instead Vitagraph became the film-producing partner. All together 15,947 feet of films were prepared on all kinds of topics subjects, for example *The Fire Fighters* (3,000 feet), *The Finest Police* in four parts (altogether 3,595 feet), and *Making a Good Citizen* (1,122 feet). According to the organisers the films that arouse most interest were the titles: *New York, Past and Present* in three parts, *The Finest*, *The Fire Fighters*, and *The Locked Door* (on the subject of fire prevention), all of which lasted a full hour.[21] The New York City's exhibit earned a number of distinctions: among them where three Grand Prizes for the entire municipal exhibit, the general excellence of illustrative photography, and finally the Department of Health for its health and sanitation. The educational exhibit in its entirety was awarded a medal of honor.[22]

Several philanthropic organisations presented their health work at the San Francisco exposition. One exhibit that attracted much attention was the International Health Commission of the Rockefeller Foundation and their work on the Eradication of Hookworm Disease in the American South (a campaign that would get a more international direction after 1915). According to Todd, the hookworm exhibit at the Hygiene section of the Department of Social Economy was a typical illustration of the practical value education about a disease could have.[23] The purpose of the exhibit was to make evident to the public the nature and importance of the hookworm disease and to emphasise the simplicity and low cost of the cure. It was well attended and became famous through its vivid features, which assembled material and pictures from their work.

On the recommendation of Pope, Philip Rauer, an expert wax worker who had executed the exhibit Der Mensch at the Dresden Exposition, was brought in from Germany.[24] He prepared models of portions of the body such as hands and feet illustrating the pathological effect of the entrance of hookworms, life-size and life-like models of children were made, showing different stages of the disease, and symptoms such as stunting growth.[25] There were also models of sanitary and unsanitary homes, maps showing the spread of hookworms over the world, photographs (of hookworm victims before and after treatment), charts, lantern slides, most of which interpreted different phases of the hookworm lesson. Two attendants, from the field, recruited from Kentucky, lectured and answered questions, and performed examinations for hookworm disease when requested by visitors.

The exhibition was planned to be of two forms: one in three dimensions as far as this was possible and the other with moving pictures to be shown in one of the moving picture theatres in the Palace of Education. In the end, however, the moving picture show came in the form of a stereomotorgraph. It was placed in one section of the booth provided with chairs, from which visitors could view about fifty slides shown on a screen. The hookworm exhibit was also awarded the Grand Prize. Some of the points considered by the jury were: 'The importance of the lesson taught by the exhibit. The efficient manner in which the exhibit taught this lesson. The far reaching influence of its activities. Effectiveness of installation'.[26]

Several countries exhibited their educational system and social work at large. Sweden, for example, presented models, statistics and photographs showing social work and social development in Sweden. Photographs of a 'Home for Sick Children' or 'Midsummer at Childrens' Summer Recreation Home at Lingslättö', where children from the urban areas could enjoy the countryside, presented prominent institutions of childcare. As it is phrased in the Official Swedish Catalogue:

> At the present time one observes in nearly all civilized countries deep currents of opinion tending to reform society, which are unlike previous attempts at reform in-as-much as they have penetrated down into the masses of our population.[27]

The history of the trade unions, collective labour agreements, workmen's protection laws, and emigration were central topics. In 1915 over one million Swedes had emigrated, mainly to the United States. The Swedish exposition was part of the efforts to encourage the emigrants to return; a movement chiefly organized by the National Anti-emigration Society. And one of the main objectives was the housing question.

As is put forward in the Official Swedish Catalogue: 'healthy and cheap dwellings are perhaps the most important condition for a successful struggle against disease, drink, immortality, and other social evils'.[28] As Anne Bachmann has discussed, the Swedish 'Own homes' movement bureau was present at the exposition to show ideal houses as well as to give assistance and advice regarding purchases of houses in Sweden.[29]

Swedish films, selected by Walter Fevrell, director of the Swedish Board of Film Censors 1911–1914, were shown in the Swedish pavilion, free of charge and once or twice a week. With emigrated Swedes as the target audience the titles illustrated Swedish everyday life, nature and improved social conditions.[30] The film screenings were part of the movement Riksföreningen för Svenskhetens bevarande i utlandet, an organisation to preserve the Swedish emigrants' national identity.[31] One anti-emigration film was actually made for the exposition, in which a Swedish-American decides to move back to the old country and build his own home, inspired by the own home colony at Bankesta.[32] The man becomes quite prosperous in the film's happy ending.

According to Robert W. Rydell, nearly one hundred million people visited the international expositions organised in the United States between 1876 and 1916. The direct and indirect impact of these key arenas for putting modernity on display was immense for spreading ideas of progress and political values,[33] and highly innovative in the manners of which the whole gamut of visual tools were put to work. Modernity was more than anything predicated on a recasting of the sensual order by privileging vision and visual representation. Moving images were pivotal in this respect, thus the ubiquitous enlisting of cinema in San Francisco at a time when the medium was on the verge of a new level of maturity concerning production, distribution and exhibition. In 1915 moving pictures were no longer a technological novelty on display for its own sake as in the 1900 fair in Paris and 1904 World's fair in St Louis. At the Panama-Pacific Exposition the enlisting of moving pictures was utilitarian. A popular and pleasurable pastime and a proven attention grabber, cinema was an ideal tool for instruction and education for audiences fully conversant with film culture. Educating the visitors using the appeal of an intermedial landscape reflects Neil Harris' term the 'operational aesthetic'.[34] How the exhibition context specifically influenced the further developments of educational moving-picture practices is still a mainly unchartered scholarly field, albeit currently attracting a new level of research attention.

The visitors went to the Palace of Education not primarily to be amused, but, according to Frank Morton Todd, to study.[35] Due to the anthological nature of sanitary displays in place, the exposition became a critical hub by putting public health on the agenda and creating added social awareness for such issues in line with progressive ideals. The visitors were offered an extraordinary opportunity to get an overview of the campaigns at work and the visual media at play that, according to Todd, 'they might never have acquired elsewhere'.[36] Furthermore, these didactic initiatives and exhibition practices would serve as a model also for future work outside the United States. To, carry on with the somewhat pompous verbiage of one of the many reports of the expo:

> 'The triumphant progress of humanity'.[37]

Notes

1. Thomas Morrell Moore, Charles C. Curran and Edward Everett Winchell, *Panama-Pacific International Exposition 1915* (San Francisco, 1913), 3.
2. Frank Morton Todd, *The Story of the Exposition: Being the Official History of the International*

  Celebration held at San Francisco in 1915 to Commemorate the Discovery of the Pacific Ocean and the Construction of the Panama Canal, vol I (New York: The Knickerbocker Press, 1921), 254–255.

3. *Department of Social Economy Bulletin* (San Francisco: Panama-Pacific International Exposition, 1913), no. 1: 13.
4. Todd, *The Story of the Exposition*, IV, 42.
5. Ibid., 32.
6. Letter signed by Alvin E. Pope, Rockefeller Foundation (RF), Record Group (RG) 5, Series 1:2, Box 19, Folder 294.
7. Todd, *The Story of the Exposition*, IV, 42.
8. Ibid., 40.
9. Todd, *The Story of the Exposition*, III, 33.
10. For a discussion on racial exploitation on early world's fairs in the U.S. see Robert W. Rydell, *All the World's a Fair. Visions of Empire at American International Expositions, 1876–1916* (Chicago & London: University of Chicago Press, 1984).
11. Gregory A. Waller has generously granted me access to his unpublished paper: "Nontheatrical Theaters: The Panama-Pacific International Exposition (1915)", presented at SCMS, March 2012.
12. "Metro Day at the Frisco Convention," *Moving Picture World* 25, no. 31 (July 1915), 843.
13. *New York State at the Panama-Pacific International Exposition*, San Francisco, California, 1915 (Albany, 1915), 11.
14. Ibid., 12.
15. Ibid., 14.
16. Todd, *The Story of the Exposition*, III, 341.
17. *New York City's Exhibit at the Panama-Pacific International Exposition. San Francisco, 1915. Report of the Chairman of the Sub-Committee in Charge* (April 1916), 5, 23.
18. *New York State at the Panama-Pacific International Exposition*, 15–16.
19. "A New Bureau of Public Health Education", *Weekly Bulletin of the Department of Health, City of New York*, III, no. 22 (6 June 1914): 179.
20. "Moving Picture Activities," *Weekly Bulletin of the Department of Health, City of New York*, IV, no. 6 (6 February 1915): 50; Florence Margolies, "Promoting Public Health", *Moving Picture World* 22, no. 10 (5 December 1914), 1359.
21. *New York City's Exhibit at the Panama-Pacific International Exposition*, 28–29.
22. Annual Report of the Department of Health of The City of New York for the Calender Year 1915 (New York City, 1916), 108.
23. Todd, *The Story of the Exposition*, IV, 61.
24. Letter signed by Alvin E. Pope, RF, RG 5, Series 1:2, Box 19, Folder 294.
25. Models of eggs, embryos, and mature hookworms were made by Dr B. E. Dahlgren. 'Information for International Jury. Special Questionnaire for Scientific, Educational and Humanitarian Exhibits', Rockefeller Foundation, RG 5, series 1:2, Box 19, Folder 300.
26. Letter to Dr Ernest C. Meyer, International Health Commission, signed by Alvin E. Pope on June 25, 1915. RF, RG 5, Series 1:2, Box 19, Folder 294.
27. *Official Swedish Catalogue: Panama-Pacific International Exposition, San Francisco 1915* (Stockholm, 1915), 141.
28. Ibid., 144.
29. Anne Bachmann, "Atlantic crossings: Exhibiting Scandinavian–American relations in scale models

and moving pictures during the mid-1910s", *Early Popular Visual Culture* 10, no 4 (2012). See also Ann-Kristin Wallengren, *Välkommen hem Mr Swanson* (Lund: Nordic Academic Press, 2013).

30. *Svensk-amerikanska utställningskommittens och Svensk-amerikanska kvinnokommittens i San Francisco slutrapport öfver insamlingsarbetet för Sveriges och svensk-amerikanernas deltagande i den internationella Panama-Pacific utställningen i San Francisco, U.S.A., 1915*: (San Francisco: Svensk-am. utställningskommittén, 1916), 33.

31. K.L., "Svenska filmer på San Francisco utställningen. Biografförevisningar i svenska utställningsbyggnaden," *Filmbladet* 1, no. 1 (15 January 1915), 2–3.

32. Unsigned, "En antiemigrationsfilm," *Filmbladet* 1, no. 3A (15 February 1915), 39–40.

33. Rydell, 1–8.

34. Neil Harris, *Humbug: The Art of P.T. Barnum* (Chicago: University of Chicago Press, 1981)

35. Todd, *The Story of the Exposition*, IV, 37.

36. Ibid.

37. Moore, Curran and Winchell, *Panama-Pacific International Exposition 1915*, 3.

19

Lyrical Education: Music and Colour in Early Non-fiction Film

Jennifer Peterson

Recent research on colour and music in early film has begun to broaden our sense of how audiences experienced cinema in the single-reel era, paying more attention to cinema's intermedial and performative contexts.[1] Much of my own research has focused on early non-fiction – particularly scenic films – which is another formerly marginalised topic of cinema scholarship.[2] This paper, which represents the beginning of a new research project, briefly considers the relationship between music and colour in early non-fiction films, exploring how and why so-called 'educational' cinema contained a lyrical imperative in the early 1910s. The educational principles of the Progressive Era (that period in the United States from the 1890s to the 1920s that witnessed social and political reform) centered for the most part on expanding access to education for the middle and working classes. Questions of emotion, lyricism, and expressiveness would seem to be removed from such concerns as democratisation. And yet non-fiction films, which were promoted as 'educational' cinema in the early 1910s, were some of the most frequently coloured subjects in early cinema, and of course these films were, like most silent-era cinema, accompanied by live music. I would like to propose that educational films from this period embody a kind of contradictory 'educational lyricism', especially when considered in the context of colour and music.

There are at least four large issues at play with this concept of 'educational lyricism': colour, music, education and aesthetics. Here I will outline some of the key questions related to these issues and indicate where research into these topics might lead us. First, the question of colour. Recent research on specific colour processes, and the difficult aspect of colour's archival preservation, has made important strides in establishing just how colourful early cinema was. But colour's larger social and cultural meanings in the cinema of this period have proved more difficult to pin down. David Batchelor has influentially argued that colour has been consistently denigrated in Western culture. As he puts it,

19 Lyrical Education: Music and Colour in Early Non-fiction Film

colour tends to be associated with so-called foreign bodies, 'usually the feminine, the oriental, the primitive, the infantile, the vulgar, the queer or the pathological'.[3] Batchelor's argument is persuasive, and certainly correct, but it lacks historical and cultural specificity.

Colour played a particularly important role in early non-fiction film genres such as travelogues and nature films, which were commonplace film genres in the 1900s and 1910s. A majority of educational films produced in the single-reel era were released with applied colour (using either tinting, toning, or stencil techniques); in the case of the additive colour systems such as Kinemacolour, about seventy percent of the titles released were non-fiction subjects. Eirik Frisvold Hanssen argues that the 1910s and 20s were, 'an era of indeterminacy and hesitation regarding the possible functions of colour', in cinema.[4] Taking a slightly different line, Joshua Yumibe argues that the brightly coloured fairy and trick films of the early 1900s gave way to a more subdued colour design by about 1909. During the transitional era, Yumibe explains, colour, while, 'still designed to work sensually, offered greater subtlety to enhance the story … provid[ing] a restrained and artistic resonance … that increased narrative intelligibility'.[5] One can connect this subduing of colour to the larger imperative of social and cultural 'uplift' that characterises the era. In fact, the flowering of educational genres in the early 1910s coincides with this muting of colour stylistics.

As my research has shown, genres such as travelogues, nature films, science films, topical news films, historical films, and the like were heavily promoted for a few years in the early 1910s, when some in the film industry thought that these genres held solid commercial potential. For the most part, advertisements and press coverage of these early educational films celebrated colour's 'naturalistic' aspects, pointing out that such films featured 'natural' or 'living' colours. But when one examines the actual films rather than their promotional materials, and especially when one considers the films in the context of their exhibition, what was touted as 'natural' often appears rather more lyrical or even fantastical. In fact, I would argue that colour in 1910s educational films was at various times either lurid or naturalistic, depending on the film, and sometimes it could be both simultaneously.

As this image from the German film *Feeding the Snakes* (Komet-Film, 1911) illustrates, not all non-fiction films from the period were equally 'genteel' or 'uplifting'; the blue-green tinting of this film arguably adds to its sensationalism (see Figure 1).[6] We might also wonder why these colours, and not red or yellow or pink tinting? Such questions about the meaning of colour tinting have proven

Figure 1: This extant print of *Feeding the Snakes* (Comet-Film, 1911) is tinted blue-green. [Image courtesy of the EYE Film Institute Netherlands.]

difficult to answer, given that such colours often lacked a stable meaning. In contrast, Pathé's renowned stencil-coloured non-fiction films defined a particular 'look' for educational cinema in the 1910s, as in the film *Burgos* from 1918.[7] The crisp match between stencil colouring and photographic image in this film is characteristic of Pathé's stenciling technique, which we can associate with the 'subdued' trend that Yumibe identifies in coloured fiction films from this era.

But consider also *The Squirrel* from 1913, a film whose colour design is less clear.[8] This is a messier film in many ways, moreover the print is faded, so the colours are somewhat difficult to make out. In the film's opening close-up of a squirrel eating a nut, what appears to be pink and yellow stencil colouring adds to the sensuality of the image, and at the same time it confers graphic legibility, setting the squirrel off from his shadowy background. I find it important that colour here can simultaneously add sensuality *and* legibility, for these are precisely the contradictory terms I intend to convey with the concept 'lyrical education'. This tension is even more apparent when one watches the actual film: the inter-titles stating 'the fore paws of the squirrel serve as hands' (tinted red) also add legibility, although only on the most basic level – the viewer might already have noticed that the squirrel is using his forepaws as hands, for example. In fact, many intertitles in educational films are redundant, simply repeating in linguistic form what we can already see in the image. Colour, however, sometimes functions in tandem with the image, as in much stencil colouring, and sometimes in counterpoint to the image, as in much colour tinting.

In addition, colour in *The Squirrel* is applied imprecisely; this is easier to see in a long shot with green, pink, and yellow colouring, bleeding beyond the edges of the areas it seems intended to demarcate. This bleeding-over-the-edges quality (which is most pronounced in the hand-painted films of very early cinema) links colour in early cinema directly to painting. In the film's long shots, in fact, the colour does not really add much to what is really a graphically muddy image. What I particularly enjoy about this film, in fact, is its shabbiness: it was clearly staged in a small terrarium, which is quite apparent in moving images but less so in still images. This staged quality is interesting in terms of the history of nature films, which were already being shot on location by Oliver Pike by this time, though it's not so nice for the squirrel, who flits around anxiously throughout the film, until he is finally caged, and spins around frantically in the last shot.

Next, to the question of music. While there is a rich body of theoretical writing on film sound, stretching back to Sergei Eisenstein, there has been little research done on the kinds of music used to accompany educational and non-fiction films in the early period. Although evidence is limited about the musical accompaniment for early non-fiction films, some traces do remain. These accounts, though prescriptive rather than descriptive, indicate that waltzes were encouraged as the default musical genre to accompany non-fiction films through the 1910s. In his regular column for *Film Index*, for example, Clyde Martin wrote in 1910, 'For industrial pictures such as the Selig release of August 1st, "Shrimps," the Urban-Eclipse release of August 24th, "Shipbuilding of Toulon, France," or the Pathé release of September 5th, "Zoological Gardens in Antwerp," a good waltz is the best, and in fact the only music that can be used'.[9] Listening to a waltz while watching a film about the shrimp industry, as Martin suggests, or the squirrel, to take our recent example, might seem incongruous, but this incongruity was in fact a defining feature of non-fiction films when they are considered in the context of exhibition. When one considers the added expressivity of colour, non-fiction films such as this one about the squirrel become a multi-media sensorial feast, rather than a sober presentation of factual information.

The waltz did not always dominate educational film screenings: by the early 1920s when film music guidebooks began to appear, musicians were encouraged to abandon the waltz in favour of a range of other material. Erno Rapée wrote a critique of the waltz in his *Encyclopedia of Music for Pictures* in 1925, explaining why they were poor accompaniments for scenic films: 'Wherein do [the emotions of the waltz] fit the grandeur of nature, the strength of towering mountains or the peaceful content of sylvan glades?'[10] Rapée recommended giving up the waltz in favour of, among other things, Dvořák's 'New World' symphony. In a similar vein, George W. Beynon in his 1921 book *Musical Presentation of Motion Pictures* called scenics 'musical landscape portraits', arguing, 'The Scenic always provides opportunity for some real music. This is the one chance in the program given to the musician to show what he can do as a virtuoso… Panoramas are very much alike on the screen, and music alone can lend the required atmosphere as a distinguishing mark'.[11] This connection between music and landscape is important, as I shall explain momentarily.

Any relationship between colour and music in these films would have been unforeseen by the film's producers, of course, given that the live musical accompaniment changed every time these films were shown, and this contingency opens up further questions about the performative nature of early cinema. Typically released on a split reel, often with a comedy, these non-fiction films' place in the variety film programme was an integral part of their experiential dynamic. The aforementioned *Shrimps* film, for example, was released on a split reel with a comedy called *Her First Long Dress*. This means that the waltz, if one were played, would likely have shifted to some other kind of music once the comedy began (marches and popular song choruses were often recommended for comedies), further emphasising the discordant quality of these films.

The third issue at play here is the question of the status of educational cinema in this period. As new scholarship has been working to establish, beginning around 1910 educational cinema was an important part of the early film industry's drive to legitimate itself as a respectable entertainment form for the middle classes. My argument about educational cinema has tended to focus on its excessive, unpredictable qualities, considering the way audiences might have interpreted these films in unforeseen ways, or even accounting for the fact that many audience members may have simply found non-fiction boring. I have never been convinced by the argument, most strongly put forth by Charles Musser, that scenic films were merely 'genteel' or even reactionary. Emphasising the lyrical dimension of non-fiction film is another way to address how these films exceed our attempts to pigeonhole them as culturally regressive.

Lastly, the question of aesthetics looms large as a kind of umbrella category encompassing the previous three issues of colour, music, and education. Aesthetic issues, not as an abstract formal concern but in terms of their connection to social and cultural practices, are in fact what primarily motivate my interest in this topic of colour. According to the tradition of synaesthesia (which Yumibe analyses in *Moving Color*), musical tones have long been thought to inspire visions of colour in some people. This has led to a host of overlapping practices involving music and colour as found in colour organs, coloured light shows, abstract painting and filmmaking and so forth.[12] The occult relationship between music and colour is a fascinating avenue of research, but to conclude, I want to follow a different line of thinking, drawing from Eisenstein, who flatly rejected any direct correspondence between musical tones and specific colours. He wrote, 'A meadow is green. The sea is green. And it is not the colour but the *content* of the one or the other that determines the theme music, not some mystical unity between the sound of the colour and the musical tone of the colour green …'.[13] As one might expect, Eisenstein was more interested in colour's potential to dialectically *clash* with other elements of a film. He argued that colour in film was important enough to be placed on an equal footing with elements of montage.

For Eisenstein, in fact, colour was not necessarily a lyrical element; rather, for him, representations of landscapes were the visual correlative to music. In his book *Nonindifferent Nature,* Eisenstein mounted an elaborate argument about landscape in cinema in which he claimed that, 'landscape lies closest to music', in its, 'pure emotionality', and that music and landscape both function to, 'emotionally express what is inexpressible by other means'.[14] I would add to this that the relationship of music to landscape is not metaphorical – it is not that one stands for the other – but additive – they both function *at the same time* to create an emotional tone. If you push this thought, in fact, scenic films begin to appear as a surprising precursor to the cinematic experiments in visual music that emerged in the 1920s by filmmakers such as Oskar Fischinger and others. In conclusion, I want to suggest that it was the open-endedness of colour that freed non-fiction film from being merely a transmitter of 'genteel' values, and instead elevated the seemingly prosaic educational film into the arena of poetics.

Notes

1. On colour in early cinema see Joshua Yumibe, *Moving Color: Early Film, Mass Culture, Modernism* (New Brunswick, NJ: Rutgers University Press, 2012); and Eirik Frisvold Hanssen, "Early Discourses on Colour and Cinema: Origins, Functions, Meanings" (PhD Diss., Stockholm University, 2006). On sound in early cinema see Richard Abel and Rick Altman (eds), *The Sounds of Early Cinema* (Bloomington, IN: Indiana University Press, 2001); and Rick Altman, *Silent Film Sound* (New York: Columbia University Press, 2004).
2. See Jennifer Lynn Peterson, *Education in the School of Dreams: Travelogues and Early Nonfiction Film* (Durham, NC: Duke University Press, 2013).

3. David Batchelor, *Chromophobia* (London: Reaktion Books, 2000), 64.
4. Eirik Frisvold Hanssen, "Symptoms of Desire: Colour, Costume, and Commodities in Fashion Newsreels of the 1910s and 1920s", *Film History* 21, no. 2 (2009), 107.
5. Yumibe, *Moving Color*, 123.
6. *Feeding the Snakes* (Komet-Film, 1911) is in the collection of the EYE Film Institute, Netherlands.
7. *Burgos* (Pathé, 1918) is available on the DVD *Exotic Europe: Journeys into Early Cinema*, co-released in 2000 by the Bundesarchiv-Filmarchiv Berlin; the Nederlands Filmmuseum, Amsterdam; and the Cinema Museum, London.
8. *The Squirrel* (Pathé, 1913) is in the collection of the British Film Institute National Archive, London.
9. Clyde Martin, "Playing the Pictures", *Film Index*, 19 November 1910, 27.
10. Erno Rapée, *Encyclopaedia of Music for Pictures* (New York: Belwin, 1925), 90.
11. George W. Beynon, *Musical Presentation of Motion Pictures* (New York: G. Schirmer, 1921), 92–93.
12. See Kevin T. Dann, *Bright Colours Falsely Seen: Synaesthesia and the Search for Transcendental Knowledge* (New Haven: Yale University Press, 1998).
13. Sergei Eisenstein, "On Colour", in Angela Dalle Vacche and Brian Price (eds), *Color: The Film Reader* (London: Routledge, 2006), 107.
14. Sergei Eisenstein, *Nonindifferent Nature*, trans. Herbert Marshall (Cambridge: Cambridge University Press, 1987), 217.

20

'Offensive and Riotous Behaviour'? Performing the Role of an Audience in Irish Cinema of the mid-1910s

Denis Condon

In September 1915, Frederick Arthur Sparling, proprietor of the Bohemian Picture Theatre, Dublin, prosecuted William Larkin on a charge of offensive and riotous behaviour for protesting in the auditorium during a screening of Life Photo Film's *A Modern Magdalen* (United States, 1915). The protest was part of an ongoing campaign by the Catholic church-based vigilance committees – led by the Dublin Vigilance Committee (DVC) – against certain kinds of imported popular culture, initially targeting newspapers, magazines and books and moving on by 1915 to theatrical shows and films.[1] Larkin played a leading role in the confrontational elements of the campaign, gaining notoriety among theatre and cinema owners as he successfully drew press attention to the DVC's activities.

Newspaper accounts of this case stand out in early Irish cinema history as providing the most extensive evidence of audience behaviour, but they also pose methodological questions. These include what the most appropriate way is to discuss Larkin's protest, which was not 'normal' behaviour but a kind of spectacular performance – honed and rehearsed – whose rhetorical intent was to suggest that he spoke for a silent majority too timid to voice their own interpretation of unacceptable images. Accounts of this case suggest that Larkin and the DVC rejected the attentive passivity apparently demanded of cinema audiences by such factors as the feature film's growing dominance on the cinema programme in order to provide a space for performances of a Catholic Irishness they thought inadequately – or sometimes insultingly – portrayed on screen. However, despite tacit – and even explicitly – judicial approval of previous protests, this case did not end altogether successfully for Larkin. Courtroom appearances by cinema employees and audience members not affiliated with the DVC offer rare glimpses of ordinary cinemagoers' responses not only to images

193

on the screen but also to the behaviour of organisations who claimed to speak for them.

The few surviving archival traces of William Larkin give little indication of why he became involved with a conservative Catholic movement in an Ireland in which the name Larkin was synonymous with labour protest. The surname Larkin is likely – particularly in the wake of the 2013 centenary commemoration of labour struggles at the time of Dublin Lockout of 1913 – to alert readers familiar with Irish history to the very different forms of protests organized by Jim Larkin – apparently no relation – militant labour leader and founder of the Irish Transport and General Workers' Union. William Larkin – thirty-three in 1915 – came from a working-class family – his father had been a wine porter – and he lived with his elderly parents and his twin brother Francis – who frequently joined William's protests – in Sherrard Avenue, a residential street of small houses north of the city centre.[2] Although his place of work is unclear, he was a clerk, and this shift in class status may have prompted his involvement with a church organisation. Certainly, his willingness to breach the bounds of respectable behaviour made him valuable to more securely middle-class and ecclesiastical members of the DVC, for whom such behaviour would have been unacceptable.

Given their shared interest in an active audience, it seems less incongruous that the *Irish Times*, one of Ireland's main daily newspapers, should draw comparisons between the DVC and Futurist Filippo Tommaso Marinetti. Writing in May 1913, the *Times*'s editorial writer commented that the manifesto the paper had recently received from the DVC

> reminds us of the proclamations which, from time to time, reach this office from Signor Marinetti, the leader of that amiable band of anarchists, the Futurists. We hasten to say that the resemblance is one of manner, not of matter. The literary artist who drafted the Committee's address has the same seriousness of purpose, the same passionate utterance, the same "intoxication in the exuberance of his own verbosity".[3]

The reasons the *Irish Times* drew these comparisons are worth exploring, but such a comparison is likely to remind early cinema scholars of the most famous essay in the field, Tom Gunning's 'The Cinema of Attractions' and of Wanda Strauven's recent re-examination of it in relation to Marinetti's discussion of variety theatre and cinema.[4] Gunning observes that Marinetti's 1913 manifesto on 'The Variety Theatre'

> not only praised its aesthetics of astonishment and stimulation, but particularly its creation of a new spectator who contrasts with the "static", "stupid voyeur" of

traditional theatre. The spectator at the variety theatre feels directly addressed by the spectacle and joins in, singing along, heckling the comedians.[5]

As a result of this constantly changing stimulation, the variety spectator could not become enthralled by the entertainment. The variety spectator became the model for the spectator of Futurist theatre, whom Marinetti promised to foster by introducing agitation into the auditorium by various means.[6] Ironically, it was precisely in the mid-1910s, when Marinetti was co-authoring 'The Futurist Cinema' (1916), that the 'trickality' of early cinema he valued was giving way to the theatricality and narrativity of Italian and world cinema.[7]

The *Irish Times*'s comparison of the DVC and the Futurists was made before the publication of 'The Variety Theatre' in September 1913, and while the item made light of the DVC, its intentions went beyond humour to express the irritation of at least certain elements of the press with the movement. Nor was the comparison too obscure for contemporary readers. The *Times* had kept its readers informed about Futurism in a series of editorial items and short articles on the movement since 1909, many of them in response to the manifestos that Marinetti sent to it.[8] However, the phrase 'amiable anarchist' was an oxymoron at the time, and the general opinion of anarchy as dangerous and destructive was epitomized by the sensational press reports and films of the Sidney Street Siege of London-based Latvian anarchists in January 1911. Although Marinetti's anarchism might be rendered amiable by his geographical remoteness and colourful iconoclasm operating wholly in the cultural realm, the same could not be said about the DVC by a Dublin-based newspaper.

The DVC was part of a Catholic Church-based movement that began in the West-coast city of Limerick in early October 1911. Its founding by a priest attached to the Archconfraternity of the Holy Family was widely covered in the press, particularly during an initial campaign against the delivery to the city's newsagents of English Sunday newspapers, which contained the details of divorce trials that the vigilance committee thought inappropriate for Catholics whose church opposed divorce.[9] As the movement spread – and it did so like wildfire – its aims were initially expressed principally as a campaign against 'evil' literature of this kind. Committees were quickly formed elsewhere in the country. The DVC was founded on the initiative of members of the Catholic Young Men's Society in early November 1911 and by the end of the month had eighteen constituent parochial committees.[10] What the committees deemed evil, however, remained vague and shifting, and their campaigns caused irritation in the press, particular such titles as the *Times* whose readership was largely Protestant and opposed to nationalism. Such irritation increased from 1913 on,

Figure 1: "A Review of the Audience", *Leader* (17 July 1915): 541.

as vigilance tactics became more confrontational. The DVC began picketing newsagents in early 1913 with the expressed aim of informing people attempting to buy certain newspapers of the unsuitability of their content but in fact – as was established later in court – physically obstructing and intimidating people. In the most widely publicised case, the Larkin brothers were arrested for obstruction outside a newsagent and fined £1 each.[11]

The Catholic and nationalist sections of the press were generally supportive of the increasing militancy of the DVC's campaign. Although not representative of the mainstream nationalist press, the cultural nationalist journal The *Leader* – whose editor and chief polemicist, D. P. Moran, advocated an 'Irish Ireland' that should be 'de-Anglicized' to become fully Catholic and Gaelic in its language and culture – is of particular interest because it expressed its support not only in words but also in some of the few images of popular audiences of the period. Beginning its first issue in September 1900 with a review of a show at Dublin's Lyric Music Hall, the *Leader* had condemned Irish variety theatres not merely because they were 'regular night-schools for Anglicisation' but

Figure 2: "Limerick to the Rescue", *Leader* (25 September 1915): 153.

because the type of entertainment that they brought to Ireland was a degenerate form of what was available in London and as a result was especially morally pernicious.[12] The reason that Dublin had become a dumping ground for such a low form, Moran contended, was that the Irish press praised what it should actually condemn. He excoriated unionist newspapers – principally the *Times* and *Dublin Evening Mail* – but reserved particular vitriol for the Catholic nationalist press – the *Freeman's Journal* and its *Evening Telegraph*, and the *Irish Independent* and its *Evening Herald*. In a cartoon that appeared in the *Leader* in July 1915, the *Dublin Evening Mail* and *the Freeman's Journal* are seen watching from the privileged vantage point of theatrical boxes a music hall production they have advertised and recommended (Figure 1). However, Moran's real target was the Irish popular audience, which the *Leader* – in very similar terms to Marinetti's condemnation of the bourgeois theatrical audience – repeatedly chastised for being too passive and in need of rousing, but here condemned for the groups among them who craved and supported degenerate music hall shows. A scathing description of the audience in verse below the cartoon described the 'dirty degenerates' into whose faces readers looked.[13]

In another cartoon published just over two months later, the *Leader* provided the reverse angle on this image (Figure 2). It was reversed not only in viewing the stage from the auditorium but also in offering a complete change in the representation of the popular audience. Unlike the first cartoon, which depicted a 'typical' degenerate audience, this image and its accompanying verse portrayed and praised the actual members of the audience of Limerick's Rink Palace, who on 7 September 1915, chased the artistes performing the variety revue *Everything in the Gardens* from the stage.[14] The Rink Palace was part of the circuit operated by Ireland's best known film exhibitor, James T. Jameson, who ran occasional weeks of pure variety revue but mostly offered programmes of pictures accompanied by one variety act. With over ten-years' experience of Irish show business, Jameson should have known his audience well enough to avoid such a confrontation, but it appears that he fell afoul of what the *Limerick Leader* termed 'Vigilance Revived'.[15] Indeed, while the image and verse in Moran's paper distinguished the 'raiders' from other members of the audience who did not take part in the protest, the *Limerick Leader* was more explicit in identifying these raiders as 'Arch-Confraternity men [who] formed themselves into an informal Vigilance Committee, stormed the Rink and requested the audience to leave quietly'.[16]

The timing of the raid on the Rink Palace suggests that the protesters were answering the call made by the leaders of the vigilance movement to intensify their campaign against variety theatres and cinemas. Addressing the movement's annual mass meeting at Dublin's Mansion House on 5 September 1915, two days before the Limerick incident, the national movement's defacto head Father Paul announced a shift in the committees' focus from literature to films. 'Pestilent literature is bad enough', he argued, 'but its dreadful havoc is outdistanced by the pernicious effects of the filthy picture screen'.[17] Justifying this on the basis that the cinemas were most popular with impressionable youths, Paul urged a plan of action on his hearers:

> We appeal to you not to frequent any amusement Hall that will not maintain a high standard of morality, and should anything improper appear on the stage or picture screen urge upon you to mark your disproval by a strong protest, and we feel that in relying upon your co-operation we shall not be disappointed.[18]

While his words were being greeted with loud applause by those in the Mansion House, the twenty thousand who could not get in were being addressed outside by William Larkin, whom the *Irish Catholic* described in its report of the events as 'the hero of so many prosecutions for making vigorous public protests that drew on him the attention of the law'.[19] Larkin also spoke to his hearers about strong protest, which he said they could perform with relative impunity because 'in consequence of cases brought against him it had been laid down by the magistrates that everyone present at a theatre, music hall, or cinema show had a legal right to manifest publicly in due measure by hissing or other protest, their disapprobation of any performance they considered objectionable'.[20]

Perhaps in his turn taking inspiration from the raid on the Rink Palace, Larkin would just a week later again test the laxity of Dublin magistrates. When he and Francis had been arrested for what appears to have been their first theatre protest at the Gaiety Theatre during a live-theatre production of the French farce *Who's the Lady?* in March 1914, the magistrate had dismissed the case and praised them for performing a public service.[21] This set the pattern for the cinema protests that followed and made cinema owners reluctant to take a case. In some cases William alone and in others both Larkin brothers would also face a magistrate for protests at the Phibsboro Picture House in June 1914 during Kinografen's film *In the Shadow of a Throne* (*I Tronens Skygge*; Denmark, 1914) and at the Pillar Picture House in February 1917 for interrupting a screenings of Fox's *The Soul of New York* (United States, 1916).[22] As well as these incidents, there were several others at which they were not arrested and the papers merely reported a disturbance, notably another protest at the Bohemian in July 1915 during a screening of Universal's *Neptune's Daughter* (United States, 1914).[23] Even in the cases where they were arrested and appeared in court, however, they merely received nominal fines, suggesting tacit approval by the magistrates concerned.

The fact that the Larkin brothers protested repeatedly at cinemas located out of the city centre – particularly in Phibsboro, at the northern edge of the city – indicates how the advent of cinema changed not only where people went for entertainment but also where protests could take place. Between 1911 and 1915, Dublin city (population: 304,802) experienced a boom in cinema construction. Many of the twenty-seven cinema licences that Dublin Corporation issued per year by 1915 were for venues located within the business core of the city, which was the customary location of theatres and other kinds of professional entertainment. However, cinemas were also located in residential areas, where professional entertainment had never been available on a regular basis before. Phibsboro's entertainment provision was radically altered when just a few weeks apart at the end of May and beginning of June 1914, two substantial cinemas, the Phibsboro Picture House and the Bohemian Picture Theatre, opened. Located about fifteen minutes walk from Sherrard Avenue, these were William Larkin's closest cinemas, offering him a choice of local venues at which to protest.

At about ten o'clock on the evening of Tuesday, 14 September 1915, he shouted repeatedly during *A Modern Magdalen* at the Bohemian, causing a large number of people to leave the cinema. Daisy Sandes, a sixteen-year-old girl sitting near him, testified in court that she earlier heard him hissing during the film's so-called 'madcap scene', in which the female protagonist Katinka danced on a table in a nightclub – before he shouted: 'This is a picture that our "Freeman's Journal" would not object to' – a reference to Ireland's largest daily newspaper's positive review – and 'It is damned near time that we called for an Irish Board of Censors'.[24] His shouts caused some girls in the audience to scream, and a general panic ensued, with many people rushing to leave the cinema. The manager, Ernest Mathewson, ordered Larkin to leave, escorting him to the door. However, Larkin then held what owner Frederick Arthur Sparling – who was also there that night – described as a kind of public meeting.[25] Larkin stood at the top of the steps leading from the street up to the box office and addressed the departing patrons on the need for film censorship. At this point, Sparling had Larkin arrested on the grounds that he had disturbed the peace. After appearances in court on 15 and 22 September the charges against him were dismissed to applause from Larkin's DVC supporters in court because disturbing the peace was not an indictable offense in an Irish theatre or cinema.[26] Determined to put a stop to Larkin's protests, Sparling prosecuted him again, this time for offensive and riotous behaviour.

Up to this point, Larkin's performance had had its intended effect. He had made his protest, had been arrested – thereby receiving the additional publicity that came with the court case – and the charges had been dismissed. However, the second prosecution was unprecedented and gave rise to some consequences Larkin had not foreseen. At this second trial, Larkin argued that his protest was legitimate because in the mad-cap scene, Katinka danced topless, a detail the prosecution and most of the witnesses disputed. The case was adjourned for a week while the magistrate viewed the film, and he concluded that it was not indecent or objectionable, imposing a fine and costs on Larkin. More interestingly, in order to prove the charge that Larkin had caused a panic, Sparling called cinema staff and audience members to testify, and Larkin's lawyers called the DVC members who had been present as defence witnesses. As a result, this is the only instance in which the views – or even the names – of ordinary members of an Irish audience were recorded. The court provided a forum for these ordinary audience members to confront the coercive behaviour of the DVC.

Like Larkin, however, these people have left very few archival traces beyond their names, addresses and professions. In all, fifteen people testified in court, including Larkin, Sparling and Mathewson. The DVC members, for the defence, were Richard Jones, chairman of the Richmond Asylum; Mrs. A Murphy of Capel Street; P.J. Walsh, a Phibsboro accountant; Philip Lavery, a justice of the peace from Armagh; and Peter Tierney, a china and glass merchant of Bolton Street. The cinema staff who testified were the operators William Jones and Scallan; advertising agent Robert Moss; and cashier Rachel Smith. Three 'unaffiliated' witnesses also spoke for the prosecution: Mrs. Evans of Grangegorman, civil servant Charles Millen and Daisy Sandes. They said similar things, perhaps best put by the youngest of them, Daisy Sandes, who worked at a retouching studio and lived with her working-class family in an artisan dwelling about ten minutes walk from the Bohemian. 'I was amazed', she commented, when asked about Larkin's behaviour. 'I did not see why anyone should object'.[27] Sandes' utter rejection of Larkin's arguments refutes the DVC's claim to speak for ordinary people too timid and accepting to speak for themselves. It seems also to mark a point at which she and other young working-class men and women were increasingly choosing a form of entertainment at which agitation in the auditorium was to be kept to a minimum.

Notes

1. For the importance of this case to the introduction of film censorship, see Kevin Rockett, *Irish Film Censorship: A Cultural Journey from Silent Cinema to Internet Pornography* (Dublin: Four Courts, 2004), 44–51.
2. http://www.census.nationalarchives.ie/ (accessed 27 August 2013).
3. "The Vigilance Committee", *Irish Times* (31 May 1913): 6.
4. Tom Gunning, "The Cinema of Attraction[s]: Early Film, Its Spectator and the Avant-Garde", and Wanda Strauven, "From 'Primitive Cinema' to 'Marvelous'", in Wanda Strauven (ed.), *The Cinema of Attractions Reloaded* (Amsterdam: Amsterdam University Press, 2006), 381–388 and 105–120.
5. Gunning, 385. Marinetti's manifestos, including "The Variety Theatre" are available in Lawrence Rainey, Christine Foggi and Laura Witman (eds), *Futurism: An Anthology* (New Haven: Yale University Press, 2009), 159–164.
6. Strauven, 115.
7. Strauven, 107–108.
8. [Editorial item], *Irish Times* (5 May 1909): 4; [Editorial item], *Irish Times* 24 August 1912): 6; "Revolution in Art", *Irish Times* (24 November 1913): 6. The *Times* would continue to report on Marinetti: "Futurism", *Irish Times* (3 December 1915): 4; "Futurism", *Irish Times* (25 March 1916): 4.
9. See for example, "English Sunday Press", *Irish Independent* (24 October 1911): 7; "English Sunday Newspapers", *Nenagh Guardian* (28 October 1911): 3.
10. "Dublin to Take Action", *Irish Independent* (2 November 1911): 7; "Obnoxious Literature: Suggested Action in Dublin", *Irish Times* (2 November 1911): 7; "Dublin Vigilance Committee", *Irish Times* (28 November 1911): 11.
11. "Evil Literature Crusade: Dublin Obstruction Charge", *Irish Independent* (4 February 1913): 5

"Dublin Vigilance Committee: Two Members Fined for Obstruction", *Irish Times* (8 February 1913): 1.
12. *Leader* (1 September 1900): 2–4.
13. "A Review of the Audience", *Leader* (17 July 1915): 541.
14. "Limerick to the Rescue", *Leader* (25 September 1915): 158.
15. "Vigilance Revived: Rink Palace Stormed", *Limerick Leader* (8 September 1915): 3.
16. Ibid.
17. "Fighting a Plague: Vigilance Committee's Crusade: Annual Procession and Meeting", *Irish Catholic* (11 September 1915): 2.
18. Ibid.
19. Ibid.
20. Ibid.
21. "'Who's the Lady?' Scene in the Gaiety Theatre", *Irish Times* (4 March 1914): 8.
22. "Row in Picture House: Ink Thrown at Picture", *Evening Telegraph* (5 June 1914): 5; "City Cinema: Exciting Episode", *Evening Telegraph* (22 February 1917): 1.
23. "Annette Kellerman at the Bohemian", *Freeman's Journal* (10 July 1915): 7.
24. All Dublin's newspapers covered the case, including: "Scene in Dublin Picture Theatre: Question as to the Morality of the Film", *Evening Herald* (11 October 1915): 5.
25. "Scene in a City Cinema: 'An Irish Board of Censors'", *Dublin Evening Mail* (11 October 1915): 4.
26. "Scene in a City Cinema: 'Irish Censor Board Wanted'", *Dublin Evening Mail* (22 September 1915): 5.
27. "Scene in Dublin Picture Theatre: Question as to the Morality of the Film", *Evening Herald* (11 October 1915): 5.

21

Tango Mad and Affected by Cinematographitis: Rhythmic 'Contagions' Between Screens and Audiences in the 1910s

Kristina Köhler

'People are crazy about the moving pictures and the tango', lamented Shaller Matthews, dean of the University of Chicago, in 1914.[1] Likening cinema to the 'new terpsichorean fad', the academic placed the medium's 'maddening' effect in relation to that of another mass-cultural phenomenon: In the early 1910s, the tango conquered dance floors throughout Europe, the United States, and Russia, spreading so rapidly that the diagnosis of 'tango mania' or 'tangoitis' became a popular dictum – and a frequent subject of parody.[2] In 1914, a British journalist noted – not without the obligatory ironic undertone: 'The world revolves no longer. It sways rhythmically to the Tango. The sun sets on the Tango. From China to Peru, or, rather, from the Argentine to Paris, it is the same story: [...] Tangoism is the ruling spirit of the day and the night everywhere'.[3]

While journalists commented on the tango phenomenon with delectation, and while devotees rushed to the dance halls *en masse* to learn and perform the new steps, representatives of public institutions, clergy, and social reformers saw the tango and other 'modern dances' as threats to social mores and public order. Their objections were directed not only against the unfamiliar new dance movements – discredited as 'nervous degeneracy'[4] – but also against their social sites, the dance halls doomed as 'brilliant entrance[s] to hell itself',[5] alluring their patrons with alcoholic drinks and the promise of body contact. It was above all the 'audaciously' physical dimension of the dance amusements, together with their mobilizing effect upon the masses' bodies – and especially those of a hitherto 'tamed' middle-class – that called guardians of public morals into action. Against the backdrop of these animated debates, the 'tango question' advanced to an emblematic and prototypical site of negotiation for the interrelations between movement, perception, and corporeality – interrelations that also concerned a number of other mass phenomena in the early twentieth century, not least the cinema. So it comes as no surprise that tango analogies also permeated the contemporary discourses on film. A German journalist commented in 1914: 'The cinematograph and the *Kientopp* have demonstrated how much we are subject to mass suggestion, just as is the case with the tango'.[6]

'Tango mania,' however, not only figures as a *negative* reference in the discourses on cinema in the 1910s, but also inscribes itself on various levels and in a far more ambivalent way into the cinema culture of that decade. I argue that if the dance crazes serve as a prominent theme in countless films produced between 1912 and 1914, they also supplied a cultural setting, perceptual pattern, and conceptual framework that influenced how films were designed, performed and experienced in that era. 'Tango mania' and its underlying rationale of an immediate movement contagion, I contend, provided a powerful image to conceptualize the new medium, and especially its kinetic and corporeal effects on spectators. Focusing on movement transmissions between screen and audience, I will show how the concept of film as an enthralling kinetic force shapes filmmaking and exhibition practices of the early 1910s, generating textual strategies and performative *dispositifs* that address, stimulate and reflect forms of a mobilized film spectatorship modelled upon the experience of social dancing.[7] With this emphasis on perceptual and experiential dimensions, my argument follows the studies of Raymond Fielding, Tom Gunning, Lauren Rabinovitz and others who have argued that early moving picture shows were not only embedded in the attraction culture of fairgrounds and amusement parks, but – more structurally – emerged from and responded to a similar fascination with speed, kineticism and movement as corporeal, kinaesthetic pleasure.[8] I claim that the same could be argued for social dancing, which was likewise part of this culture of sensorial excitement, and which relied on similar forms of corporeal and physiological stimulation. To illustrate my argument, I will discuss two film practices that became especially popular under the influence of 1910s dance crazes: 1) dance instruction films and 2) film comedies picking up on the motif and kinetic principle of 'contagious' dances.

'I can't stop doin' it': 'Tango mania' and the concept of movement contagion

The recurrent invocation of the 'tango craze', 'tango mania' or 'tangoitis', with their medico-pathological metaphors, constitutes the starting point of my analysis. Equally employed by dance supporters and opponents, these terms conceive of dancing as a 'contagious' movement transmitted almost automatically from one body to another. To understand the phenomenon of 'tango mania', it is important to note how little this conception of an enthralling dance movement has to do with the actual choreographic and gestural patterns of the tango – a dance that, as Yuri Tsivian has pointed out, is not so much based on impulse, disinhibition and kinetic excess, but characterized instead by slow, controlled and pausing movements.[9] Rather than describing the specific qualities of the dance itself, 'tango mania' illustrated the dance's massive popularity and rapid propagation, which were significantly supported by early-twentieth-century media networks. Yet, more than just a sudden 'media effect', the 'tango fever' had also been prepared by a broader international circulation of new social dances starting with ragtime dances in the 1890s (such as the Cakewalk or the One-step) and the so-called 'Animal Dances' (most famously, the Turkey Trot, the Bunny Hug, and the Grizzly Bear) by 1910. When the tango craze was triggered, social dancing already constituted an established cultural practice and mass entertainment relying on a fully developed infrastructure anchored in early-twentieth-century amusement and leisure cultures. Finally, the rather curious association of the tango with the concept of a 'contagious' movement drew on a number of established cultural narratives and concepts: Besides the references to the St. Vitus dancing pathology that had occurred during the Middle Ages,[10] the idea of dance as a 'contagious' phenomenon was also supported and promoted by a discursive and scientific context around 1900 in which new conceptions of movement as energy (from Marey's movement studies to Bergson's concept of the *élan vital*) emerged.[11] As Rae Beth Gordon has shown, the idea of early cinema as 'contagious' movement notably echoed turn-of-the-century psychiatric and physiological theories interrogating phenomena such as psychological automatism and unconscious imitation.[12] Like these medical discourses, the trope of 'tango mania' relies on a conceptual blending of the mental and the physiological that – together with its energetic conception of movement – made it an ideal, although highly ambivalent image to negotiate cinema's potential for kinetic and corporeal transmission.

'Moving Pictures to teach the Tango': Dance instruction films and the 'spectator-dancer'

The public's 'voracious appetite' for new dances led to a growing demand for dance instruction.[13] Along with an unprecedented boom in dancing schools, dance instruction became a lucrative business for the emerging media and entertainment industries: While the music industry provided musical scores for the latest tango tunes, as well as phonographs and records for domestic dancing, newspapers and magazines published photomontages of the latest dance steps; numerous dance manuals and advice books completed this merchandise with their detailed explanations, pictures and step diagrams. In the same year, several film companies – especially, but not exclusively, in the United States – began to produce dance instruction films.[14] Advertisements for these films highlighted the medium's specific effectiveness in transmitting dance steps. Kalem's *Moving Picture Dancing Lessons* (United States, 1913) is praised by a German distributor as a film, 'in which the most modern dances like the Tango, the Turkey Trot etc. are not only *shown*, but *taught* step by step. The theatre audience will be able to dance after having watched this movie'.[15] The didactic concept relied on the (rather optimistic) idea that by merely watching these films, spectators – even 'wall flowers', people who 'just can't learn', and others who are 'awkward dancers' – would be able to perform the dances: '*anyone* seeing the pictures can become a perfect dancer'.[16] These promotional descriptions of cinema as an ideal 'dancing teacher' obviously conceal the often-lengthy, laborious and complex process of learning new dance techniques, and imagine the kinetic transmission between screen and audiences as merely an effect of the cinematic apparatus. Yet, it is noteworthy that, in spite of their simplified logic, these advertisement discourses conceive of cinema as a medium where the visual and the corporeal would be intrinsically connected – a concept that is structurally related to a film-theoretical ideas that were at the same time extensively discussed in the cinema reform movement and in 'physiognomic' approaches.[17]

The dance instruction films themselves were similarly designed to strengthen the supposed sensorial connections and to tie the experience of watching dances to a kinaesthetic, bodily response. Advertising texts and pictures, catalogue descriptions, and reviews indicate that films like *Moving Picture Dancing Lessons* and *Dances of Today* (United States, 1914) employed specific filmic devices, such as editing and close-ups, to facilitate the learning of dance steps.[18] In *Moving Picture Dancing Lessons*, for example, dance instructor McCutcheon first performs the steps for men and women separately; then the couple dances the complete choreography together.[19] Close-ups – especially of the dancers' feet – were integrated as well, for example in Victor-Universal's *Dances of Today* (United States, 1914). The camera's proximity to the dancers was supposed to guarantee the steps' optimal visibility so 'that every movement might be plainly distinguished by the spectator; that the spectator might be able to fasten the various movements in the mind's eye'.[20]

As this source indicates, spectators who watched these films in cinemas or vaudeville theatres had to memorise the dance steps in order to practice them afterwards. There is some evidence however that these films might also have been projected and performed in specific ballroom settings, encouraging audiences to learn the steps and move *while* watching the movies. In 1914, *The Moving Picture World* reported on a project in Buffalo, New York, where local theatre manager Harold Edel was planning the construction of a gigantic dance pavilion equipped with a cinema screen:

> In the center will be suspended a huge screen, on which moving pictures showing the latest steps in dancing will be presented. These will take the place of regular dancing instructors. The pictures will be visible on both sides of the screen. Mr. Edel says he is planning to use 'The dances of today', by the Universal Company, and 'Motion Pictures Dancing Lessons', by the Kalem Company. After the various steps are shown and practiced by the dancers, the instructions are ended. A varied program of regular pictures is then given for the delectation of the patrons, who at the same time may indulge in dancing to their heart's content.[21]

Although it remains uncertain whether Edel's plans for the dance pavilion in Buffalo were indeed realised, this report indicates that dance instruction films of the 1910s at least inspired *fantasies* of film exhibition and performance practices in ballrooms. Strikingly, the whole setting imagined by Edel was designed to facilitate a *simultaneity* of film reception and dance practice. The spatial arrangement of the double-sided projection screen placed in the middle of a huge dance floor would allow the dancing couples to freely circulate within the space without losing sight of the projected instructions. Supported by a musical score especially composed for these films and performed by a live band, the dancers could 'synchronize' their body movements with the dance instructions shown onscreen.[22] In this unusual setting, the instruction film serves as a movement *initiation* transforming the film spectators quite literally into dancers. Edel even planned to extend this logic of kinetic synchronisation between the screen and the audiences beyond the use of instructional films by projecting what he referred to as 'regular pictures'. In this case, the movements onscreen and on the dance floor would no longer be regulated by filmic instructions, but solely orchestrated by the *rhythmic* correspondence between visual and acoustic moves within the setting. Along with this idea of a mode of cinematic reception that would rely on film's rhythm, rather than on its representational qualities, this *dispositif* evokes a cinematic subject that could be considered as the 'spectator-dancer' – in analogy to Lynn Kirby's concept of the 'spectator-passenger'.[23] Similar to the railroad experience that Kirby refers to as proto-cinematic, projects such as Edel's cinematic ballroom demonstrate the extent to which practices of dancing prepared and modelled a specific form of cinematic

Figure 1: *Kri Kri e il tango* (Italy, 1913).

spectatorship where the act of *watching* the moving pictures coincides with (and is possibly intensified by) the corporeal *experience* of dancing.

Movement contagions as contact zones: Infectious dances in the comic genre

Concepts of a 'dancing spectator' are also negotiated in a number of film comedies that take up the motif of an enthralling dance movement seizing human bodies, objects, and furniture alike. This micro-narrative, a variation of the chase, already occurs prior to 1910 in European film comedies such as Alice Guy's *Le Piano Irresistible* (France, 1907) or Louis Feuillade's *La Bous-Bous-mee* (France, 1909).[24] Yet, in the 'tango-years' 1913/14, this motif recurs so abundantly under illustrious titles such as *Gavroche et la valse obsédante* (France, 1913), *The Turkey Trot Town* (United States, 1914), *The Tango Craze* (United States, 1914), *The Epidemic* (United States, 1914) and *He Danced Himself to Death* (United States, 1914) that a writer in the *Moving Picture World* complained by 1914 that 'there is nothing in it that is new'.[25]

I argue that these 'dancing mania comedies', like the dance instruction films, can be viewed as meta-filmic reflections on the function of movement as a principal vector within and beyond the diegesis. In *Kri-Kri e il tango* (1913), a

21 Tango Mad and Affected by Cinematographitis

Figure 2: *Kri Kri balla* (Italy, 1915).

film from the Italian comic series *Kri Kri* (1912–1915), the 'contagious' movements seem to virtually 'infect' the filmic medium in its content and form.²⁶ Under the perturbations of a jealous rival, the protagonist Kri Kri dances an 'unstoppable' tango with his dancing partner Lea. In their boisterous dance, they pull down the concert podium, leap backwards over a sofa, fall over a balustrade into the water and (by reverse-motion) back out of the water. Kri Kri's excessive dancing becomes the overall principle structuring the flux of the images and the continuity of the editing, connecting different scenes and rooms. This excessive dancing culminates in the last scene: When Lea dances with the rival, Kri Kri ropes up the dancing couple and then unrolls the rope so impetuously that they start to gyrate at an incredible speed. This kinetic excess even seems to entrain the camera to twirl with the dancers – mounted 'on a rotating platform so that the dancing crowd spins round while the main couple, slightly rocking, is kept permanently in frame (MCU)'.²⁷ As Ivo Blom has noted,²⁸ the combination of the rotating camera with a variant of a POV shot produces a particular mode of spectatorial address, and a quite paradoxical perspective: In one single shot, the vertiginous rotation is seen from the dancers' dynamic point of view, while they appear at the same time *within* the image. While this composition curiously interlaces subjective and objective views, it also inverts the roles of spectator and performers. Engaged in the vertiginous camera movement, the film spectator now seems to be 'looked upon' by the crowd *in* the scene.

In a later film from the Kri Kri series, *Kri Kri balla* (1915), cinema's 'contagious' effects are revealed even more virtuosically. Eager to perform the balletic pirouettes that he has seen on a theatre stage, Kri Kri applies the unleashing rope trick (as presented in *Kri Kri e il tango*) to himself. The effect is, as stated in the intertitles, 'an epidemic – that spreads quickly – and does not even spare the cinema spectators'.[29] In the film's final scene, the action is transposed from sets like a market place, a street and a soirée into a cinema theatre: Upon the sight of a vertiginous camera rotation on the screen-in-the-film, the spectators-in-the-film start to pirouette simultaneously as if 'infected' by the filmic images. With this self-reflexive *clin d'œil*, the film not only comments on cinema's role in the propagation of the 1910s 'tango mania', but also presents cinematic movement itself as a 'contagious' and continuous flow of energy. With a quite immersive potential, this kinetic vector connects bodies and places *within* the diegetic universe, but also creates transitions and contact zones between spheres that are usually thought of as ontologically distinct: the profilmic, the diegetic and the spectator's realm. By self-reflexively integrating the 'dancing spectator' into the film, *Kri Kri balla* suggests an understanding of the relation between the filmic dances and the audiences' bodies as a co-presence, similarly to a ballroom setting where the spaces of performance and spectatorship are permeable and can – at least potentially – interact with each other.

It is impossible to ignore the parodic tone of Kri kri's 'dancing spectators' – a tone that indicates that such depictions of spectators-*in*-the-film do not, of course, document actual viewer behaviour. As Miriam Hansen, Thomas Elsaesser, and others have argued, parodies of a primitive film spectator actually address or train a more 'mature' public;[30] for their comic effect relies on spectators' awareness that such instinctive reactions are inappropriate. At the same time, such self-reflexive visions of a 'dancing spectator' can also be understood as ironic and imaginary alternatives to the idea of the disciplined, immobile spectator, which, as Hansen has shown, emerged at around the same time.[31] Images and fantasies of a 'dancing spectator' thus constitute a highly ambivalent figure within arising conceptualizations of spectator-film relations in the 1910s. If, on the one hand, they negotiate the possibilities of a mobilised, active, and physically involved spectatorship – a figure of potential subversion within the regulated space of the cinema – on the other, they point to the allegedly manipulative, suggestive and compulsory impact of cinema on the masses. Modelled upon a dual logic similar to Kri Kri's rope that inhibits *and* unleashes the dance movements, filmic and discursive fantasies of the 'dancing spectator' conceive of film spectatorship as an experience where mobility an immobility, corporeal and mental effects are intrinsically interwoven.

Conclusions

Both the instructional dance films and the 'dance mania comedies' refer to the idea of 'contagious' movement as a powerful image to epitomize the impact of the cinematic medium and to shape film-viewer relations. Although the examples come from different national contexts and employ different strategies, they all conjure up cinema's kinaesthetic potential to 'set the spectator in motion'. At the same time, I have argued, they articulate (and emulate through cinematic means) a very fundamental assumption of the conditions and effects of movement perception in dance: namely, the idea that the experience of dance constitutively goes along with a dynamised perception. If, on the one hand, we can read these film-viewer relations as symptomatic of cinema's transitional period in the 1910s, negotiating and oscillating between a 'cinema of attractions', with its corporeal-kinetic mode of address, and a cinema of narrative integration, evoking a more classical form of spectatorship, we might – on the other – put this phenomenon in a larger historical context. For conceptions of a dancing spectator persist far beyond the 1910s dance crazes. They recur more metaphorically, for example, within a number of film-theoretical writings in the 1920s, such as those of Béla Balázs or Dziga Vertov, who use the trope of the 'dancing spectator' to underline the somatic dimension of movement experience in film.[32] More recently, similar questions have been addressed within phenomenological and sensory film theory (as developed by Vivian Sobchack, Laura U. Marks, Jennifer Barker and others).[33] In a similar, though more playful and ironic way, the dance instruction films as well as the *Kri Kri* comedies shape the cinematic experience as a visual *and* corporeal one, and cinematic perception as intrinsically linked to the interplay of (im)mobility; thus, I would argue, conceptions of a spectator-dancer could be understood as early negotiations of a film phenomenology *avant la lettre*. And yet, in scarcely any other context can the concept of the dancing spectator be taken so literally as under the influence of the 1910s dance crazes.

Notes

1. "Michigan", *The Moving Picture World* 21, no. 8 (August 1914): 1117. I wish to thank the participants of the Twelfth International Domitor Conference 2012 for inspiring discussions and

fruitful input. Furthermore, I am indebted to Nicholas W. Baer for his help with the English version of this text and the stimulating discussions on 'viral' media dynamics.

2. For a fuller survey of the dance fads of the early 1910s, see Lewis A. Erenberg, "Everybody's Doin' It: The Pre-World War I Dance Craze, the Castles, and the Modern American Girl", *Feminist Studies* 3, no. 1/2 (Autumn 1975): 155–170; Mark Knowles, *The wicked waltz and other scandalous dances: Outrage at couple dancing in the 19th and early 20th centuries* (Jefferson, N.C. and London: McFarland, 2009). For the Russian context, see Yuri Tsivian, "The Tango in Russia", *Experiment: A Journal of Russian Culture* 2 (1996), 307–334.

3. S. Beach Chester, *The Secrets of the Tango: Its History and How to Dance It* (London: T. Werner Laurie, 1914), 7.

4. "Pastors Approve Ban on the Tango", *The New York Times* (5 January 1914): 5.

5. Ernest Bell, *War on the White Slave Trade: Fighting the Traffic in Young Girls* (Chicago: GS Ball, 1910), 50–51.

6. "Eine gerechte Würdigung des Kinos", *Kinema* 4, no. 5 (January 1914): 7. All translations are my own unless otherwise indicated.

7. With the concept of 'movement contagion', I follow the seminal works of Rae Beth Gordon as well as a number of publications from dance and theatre studies, which retrace the concept of 'contagion' in discourses on stage-audience relations. See Rae Beth Gordon, *Why the French Love Jerry Lewis: From Cabaret to Early Cinema* (Stanford: Stanford University Press, 2001); Susan Leigh Foster, "Movement's contagion: The kinesthetic impact of performance", in Tracy C. Davis (ed.), *The Cambridge companion to performance studies* (Cambridge: Cambridge University Press, 2008), 46–59; Erika Fischer-Lichte, "Zuschauen als Ansteckung", in Mirjam Schaub and Nicola Suthor (eds), *Ansteckung: Zur Körperlichkeit eines ästhetischen Prinzips* (München: Fink, 2005), 35–50.

8. Raymond Fielding, "Hale's tours: Ultrarealism in the pre-1910 motion picture", *Cinema Journal* 10, no. 1 (1970): 34–47; Tom Gunning, "The cinema of attractions: Early film, its spectator and the avant-garde", in Thomas Elsaesser (ed.), *Early Cinema: Space, Frame, Narrative* (London: BFI, 1991), 56–62; Lauren Rabinovitz, *Electric Dreamland: Amusement Parks, Movies, and American Modernity* (New York: Columbia University Press, 2012).

9. Yuri Tsivian, "Russia, 1913: Cinema in the Cultural Landscape", in Richard Abel (ed.), *Silent Film* (New Brunswick: Rutgers University Press, 1996), 194–216, 207.

10. For a critical account on the narrative of the medieval dancing mania and its reception in the early twentieth century, see Gregor Rohmann, "The Invention of Dancing Mania: Frankish Christianity, Platonic Cosmology and Bodily Expressions in Sacred Space", *The Medieval History Journal* 12, no. 1 (2009): 13–45; Astrid Kusser, *Körper in Schieflage: Tanzen im Strudel des Black Atlantic um 1900* (Bielefeld: Transcript, 2013).

11. See for example Christoph Asendorf, *Ströme und Strahlen: Das langsame Verschwinden der Materie um 1900* (Giessen: Anabas, 1989).

12. See Gordon, *Why the French love Jerry Lewis*, 1–27.

13. See Knowles, *The wicked waltz*, 111–124.

14. For reasons of source availability, I focus on examples from a US-American context in this article. A more detailed analysis of the phenomenon (including examples from the European context) will be included in my dissertation, where I also relate these early practices to dance instruction films and cinematic ballrooms in the 1920s. For the latter, also see Michael Cowan, *Technology's pulse: Essays on rhythm in German modernism* (London: igrs books, 2011), 187–189.

15. Advertisement from *Die Lichtbild-Bühne* 2 (January 1914): 2–3. My emphasis.

16. "News Items of the Kalem Company", *The Evening News* (November 1913): 7. My emphasis.

17. See Scott Curtis, "Aesthetics as Applied Physiology: Corporal Understanding in the Kino-Debatte", in Leonard Quaresima and Laura Vichi (eds), *The Tenth Muse: Cinema and the Other*

     Arts/La decima musa: il cinema e le altri arti (Udine: Forum, 2001), 407–413; Jörg Schweinitz, *Prolog vor dem Film: Nachdenken über ein neues Medium 1909–1914* (Leipzig: Reclam, 1992); Michail Jampolski, "Die Geburt der Filmtheorie aus dem Geiste der Physiognomik", *Beiträge zur Film- und Fernsehwissenschaft* 27, no. 2 (1986): 79–98.

18. At the current state of my research, I could not retrieve any surviving copies of these 1910s dance instruction films; my analysis thus relies on extra-filmic sources.
19. "Dancing Lessons Pictured", *The Moving Picture World* 18, no. 3 (October 1913): 248.
20. "A Universal Tango Picture. Sebastian and Allen, Famous Vaudeville Team, Pose For Special Dance Feature", *Moving Picture World* 19, no. 5 (January 1914): 554.
21. Billy Bison, "North Western New York", *The Moving Picture World* 19, no. 7 (February 1914): 854.
22. The musical scores are mentioned in several reviews and advertisements, for example *The Moving Picture World* 18, no. 3 (October 1913): 240 and 248.
23. Lynne Kirby, *Parallel tracks: The railroad and silent cinema* (Durham and London: Duke University Press, 1997), 4.
24. For a detailed analysis of *La Bous-bous-me*, see Gordon, *Why the French Love Jerry Lewis*, 156–166.
25. Review of the film *Tango troubles*, *The Moving Picture World* 20, no. 12 (June 1914): 1689.
26. On the *Kri Kri*-series, see Peter von Bagh (ed.), *Il comico e il sublime/The comic and the sublime* (Recco: Le Mani, 2006). My film analyses of *Kri Kri e il tango* and *Kri Kri balla* are based on archival copies from the EYE Filminstituut Amsterdam.
27. Tsivian, "Russia, 1913", 208–209.
28. Ivo Blom, "All the same or strategies of difference: Early Italian comedy in international perspective", in Anna Antonini (ed.), *Film and its multiples/ Il film e i suoi multipli* (Udine: Forum 2003), 465–479, 470.
29. My translation from the Dutch copy: 'En dat wordt eene epidemie – Die zich snel voortplant – zonder zelfs de bioscope bezoekers te sparen.'.
30. See Miriam Hansen, *Babel & Babylon: Spectatorship in American Silent Film* (Cambridge, Massachusetts and London: Harvard University Press, 1994), 25–30; Thomas Elsaesser, "Discipline through Diegesis: The Rube film between attraction and integration", in Wanda Strauven (ed.), *The Cinema of Attractions Reloaded: Film Culture in Transition* (Amsterdam: Amsterdam University Press, 2006), 205–223.
31. See Hansen, *Babel & Babylon*, 23–59.
32. See Béla Balázs, *Schriften zum Film* (München: Hanser, 1984, vol. 2), 91; Dziga Vertov, *Kino-Eye: The writings of Dziga Vertov* (Berkeley and Los Angeles: University of California Press, 1984).
33. See Vivian C. Sobchack, *The Address of the Eye: A Phenomenology of Film Experience* (Princeton: Princeton University Press, 1991); Laura U. Marks, *The Skin of the Film: Intercultural Cinema, Embodiment, and the Senses* (Durham and London: Duke University Press, 2000); Jennifer M. Barker, *The Tactile Eye: Touch and the Cinematic Experience* (Berkeley, Los Angeles, and London: University of California Press, 2009).

PART IV

Intermedial Performance

22

Screening Sensations and Live Performance: the Creative Blending of Traditional and New Projected Media at the Start of the Twentieth Century

Ludwig Maria Vogl-Bienek

Do you see the screen?

Do you see the screen? When people assemble to gaze at a white wall or screen, they usually don't actually want to see that surface. We don't consider this behaviour as absurd because we are familiar with this cultural tradition and the related expectation that we will see something moving, attractive or informative appear there (Figure 1).

Technically, the projection surface, the screen, has always stayed the same. This principle applies for all forms of projection media and, figuratively speaking, for their history as well. The screen was firmly established as a part of international cultural life at the end of the nineteenth century. The rapid success of standardised photographic slides and cinematography at the turn of the twentieth century owed much to this art of projection and was historically regarded as a part of it.

The long history of performances with the magic or optical lantern, or simply the projection apparatus, culminated in the establishment of the cultural, economic, artistic and technical bases for these related screen media at the end of the nineteenth century. Above all, the new media of cinematography and photographic lantern slides used the same arrangement or dispositif between screen and audience which had been common for decades. The same was true for the theatrical principle of the performance: the appearances on screen were carefully arranged in a dramaturgical timeline and were always part of a live performance including lecturers, narrators, reciters, singers and musicians. This

Before and behind the screen at the Polytechnic during the exhibition of the dioramic effects of the siege of Delhi.   p. 306.

Figure 1: The gathering shown in Fig. 1 about 1860 at the Royal Polytechnic Institution in London depicts an audience who have come to see the siege of Delhi. In the decades before 1880, this venue was famous for its spectacular "dissolving views" or "dioramic effects" accompanied by lectures, vocals, music and well prepared sound effects. Source: John Henry Pepper, The Boy's Playbook of Science (London, New York: Routledge, Warne and Routledge, 1862), 307. [Courtesy David Francis Collection.]

constellation also enabled the creative blending of traditional and new projection media within the same performance.

Wondrous apparitions

By the late eighteenth century, audiences in Europe were well acquainted with elusive projections on a white wall as orchestrated by a performer. In 1774, this experience allowed the young Johann Wolfgang Goethe a felicitous metaphor in his novel *The Sorrows of Young Werther*:

> Wilhelm, was ist unserem Herzen die Welt ohne Liebe!

> Wilhelm, what is the world to our hearts without love! It's like a Magic Lantern without light! Just put in the small lamp and the most colourful pictures appear on your white wall! And even if it were nothing more than that, than transient phantoms, it would still make us happy to stay in front of it like young boys being charmed by these wondrous apparitions.[1]

In Goethe's metaphor, the German word 'Zauberlaterne' for Magic Lantern could also be translated as the 'enchanting lantern' because it focused on the emotional transformation we may experience as spectators in front of these wondrous apparitions of light. Solely made of light they are able to appear and disappear in an instant and they may be transformed and moved easily without leaving any trace on the surface. In 1786 Goethe supported Siegismund Gottfried Dittmar in his suggestion to use the magic lantern as a means to introduce children to natural history.[2] But he was a theatre man and so, in his later years, he was particularly interested in the use of the lantern on stage, as stronger light sources became available. He was interested primarily in the utilisation of phantasmagorical techniques in his tragedy *Faust*, e.g. the apparition of the 'Erdgeist' ('the earth-spirit'). 'Helena', in the interlude to *Faust*, was called a, 'classical-romantic phantasmagoria' ('klassisch romantische Phantasmagorie') and Goethe experimented with a magic lantern at the time when he was working on this act of *Faust* II.[3]

The magic lantern changed considerably throughout Goethe's lifespan (1749–1832). Goethe observed this development; he wasn't a protagonist in the art of projection, but rather an attentive contemporary witness and a practitioner. As a young writer he succeeded in expressing the enchantment he experienced with the magic lantern. He saw the educational potential of projection. Furthermore, he was interested to fathom how projection techniques could be applied on stage. These are the outlines of experience on which the art of projection's field of action was based in the nineteenth century: entertainment and education. Both could only work, if the art of projection was carefully nurtured within carefully staged live performances.

Entertainment – education – performance

In the second half of the nineteenth century, all the authors of specialist literature on technique and composition of magic lantern shows agreed that the close connection between education and entertainment had to be considered an essential characteristic of the medium. Exemplary in this respect is the handbook *Die Projektionskunst* (*The Art of Projection*) by the German company Liesegang, which was published in twelve revised editions between 1870 and 1909. The first known edition is the fifth edition of 1876. All give the same fundamental description:

> Of the different ways to instruct entertainingly and to entertain instructively the one taken by the art of projection has to be counted, undoubtedly, as one of the most effective, yes, if we should believe Abbé Moigno, it is even the safest way to the education of the general public.[4]

One technical improvement of the projection apparatus that was of great necessity to reach the general public and to establish the screen as a social and cultural medium was the new and enhanced brightness of the lantern's illuminants. As we see from manuals such as *Die Projektionskunst*, it was now possible

PERFORMING NEW MEDIA, 1890–1915

Figures 2–5: A dissolving view apparatus with three projection units (objectives); the transformation from summer to winter; the combination of the Aurora Borealis and The Emigrant Ship which featured dissolves, superimposition and moving effects. [Courtesy Willem Wagenaar Collection.]

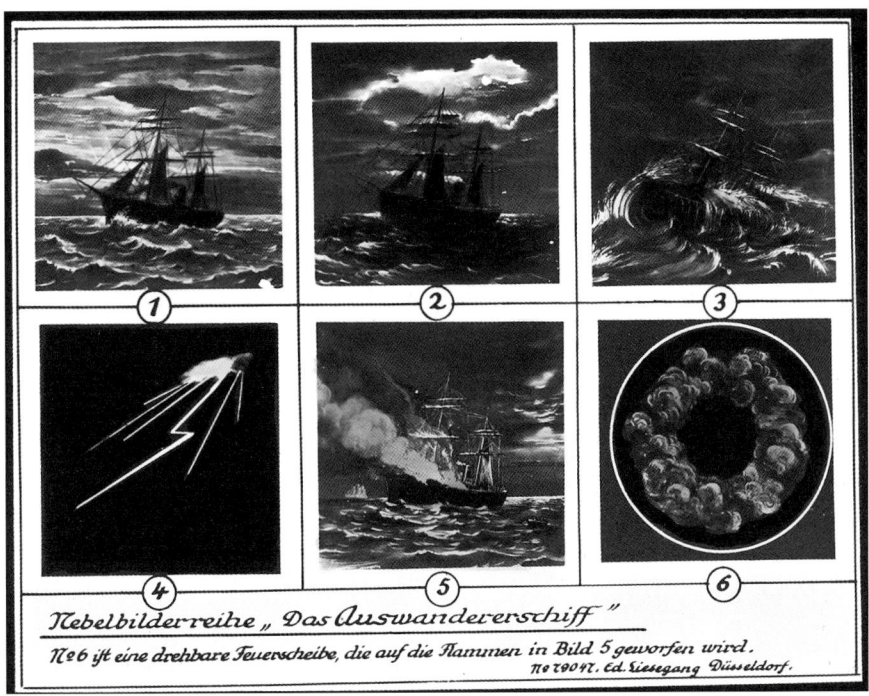

to show images that were more detailed to bigger audiences in theatres, auditoriums, church halls and classrooms. The intensely bright 'lime light' became the most important light source for the elaborate art of projection throughout the entire nineteenth century. Only at the end of this century would it start to be replaced by electric light.

Companies belonging to the optical industry supplied show-people with all of the implements required to stage a good performance with projected images and effects: instruments, attachments and slide series with and without lecture readings. The offers were announced in catalogues, manuals and magazines and this literature provided the practitioner with technical and organisational know-how. From the information collected and published by these companies, it is clear that the tradition of projection had become firmly established by 1890.

The creative blending of old and new projected media at the start of the twentieth century

A contemporary witness who was actively involved in this historical process was the German lantern and slide manufacturer Franz Paul Liesegang who edited the twelfth and last edition of *Die Projektionskunst* in 1909. In the 1890s he joined the family business which had been founded in 1854. He was an experienced creator of lantern shows and an exhibitor of early films as well as a competent researcher in the history of projection.

In a lantern lecture from 1918, he offered a retrospective overview on the history of projection using sixty-six photographic lantern slides to illustrate the history *Vom Geisterspiegel zum Kino* (From Magic Mirror to Cinema).[5] A considerable part of this lecture was devoted to 'dissolving views'. Technically and compositionally they were the most complex technique in the art of projection in the nineteenth century. Using several projection units (lanterns), the images were dissolved in smooth transitions, superimposed onto each other as each one vanished into the next (Figures 2–5).

In 1907, Liesegang, taking the stance of a showman, still didn't consider the traditional dissolving views as obsolete. At this time the company already offered a choice of various cinematographs in their catalogues and were advertising them as an enormous enrichment for shows, because of the lifelike nature of the new animated photographs. However, in this catalogue Liesegang recommended the creative blending of traditional and new projected media as well. He began with a description of *The Emigrant Ship*, one of the best known effect pieces: '… which sails in fine weather, is surprised by a thunder storm, is then hit by

Figure 6: "Prätor Kinematograph mit Zela-Laterne – für stehende und lebende Lichtbilder." ("Prätor cinematograph with Zela lantern – for still and animated lanternslides."), Advertisement by Liesegang. [Courtesy Deutsches Museum Munich.]

lightning, catches fire and finally drifts about as a sad wreck'.[6] After another example, Liesegang follows on:

> The aforementioned will offer a nice variation to the cinematographic performances. Even more I am thinking of a coherent presentation in which dissolving view-apparatus and cinematograph would go into action complementing each other. Let us take a 'Travel Around the World' as an example, same will consist of a number of coloured photographic slides, some dissolving views and several films and can be arranged variably – for instance in the following manner: first of all some beautiful slides are projected showing views of the starting point and the journey to the seaport; then the cinematograph is initiated and we see a magnificent moving image: the departure of the ocean steamer. The ship is soon on the open sea. Now, the dissolving view apparatus creates an image of the ocean seen from the ship the way it shows itself at sunset: the floods shine resplendent in glorious red. Such an effect, as easily as it may be achieved, creates an impression beyond words. But gradually the second lantern comes into action, the crimson of the sunset fades to blue, night falls, moon light glistens on the waves – One continues in the indicated manner, here and there activating a suitable dissolving view (i.e. Fata Morgana in the Desert, Niagara with Rainbow etc.) and a moving image, such as Street Scene in Paris and the like.[7]

Seen from the angle of successful live-performances, Liesegang's view was to see

Figure 7: "Dreifacher Apparat Modell 34 – mit Kinematograph."
("Triple apparatus model 34 – with cinematograph."),
Advertisement by Liesegang.
[Courtesy Deutsches Museum Munich.]

Figure 8: Double Dissolving Stereopticon. Advertisement by Chicago Projecting Company.
[Courtesy David Francis Collection.]

Figure 9: The blending of lantern slides, dissolving views and films announced as basis for a successful business. Advertisement by Chicago Projecting Company.
[Courtesy David Francis Collection.]

the new opportunities presented by combining the old and the new projected media rather than focus on the distinctions between the old (the magic lantern) and the new (film). Consequently, many companies, such as Liesegang's (Figures 6 and 7) and the Chicago Projecting Company (Figures 8 and 9), offered projectors which enabled professional show people, social organisations and educational institutions to present films and photographic slides as well as dissolving views. Regarding the apparatus, Liesegang continued:

> Now, which apparatus arrangement is necessary for this? As mentioned above, any available cinematograph can be used, even those on the list that are complemented as a dissolving view-apparatus, indeed, for this purpose, depending on the kind of effect slides that shall be projected, one or two further lanterns are necessary.[8]

Liesegang's suggestion was based on a long lasting tradition of profound knowledge, creative experience and the solid technical infrastructure of the art of projection. Internationally, millions of people were used to watching the screen, expecting to see 'wondrous apparitions', moving, attractive or informative. The established screen was a reliable basis for the rapid development of cinematography in the twentieth century while lantern lectures were still in use. The periodisation of both pre-cinema history and cinema history as found in the dominant histories does not do justice to the embedding of early film into live lantern performances. This raises the question as to when and to what extent the different options of live presentation in the art of projection including early cinema were given up for a business model of automated performances, as we can describe the self-contained nature of the presentation of a sound film.

To look at the screen as the infrastructural element connecting traditional and new visual media generates particular historical insights related to these media and their inter-relationships that are different from the habitually continued technical and teleological periodisation of traditional film history. Albeit, this question has been debated for quite some time now. A rather impressive contribution to this debate was offered by Charles Musser in his work, *The Emergence of Cinema*, published more than twenty years ago. In it he argued the need for a distinct history of screen practice as a field of study that needed to be defined and pursued.[9] But screen practice beyond film has remained the domain of relatively few specialists who know how to find slides and historical evidence in either uncatalogued archives or private collections. To highlight an understanding of the art of projection, as I have suggested here, contributes to the development of a history of the screen as a relevant part of the overall cultural infrastructure, especially at this vital transitional period around 1900.

Translated by Franziska Bienek.

Notes

1. Johann Wolfgang Goethe, *Die Leiden des jungen Werther* (Leipzig: Weygandsche Buchhandlung, 1825), 74–75.
2. See Renate Grumach (ed.), *Goethe, Begegnungen und Gespräche* (Berlin, New York: Walter de Gruyter, 1977), 31.
3. See Christoph Perels (ed.), *"Ein Dichter hatte uns alle geweckt", Goethe und die klassische Romantik* (Frankfurt am Main: Freies Deutsches Hochstift, Frankfurter Goethe Museum, 1999), 169–179.
4. *Die Projektionskunst für Schulen, Familien und öffentliche Vorstellungen*, 5th edition (Düsseldorf: Verlag des photographischen Archivs. Ed. Liesegang, 1876), 1.
5. Franz Paul Liesegang, *Vom Geisterspiegel zum Kino. Vortrag zu einer Reihe von 66 Bildern* (Düsseldorf: Ed. Liesegang, 1918).
6. *Preisliste über Kinematographen, Apparate zur Darstellung lebender Lichtbilder* (Düsseldorf: Ed. Liesegang, 1907), 13. [Assigned to Franz Paul Liesegang.]
7. Ibid.
8. Ibid.
9. See Charles Musser, *The Emergence of Cinema: The American Screen to* 1907 (Berkeley, New York: University of California Press, 1990), 16–54.

Le spectacle de lanterne magique considéré sous l'angle de la conférence : quelques traces écrites d'une performance orale

Alain Boillat

L'objectif des recherches dont j'aimerais exposer ici quelques résultats consiste à examiner, à partir de sources de la fin du XIXe siècle et de la première décennie du XXe, la façon dont a été envisagé l'accompagnement verbal oral des séances de lanterne magique dans des textes le plus souvent édités par des fabricants d'appareils et de plaques. Cette étude s'inscrit dans le prolongement des réflexions sur le 'bonimenteur' du cinéma des premiers temps qui ont été initiées dans le sillage du colloque de Brighton de 1978[1] puis notamment développées, pour les vues animées, dans les travaux de Germain Lacasse. On le sait, le spectacle de la lanterne ne convoquait pas uniquement la dimension visuelle, comme le souligne, en 1897, Eugène Trutat dans son *Traité général des projections*: '[…] il ne suffit pas de projeter sur la toile des tableaux excellents, convenablement éclairés et se succédant sans accident, il faut aussi accompagner ces exhibitions d'un commentaire parlé qui leur donne toute leur valeur'.[2] La 'technique' ne concerne dès lors pas seulement les manipulations des différents composants de la lanterne mais aussi le maniement des mots.

Cet impensé qu'est la parole

Pourtant, force est de constater que la question de l'accompagnement verbal des vues occupe une place mineure dans les manuels consacrés à la lanterne, qui se concentrent presqu'exclusivement sur la description des différents types d'appareils et sur la formulation de recommandations quant à leur utilisation, sorte de *vade mecum* pour projectionniste plutôt que 'traité' destiné aux conférenciers (ce terme fût-il présent dans le titre de l'ouvrage). En effet, si les auteurs de ce type de publications – souvent impliqués par ailleurs dans la conception et la commercialisation des appareils, à l'instar de Molteni et Mazo qui possèdent leur propre marque, ou de Coissac qui travaille pour le groupe Maison de la

Bonne Presse – rendent compte avec minutie du fonctionnement des sources lumineuses, des condensateurs ou des plaques, ils laissent dans l'ombre (comme devait l'être parfois, de façon littérale, le conférencier dans la salle) la dimension oratoire. Cette posture n'est pas étonnante chez un fabricant comme Molteni qui conçoit sa publication comme un simple mode d'emploi,[3] mais l'attention consacrée à la parole n'est, somme toute, guère plus aiguë chez des auteurs comme Trutat ou Coissac qui, pourtant, se réclament d'une grande expérience dans l'art de la conférence et se montrent soucieux de conférer une dimension 'théorique' à leur opus.[4] Sans doute ces auteurs partent-ils du principe qu'il ne leur incombe pas de traiter de la conférence proprement dite, dans la mesure où l'étude de celle-ci relève d'autres domaines. Significativement, lorsqu'il en est question, Eugène Trutat se réfère à Gustave Larroumet, membre de l'Académie des Beaux-Arts et ancien professeur de rhétorique, dont il cite *in extenso* sur quatre pages une définition de la conférence érigée en 'genre'.[5] Il accorde donc une certaine place à la parole, mais délègue ce sujet à une instance jugée plus compétente, bien que celle-ci ne discute aucunement le cas spécifique de la projection. Ce n'est de toute évidence pas de la conférence que les auteurs de manuel entendent instruire leur lectorat. Pourtant, à les lire, on constate à quel point leurs recommandations (en particulier concernant la préparation de la salle et l'utilisation d'accessoires) postulent des dispositifs différents dont chacun octroie une place spécifique au conférencier et à l'opérateur avec lequel il interagit.[6] De ce fait, même les descriptions les plus 'étroitement' techniques ne manquent pas de nous livrer, indirectement, des informations quant à l'activité du conférencier.

Étant donné la démarche de légitimation culturelle qui sous-tend le discours de ces spécialistes, la projection est majoritairement envisagée comme un outil pédagogique. Or, cet usage ne pouvant faire l'économie de la parole, il est d'autant plus étonnant que les auteurs de manuels s'attardent si peu sur celle-ci. En fait, la présence du verbe n'est pas niée – au contraire, on ne cesse d'en souligner l'importance – , mais demeure souvent implicite. En outre, le contexte pédagogique contribue à déterminer un certain rapport du texte proféré à l'image projetée qui semble aller de soi. Comme l'ont montré François Albera et André Gaudreault à propos du cinéma des premiers temps,[7] il convient de distinguer deux séries culturelles, celle de la 'conférence-avec-projection' et celle de la 'projection-avec-boniment'. La plupart des ouvrages considérés ici prônent un modèle basé sur la subordination de l'image au texte, tout en n'accordant paradoxalement qu'une place ténue à la part verbale de la projection.

Même si la conférence a laissé très peu de traces et constitue une sorte d'impensé dans les discours de l'époque sur la projection, il nous paraît important d'inclure la performance orale dans l'étude historique des appareils, car elle participe grandement de leurs usages.

Les images au rythme des mots

Peu abordée en tant que telle, la conférence l'est par contre quant au lien qu'elle est susceptible d'instaurer avec les images projetées. En effet, tant Trutat que Coissac se demandent si la parole doit être proférée simultanément aux images. Tous deux recommandent d'écarter la présentation d'un exposé complet proféré préalablement à l'ensemble des projections, et proposent une solution intermédiaire qui consiste à faire une introduction sans projection – de sorte que la salle demeure éclairée et la performance du conférencier visible – , puis, après avoir baissé la lumière, d'annoncer et de commenter brièvement les tableaux pendant la projection.[8] La simultanéité de la profération verbale et de la projection conduit les auteurs à réfléchir aux modalités de communication entre l'orateur et l'opérateur au moment du changement de vue. Trutat et Coissac préconisent à cet égard la plus grande discrétion. Tandis que Coissac mentionne la possibilité d'utiliser une lampe de pupitre permettant au conférencier, en plus de 'lire ou consulter des notes' dans l'obscurité, d'envoyer un signal optique lumineux à son assistant,[9] Trutat recommande l'usage d'un avertisseur électrique, 'signal muet indispensable' car, selon lui, 'rien n'est plus fatigant que d'entendre continuellement: 'Voulez-vous changer la vue ?'; ou bien: 'Donnez-nous le tableau suivant'.[10] Il déconseille en outre le recours jugé trop bruyant à une clochette, soit, précisément, à l'instrument auquel font référence les *lantern readings* britanniques, où ce tintement fait partie du rituel de la projection. En effet, tous les livrets commercialisés par l'éditeur Riley Bros comportent une note liminaire visant à sensibiliser les usagers amateurs au problème de la coordination avec l'opérateur:

> It is [...] recommended [...] not to adopt the too commun mode of signalling to the operator at one time rapping with the pointer, at another giving directions with the voice. The customary *"rat-tap-tap"* alternating with *"now then, if you please, the next picture"* has a grotesque effect on the audience [...]. The use of a Small table-bell [...] will be found to be a much better way.[11]

D'ailleurs, le moment où le signal doit être donné par la clochette est indiqué dans les textes des livrets proposés par les éditeurs de plaques, qui ont été segmentés en parties numérotées conformément à chacun des tableaux de la série et émaillés de mentions 'B' (pour 'Bell'). Cette convention témoigne d'un souci d'introduire, dans le flux de paroles, des points de synchronisation avec les images. Si Trutat condamne la réduction du texte à de brèves mentions ou au seul titre de la vue, c'est en raison d'une 'difficulté réelle pour l'orateur de rendre acceptable cette suite trop rapide de tableaux':[12] la parole exerce un contrôle absolu sur la fréquence d'apparition des vues. Afin d'équilibrer monstration et narration verbale, Trutat évalue à une cinquantaine d'images le nombre de vues souhaité pour une conférence dont la durée idéale est estimée à une heure: '[C]'est là un maximum qu'il ne faut dépasser qu'exceptionnellement, car certaines vues ne pourront rester sur l'écran que bien peu de temps, et le manipulateur sera obligé de marcher à grande vitesse'.[13] Les raisons de cette recommandation ne sont pas seulement pratiques, mais résultent d'une certaine conception des liens entre les images et la parole. Dans *Silent Film Sound*, Rick Altman compare la pratique lanterniste de John Stoddard avec celle de Burton Holmes et montre qu'elles s'inscrivent dans deux paradigmes fort différents: l'une se définit par la subordination totale des images au texte, l'autre par une certaine autosuffisance conférée aux images.[14] Il s'agit là de deux manières de gérer le rythme d'apparition des vues, l'image étant envisagée soit comme une ponctuation *discrète* du discours, soit comme le maillon d'une chaîne continue.

Dans un paragraphe du *Manuel pratique du conférencier-projectionniste* étonnamment absent du plus volumineux *Traité des projections* paru trois ans auparavant, Coissac aborde la question de la fréquence des changements d'image en soulignant certaines limites du cinématographe lorsqu'il est utilisé dans un contexte pédagogique:

> Les projections animées présentent certainement un grand intérêt, mais il ne faudrait cependant pas en abuser; beaucoup plus vite que les projections fixes, elles deviendraient une cause d'ennui et de fatigue [...] parce qu'il est bien difficile d'accompagner d'une explication intéressante, instructive, complète, les multiples phases de la scène projetée. [...] Seule la projection fixe, par l'étude du détail [...] rend ce concours [à l'enseignement] possible.[15]

Pour Coissac, l'avantage de la projection fixe est d'assurer la subordination de l'image à la parole, la première faisant office d'illustration au sein d'une démonstration avant tout verbale. Ce futur historien du cinéma est donc conduit à déprécier, dans ce cas particulier, l'usage des images animées. Cet argument avancé en 1908 sera fréquemment convoqué dans les discours sur l'utilisation de l'image dans un contexte éducatif; ainsi, dans un numéro du *Fascinateur* (dont Coissac fut longtemps le rédacteur en chef) datant de 1923, un curé de province fait l'apologie des tableaux figurant au catalogue de la Bonne Presse et prédit le succès des confrères ayant fait l'acquisition de plaques. Il s'adresse à eux en ces termes: 'Vous pourrez alors, grâce à la projection fixe, faire œuvre parfaite d'éducateur, travailler peu à peu votre auditoire sans crainte d'exalter l'imagination et ses nerfs, insister sur les vues qui le frappent davantage. Aussi, je comprends pourquoi, dans tous les milieux [...], on revient de plus en plus à la projection fixe'.[16] Il semble bien que, jusqu'à la généralisation du film didactique parlant au moins, cette préférence pour la lanterne ait persisté chez des pédagogues qui entendent user avant tout de la 'magie' du verbe.

Les Narrations: la conférence dans le texte

Parmi les ouvrages consacrés à la lanterne, l'éditeur parisien Mazo publie, parallèlement à *La projection en pratique* et au *Grand manuel de projection*[17] dus au conférencier Alber, un volume du même auteur spécifiquement dédié aux conférences, *Les narrations du prestidigitateur Alber*.[18] L'avant-propos de cette anthologie de textes destinés à être lus lors de séances de projection débute par la déclaration d'intentions suivante:

> Un livre de contes, me direz-vous, mais nous en avons et pour ne citer que les principaux, les contes de Perrault [...] nous suffisent amplement. C'est très vrai, si vous ne voyez dans ce livre qu'un recueil de contes, légendes ou pièces en vers pour la lecture [...] *Aussi faut-il considérer ce recueil à son véritable point de vue, c'est-à-dire comme une suite de légendes, devant accompagner des gravures et non pas des gravures dans un livre, mais des images projetées.* C'est la partie d'un tout récréatif. L'œil doit être amusé par les gravures, mais l'oreille doit en même temps recevoir une explication et c'est l'ensemble de ces deux sensations qui permet à une projection de présenter son maximum d'intérêt.[19]

Dans ce texte liminaire, l'auteur revendique le fait que les textes narratifs proposés sont *spécifiquement* conçus en vue d'accompagner des images, et plus précisément dans le contexte de la projection. Il a conscience de se référer à un 'médium' donné (proche mais néanmoins distinct du livre illustré),[20] défini par la coprésence de la voix et de l'image, en des termes – l'oreille s'associant à l'œil pour percevoir un 'tout' audiovisuel – qui ne sont pas sans parentés avec les discours contemporains des pionniers du cinéma sonore. L'intérêt des textes rassemblés ne résiderait donc pas, selon Alber, dans leur contenu narratif proprement dit, mais dans l'adaptation de ces récits aux conditions du spectacle lanterniste. Or il apparaît qu'outre la concision des formules et le découpage en parties numérotées correspondant aux différentes vues commercialisées par Mazo sous forme de séries (composées en général de 12 'tableaux', dont le prix global est mentionné en note de bas de page à la fin de chaque histoire),[21] ces *Narrations* ne se distinguent pas fondamentalement, du moins en ce qui concerne les contes, des livres illustrés, si ce n'est que la hiérarchie entre le texte et l'image y est inversée, ainsi que l'explique leur auteur:

> Vous vous rappelez que ce qui vous charmait dans votre enfance au moins autant que les images, c'était le "boniment" du montreur. La projection, comme la lanterne magique, a besoin de l'accompagnement explicatif. Dans certains cas, dans des conférences, par exemple, c'est la projection qui accompagne le

conférencier et explique ses paroles par des images. Ici, nous envisageons le cas contraire, où les images amusantes ont besoin d'être expliquées, commentées.²²

Si, comme la plupart des auteurs de traités de projection, Alber prend soin de distinguer son objet (la 'projection') de la lanterne magique, quant à elle associée à un contexte supposément infantile, il n'en précise pas moins que la fonction principale des séances prévues dans son ouvrage réside dans le divertissement. Sa pratique s'inscrit bien, pour reprendre la notion mentionnée ci-dessus, dans la série culturelle de la 'projection-avec-boniment': les guillemets appliqués par Alber au mot 'boniment' dénotent certes une distance par rapport au contexte forain et itinérant, mais il se réclame néanmoins, par le choix de ce terme, d'une visée similaire. C'est pourquoi ses textes se caractérisent par un régime énonciatif mixte où le *discours* prime dans certains passages sur l'*histoire* (au sens de Benveniste), notamment lorsqu'il s'agit de renvoyer à l'activité de perception visuelle,²³ ou au caractère spectaculaire et grandiose du spectacle projeté, considéré comme une 'scène',²⁴ c'est-à-dire comme le produit d'une représentation. L'adaptation au public supposé constitue un principe: le narrateur prend par exemple la peine, après avoir cité une célèbre phrase du *Petit chaperon rouge* tel que popularisé par Perrault, de préciser ce qu'elle 'veut dire en français d'aujourd'hui'.²⁵ Par ailleurs, en orientant la lecture de l'image grâce à la mise en évidence d'éléments spécifiques (en particulier des motifs situés à l'arrière-plan),²⁶ à l'identification de figures clés ('Le personnage qui parle est celui qui est au milieu, Mohammed Ben-Ali est d'un côté, et le capitaine du navire de l'autre')²⁷ et à la formulation d'hypothèses narratives,²⁸ les textes visent, comme l'a suggéré Jean Châteauvert à propos du bonimenteur de cinéma,²⁹ à 'éduquer le regard du spectateur'. Ainsi, comme Burch l'avait noté,³⁰ certains textes renforcent la continuité narrative entre les vues: lors du passage d'une scène diurne à une scène nocturne grâce au procédé des *dissolving views*, on nous dit par exemple à propos d'un personnage désormais absent: 'Le berger *que nous avions vu tout à l'heure* ramenant son troupeau est rentré dans sa chaumière'.³¹ En de rares cas, cette démarche occasionne une explicitation de certains codes visuels, comme dans cet exemple-ci, extrait de l'*Histoire de deux gendarmes et d'un voleur*:

> 3ᵉ Tableau. – Nous voyons dans ce tableau la suite de la scène de l'arrestation, scène vue de dos, cette fois. Cette volte-face était nécessaire pour bien démontrer le stratagème, le truc employé par l'adroit coquin afin de se soustraire à la poigne des gendarmes.
>
> 4ᵉ tableau. – Continuation de la conduite des gendarmes.³²

Le 'volte-face', c'est-à-dire le changement de point de vue radical apporté à une scène identique (au détriment de ce qui deviendra 'l'axe de jeu' dans le futur cinéma classique), est explicitement motivé par le gain cognitif que nous confère l'image suivante. À une époque où la constance du point de vue par rapport à la scène était dominante (en particulier dans les histoires comiques racontées par une juxtaposition de dessins publiés dans la presse ou dans les images d'Épinal), le commentaire prend soin d'expliciter la logique du 'montage' en précisant qu'il s'agit de la même scène vue sous un autre angle. On peut imaginer que le bonimenteur de cinéma ne s'y prenait pas autrement pour expliquer le passage de l'extérieur à l'intérieur (et le 'bégaiement' temporel subséquent) d'une bande comme *Life of an American Fireman* (1903),[33] qui reprend par ailleurs un célèbre motif de la tradition des spectacles de lanterne magique.

Lantern readings: réappropriations orales de l'écrit

Dans l'ouvrage publié par Mazo, certains textes sont présentés comme des résumés ou des compilations de textes préexistants.[34] De telles opérations de reformatage de sources en vue de l'adaptation à la projection ne sont cependant pas le seul fait du prestidigitateur Alber, puisque les éditeurs anglais avaient pour habitude de joindre des livrets aux séries de vues qu'ils commercialisaient. Le riche fonds des *lantern readings* de la Cinémathèque française, diversifié dans les pièces qu'il contient (histoires d'édification du public populaire, récits adaptés à la projection, descriptions de lieux touristiques, etc.), permet de se faire une idée assez précise de ce type d'écrits. On constate notamment que ces livrets, tout comme les manuels, ne contiennent que peu de consignes quant à la prestation orale du conférencier. Le langage utilisé, très littéraire, n'est guère empreint de style oralisé. Rarement, les textes sont précédés d'une introduction 'réflexive' livrant consignes ou intentions. On en trouve toutefois quelques-unes, notamment dans un fascicule comprenant une série de monologues dont l'auteur anonyme se présente comme un lanterniste ayant mis par écrit l'une de ses conférences à succès, *How Bill Adams Won the Battle of Waterloo*; il précise d'entrée de jeu le caractère peu littéraire de son texte, qu'il présente comme une transposition scrupuleuse d'une performance orale ('I have written it – commencing with the introductory remarks leading up his remarkable parable in his own peculiar vernacular – exactly as I tell it myself'). Ici, la performance orale est posée comme première, antérieure à l'écrit.

En fait, les phénomènes relevant de l'oralité ne se jouent pas tant dans la rédaction des textes que dans l'usage qui a été fait de ces livrets par les conférenciers, dont témoignent les documents conservés dans ce fonds. En effet, ils portent la trace d'une appropriation personnelle des utilisateurs qui se manifeste de deux manières: il peut s'agir soit d'indications manuscrites ajoutées

233

au texte fourni par l'éditeur par un conférencier faisant fi des conditions de location du document sur lequel figure, à l'encre rouge, le tampon 'This book must not be marked', soit de fascicules entièrement confectionnés par les orateurs eux-mêmes à partir d'ouvrages existants (à l'instar des versions abrégées de récits populaires de la collection Penny Reading Books, par ailleurs accompagnés d'illustrations). Dans ce second cas de figure, le conférencier a indiqué à la main le numéro de la vue correspondante afin d'instaurer des points de synchronisation et, à l'instar de l'exhibiteur de vues animées, effectue un travail de collage et d'agencement pour constituer le programme d'une séance. Les séries de tableaux et les livrets mis à disposition par les éditeurs constituaient par conséquent des produits semi-finis, parachevés par des pratiques relevant de l'*oralité*, dans le sens large que Paul Zumthor a donné à cette notion. C'est pourquoi il est difficile de les théoriser comme des phénomènes homogènes, mais passionnant de les étudier dans leur singularité matérielle. Si nous ne disposons d'aucune trace sonore témoignant de l'activité des bonimenteurs, de tels textes permettent d'examiner les étapes préparatoires de cette parole vive et, selon les cas, offrent la possibilité d'une confrontation avec les vues elles-mêmes; mais ce serait là, précisément, un autre sujet de conférence.

Notes

1. Voir Martin Sopocy, "Un cinéma avec narrateur: les premiers films narratifs de James A. Williamson", *Cahiers de la Cinémathèque* 29 (1979): 108–125.
2. Eugène Trutat, *Traité général des projections* (Paris: Charles Mendel, 1897): 351.
3. Alfred Molteni, *Instructions pratiques sur l'emploi des appareils de projection* (Paris: Molteni, 1878; 1881; 1884).
4. Trutat, *Traité*; G.-Michel Coissac, *La théorie et la pratique des projections* (Paris: La Bonne Presse, 1905).
5. On y lit notamment les éléments de définition suivants: 'La conférence est une causerie, elle doit être improvisée. [...] il faut que tout orateur respecte les deux lois essentielles du genre: la première est d'être naturel, la seconde de ne pas écrire', (Trutat, *Traité*, 349). On retrouve une conception similaire chez Coissac: 'L'œil exercé du conférencier de profession remarque vite quand le public se fatigue [...]. Selon l'impression qu'il en a, il oriente son improvisation dans un sens ou un autre', (*La théorie*, 421).
6. À propos de la place du conférencier dans le dispositif de projection, voir notre article "The Lecturer, the Image, the Machine and the Audio-Spectator. The Voice as a Component Part of Audio-Visual Dispositives", dans *Cinema Beyond Film: Media Epistemology in the Modern Era*, sous la direction de François Albera et Maria Tortajada (Amsterdam: Amsterdam University Press, 2010): 215–231.
7. André Gaudreault et François Albera, "Apparition, disparition et escamotage du bonimenteur dans l'historiographie française du cinéma", dans *Le muet a la parole*, sous la direction de Giusy Pisano et Valérie Pozner (Paris: AFRHC, 2005): 167–200.
8. Trutat, *Traité*, 353–354; Coissac, *La théorie*, 416.
9. Coissac, *La théorie*, 89.

10. Trutat, *Traité*, 342.
11. Collection de la Cinémathèque française. Nous remercions vivement Laurent Mannoni et Laure Parchomenko de nous avoir accueilli dans leurs murs et donné accès à ce fonds.
12. Trutat, *Traité* 353.
13. Ibid., 355.
14. Rick Altman, *Silent Film Sounds* (New York: Columbia University Press, 2004): 55–72.
15. G.-Michel Coissac, *Manuel pratique du conférencier-projectionniste* (Paris: Bonne Presse, 1908): 22–23.
16. M. l'abbé Agar, "L'apostolat aidé par la projection lumineuse", *Le Fascinateur* 185 (octobre 1923): 361.
17. Dans cet ouvrage, Alber note: "Il est nécessaire d'employer un accessoire qui ne s'achète pas, mais qui est le puissant auxiliaire d'une bonne lanterne, c'est la parole de l'opérateur, ce sont les explications qu'il donne", (*Le grand manuel de projection* [Paris: Mazo, 1897]: 163). L'auteur regrette que les ouvrages relatifs à la lanterne n'aient jamais guidé le lecteur dans la confection de "légendes".
18. Alber, *Les narrations du prestidigitateur Alber* (Paris: E. Mazo Éditeur, 3e éd. non datée [1ère éd. 1895]). Nos remerciements à Thierry Lecointe pour nous avoir prêté son exemplaire de cet opus rarissime.
19. Alber, *Les narrations*, 3 (*nous soulignons*).
20. On retrouve une comparaison identique chez Coissac: "La projection est à la conférence ce que la gravure, l'illustration est au livre", (Coissac, *La théorie*, 415).
21. Le client peut choisir, dans le catalogue de l'éditeur Mazo, entre une feuille chromolithographique comprenant l'ensemble des tableaux à partir de laquelle il composera les vues à projeter ou, pour un prix plus élevé, ces mêmes tableaux déjà 'montés sur verre mince'.
22. Alber, *Les narrations*, 8.
23. On trouve en effet de nombreuses occurrences du verbe 'voir' à la première et à la deuxième personne du pluriel, ou des expressions telles que 'sous *nos* yeux', qui postulent également un renvoi à une situation d'énonciation. Voir par exemple: 40, 43, 46, 87, 131 et 255.
24. Voir par exemple: 115, 118, 125 et 148.
25. Alber, *Les narrations*, 24.
26. Voir par exemple: 47, 149, 265.
27. Alber, *Les narrations*, 47.
28. Par exemple dans *Le nain au long nez*: 'Il est probable, d'après ce que nous voyons, que la vieille sorcière continua pendant ce temps-là ses enchantements diaboliques', (Alber, *Les narrations*, 43 ; *nous soulignons*).
29. Jean Châteauvert, 'Le cinéma muait', *Iris* 22 (1996): 107.
30. Noël Burch, *La lucarne de l'infini* (Paris: Nathan, 1991): 149; 228–231.
31. Alber, *Les narrations*, 138 (nous soulignons).
32. Alber, *Les narrations*, 263.
33. Voir Burch, *La lucarne*, 196–197.
34. À propos de la série intitulée *Les mots historiques* et de ses images extraites d'un livre illustré, Alber précise: '[l'auteur] nous pardonnera de nous être simplement inspiré de son texte, de l'avoir élagué, raccourci et sûrement diminué d'intérêt. On comprendra aisément qu'une séance ne peut comporter la matière d'un grand volume in-4 auquel il sera toujours facile de se reporter pour les détails complémentaires', (Alber, *Les narrations*, 157).

Getting to Know the Dutch: Magic Lantern Slides as Traces of Intermedial Performance Practices

Sarah Dellmann

Around 1900, only wealthier citizens could afford a trip abroad and encounter the inhabitants of other countries 'on location'. What most people could come to know about other people and remote places was to a large extent dependent on mediation. In this essay, I will argue that the dimension of performance should be taken into account when analysing visual material which was shown in these mediated encounters. Taking popular images of the Dutch as an example, I will propose a method of tying intermediality and performance practices together in the study of the communicated meaning(s) of an image.[1]

The media landscape of the late nineteenth century was – as it is today – highly multimedial. Popular mass media such as lantern slides and stereoscopic photographs were sold on an international market and were seen by people around the globe. Images of the Netherlands were present in all visual media of that time. In my archival research the same visual motifs occur in various media formats: city views with canals and people in traditional clothing appear in picture postcards, magic lantern slides, stereo cards, illustrated magazines, films, and advertising trade cards – to name some very popular visual media of the time. Maybe it is not surprising to find that manufacturers offered their images in different media and formats (e.g. the American Keystone View Company offered photographs for use in schools as both lantern slides and stereoscopic cards from the same negatives;[2] and the Dutch enterprise CAPI offered the same sets of images for projection on slide sets and on film strips[3]). However, what really struck me was to find that identical images were used in different publications in different countries.[4] As illustrated here, the same photograph was printed in a British tourist guide book,[5] with the caption referring to the children as 'waiting for the tourist' (Figure 1). The image was also sold as

Figure 1: 'The Harbour of Marken', Charles E. Roche, *Things Seen in Holland* (London: Seeley and Co. Limited, 1910): 219.

educational material in the United States. The text of the accompanying lecture card stated that these children went to school in wooden shoes (Figure 2).⁶

These findings revealed to me that information on the Netherlands and the Dutch was not determined by neither medium technology nor motif. If neither medium nor motif are the key to determine the meaning which these images communicated, and if we are still convinced that non-fiction images do not convey completely arbitrary information, we should study how meaning for a reader in each instance was created by a very specific combination of image and text.

Frank Kessler, in his study of titles and catalogue entries of early non-fiction films, has drawn attention to the importance of extra-filmic and paratextual

Figure 2: 'Dutch Children in Native Costume. Fishermen. Boats', Slide P287 (V12206) of unknown set (Meadville: Keystone View Company, after 1905), 3.5 inches by 4 inches.
[Private collection Gwen Sebus, Netherlands.]

references for understanding films of this kind. He found that titles of non-fiction films were often more descriptive than those of fiction films. That way, the non-fiction film titles enunciated the images and oriented the viewer as to what to expect.[7] Catalogue descriptions proposed a written narrative to accompany early non-fiction films and thereby offered a structure for an understanding of such films.[8]

For some of the historic visual material with images of the Netherlands and the Dutch, I began to find paratextual information such as title, caption, catalogue description, reviews and lecture material. Precisely how were written commentary and a non-fiction image combined to 'make sense'? What was also apparent was that in the case of registered media such as the magic lantern and film, where the same slides and films were screened and re-screened at different places and times and for different audiences and by different performers, that information on the Dutch was always being mediated *and* performed at the same time. This understanding made aware acutely of the fact that particular archival objects (such as the lantern slide and film) embody traces of performance, i.e. they were

24 Getting to Know the Dutch

Figure 3: 'Rotterdam, Post Office', slide 1 of *Holland and the Hollanders* (London: York & Son, fifty slides, 1900). 3.25 inches by 3.25 inches. [Private collection Gwen Sebus, Netherlands.]

part of a practice which brought together the visual imagery and other elements *in performance*.

The Rotterdam Post Office in performance

The image (Figure 3) shows the first slide of from the slide set *Holland and the Hollanders*, titled 'Rotterdam, Post Office'.[9] An advertisement in the trade press made it possible to date the first publication to 1900[10] and a reading to the slide set is available in the library of the British Film Institute.[11] What can be extracted from these heterogeneous sources with regard to this question: what were audiences told about this lantern slide when it was performed?

The photographic image of the lantern slide shows a huge building, four floors high, with its front to a large, paved square. About a dozen people stand on the otherwise empty square, but they are too far away to be studied in detail. From

239

the image alone, we can infer that this building existed, and this is what it looked like. The first piece of paratextual information comes from a piece of paper glued onto the glass plate with the slide title.[12] It informs us that the building on the image is the post office of Rotterdam; we thus learn that Rotterdam had a post office and we know that the central square is situated in this Dutch city.

Different comments to accompany this image are imaginable; a number of people could show interest in it: the press department of the postal service, tourists who saw this building, local historians of Rotterdam, architects, lantern slide collectors and researchers in media history – and all are likely to comment on this image differently, depending on their interests. Or, to put in another way: all would perform the image differently. These multiple possibilities notwithstanding, it is rather obvious that this lantern slide was intentionally produced to be projected in a lantern slide show on the Netherlands. The projection of the slide set was designed to be accompanied by a specially prepared spoken commentary. The title of both the slide set and the reading, *Holland and the Hollanders*, made me expect specific information for a slide titled 'Rotterdam, Post Office' such as information on Rotterdam and its population, information on the building and the postal system of the Netherlands. Given that this was the first slide of the slide set, I would not be surprised to read a description of a tourist arriving in Rotterdam. Here is the entire quotation from the reading for this slide:

> This is a very useful, but not very ornamental building: some of the post offices in Holland – Amsterdam for instance – are very handsome structures, and with every convenience. One of the first things that strike the tourist on his first visit to Holland is the extreme cleanliness of everything and everybody. If ever a nation believed implicitly in soap and water it is the Dutch. Another thing is the deliberation with which everything is done: there is no haste. In this very post office, I remember, says a recent tourist, seeing a man putting postage stamps on about a hundred circulars. I first saw him about 10 o'clock; he had just bought a sheet of stamps and was leisurely separating them: he then seated himself at the table, and taking a stamp in his right hand by one corner, carefully applied his tongue to about half of it; he then took the wet part in his left hand, and proceeded to moisten the remainder; he next turned the stamp over to see it was 'head uppermost,' and laid it carefully on the circular; after pressing it in close contact with the ball of the thumb, he took out his pocket-handkerchief, and making a little pad of it, finished the operation. I saw him do several in exactly the same way, and then took the steam tram from the Cool Singel to Schiedam and back; I then looked in at the Post Office to make an inquiry, and my young friend was still going steadily on with his job.[13]

The lecture met all of my expectations as it provided detail and context as expected from a travelogue, including detail on working routines inside this post office. However the textual commentary also moved beyond the descriptive as it entered into an evaluation of both taste, character and Dutchness. The passage starts with both generic and generalised subjects ('the tourist', 'a nation', 'the Dutch', 'everything'). After these generic subjects are introduced they are qualified with characteristics, and these characteristics are of an evaluative kind ('useful, but not very ornamental', 'deliberation', 'no haste'). By adopting the voice of an authoritative speaker, particular values are asserted; the norm against which something is judged as ornamental or what is considered to be hasty stays implicit. This judgment passes as description by validating the statements through an authoritative speaker's position. ('In this very post office, I remember, says a recent tourist').

The lecture is written in the first person so that its reader, when performing the text in public, can assume the role of being both knowledgeable and opinionated on this subject. The use of the formulation 'recent tourist' does two things. Firstly, the deictic reference ('recent') presents the statement as being current and avoids dating. When read out during the performance of the slide show, the statement is presented as valid every time that these words are spoken. Secondly, the perspective offered by the anonimised 'tourist' is validated by the lecturer's use of it. In the performance of the slide, the 'recent tourist' serves as an authentic eyewitness. The use of this account ensures that the lecturer cannot be held accountable for the eyewitness evidence expressed within it. It is almost impossible to contest an eyewitness, all the more if the audience members did not make alternative experiences. The incontestability of the 'recent tourist's' statement in turn strengthens the authority of the lecturer as the words which he/she reads out pass as valid.

We can find another trait of authenticity when we remember that the commentary was read out as part of a performance where an audience was looking at the projected image of the Rotterdam post office. In this case, the generic subjects of the commentary are concretised by tying them to something that has just happened, 'recently', and in 'this very post office' which we doubtlessly see so clearly on the screen. The text in this way becomes anchored to the image and together, it can be argued, they both reinforce and guarantee the commentary's truthfulness.[14]

Documenting traces of performance practices

Seeing particular historic visual material, like the lantern slide of the Rotterdam post office, as a trace of a performance practice implies an understanding of the historic image-object as an element within a set of intermedial relationships.

Only in performance are these images embedded in a setting (i.e. educational, touristic, anthropological) and linked potentially to music, commentary, texts and songs. Only in intermedial performances do such objects (such as a lantern slide) in fact become *meaningful* objects. In such mediated encounters, audiences received information on the Netherlands and the Dutch from the performance, not from the 'pure' image and not from the 'pure' text. This understanding should now change the status of the archival object. The lantern slide from 1900 is no longer a distinct, self-contained entity but an element that was historically within varying and complex situations.

For archivists, librarians, and curators, this perspective should lead to rethinking the practices of cataloguing such collections. If the object only makes (historical) sense within performance, the necessarily object-centred databases of their collections should also include relevant contextual information on venues, locations, lecturers, publicity and programmes. This is now better enabled through the use of relational field databases through which apparently diverse objects can be brought together systematically. The born-digital web resource LUCERNA (www.slides.uni-trier.de) on the magic lantern and its uses is a good example of how information on different types of objects, scattered across a range of different collections, can be brought together. This is not only invaluable but also essential when we recognise the need to move beyond an understanding of the single object. Bringing objects and information together from heterogeneous sources is a necessary condition for research into the intended, possible and probable meanings of historic visual material in performance.

For scholars, to consider performativity in intermedial research is to engage with questions that address the production of cultural meaning. Every performance is situated in a setting defined by technological limits, existing and available media, theatrical and social conventions and the nature of the audience. The place and time of a performance are important determinants. Each venue – a fairground show, a university's lecture theatre, an advertisement in a trade press – provides a broad horizon of possibilities as do the narratives of a society as expressed through the conventions of genre, general beliefs and pictorial and narrative traditions.[15]

Through performativity we can move beyond the established research perspective of film studies that focused on the apparatus and sketched an ideal spectator that received the univocal film 'text'. We can move beyond mere object descriptions and personal interpretations of isolated media texts. By taking into account performance, we begin to understand that the meaning which is attributed to an image is situated within a very particular setting and very *time specific*, even when standardised, internationally distributed, and supposedly universally comprehensible images are involved. Studying images via performativity does not offer a univocal answer to the question what an image means or meant. On the contrary, performativity is a strong argument against claims to represent a historic object 'as it was in and of itself'.

Approaching historic visual media through performativity raises a very important ethical consideration. When we understand that early screen images are not stable historical entities but functioned as elements within an audio-visual performance, we can challenge with the historic material object that does not change over time any notion that the early screen object is fixed and contained within particular historiographical narratives such as linearity, teleology and essentialism. Through the perspective of performance, we can trace the operations that generated meaning and the functions of these generated meanings in various settings; through the perspective of performance we become aware of the mutable nature of the early screen object.

After these considerations, the answer to the question is not so much *what* but rather *how* people around 1900 got to know the Dutch. The answer is a fairly short one. Most people did not get to know *the* Dutch as they only met the Dutch *in performance* – and that was their only possible way of getting to know the Dutch.

Acknowledgements: The author thanks Gwen Sebus for the permission to publish scans of lantern slides from her private collection as well as all members of the Magic Lantern Society who shared their knowledge about the subject.

Notes

1. The expression 'performance of an image' in this essay explicitly refers to planned or exercised *practice*. I do not restrict the term 'performance' to practices of showmanship alone but use it for *any practice in which these images were shown to an audience*. This includes e.g. slide projection in educational settings, and in a slightly metaphorical way, I consider the printed images in illustrated mass media (magazines, brochures, advertising trade cards etc.) also as the performance of an image.

2. For example see the introduction, 'How to use this visual unit', in a booklet for teachers: 'After the slides have been presented and discussed by the children, then the *duplicate stereographs*, which have the same numbers as the slides, should be laid out on the room reference table or in the school library, or be made available for passing around the class', Zoe A. Thralls, *Three Progressive Small Nations. The Netherlands, Belgium, and Denmark*. Keystone Geography Units. Stereographs and Lantern Slides. Unit XXX. (Meadville: Keystone View Company, 1938), 1. Emphasis added. Private collection Gwen Sebus.

3. 'Onze bekende en veel gevraagde "Lichtbeelden voor allen" (zie blz. 12) leveren wij ook op kino-film-stroken afgedrukt', CAPI, *Catalogus No. 40 van lantaarnplaatjes, lichtbeelden op filmstrooken enz.* (Amsterdam, Den Haag, Nijmegen and Groningen: CAPI, ca. 1922), 28. Private collection Henc de Roo.

4. For a discussion of several cases see Sarah Dellmann, 'To and From the Magic Lantern. Reappearing Photographic Images of the Netherlands in Various Media', *The New Magic Lantern Journal* 11, no. 3 (December 2012): 14–16.
5. Charles E. Roche, *Things Seen in Holland* (London: Seeley and Co. Limited, 1910).
6. 'How should you like to go clump, clump, clump to school in great wooden shoes? These children do not mind it, for most of them never had any other kind. Their fathers and mothers wear shoes just like theirs. People all over Holland wear wooden shoes', Keystone View Company, *School Children, Marken, Holland*, lecture card for the lantern slide, 'Dutch Children in Native Costume. Fishermen. Boats', Slide P287 (V12206) of unknown set (Meadville: Keystone View Company, in/after 1905), 3.5 inches by 4 inches. Unknown private collection.
7. Frank Kessler, 'Was kommt zuerst? Strategien des Anfangs im frühen *nonfiction*-Film', *Montage/AV* 12, no. 2 (2003), 103–118.
8. Frank Kessler, 'Narrer la non-fiction dans les catalogues des premiers temps', in Alice Aurelitano, Valentina Re (eds), *Il racconto del film / Narrating the Film* (Udine: Forum, 2006), 39–49.
9. York & Son, *Holland and the Hollanders*, lantern slide set of fifty slides, 3.25 inches by 3.25 inches (London: York & Son, 1900). Private collection Gwen Sebus.
10. 'New Lantern Slides' [Advertisement by York & Son], *The Optical Magic Lantern Journal and Photographic Enlarger* 11, no. 136 (September 1900), xiii.
11. Anonymous, *Optical Lantern Reading Holland and the Hollanders* (London: York & Son, 1900). BFI Reuben Library. These 'readings' or 'descriptive lectures' were small booklets that provided a comment on each slide for the respective set. Most readings were issued between the mid-1880s and the 1900s and were mostly sold separately to the slide set. Hired lecture slide sets usually included a reading.
12. In addition, information can come from this lantern slide as object, e.g. the manufacturer's trade mark in one corner and a number. From the material (emulsion, type of glass), information on manufacturing processes can be deduced. As this article focuses on the image in projection, I did not investigate the material qualities of each slide.
13. Anonymous, *Optical Lantern Reading Holland and the Hollanders*, 4–5.
14. This slide set was also distributed in the Netherlands. It is improbable that Dutch lecturers in the Netherlands read out the English reading when presenting this slide set. Little is known about lantern slide sets and performances, even less is known about the use of the readings. Therefore readings only provide a guide to the *possible* commentary delivered to accompany a slide.
15. Alison Griffiths' conclusions on the impact of metanarratives in ascribing meaning to early ethnographic film can be applied more broadly: 'The challenges to historians in accounting for the role of such powerful but implicit metanarratives and the vicissitudes of reception suggests some of the difficulties in determining how the meanings of ethnographic films and photographs were negotiated in the early part of this century'. Alison Griffiths, *Wondrous Difference: Cinema, Anthropology, and Turn-of-the-century Visual Culture* (New York: Columbia University Press 2002), 121.

25

20 Minutes or Less: Short-Form Film-and-Theatre Hybrids – Skits, Sketches, Playlets, and Acts in Vaudeville, Variety, Revues, &c.

Gwendolyn Waltz

Mister Earth has waited these long, long years
For his wandering comet love,

Begins the verse of Gus Edwards and Harry B. Smith's 'The Comet and the Earth', sung in Florenz Ziegfeld's *Follies of 1910*.[1] The vocalist shared the stage with a motion-picture screen on which was projected a specially made Edison film with the disembodied visages of Harry Watson as the earth and Anna Held as the comet, and a bevy of tiny faces of Ziegfeld chorines in Held's wake as the comet's tail. Several years ago at the Library of Congress in Washington, D.C., I was thrilled to identify this and two other films from the George Kleine Collection as moving pictures that were made for short-form, film-and-theatre hybrid performances.[2] I also discovered a number of microfilmed scripts – originally filed with the federal Copyright Office – for multi-media playlets and stage acts that combined film with live performance. Usually, the film in a hybrid production is known to us only as a drama critic's all-too-brief reference to the inclusion of a motion picture, thus the Kleine Collection films are unique documents of multi-media performance that offer us opportunities to study in depth the mechanics of specific stage acts, as well as how contemporary film techniques were (and were not) integrated. Without the films to view, however, this article will serve as an introduction to the motion pictures and their hybrid staging. Further, the essay will place these films in their larger contexts, especially how they functioned in variety entertainments, related to other film-and-live-performance acts, took a role in defining copyright law, introduced modern technology and subject matter to nineteenth-century minstrelsy, and even possibly influenced some of Buster Keaton's comic 'bits'.

By September 1896 in the United States, film began to be integrated into

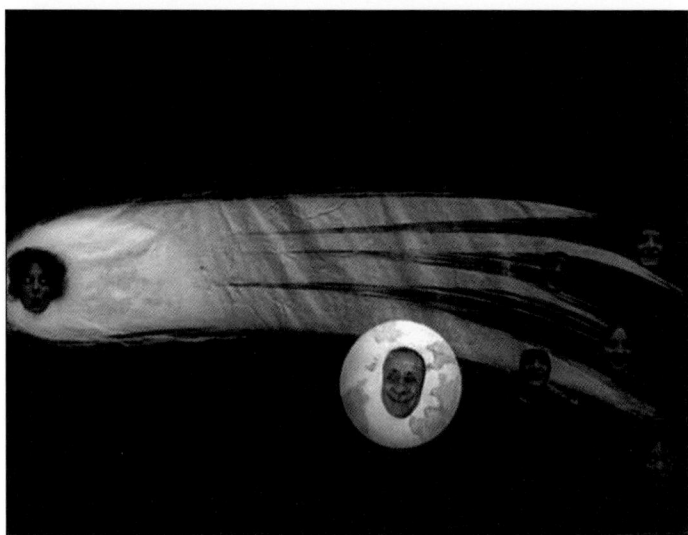

Figure 1: *The Comet* (Edison, 1910), George Kleine Collection.
[Courtesy of the Moving Image Section of the Library of Congress, Washington,

full-length dramatic productions.³ Soon afterwards, motion pictures were incorporated in shorter theatrical compositions, such as sketches, twenty- to thirty-minute playlets, song or dance numbers, technologically spectacular 'effects scenes' (often recycled in vaudeville after appearing in a melodrama or musical revue), stage acts, monologues, and motion-picture scenes that alternated with, or led into, live entertainers's entrances onstage. Short-form hybrids began to appear in variety entertainments where the whole of a performance was divided into numerous components. For instance, the non-narrative structure of vaudeville or a minstrel show channeled consecutive components in a swift flow of staging and created rhythms and crescendos of tension, while the extremely loose narrative of a musical revue provided a pretext for a series of unrelated amusements. Components were brief, so they allowed people experimenting with hybrid forms the focus and flexibility to explore new production techniques made possible when film and live performance were intermingled.

'The Comet' was presented as an illustrated song, with its two verses each visualised as a flirtatious flight across the sky of Held's comet towards Watson's moon, climaxing in a moment of facially expressive intensity (when the faces become superimposed) before Held and her chorus pass. Watson 'mugs' in his signature comic persona, soon to be popularised in the George Kleine – then Essanay – 'Musty Suffer' film series. Held emphasises her famous 'misbehavin' eyes.' In the publicity that began the 'Anna Held craze' of the 1900s, Held had been heralded as 'the comet of the century's end',⁴ and here, in this film, her status as a star performer is combined in reference to the passing of Halley's comet only months before the *Follies* opening.

Other celestially themed hybrids predated this act. Almost a decade earlier (1901), British music-hall performer Percy Honri had sung Frederick Norton's 'Oh, Mr. Moon' to a film of his lunar self playing the banjo.[5] Additionally, we easily can make an associative leap to Georges Méliès's *L'Éclipse du soleil en pleine lune*. *L'Éclipse* was produced for the 1907 revue *Cigale* at the Folies-Bergère – the very theatre from which Held had been lured by Ziegfeld to New York and which influenced Ziegfeld's revue format and showgirl glorification in his own *Follies*, which also premiered in 1907 (reportedly at Held's suggestion). In Ziegfeld's *Follies*, the more overt sexuality of the Parisian Folies was translated and made acceptable to strait-laced American audiences by clouding or teasing erotic content. We see this in comparing the two films: Ziegfeld's moon is more puerile than Méliès's lascivious sun, reacting to the female comet's advances with the bashful, comic sexuality of a burlesque comedian fiddling with a necktie. In both films the female is the initiating party, in confident motion towards the male, although the encounter of Ziegfeld's couple seems *hardly* as satisfying as that of Méliès. The Edison film is not as technically sharp as Méliès's; the two segments look much like experiments in double-exposure, with the camera operator estimating how the images will line up and relate to each other in size.

This self-contained film-and-musical number was moved around the programme of the *Follies of 1910* during the run of the show.[6] Self-containment and maneuverability were important, since the employment of revue performers was often temporary. Therefore, the order of acts had to be flexible, although sometimes an act's placement was indicated specifically in the script, such as with Frank D. Thomas's 'Bathing Scene' for the Ziegfeld *Follies of 1907*. Thomas's scenario unfortunately does not survive at the Library of Congress. However, its place is indicated in the *Follies* script, act 2, scene 9: 'The Surf. A vitascope effect with girls [sic] heads and shoulders looking through a drop. The picture thrown on the drop represents waves in motion. The girls jumping the waves, screaming and laughing. Imitation of the noise of surf.' The effect's patent also survives, with illustrations of the motion-picture screen, with its star-trap openings through which the chorus of Gibson Bathing Girls frolicked in the filmed ocean surf.[7]

Beginning in 1900, actor Adolph Zink performed a quick-change act in vaudeville, entering and exiting the stage to perform 'live' impersonations, then making his costume changes while a motion picture displayed his supposed antics with his dresser backstage: Zink, a 'little person', combines gags about his size, boyish appearance, pugnacity (reported in newspapers), a 'No Smoking' sign, and the cross-dressing material in his act. The photographic quality of the surviving Edison film at the Library of Congress (catalogued as '[Dressing room scenes – Adolph Zinc (sic)]') suggests it may be a remake of Zink's original film, perhaps circa 1903 when Zink and his manager, Edwin Miner, won a federal lawsuit and probably took advantage of the resulting publicity. '[Dressing room scenes]' is incompletely edited, with a series of close-ups appearing together at the end of the film, which also supports dating it later. Information from 1903 managers's reports on the Keith-Albee circuit confirm that the film's cuts in action between costume changes indicate places where Zink appeared onstage in alternation with the filmed sequences of his fifteen to twenty minute act; for example, 'does imitations . . . making changes back of the scenes while the biograph sheet is dropped between each change, and moving picture views of his making the changes are shown on the sheet'.[8]

The Circuit Court case of *Barnes vs. Miner*, published in *The Federal Reporter*, vol. 122, may be an unusual place to find script and performance information, yet it is an excellent source: since it is testimony, it is superbly detailed. We learn, for instance, that Zink entered the stage, announced his impersonations, then he prepared his audience and cued his film operator as he exited for his first transformation by saying, 'Remember that good goods come in little packages. I trust you will like this little package. I now invite you all to my dressing room to watch me make my quick changes'.[9] Clarifications are made about the roles Zink portrayed in his protean act: in the motion picture, Zink dons the Salvation Army costume of Edna May as she appeared singing 'Follow On' in *The Belle of New York*, then he's ruffled and petticoated as Lottie Collins to perform her signature 'Ta-Ra-Ra-Boom-De-Ay', and finally he becomes 'Bath House John of Chicago' for his onstage song, 'Reggie, the Reigning Rage'. A May Irwin imitation is also mentioned in the legal document and managers reports, but is not included in the film, where Zink is also seen in close-up shots making up his face as another male character, not identified in testimony.[10] The court case, further, provides the script and description of 'X-Rays of Society', performed in 1897 by Hattie Delaro Barnes, the plaintiff, who charged Miner and Zink with copyright infringement: the theft of her idea for a quick-change act incorporating moving pictures. The judge questioned the morality of Barnes's act, which showed her undressing down to her bloomers in the film (International Film Company, 1897). Unlike Zink's performance, her act had copyrighted dialogue. Barnes performed three songs, including an Anna Held imitation.[11]

Creative property and its ownership were becoming defined legally at the turn of the twentieth century. For artists using hybrid forms, the *Barnes vs. Miner* judge's ruling to dismiss the case clarified that ownership did not apply to a 'mere idea' taken from another performer. Ownership only applied to property that was 'substantial or material'.[12] Subsequent multi-media presenters could more carefully protect their innovations through copyrights for dramatic compositions and patents for special-effects technology, but conceptual ideas had a freer exchange and could be built upon.

We see this kind of creative addition and interplay, for example, in the work of writers and performers in minstrelsy. While blithely perpetuating the degrading racial stereotypes of blackface performance, early-twentieth-century Caucasian minstrels also were changing minstrel-show structure, experimenting with elements that pushed minstrelsy in the direction of musical revue. Technology was one of these, both as topical material and with hybrid effects as a mode of presentation.

Such is the case with what seems to be a rushing-to-the-theatre entrance film at the Library of Congress. Five men and a dog run down residential and city streets and over hilly terrain, travelling by automobile, trolley, train, horse-drawn buggy, and nearly by ferry, and dash into a theatre building. The theatre shot is the fourth of more than a dozen, which make no sequential sense and appear to be unedited and arranged in the order in which they were filmed. The Kleine Collection title, '[Elks late for rehearsal]', suggests the film could have been made for an amateur performance of the Elks Club, an organisation to which many minstrels belonged. Clubs with regional networks, such as the Elks, provided social homes for performers on tour. Local members welcomed travelling performers by producing private entertainments, as evidenced in newspaper reports.[13] Could this film have been used for a benefit performance or carried on tour by a minstrel troupe for appearances at Elks functions across the United States?

Alternatively, of course, the film may have been used professionally. Lew Dockstader incorporated alternation-form hybrid effects for several years in his minstrel shows, working with Edwin S. Porter, and '[Elks]' is tentatively attributed to Edison in the Kleine catalogue. Charles Musser has written about Porter's special theatrical projects at Edison, such as Dockstader's *Minstrel Mishaps*, in which Dockstader played all the roles in a minstrel show, and another film – involving this blackface comedian and an actor made up to look like President Roosevelt – that was intercepted by federal officers, so it never was shown onstage.[14] Dockstader also employed magic-lantern effects as scenery for his tour-guide 'Rubberneck Hack' and flying-pickle airship monologues. By October 1904, film was added to this and 'Dockstader was blown to earth by kinematograph' before he parachuted to the stage to deliver a monologue.[15] Also, circa 1905 in 'The Pursuit', a chase film was used by Dockstader's company.[16] Perhaps this is '[Elks late for rehearsal]'?

The prolific writer, composer, producer, and jack-of-all-trades Jean Havez was an integral part of these hybrids when he worked as Dockstader's company manager, publicist, and 'idea man'. While with Dockstader, Havez also took seven months preparing (with Porter/Edison) and producing (with W.C. Youngson) *Spook Minstrels*, the hybrid behind-the-screen 'talkie' act that Rick Altman has researched at length. Announced at the end of 1904, *Spook Minstrels* premiered early in 1905 and was playing vaudeville as late as 1911.[17] During this same time, 'Everybody Works But Father', a song Havez wrote for Dockstader, became enormously popular, and was filmed by both Edison and American Mutoscope & Biograph in November 1905. Biograph advertised a mode of hybrid presentation: 'A Decided Novelty for Illustrated Song Singers . . . No slides are necessary. . . . if you sing it just as it is written you can't get away from the pictures'.[18] Interestingly, the sheet music was published under two separate covers by Helf & Hager (1905), one with Dockstader in blackface and one without. I have not come across any other minstrel music marketed this way. Furthermore, Biograph made blackface and whiteface film versions, shot by G.W. Bitzer. Were these coordinated by Biograph in a business relationship with the music publisher, who is credited in the films's Biograph *Bulletin*? It is an interesting puzzle.

In 1914, Havez wrote and produced *Curse You, Jack Dalton*, another hybrid, with a surviving script at the Library of Congress. Possibly based on a vaudeville turn by Joe Cook (ca. 1912), this playlet became a vehicle for former minstrel 'Happy Jack' Gardner, who spoke a monologue that accompanied his interaction with the filmed characters of an onscreen melodrama that, 'when the villain becomes too intolerably villainous', ended with Gardner shooting him: 'and the photograph wretch drops to the photograph floor, photograph dead'.[19] Echoing Barnes's suit against Zink, Havez threatened legal action against Florenz Ziegfeld when Channing Pollock wrote 'Commotion Pictures',[20] a revue sketch for the *Ziegfeld Follies of 1915* in which Ed Wynn appeared in the auditorium of the New Amsterdam Theatre as a motion-picture director, shouting orders that the performers – seen onscreen as film images – obeyed. Of course, besides the Joe Cook precursor, Havez's own act followed closely on the heels of Winsor McCay's vaudeville act with *Gertie the Dinosaur*, novel for its own interaction between a live performer and filmed character. The Ziegfeld film scene was exported to London's Alhambra Theatre, where the Follies performers took direction from Jack Morrison in a music-hall sketch now titled 'An Early Morning Rehearsal'; it is not clear whether this was a typical progression of an act from revue to variety, or a means by which Ziegfeld evaded Havez's copyright suit in the United States.[21]

The extensive experience of Jean Havez with film-and-theatre hybrids may have influenced some of his work in later years when he was a comedy writer for motion pictures. He wrote for Keystone, Conklin, Laurel and Hardy, Arbuckle, Lloyd, and Keaton from 1915 to 1925. Although Havez is not credited for *The Playhouse*, might elements of *Minstrel Mishaps* have been restyled in the opening dream sequence where Keaton plays all the roles? And, besides the Three Keatons's familiarity with Winsor McCay from concurrent vaudeville engagements, as possible influences for the beginning of the dream sequence in *Sherlock, Jr.* (1924), the family's relationship with 'Happy Jack' Gardner as fellow members of the summer actors's colony in Muskegon, Michigan cannot be discounted,[22] nor can we ignore Havez's direct influence as one of the film's credited writers. Buster's famous liminal crossing from 'life to film' may have origins in stage-and-screen multi-media and be a rendering in one medium of meta-referential experiments that began in the hybridization of two.

To anyone who has viewed surviving films from hybrids, it is clear that the value of these discoveries is *not* in their filmic quality. This can be expected, since they are snippets of action separated from the larger context of their original performances – we may reconstruct ways they were used, yet not recover the experiences they created. Rather, importance lies in the fact that a number of these limited-use films actually exist as artefacts. They offer a glimpse of an innovative, medially interactive approach to presentation on the stage, while widening our understanding of early film's many applications and its reception by people involved in, and entertained by, the artistry and business of amusement more than a century ago. Hybrids challenge traditional historiographies, replacing linear models of development with spectrums, continuums, and overlays that not only are more accurate, but also are more richly nuanced. It will benefit not only film studies, but also theatre, dance, and performance studies for us to gather together materials related to hybrids so we can think about them as more than individual novelties. Their unique performance contexts should not be discounted and are our starting points, of course, but we can examine hybrids in other, larger frameworks, such as comparing them nationally and internationally, examining the roles they played in entertainment enterprises that had inter-medial financial holdings, and tracing the history of creative, conceptual experimentation regarding the imaginatively-possible relationships between real-life and reel-life – a type of experimentation that continues to this day in multi-media theatre, dance, and music performance (now with digital technology), as well as in the related, self-referential interplay of 'reality' and 'the movies' on the screen in the tradition of *Sherlock, Jr.* or 'Out of the Inkwell'-style animation.

Notes

1. Gus Edwards and Harry B. Smith, "The Comet and the Earth" (New York: Jerome H. Remick, 1910). The song/scene was titled 'Mr. Earth and His Comet Love' in theatre programmes; New York reviews credit Eleanor St. Clair as the vocalist, while programmes on tour credit Lillian St. Clair.

2. *The Comet* (Edison, 1910), '[Dressing room scenes – Adolph Zinc (sic)]' (Edison, [190?], and '[Elks late for rehearsal]' ([Edison], [1905?]) in the George Kleine Collection, Motion Picture, Broadcasting, & Recorded Sound Division, Library of Congress, Washington, D.C.

3. *Bullfight* (Gray Latham and Eugène Lauste, Eidoloscope Co., 1896) was inserted as a filmed scene in Rosabel Morrison's stage production of Theodore Kremer's drama *Carmen*. See Gwendolyn Waltz, "'Half Real-Half Reel': Alternation Format Stage-and-Screen Hybrids", in André Gaudreault, Nicolas Dulac, and Santiago Hidalgo (eds), *A Companion to Early Cinema* (Wiley-Blackwell, 2012), 360–361. Recently, Paul Spehr drew my attention to "John Mishler's Busy Five Hours", *New York Dramatic Mirror* (25 July 1896): 8, in which Morrison's manager, Ed Abram[s], is credited with adding Latham's Eidoloscope and film.

4. Linda Mizejewski, *Ziegfeld Girl: Image and Icon in Culture and Cinema* (Durham: Duke University Press), 47. Mizejewski interprets the act as a trick boasting 'Held's refusal that year of a five-thousand-dollar moving-picture ... contract', 139.

5. Peter Honri, *Working the Halls* (Farnborough: Saxon House, 1973), 107 and 109 (illus. 105–106). Two versions of the Mitchell and Kenyon film survive at the British Film Institute, London.

6. Information from a [New York] programme places the illustrated song in act 2, scene 13, while on tour in Chicago it appeared in act 1, scene 5: Herbert G. Goldman, *Fannie Brice: The Original Funny Girl* (New York: Oxford University Press, 1992), 229 and 'Follies Inaugurate', *The Billboard* (10 September 1910): 8.

7. Frank D. Thomas, 'Bathing scene' (New York: 13 March 1907), U.S. Copyright D 10129; records suggest no text was submitted to the Copyright Office. Harry B. Smith, *Follies of 1907: A Review of the Year* (New York: 9 and 20 July 1907), U.S. Copyright D 10933, 42, microfilm: Copyright deposits, 1901–1922, class D dramas; Manuscript Division, Library of Congress. Frank D. Thomas, 1907, Illusion Apparatus, U.S. Patent 863,470, filed 9 April 1907, and issued 13 August 1907. The stage effect premiered in vaudeville 'in 1906 at Keith & Proctor's Fifth Avenue Theatre', and was recycled after the *Follies of 1907* for Joseph Hart's vaudeville sketch *The Bathing Girls* (1910), which was assimilated into Lew Fields's musical comedy *The Summer Widowers* (1910). See 1911 advertisement in *Variety*, [n.d.] http://fultonhistory.com, Document: Variety 1911 – 0257.pdf. For more about Thomas, see Gwendolyn Waltz, "Filmed Scenery on the Live Stage", *Theatre Journal* 58, no. 4 (December 2006): 547–573.

8. H.A. Daniels, "Criticism of Keith's Theatre, Philadelphia, Pennsylvania, Nov. 9th", Managers's Report Books, vol. 1, 62, Keith/Albee Collection, Special Collections, University of Iowa Libraries, Iowa City, Iowa. Film scholar Matthew Solomon graciously shared his notes on Zink from this collection. In 1905, evidently connected with an appearance at the Palace Theatre, London, Horace Goldin published a 'prospectus' for a similar hybrid quick-change act: "Stage

Representation. Comprising Bioscopic Effects, in Combination with the Acting and Dialogue of an Artiste or Artistes"; see General Reference Collection, British Library, London. Stephen Bottomore has published Goldin's text in "News, Reviews and Notes", *Early Popular Visual Culture* 5, no. 2, 225–226. Films from similar behind-the-scenes hybrid acts of other performers survive at the British Film Institute.

9. *Barnes vs. Miner, Federal Reporter*, vol. 122 (St. Paul: West Publishing Co., 1903), 480 and 485.

10. Ibid. and "Temple Theater, Detroit, Michigan, Week of Dec. 7, 1903", Managers's Report Books, vol. 1, 103, Keith/Albee Collection, Special Collections, University of Iowa Libraries.

11. *Barnes vs. Miner,* 482 and 484.

12. Ibid., 492; see also Siva Vaidhyanathan, *Copyrights and Copywrongs: The Rise of Intellectual Property and How It Threatens Creativity* (New York: New York University Press, 2003), 90–91.

13. For example, "Elks Preparing to Entertain Primrose Minstrels", *Albuquerque Citizen* (23 October 1907): 5, and "Elks Social Season", *Daily Press,* Newport News, Virginia (3 March 1903): 3: "... Jean Havez and Various Others Besides Dockstader Himself Contributed to An Enjoyable Impromptu Program".

14. Charles Musser, *Before the Nickelodeon: Edwin S. Porter and the Edison Manufacturing Company* (Berkeley: University of California Press, 1991), 275 and 321–322. For a fuller account of the Dockstader-Roosevelt film, see Terry Ramsaye, *A Million and One Nights: A History of the Motion Picture Through 1925* (New York: Simon and Shuster, 1926/1986), 434–439. The incident was well chronicled in 1904–1905 newspapers.

15. "Dockstader's Minstrels", *New York Times* (4 October 1904), and "Article 6 – No Title", *New York Times* (2 October 1904), http://select.nytimes.com/gst/abstract.html?res= F50617F7355F13718DDDAB0894D8415B848CF1D3.

16. "Columbia Theater", *Evening Star*, Washington, D.C. (5 December 1905): 16. 'The Pursuit' was the entertainment's third part, 'with the chase cleverly carried out in motion pictures'.

17. Rick Altman, *Silent Film Sound* (New York: Columbia University Press, 2004). The Library of Congress's newspaper search engine and database, chroniclingamerica.loc.gov, contains *Spook Minstrels* articles dating performances from February 1905 to September 1911. In 1918, George Layton (who later teamed with Frank D. Thomas, mentioned above) was credited with originating the idea for *Spook Minstrels*. See *Evening Public Ledger*, Philadelphia (21 December 1918): 14. Production details regarding the act and film are provided in an interview with Layton, "Making a Moving Film 2,000 Feet in Length", *Minneapolis Journal* (15 November 1905): 3. Copies of *Spook Minstrels* survive in shorter lengths at the Museum of Modern Art Film Library, New York, and British Film Institute.

18. Kemp Niver (comp), *Biograph Bulletins, 1896–1908* (Los Angeles: Locare Research Group, 1971), 231. Both versions of the film survive: *Everybody Works But Father* (Blackface) and (Whiteface), (G.W. Bitzer, American Mutoscope and Biograph, 1905) in the Paper Print Collection, Motion Picture, Broadcasting, & Recorded Sound Division, Library of Congress.

19. "'Curse You, Jack Dalton'", *New York Times* (26 July 1914). Jean C. Havez's *Curse You Jack Dalton* survives on microfilm: (New York: 30 June 1914), U.S. Copyright D 37491, Copyright deposits, 1901–1922, class D dramas, Manuscript Division, Library of Congress.

20. "Follies a Big Hit", *Variety* [n.d.], 10, http://fultonhistory.com, Document: Variety 1915 – 1175.pdf; Joe Cook is also mentioned in this article.

21. Programme, Alhambra Theatre, London, week ending 14 August 1915. Collection of the author.

22. "The Gardners", Ron Pesch, *Actors' Colony at Bluffton, 1908–1938: Buster Keaton and the Muskegon Connection*, http://www.actorscolony.com/Gardners.htm.

26

Between Karagöz and Cinema: Connectivity, Mobility, Collectivity

Canan Balan

The earliest comedy film series of the declining Ottoman Empire, named after its main character *Bican Efendi*, were made between 1917 and 1922. This was an exceptionally turbulent and cosmopolitan period for the city of Istanbul in the twentieth century. With the start of the Russian Revolution in 1917, many White Russians moved to the capital of the Ottoman Empire for a short period before settling in Europe and Istanbul was occupied by the French, British and Italian armies between 1918 and 1923. Under these circumstances, it would not be wrong to assume that the encounters between the local and the global gained new meanings at an accelerated rate during this period. These new meanings for the understanding of the context of early cinema did not only involve a hybridisation of the spectatorship culture but also a hybridisation of different media.

One of the two extant silent films that were made in Istanbul is from the early slapstick series, Bican Efendi. It is an eccentric example of the intermedial aspect of cinema in this period. The series was among the most popular Turkish films of its time; the first was made in 1917, the sixth and final film was made in 1921. The titles are *Bican Efendi the Cautious* (1917), *Bican Efendi Seeking Money* (1918), *Bican Efendi the New Rich Man* (1918), *Bican Efendi the Teacher* (1921), and *The Dream of Bican Efendi* (1921). The only one that has survived was made in 1922 and was named *Bican Efendi the Steward* (a.k.a. *Bican Efendi Vekilharç*, Şadi Fikret Karagözoğlu, Turkey). This particular film stands at the intersection of early cinema and the Ottoman shadow-play, Turkish and Western theatre and public storytelling. This study will concentrate mainly on the connection between shadow-play and cinema and on the means with which *Bican Efendi the Steward* made a fusion of these two types of spectacles, while considering the modes and the places of their interaction with the spectators. Before focusing on this interplay, however, it is best to mention other translations, intermedialities and intertextualities revealed by this one particular film.

Bican Efendi the Steward was an adaptation of a theatre play written by İbn-ür Refik Ahmet Nuri, who would later dedicate the play to Şadi Karagözoğlu, the director and the main actor of *Bican Efendi the Steward*. He was a theatre actor before moving into the film business. The reason this play was dedicated to him was the writer's wish to honour Karagözoğlu's efforts in making the play famous by turning it into a film, as well as his success in bringing the role to life as a leading actor in the play itself. However, the play was not original since İbn-ür Refik Ahmet Nuri had re-written it from a French play, entitled *Le Prétexte*.[1] The original play was adapted into a Turkish context and first performed at the Istanbul City Theatre in 1916.[2] The Turkish play was named *Hisse-i Şayia*, which is literally translated as, 'a share in a collective property'. This 'share in a collective property' was seemingly given as the title of the play for it was about the parents' role in determining their children's partners in marriage. However unintentional it may be, from the perspective of the translatability of these media, the title of the play was not the only 'share in a collective property' as the film was an adaptation that drew upon the French and Turkish origins of the play.

Karagöz as the harbinger of film in the Ottoman lands

Bican Efendi the Steward is very connected to the history of Turkish shadow-play – Karagöz – especially through its director and lead actor, Şadi Karagözoğlu ('the son of Karagöz') who was a grandson of a Karagöz master. Shadow-play was brought to the Ottoman lands in the sixteenth century supposedly from either Indonesia, China or India. It then evolved into Karagöz, named after the main character of the show. Karagöz was widely performed with slight differences in a wide geographical area that included most of the Balkans and the Middle East. Karagöz is formed by the colourful reflections of two-dimensional puppets on a thin white cloth called the curtain. The curtain is lit from behind and the puppets are manipulated with long sticks by puppeteers beneath the curtain / screen. The show is based on the adventures and misadventures of two funny figures who constantly misunderstand each other and they are voiced by the puppeteers.

It is interesting to explore the common ground between the performances of Karagöz and early cinema, even though they first appear to be quite different media. Shadow-play shows encouraged an awareness of the act of watching and even invited the audience to participate in changing the direction of the action during the performances. Most of the lines, dialogue and poems cited in the prologue and the epilogue are in visual terms and self-reflectively refer to the concept of spectacle by 'staging', 'mirroring' and 'reflecting' the world on the 'curtain' (which is also the word for cinema screen in Turkish). This constant call for attention to spectacle within the spectacle was not only verbal, but also made visible. The characters of the shadow-play often suddenly shift forms by becoming animals or sometimes even random objects such as an umbrella, a jar or binoculars. By way of example let us say that Karagöz annoys some witches in one play. They then turn him into an animal or in another such scene, 'a snake eats his donkey's head after which Karagöz experiments with the possible uses of a headless donkey'.[3] The temporal elements of trick photography and *féerie* films were therefore somewhat familiar to the audience of Karagöz as both shows would feature figures that would unexpectedly and swiftly appear, disappear or be transformed.[4]

The second shared territory of early cinema and Karagöz performances in Istanbul was the fact that until the mid-1910s, the film programmes occasionally also included Karagöz performances. Alternatively, and in the same period, they would often share the same venue in for example a theatre, coffeehouse or circus. In the month of Ramadan, the two shows would be organised together to compose 'a fairylike spectacle'.[5] If there was a festival, carnival or a celebration of some sort, the same programme could also be extended to include pantomimes and cantos (light-hearted songs performed by female singers in cabaret style; a popular musical genre of the late nineteenth and early twentieth centuries). The same exhibition pattern was also found in Beirut and Damascus, where cinema shows would also share the same tent with Karagöz performances.[6]

Bican Efendi

Early cinema and Karagöz did not only intersect in the same venues. The intersections would also take place within the same medium. In a surviving shadow-play text, Karagöz visited the cinematographe,[7] while characters that resemble both Karagöz and Chaplin's fictional character of the Tramp would take part in films like *Bican Efendi the Steward* of 1922. In each episode of the series, Bican Efendi, the hero whose name is also the title of the film, has a new job from which he is fired. His marginalised social status as the basis for the film's humour is considered an imitation of Chaplin's films by film historians such as Nijat Özön and Giovanni Scognomillo.[8] A close examination of Karagöz and Chaplin's cinema enables us to see the parallels between the two. This series is also reminiscent of the Ottoman shadow-theatre character of Karagöz. Both spectacles revolve around a character whose unpredictable nature leads to extraordinary adventures, and in both texts the main characters have unfixed identities along with a wide range of varying hobbies, professions and interests. They also change roles from being a father to a newly wed and a single man. Hence, a more suitable approach would be to perhaps consider both *Karagöz* and Charlie Chaplin as the main sources of inspiration for this intermedial series. Neither of them have stable family lives or sources of income; they both change jobs very often, and they always play playful and carefree characters. If we look into the synopses of other Bican Efendi sequels, it is possible to see he too changes jobs often, has little or no family ties and is always in search of finding his way out of petty troubles. All these three characters experience mishaps with objects by misusing or overusing them. Chaplin, for instance, directs the fire hose towards the people instead of the burning house (*The Fireman*, Unites States, 1916), while Bican Efendi is unable to shovel the soil. Chaplin may drag a man with a ladder without even noticing (*The Pawnshop*, United States, 1916), while Bican Efendi has a hilariously manic moment with an umbrella. Perhaps unlike grounded Karagöz but similar to Chaplin's tramp, Bican Efendi is often clumsy, as in the scene when he fails to properly sit on an ordinary secure chair or when he beats the air instead of a man he is fighting with.

Bican Efendi the Steward is the third of a series of slapstick comedies made in 1922 by the former theatre actor, Şadi Karagözoğlu. His surname, which as mentioned means son of Karagöz, was chosen deliberately by the actor himself after the surname law (mandating surnames be registered for every citizen) in Turkey in 1934. The film was funded by the Army Film Centre. It was the first national film production company and along side the Bican Efendi series it produced a number of early feature-length films of Turkey, some of which addressed the War of Independence and the occupation of Istanbul by the Entente Powers after the First World War.[9]

After the National Film Archive burnt down in 1959, *Bican Efendi the Steward* remained as only one of two surviving silent films made in Turkey.[10] Unfortunately, this only extant copy of Bican Efendi had been left unedited until a Turkish film historian, named Nijat Özön, found the copy and edited the film himself according to its synopsis.[11] The film in this new version is mainly composed of unrelated fragments, which makes it perhaps closer to the non-linear narration style of Karagöz.

Although this print is in this re-edited form and is around four minutes shorter than the original length. I would argue there is still value in investigating it in terms of its relationship to Karagöz and the cinema of Charlie Chaplin. The film offers some of the significant characteristics of early cinema such as

Figure 1: Still from *Bican Efendi the Steward*.

voyeurism and self-reflexivity most notably with a keyhole shot and some belly-dance scenes. The film also includes various scenes that function almost like a silent laugh track. In order to emphasise the humour derived from the main character's clumsiness, supporting actors are shown to laugh at him while holding their bellies.

Bican Efendi's beard, his gestures and his posture look similar to those of Karagöz in the shadow-plays as both have hunchbacks and stand with their arms half-raised most of the time. Bican Efendi's body language, in the way he walks or climbs up stairs, also resembles the body movements of Chaplin.

In Bican Efendi we see fighting as part of a light-hearted spectacle. This is not unlike children's cartoons where nobody is seriously injured or dies and if they do, they recover soon afterwards. In shadow-plays, Karagöz and his fellow friend Hacivat beat each other up as part of their ordinary conversations and this is a way of keeping the conversation witty, alive and animated. What is perhaps even more interesting about Bican Efendi's fight scenes is that we also see somebody watching the fights in the same frame. Indeed, the spectator within the frame is much more than a silent witness to Bican Efendi. He also directs the audience's attention in terms what to look at and how to respond to it such as encouraging the audience to laugh at particular actions. In one such scene, one of the characters points Bican Efendi towards the camera while he is unsuccessfully trying to shovel. His desperate attempts at holding the shovel tightly and hitting the ground is shown for a while and then he sees someone else trying to shovel and he tells that person off for not managing to do it despite his own failure at shoveling. The man who he scolds now in turn directs the attention of the audience to the clumsiness of Bican Efendi. He looks and smiles at the camera while his hands point to Bican Efendi as he falls. The observer's self-reflexive action, one which steps outside of the diegetic space and engages with film's audience, breaks through the theatrical fourth wall. Afterwards, we see the same man laughing in an exaggerated manner even after Bican Efendi has disappeared from the screen. In the next scene, we see another man at another garden doing the same thing. Bican Efendi comes in, takes the shovel, begins digging but upon noticing his failure, this new man looks at the camera and laughs. It is unclear whether this repetition was deliberate or was something created during the film's re-editing, but it still tells us about a deliberate choice to place the spectator within the frame in a very particular way. Two shots later we see another fight between Bican Efendi and possibly a salesman where there is a third person merely watching as they fight.

These fight scenes in *Bican Efendi the Steward* may have been inspired by the quarrels of Karagöz and his fellow friend Hacivat. The inspiration for scenarios of this kind can also be traced in the cinematic cultures of other countries, such as Egypt and Syria, where Karagöz had been among the main forms of spectacle until the twentieth century. Indeed Terri Ginsberg and Chris Lippard claim that the Egyptian farcical comedy films as well as the Syrian comedy films mirrored the jokes expressed by the relationship of Karagöz and Hacivat.[12]

It is probably not a surprise that I reiterate what has been said in different contexts about the self-referentiality of early cinema, but I would like to underline the placement of the spectator within the frame as a distinctive aspect within the Ottoman arts of spectacle, in particular in Karagöz. Karagöz, as the main character of the show, frequently plays the spectator. He'll appear as a voyeur, particularly in the love scenes between the frivolous woman and the dandy. In some plays, Karagöz, from his window, listens to the young couple discussing their relationship in the garden and interferes with it, but rather awkwardly, as he never receives any response. By distortedly repeating what the lovers say or commenting on their attitude towards each other, Karagöz poses as a humorous interlocutor for the audience. In these scenes, he seems to direct his speech towards the audience without, however, any immediate contact. Such active witnessing might posit him both as narrator and spectator. This voyeuristic position was perhaps strengthened by the medium's limitations, as the puppets could appear on screen only in profile without the perspective of a three dimensional space. In the same scenes, three characters could hardly face each other and when they converse with one another, for example, they cannot walk past each other or turn around.[13]

As a loose adaptation of a theatre play, the synopses of Bican Efendi are also reminiscent of other Turkish theatre plays of this time. Theatre critic Beliz Güçbilmez finds one distinct characteristic of plays staged in Turkish at the turn of the century. According to her, these plays gave no background information about the characters nor do they seem to care about any past events that might have affected the present.[14] Rather, these plays focus on a rupture in the present, around which the entire story evolves and revolves. The plots of different Bican Efendi films may also be considered to be only about a crisis in the present moment, such as a young couple facing difficulties on their wedding day. However, since there are no intertitles and the absence of seamless, linear flow in the editing of this surviving print, it is perhaps a bit too speculative to question the film's narration. What is undeniable is the intermedial nature of the early cinema practice in Turkey and its connections to 'traditional' performing arts and particular patterns within global silent film in terms of narrative, character and acting.

Viola Shafik's work on Arab Cinema revealed that Turkish cinema was certainly not the only national cinema that had strong connections with shadow-play and Western cinema. *Al-Sa'alik* made in 1967 by Yusuf Ma'luk raised discussions over the influences on the film. While the actor in the film claimed Laurel and Hardy to be the main sources of inspiration, Shafik makes a convincing argument in regards to Karagöz and his fictional partner Hacivad (or 'Hiwaz' in Syrian) as being another important source for the representation of the constant struggles of two 'clever and cunning' characters.[15]

Bican Efendi the Steward, as a film adaptation of a Turkish theatre play, which was itself an adaptation of a French play, performed and directed by a former theatre actor whose surname was derived from the famous shadow-play character Karagöz. The shadow-play tradition of Karagöz also provided the source for the self-conscious device of the spectator within the film serving as the audience's guide to the diegetic action. Many contemporary Turkish films along with their Egyptian and Syrian counterparts are still considered to have their roots in Karagöz and silent cinema. These intermedial, international and inter-relational circumstances of the early twentieth century gave birth to cultural practices that very much represented their co-ownership in a collective cultural property.

Notes

1. 'Re-writing' here refers to a vernacularisation process that involved the changing of events, names and the spaces according to a local context. The original play itself consisted two acts while the remaking of it had three acts. While the film, *Bican Efendi the Steward*, which was inspired by this text, was shaped by different national contexts (i.e. Turkish shadow-play and American cinema), the text was also influenced by both the French and Ottoman contexts. Vasfi Rıza Zobu, a former theatre actor from this period, claims in his memoirs that the play was localised to such an extent that even the experts of French theatre were unable to track the original source, *Le Préxte*. See Vasfi Rıza Zobu, *O Günden Bugüne* (Istanbul: Milliyet Yayınları, 1977), 464–465; The reference to *Le Préxte* and the dedication to Şadi Karagözoğlu can be seen in the collection of İbn-ür Refik Ahmet Nuri's play. See Mehmed Rebii and Hatemi Baraz, *İbn-ür Refik Ahmet Sekizinci*, Vol. II (Ankara: T.C. Kültür Bakanlığı Yayınları 2001), 167–227.

2. Refik Ahmed Sevengil, *Türk Tiyatrosu Tarihi*, Vol. 5 (Ankara: Maarif Basımevi, 1968), 217. There also seems to be another interesting connection for early film history here, as the writer of this play, Daniel Riche, one year after publishing *Le Prétexte* in 1906, became a scriptwriter for Pathé-Frères. According to Laurent le Forestier's entry in *Encyclopedia of Early Cinema*, Riche also directed various dramas, comedies as well as adaptations and he became the vice-president of *Société des Auteurs de Films* in 1918. See Laurent Le Forestier, "Daniel Riche", in Richard Abel (ed.), *Encyclopedia of Early Cinema* (London: Routledge. 2005), 552.

3. Dario Mizrahi, *Diversity and Comedy in Ottoman Istanbul: The Turkish Shadow Performances* (Ph.D. Dissertation, Columbia University, 1991), 81.

4. On the temporal characteristics of early cinema see Tom Gunning, "'Now You See It, Now You Don't': The Temporality of the Cinema of Attractions", *Velvet Light Trap* no. 32 (Fall 1993): 3–12.

5. *Stamboul* (31 January 1898), 3.

6. See Elizabeth Thompson, *Colonial Citizens* (New York: Columbia University Press, 2000), 198.

7. For the particular shadow-play text where Karagöz visit the cinema show see Cevdet Kudret, *Karagöz*, Vol. I (Istanbul: YKY, 2004), 123–159.

8. See Nijat Özön, *Türk Sineması Tarihi* (Istanbul: Artist Reklam Ortaklığı Yayınları, 1962) 54–55. Giovanni Scognomillo, *Türk Sinema Tarihi*, Vol. I (MetisYayınevi, Istanbul, 1987) 32.

9. This film was realised by the National Veteran's Society, which was an extension of the National Army Film Center. *Bican Efendi the Steward*'s wide reception and the public's appreciation of it were used to obtain the legal rights for the making of a new film project of *Darülaceze*, an Ottoman national hospice for the elderly and the disabled. This new project was, however, assigned to the film company of Sigmund Weinberg, a Romanian citizen residing in Istanbul. Weinberg is a significant figure in the film history of Turkey. He had organised some early film screenings in Istanbul in 1897, made newsreels in Istanbul and trained the first local filmmakers of Turkey. The producers of *Bican Efendi the Steward* made official complaints by stating that they should be given preference to a 'lame foreigner' and justified their position by saying that they had produced a film of such great a success as *Bican Efendi the Steward*. These complaints were regarded as misleading and the legal rights of making the new film remained with Sigmund Weinberg, who in the end finished the film in 1922. This case was more than a mere competition between two cinema companies as it also reflected the complexity of the international dynamics as well as the nationalist response to them in the early film market in Istanbul. The official documents containing the exchange between the Army Film Center and Darülacaze are published in Turkish. See Ali Özuyar, *Devlet-i Aliyye'de Sinema* (İstanbul: de ki, Yayınları 2007), 45–51.

10. It is worth mentioning that the other surviving film *Binnaz* (Ahmet Fehim, Turkey, 1919) was also an adaptation from a theatre play.

11. Interview I carried out with film historian Giovanni Scognomillo.

12. Terri Ginsberg, Chris Lippard, *Historical Dictionary of Middle Eastern Cinema Historical Dictionaries of Literature and the Arts* (Maryland: Scarecrow Press, 2010), 361.
13. Mizrahi, 81.
14. Beliz Güçbilmez, *Zaman, Zemin, Zuhur: Gerçekçi Türk Tiyatrosunda Minyatür Kurgusu* (Istanbul, Deniz Kitabevi, 2006)
15. See Viola Shafik, *Arab Cinema History and Cultural Identity* (Chairo: American University in Chairo Press, 2007), 83–84; The official documents containing the exchange between the Army Film Center and Darülacaze are published in Turkish. See Ali Özuyar, *Devlet-i Aliyye'de Sinema* (Istanbul: de ki, Yayınları, 2007), 45–51.

27

Entre nouveauté et continuité : Le spectacle cinématographique serait-il une émergence des ombres françaises?

Thierry Lecointe

> Séparé de son public par un écran, [...] avant de livrer son œuvre, il [...] a fallu préparer, choisir ses lumières, [...] élaborer un texte, le compléter par un bruitage et une musique adéquate, monter un scénario et étudier la mise en scène. [...] Une séance [...] est une merveilleuse cure de silence et de calme. [...] Texte, dialogues, musique et éventuellement bruitage servent de soutien à l'image. Il est nécessaire que les scènes soient suffisamment significatives pour se passer du secours de la parole. Pour la partie musicale: [...] il faut se méfier des œuvres orchestrales, qui n'ont pas été faites pour cela. La partie sonore et la partie visuelle doivent être synchronisées très exactement. [...] Enfin, le silence convient parfaitement [...]. Une sonorisation perpétuelle est plus gênante qu'un manque total de sonorisation. Ce n'est pas du cinéma.[1]

Que d'analogies avec le cinéma muet! J'ai donc soupçonné un lien tangible entre les ombres françaises – ce texte tiré d'un manuel de montreurs d'ombres de 1959 s'y réfère – et les séances cinématographiques des premiers temps. J'entends établir un rapport entre l'organisation des spectacles d'ombres françaises et celle qui allait être progressivement mise en œuvre dans le cadre des séances cinématographiques. En somme, le cinématographe (français) ne se serait-il pas approprié la scénographie des ombres françaises afin d'être perçu, non plus comme une simple nouvelle attraction, mais comme un spectacle à part entière ? Pour valider cette hypothèse, il convient de trouver des liens entre ces deux attractions d'un point de vue conjoncturel.

Sans rentrer dans une étude historique du théâtre d'ombres, rappelons que ce spectacle fut (re)mis en valeur le 27 décembre 1886, par Rodolphe Salis (qui en a véritablement réinventé le concept au point de le baptiser ombres françaises) dans son cabaret parisien de Montmartre, le Chat Noir. Salis s'entoura des meilleurs dessinateurs, illustrateurs, chansonniers et compositeurs musicaux que pouvaient alors compter les milieux artistiques parisiens. Les ombres françaises du Chat Noir devinrent alors entre 1887 et 1897, année du décès de Salis, un spectacle parisien incontournable. Les représentations étaient constituées de véritables pièces de théâtre articulées autour de solides scénarii déclinés en tableaux (jusqu'à 30) dont la plus célèbre fut *L'Épopée*, une pièce militaire napoléonienne en deux actes à laquelle je ferai principalement référence. Des représentations ont également eu lieu dans d'autres théâtres et cabarets parisiens durant cette période. Jusqu'au début des années 1900, c'est essentiellement les ombres françaises de Dominique Bonnaud (un chansonnier qui fit ses armes au Chat Noir) qui étaient projetées. La naissance de ces deux types de spectacle à Paris ainsi que la relative proximité des principaux lieux de diffusion des ombres et des vues animées dans la capitale dénote donc une réelle connexion géographique et temporelle entre le cinématographe et les ombres françaises.

Des éditeurs littéraires communs

L'inventaire suivant montre le lien entre ombres et cinématographe du point de vue éditorial.

Ouvrages traitant des ombres animées:

H. Fourtier, *Manuel pratique de la lanterne de projection* (Paris: A. Laverne et Cie, 1889).

Bertrand Victor Effendi, *Les silhouettes animées à la main* (Paris: Charles Mendel, 1892).

H. Fourtier, *La pratique des projections* (Paris: Gauthier-Villars, 1893).

Lemercier de Neuville, *Les pupazzi noirs, ombres animées* (Paris: Charles Mendel, 1896).

Alber (prestidigitateur), *Les théâtres d'ombres chinoises* (Paris: Elie Mazo, 1896).

Ouvrages traitant des ombres animées et du cinématographe:

Eugène Trutat, *Traité général des projections, tome 1, projections ordinaires* (Paris: Charles Mendel, 1897).

Alber et A. Hégé, *Le grand manuel de projection. Guide de l'amateur* (Paris: Elie Mazo, 1897).

Ouvrages traitant du cinématographe:

A.L. Donnadieu, *La photographie animée, ses origines, son exploitation, ses dangers* (Paris: Charles Mendel, 1897).

Georges Brunel, *La photographie et la projection du mouvement. Historique, dispositifs, appareils cinématographiques* (Paris: Charles Mendel, 1897).

Louis Gastine, *La chronophotographie* (Paris: Gauthier-Villars, 1897).

Eugène Trutat, *La photographie animée* (Paris: Gauthier-Villars, 1899).

On constate à la lecture de cet inventaire que, dans un premier temps, trois éditeurs spécialisés dans la photographie et la projection ont à la fois traité des projections d'ombres et cinématographiques, et que, dans un second temps, les ouvrages abordant l'usage de la lanterne de projection y associent le théâtre d'ombres. Les lecteurs qui s'intéressaient aux projections cinématographiques n'ont de ce fait pas pu ignorer celles faites dans le cadre des ombres françaises.

Des procédés techniques et des problématiques d'exploitation communs

L'élément central commun au théâtre d'ombres, au cinématographe et aux projections fixes, c'est la lanterne. Ces différentes formes de projections relèvent souvent, comme l'ont dit André Gaudreault et Philippe Gauthier, de mêmes séries culturelles.[2] N'oublions pas l'écran, interface entre l'exhibiteur et son public. Si la lanterne et l'écran constituent les points communs en ce qui a trait au dispositif, le spectacle d'ombres françaises va révéler des problématiques identiques à celles que rencontrera ultérieurement le cinématographe. On présenta ainsi *L'Épopée* comme un spectacle mettant en scène 'quinze mille personnages, tous parfaits de contour et de mouvement'.[3] La presse ajouta au cours des semaines suivant la première:

> Caran d'Ache […] eut l'idée de projeter sur la toile les silhouettes avec la netteté et l'exactitude absolues […], tout cela avec […] une perspective vraiment admirable […]. Il faut voir l'effet produit par ces milliers d'hommes alignés, présentant tout à coup les armes d'un même mouvement automatique, pendant que l'empereur passe dans les lignes suivi d'un nombreux état-major; sa silhouette va en diminuant à mesure qu'il s'éloigne à l'horizon.[4]

> Une série de tableaux en ombres chinoises, dont l'effet est si prodigieux qu'il donne l'impression saisissante de la réalité même […]. Il y a dans chacun de ces tableaux un mouvement, une vie incomparable; il y a dans chacune des moindres silhouettes un caractère surprenant de vérité.[5]

Les premières appréciations développées furent donc, comme au cinématographe, la netteté des tableaux, la qualité des mouvements et des effets de perspective, ainsi que le réalisme des scènes. Si à l'origine, les ombres étaient monochromes, vers 1891 les auteurs commencent à introduire quelques effets de couleur:

> On a élevé la lanterne magique et les ombres chinoises à un niveau véritablement artistique. Il y a des dessinateurs comme Henri Rivière, […], Caran d'Ache, […] qui sont arrivés, dans le petit cadre doré qui sert de scène, à nous donner l'illusion exacte de la perspective, et même de la couleur. Il y a des paysages, avec des nuages mobiles se reflétant dans l'eau, qui ont tout le frisson du rêve, tout le *flou* des paysages de Corot.[6]

Alber donne quelques indications sur les procédés de colorisation, qui pouvaient reposer sur la projection par d'autres lanternes de plaques dessinées colorées ou de photographies teintées chimiquement utilisées comme décors de fond, ou encore sur la projection au travers de verres opaques teintés (boîtes à lumière[7]) pour restituer des ambiances particulières.

Outre les procédés visuels,[8] une sonorisation semblait indispensable. Un accompagnement musical illustrait tout le 'drame épique et muet'[9] de *L'Épopée*: 'une marche guerrière retentit au piano, le rideau se lève. [...] pour augmenter l'illusion, dans la coulisse il y a une dizaine de compères qui [...] jouent de la musique'.[10] L'orchestration n'est pas le seul élément sonore du spectacle, des bruits de coulisse et des voix se faisant également entendre, comme au théâtre: 'une dizaine de compères qui font les commandements militaires d'une voix sonore, [...] battent la caisse et fument de grosses pipes dont la fumée, [...] donne la sensation exacte de la bataille'.[11] Le spectacle comportait également les fameux boniments ayant fait la réputation de Salis. Ce dernier présentait d'abord le spectacle:

> Gentilshommes, [...] nous allons ressusciter devant vous l'épopée impériale et ranimer en vous la fibre chauvinesque en faisant défiler sous vos yeux éblouis les évènements qui ont eu lieu quatre-vingt ans avant le général Boulanger. Et maintenant, au rideau![12]

Salis intervenait ensuite régulièrement durant la représentation. 'Les divers tableaux de *L'Épopée* défilent', rapporte *L'Univers illustré*, 'commentés par les interprétations étourdissantes du gentilhomme-cabaretier'.[13] 'Salis lance des Vive l'empereur!', sa 'verve abracadabrante contribue encore à égayer les représentations de *L'Épopée*'.[14] Alber reprit les recettes de Salis: 'nous ne saurions trop insister sur ce point que le texte, l'application parlé, le boniment en un mot, qui accompagne une scène d'ombres a une énorme importance'.[15] Lemercier de Neuville souligne pour sa part le travail du 'récitant'.[16]

Sans préjuger de ce qu'allait devenir le cinéma des premiers temps, il faut bien constater que, tant aux plans visuel et sonore, ses propres problématiques étaient déjà intégralement posées dans les spectacles d'ombres françaises.

Lumière et Méliès: une certaine connaissance des ombres françaises

L'Épopée semblait être devenue un spectacle incontournable au début de l'année 1887, comme en témoigne *L'Univers illustré*:

> Rien de plus justifié, de plus légitime que le succès immense et sans précédent de ce spectacle. La presse entière l'a constaté; et le retentissement s'en est prolongé si loin, que nous trouvons, ces jours passés, dans des journaux américains et finlandais, des chroniques entières consacrées à le célébrer. Voilà plusieurs

semaines que *l'Épopée* [sic] est l'attraction parisienne par excellence. Toutes les illustrations, toutes les notabilités en tout genre y ont successivement défilé, depuis le général Boulanger jusqu'au prince de Suède, sans parler des écrivains, des peintres, des savants, des hommes politiques en renom. Les femmes du monde ne sont pas les moins empressées à se faire conduire au Chat-Noir [...]. D'ailleurs, il faut y être allé: la mode l'exige désormais. Aussi l'empressement est-il extraordinaire, et on se dispute jalousement les cartes d'entrée pour pénétrer dans cette petite salle du second étage de l'hôtel du seigneur Salis, qui ne peut guère s'ouvrir, chaque soir, que pour une centaine de privilégiés.[17]

On se croirait au Grand Café neuf années plus tard. Un tel succès a-t-il pu échapper à Antoine Lumière et ses fils, qui avaient 23 et 25 ans en 1887, ou encore à Georges Méliès (26 ans)? Madeleine Malthête-Méliès relate que son grand-père, installé à Paris fin 1884, fréquenta le cabaret de Salis.[18] Méliès se rendait également au théâtre Robert-Houdin avant qu'il n'en devienne le propriétaire le 1er juillet 1888. On y voyait, entre autre, des attractions d'ombres animées, dont les pupazzi de Lemercier de Neuville. Maurice Bessy et Lo Duca attribuent des ombres chinoises à Méliès en 1890.[19] Jehanne d'Alcy rapporte cependant dans un rapport de la commission historique de recherche n'avoir jamais vu de spectacle d'ombres initié par Méliès dans son théâtre.[20] Ce dernier n'ignorait pourtant rien des ombres et y fait référence dans ses souvenirs.[21] Par ailleurs, Méliès connaît le prestidigitateur Alber, grand praticien des théâtres d'ombres de salon et rédacteur en chef de la *Revue de la prestidigitation* diffusée par l'association syndicale des artistes prestidigitateurs, groupement rival à celui de Méliès.[22] Méliès rencontra enfin à Londres Félicien Trewey, magicien mais surtout ombromane, qui devint l'un de ses amis intimes.

Du côté des Lumière, les liens avec les ombres françaises sont peut-être plus ténus. Antoine fréquenta sûrement le Chat Noir. Louis, davantage confiné à Lyon, n'ignorait sans doute rien des susmentionnés ouvrages de Fourtier, qui publia en outre de nombreux livres techniques sur la photographie entre 1889 et 1895. Par ailleurs, Fourtier écrivit régulièrement dans la revue fondée par Paul Nadar, *Paris-Photographe*, dans laquelle Auguste et Louis cosignèrent également des articles. Enfin, rappelons que l'un des amis de la famille Lumière n'est autre que Trewey, qui deviendra concessionnaire et imprésario du Cinématographe en Angleterre, et acteur occasionnel dans quelques vues Lumière.

Ce que le cinématographe doit peut-être aux ombres françaises

À l'issue de la première projection publique du Cinématographe le 28 décembre 1895, dans le sous-sol du Grand Café du boulevard des Capucines à Paris, *Le Progrès*, périodique lyonnais, fut le premier à rendre compte, le lendemain, de l'évènement. On y relata assez sobrement l'admiration des spectateurs pour 'les résultats que M. Lumière a obtenus avec son nouvel appareil'.[23] Le journal parisien *La Poste* rapporta qu'on y vit 'un spectacle vraiment étrange et nouveau'. Mais au fil de l'article, on y décrit essentiellement 'leur ingénieux appareil' produisant 'des effets bien plus surprenants [que] les zootropes chers à nos premiers ans'. Le chroniqueur ajouta que 'la beauté de l'invention réside dans la nouveauté et l'ingéniosité de l'appareil', extrapolant sur son usage potentiel 'lorsque ces appareils seront livrés au public'[24] sans presque y entrevoir la future demande spectatorielle. *Le Radical* présenta la 'nouvelle invention, [des frères Lumière comme] une des choses les plus curieuses de notre époque', tout en précisant que 'leur œuvre sera une véritable merveille s'ils arrivent à atténuer, sinon à supprimer, [...] les trépidations qui se produisent dans les premiers plans'.[25] Dans *L'Univers illustré*, on vanta les mérites d'un 'curieux appareil [qui] donne vraiment l'illusion d'une photographie vivante', puis on fit un descriptif détaillé de la 'série de 11 plaques photographiques présentées pour la première fois à leurs invités le samedi 28 décembre' les qualifiant '[d']expériences [...] tout simplement merveilleuses'.[26]

À la lecture de ces comptes rendus, on doit bien admettre que, tout en étant admiratifs face à ce nouvel appareil, les chroniqueurs ne mettent pas en exergue la notion de spectacle même si le terme est employé une fois. C'est bien l'appareil qui est mis en valeur plus que le contenu des diverses photographies vivantes projetées. Aucun de ces articles ne rappelle les qualificatifs employés à propos des ombres françaises par *L'Univers illustré* en 1887: 'C'est un spectacle véritablement unique et merveilleux [...], une série de tableaux en ombres chinoises, [...] qu'ils semblent comme une évocation'.[27] On peut, dès cette séance historique au Grand Café, envisager les futures difficultés auxquelles allait être confronté le Cinématographe dans son développement commercial. En fait, cette attraction d'une durée totale de trente minutes n'était constituée que d'une dizaine de films sans lien narratif entre eux et dont chacun ne durait qu'une minute. Ce modèle allait-il s'avérer suffisamment attractif pour maintenir une affluence pérenne du public, passé l'engouement suscité par la nouveauté de cette invention?

Ni le dispositif, ni le format des films n'allait évoluer durant plus de deux années. Ainsi, un forain confirma des métrages 'de 20 m, quelques fois de 60 m de long'.[28] Méliès relata que, dans les années 1896–1900, 'les films [...] avaient 20 et 60 mètres au maximum',[29] tandis que Jasset affirma que 'la longueur générale des films en 1898–1899 était encore de vingt mètres'.[30] L'analyse de la filmographie française de 1896/1897 atteste de rares films d'un métrage supérieur à 20 mètres et ne révèle aucune bande excédant 60 mètres.[31] Dans un contexte de stagnation des formats des films, de quasi-absence de renouvellement des sujets et d'organisation inchangée des séances, le spectacle cinématographique était en récession depuis décembre 1896.[32] Cela n'a échappé ni à Lumière, ni à Méliès, lesquels, vu la conjoncture fin 1897, allaient procéder à une redéfinition de leurs films. Il convenait de rompre avec les simples 'photographies vivantes' et de produire désormais des vues dont une narrativité devait clairement se dégager.

Y-a-t-il causalité entre l'évolution des films Lumière et Méliès et une analyse que ces derniers auraient pu effectuer des atouts générant le succès des ombres françaises pendant plus de dix ans? C'est la piste que je suggère dans la mesure où ils furent les initiateurs des premiers films à tableaux. *L'Épopée* était annoncée comme une pièce relatant 'l'histoire du premier empire en trente tableaux',[33] soit 'pendant plus d'une heure'.[34] Trois éléments fondamentaux se dégagent de cette description: une histoire, ce qui présuppose un scénario, une progression narrative mise en œuvre par une succession de tableaux[35] et une durée significative permettant de valider la notion de spectacle.

Des films reprenant la conjonction de ces trois paramètres (scénario, tableaux, durée) allaient enfin voir le jour en 1898. À l'exception de la *Passion du Christ* en 12 tableaux tournée par Lear au printemps 1897,[36] dont le périmètre et le dispositif d'exploitation demeurent difficiles à évaluer, le premier film sériel témoignant d'une augmentation significative du métrage possiblement influencée par le modèle des ombres françaises est une production Méliès sur le naufrage du Maine (nos 144 à 147) sortie le 1er mai 1898. Georges Sadoul envisag l'aboutage des quatre tableaux, soit 100 mètres au total, lors des projections: 'les quatre films sont mis bout à bout'.[37]

Lumière de son côté intègre au sein de son catalogue une série plus ambitieuse, montrée pour la première fois le 15 mai 1898 à Lyon. Intitulée *Courses de taureaux*,[38] elle est composée de douze bobines d'un métrage standard d'environ 20 mètres dont chacune constitue un tableau. Ce film monté, souvent recomposé par les exploitants, fut diffusé sous forme d'une bande continue de 8 à 12 voire 13 bobines. Il s'inscrit donc en 1898 comme le premier véritable long métrage (dans le contexte de l'époque où un métrage de plus de 200 mètres représentait dix fois la longueur de la quasi-totalité des films sur le marché français). Ce film, réduit à tort comme une simple actualité, fut construit avec un réel souci de mise en valeur de la théâtralité, narrativité et dramaturgie de la corrida. Il eut un succès international, preuve de l'efficacité de sa construction narrative.

Figure 1: *Catalogue des films en location 1925–1926* (Paris: Maison de la Bonne Presse).

Ce n'est qu'en mai 1899 que Gaumont propose son premier film à tableaux: *La Passion* (220 m – 11 tableaux), plagiat de la version Lumière sortie en novembre 1898. Méliès réitère dans ce genre avec, en septembre 1899, *L'Affaire Dreyfus* (240 m – 11 tableaux). Pathé, en retard sur ses concurrents, sort en juillet 1899 une *Course de taureaux à Roubaix* d'à peine 60 mètres avant de réaliser en septembre un plagiat de *L'Affaire Dreyfus* de Méliès (155 m – 8 tableaux). Enfin, Méliès sort en décembre *Cendrillon* en une seule bande de 120 mètres et 20 tableaux. Les films français évoluèrent grâce à des structures narratives s'inspirant de séries culturelles préexistantes, notamment les ombres françaises, et, contre toutes idées reçues, les forains intégrèrent dès leurs sorties au sein de leurs programmes[39] ces films d'un nouveau format, redonnant de ce fait un second souffle à ce spectacle.

La survivance des ombres dans les années 1900, dans quelques salles dédiées, les salons privés et les patronages, entretenait une interconnexion avec le cinématographe. Ainsi, le lien ou la comparaison entre ces deux spectacles était toujours vivace en faisant presque deux rivaux:

> Mais, dira-t-on encore, l'ombre chinoise et le cinématographe ne sont-ils pas deux ennemis jurés et l'ombre peut-elle supporter la comparaison avec son omnipotent confrère. [...] il y a entre ces deux projections toute la différence qu'il y a entre une photographie et un tableau. Celui-ci est factice mais aimable, celle-là est réelle mais brutale. Le Cinématographe enfin c'est la *Vie*, les ombres c'est l'*Art*.[40]

Enfin, cette illustration n'est-elle pas un parfait résumé du lien entre les ombres et le cinéma?

Notes

1. J.-G. Salvagniac, *Spectacles d'ombres* (Paris: Éditions Billaudot, 1959), 3–11.
2. André Gaudreault et Philippe Gauthier, "Les séries culturelles de la conférence-avec-projection et de la projection-avec-boniment: continuités et ruptures", dans *Beyond the Screen: Institutions, Networks and Publics of Early Cinéma*, sous la direction de Marta Braun, Charlie Keil, Rob King, Paul Moore et Louis Pelletier (New Barnet: John Libbey Publishing, 2012), 233–238.
3. Gérome, "Courrier de Paris", *L'Univers illustré* (8 janvier 1887): 18.
4. Gérome, "Courrier de Paris", *L'Univers illustré* (15 janvier 1887): 35.
5. "Une représentation de 'L'Épopée' au Chat-Noir", *L'Univers illustré* (12 février 1887): 106.
6. Richard O'Monboy, "Courrier de Paris", *L'Univers illustré* (21 novembre 1891): 563.
7. Alber, *Les théâtres d'ombres chinoises* (Paris: E. Mazo, 1896), 28.
8. En 1887, les iconographies montrent un cadre de l'écran circulaire comme dans les projections fixes; en 1897, le cadre est rectangulaire comme au cinématographe.
9. Gérome, "Courrier de Paris", *L'Univers illustré* (8 janvier 1887): 19.
10. Gérome, "Courrier de Paris", *L'Univers illustré* (15 janvier 1887): 35.
11. Ibid.
12. Ibid.
13. "Une représentation de 'L'Épopée' au Chat-Noir", *L'Univers illustré* (12 février 1887): 106.
14. Ibid.
15. Alber, *Les Théâtres d'ombres chinoises*, 32.
16. Lemercier de Neuville, *Les Pupazzi noirs – Ombres animées* (Paris: Charles Mendel, 1896), 39.
17. "Une représentation de 'L'Épopée" au Chat-Noir", *L'Univers illustré* (12 février 1887): 106.
18. Madeleine Malthête-Méliès, *Méliès l'enchanteur* (Paris: Hachette, 1973), 94–95.
19. Maurice Bessy et Lo Duca, *Georges Méliès mage* (Paris: Prisma, 1945), 30.
20. Source que je dois à Frédéric Tabet.
21. Georges Méliès, *La vie et l'œuvre d'un pionnier du cinéma*, édition établie par Jean-Pierre Sirois-Trahan (Paris: Les Éditions du Sonneur, 2012), 35.
22. Source Frédéric Tabet.
23. *Le Progrès* (29 décembre 1895).
24. *La Poste* (30 décembre 1895).
25. *Le Radical* (30 décembre 1895).
26. E.R., *L'Univers illustré* (4 janvier 1896).
27. "Une représentation de 'L'Épopée' au Chat-Noir', *L'Univers illustré* (12 février 1887): 106.
28. *Le Journal d'Amiens, indicateur de la Somme* (19 juin 1897).
29. Georges Méliès, *Ce Soir* (23 décembre 1937), dans Marcel Lapierre, *Anthologie du cinéma* (Paris: La Nouvelle Edition, 1946), 46.
30. Victorin Jasset, *Ciné-Journal* (21 octobre 1911), dans Lapierre, *Anthologie du cinéma*, 83.
31. La filmographie Méliès est symptomatique: sur 129 titres parus en 1896/1897, seulement quatre en 1897 comportent deux bobines et deux films mesurent 60 mètres (annoncés originellement à 75 m). "*Le Tzar en France Cortège impérial à Paris* (60 mètres de longueur environ)", film Pirou inscrit dans une liste Georges Mendel (reproduite dans Victor Perrot, *Vieux papiers d'un vieux cinéphile de 1895 à 1914*, Bulletin de la société "Le Vieux Papier" [Autun: impr. L. Taverne et Ch. Chandioux, 1937], 3ème de couverture) lorsqu'il est associé à deux autres bandes de 20 mètres du même répertoire, est annoncé par la presse d'une durée de 6 à 10 minutes, voir: *L'Intransigeant*

(23 octobre 1896) et *L'Express de Mulhouse* (21 novembre 1896), cités dans Jacques et Chantal Rittaud-Hutinet, *Dictionnaire des cinématographes en France (1896–1897)* (Paris: Honoré Champion, 1999), 318–367.

32. Voir mon article "L'année 1896 en France: état des lieux sur les représentations Lumière face aux concurrents, à Paris et en Province", dans *Les cinémas périphériques dans la période des premiers temps: actes du 10e Congrès international Domitor*, sous la direction de François Amy de la Bretèque, Michel Cadé, Jordi Pons i Busquet et Angel Quintana (Perpignan: Presses universitaires de Perpignan, 2010), 75–99.

33. Gérome, "Courrier de Paris", *L'Univers illustré* (8 janvier 1887): 18.

34. Gérome, "Courrier de Paris", *L'Univers illustré* (15 janvier 1887): 35.

35. Une forme de progression narrative se retrouve dans les tapisseries flamandes du XVIe siècle: *La Parabole du fils prodigue* en 7 tableaux, *L'Histoire de Jacob* en 4 tableaux (exposées aux Hospices de Beaune).

36. Diffusé à Milan, *La Sera* (22–23 juin 1897), dans Aldo Bernardini, *Cinema muto italiano 1896/1904* (Bari: Editori Laterza, 1980), 175.

37. Georges Sadoul, "Les apprentis sorciers (d'Edison à Méliès)", *La Revue du Cinéma* no 1 (octobre 1946): 40.

38. Voir Thierry Lecointe, *Le Cinématographe Lumière dans les arènes* (Montpellier: UBTF, 2007).

39. Cf. programmes dans Jacques Deslandes et Jacques Richard, *Histoire comparée du cinéma*, tome 2 (Tournai: Casterman, 1968), 139–155–163.

40. Dans G. M., "Les ombres chinoises", *La Vie au Patronage* no 3 (15 juillet 1909): 170–171.

28

'Performed live and talking. No kinematograph': Amateur Performances of *Tableaux Vivants* and Local Film Exhibition in Germany around 1900

Daniel Wiegand

Around 1900, when the term 'living pictures' (or 'lebende Bilder' in German-speaking countries) was used, it most likely referred either to the new phenomenon of cinematograph shows or to the older but still persisting tradition of *tableaux vivants*. Apparently, the term expressed in both cases that there was something in the pictures that made them alive: in film the life-like movement of images, in *tableaux vivants* the physical presence of actors emulating a painting. Thus, while both media certainly presented pictures, the term 'living' seems to have referred to two different things. In 1913, German author and scriptwriter Paul Lindau aptly claimed that only with the emergence of film had the 'truly animated and living picture' come into being. He argued that life was tantamount to movement and that therefore a *tableau vivant*, with bodies frozen into standstill, 'was actually the exact opposite of what the words denote'.[1] As Lindau suggests, the historical concurrence of film and *tableaux vivants* at the turn of the century can be seen as a striking example of 'the simultaneity of the non-simultaneous', a temporal overlap of one medium highly indebted to nineteenth-century visual culture and another representing the advent of mass culture and expressing a more modern conception of life itself. One could go on to say that while *tableaux vivants* fixed life (largely defined as something coming from the inside) into signifying images, film on the contrary opened up images to life, now defined as movement. However, statements like Lindau's are rare. For the most part, film was not discussed as a competitor to *tableaux vivants*; indeed, the latter were popular in variety theatres and amateur theatricals well into the 1910s and beyond. We must assume, then, that contemporary audiences enjoyed *tableaux vivants* as much as film programmes or that if there were indeed something old-fashioned about the older medium, audiences did not immediately react to it in terms of conspicuous dislike.

This article presents some of the findings of a case study in the Bavarian town of Nördlingen, from which we can, I believe, infer the situation in other German small towns as well.[2] Comparing exhibition contexts and modes of reception of film and *tableaux vivants* in small towns provides useful insights into the simultaneity of the two media and what Charles Musser calls 'a field for intertextual reception'.[3] Musser explicitly refers to *tableaux vivants* in vaudeville circuits to make his point that audiences around 1900 were knowledgeable and well-versed in various visual media and thus frequently involved in 'making judgments and comparisons in relationship to other cultural works'.[4] One might add to Musser's discussion that audiences were likely to compare not only subject matter but also the media's respective formal characteristics. It is for this reason that I prefer to use the term 'intermedial' instead of 'intertextual reception'. The media landscape of small towns lends itself especially well to such an investigation since the range of media was usually narrower than in big cities and directed towards a rather homogeneous audience. In the following, I want to investigate in which exhibition contexts shows of *tableaux vivants* and films were performed, what kinds of reception modes they may have provoked and how they could have been seen in relation to each other by contemporary audiences.

Films were shown in Nördlingen from 1900 on, mostly on the annual fairground.[5] The town had about eight thousand inhabitants at that time and we can assume that most of them were eager to see the new attraction – at least the Catholic regional newspaper strongly recommended them.[6] Shows came from outside town by way of travelling exhibitors and could be seen only once or twice each year. *Tableaux vivants* on the other hand were a well-known medium even before the turn of the century and did not come from outside but were mostly staged by members of local or regional associations, who in most cases also appeared on stage. The only case of an itinerant show in Nördlingen that might have included *tableaux vivants* was a travelling theatre group presenting the Passion Plays. In its advertising, this group apparently wanted to make sure that their show was not to be confused with film: 'Performed live and talking. No kinematograph' ('Lebend sprechend aufgeführt. Kein Kinematograph').[7] In contrast, none of the local associations made such an explicit distinction, probably because *tableaux vivants* had a longer tradition in the town's cultural landscape and did not need to be explained. Also, the respective exhibition contexts were demarcated quite clearly. While films were shown in mixed programmes in rather informal contexts such as the fairground or carnival shows, local *tableaux vivants* exhibitions took place during official and prestigious festivities that displayed and negotiated the town's local, regional, and national identity. Among these events were the military association's anniversary, celebrating the victory of the Franco-Prussian War; the one-hundredth anniversary of Bavaria; and the local fire brigade's fiftieth anniversary, which was perhaps Nördlingen's most outstanding event in 1905.[8] As a rule, *tableaux vivants* shows were thematically related to the purpose of the celebration: war anniversaries would show military views, Bavaria was celebrated with *tableaux vivants* of its past kings, and the fire brigade staged pictures of a fire rescue. Thus, compared to film, the emphasis of *tableaux vivants* was not on varied entertainment but on their connection with the town's history, culture, and identity. Since both the fairground and the anniversaries were outstanding public events, we can assume that film and *tableaux vivants* shared more or less the same audiences. However, they were embedded in rather different social contexts, serving different ends.

What did *tableaux vivants* shows look like? Most consisted of coherent picture sequences or 'cycles' that would sometimes even tell a story or represent an ongoing action. Instructions for performances could be found in manuals that were printed and distributed by publishers specialising in amateur pastimes. They appeared in Germany from the second half of the nineteenth century until after First World War and well into the 1920s. Two of the manuals that were used in Nördlingen are still extant. While *Kriegs-Scenen* (*War Scenes*),[9] a popular sequence of twenty-eight military views, had been in print since the 1890s, *Die Feuerwehr im Kampfe mit dem entfesselten Element*[10] (*The Fire Brigade's Fight against the Raging Element*), was written by a member of Nördlingen's voluntary fire brigade for the very occasion when it was first staged: the fire brigade's fiftieth anniversary in 1905. These two manuals represented two genres that were popular in film, too, but have in fact a longer history as *tableaux vivants*: military views and views of the fire brigade. In the following, I want to briefly examine these two genres in their respective mediums.

Military views

While early military films mainly met a demand for actualities and news reporting,[11] most German *tableaux vivants* of this genre dealt with the past, e.g., with the Franco-Prussian War in 1870/71. Picture sequences such as the one staged in 1906 in Nördlingen had above all a commemorative function. As the introductory remarks in *Kriegs-Scenen* claim, the sequence was supposed to '*move* the important events of 1870/71 *closer* to the present and *put it in front of the eyes* of those who were not so lucky as to be involved'.[12] Military *tableaux vivants* were thus meant to construct a collective cultural memory, to mirror and to strengthen national identity by illustrating certain 'German values': bravery, patriotism, or endurance. By making recourse to a set of stereotyped and oft-repeated images, they also delegated fixed social roles to certain groups. Women, for instance, were frequently portrayed waiting while their men and sons were in the field.

Four different aspects shaped these military *tableaux vivants* as *performances* and contributed to their commemorative function: first, the performers were physically present. Second, they did not move. Third, the actors were probably known to most in the audience because they were members of the associations. And fourth, in many cases, the actors were or had been a part of what was shown on stage in real life. This was most obvious in the case of the firemen who posed as themselves but also true in the case of military views staged by associations of war veterans who had actually fought the Franco-Prussian War. The *tableaux vivants* that were staged in Nördlingen for the one-hundredth anniversary of Bavaria were described as follows: 'For the last picture … the old guard of the War Veteran Association from Kleinerdlingen appeared as well as bailiff Bohl from here. They were all standing on the battlefields in the past and are now on the peaceful stage'.[13] By staging past war scenes and using actors who had actually 'been there', *tableaux vivants* could evoke a sense of the national past as still embodied by people living within the community. While the usage of actual war veterans created a physical continuity with the past and thus enabled an almost auratic 'charging' of the performance,[14] *tableaux vivants* could not offer the kind of indexical relationship with past and distant events that was expected from cinematographic depictions of warfare. As Stephen Bottomore has shown, audiences of military films often demanded that the films show them the actual time, place and people involved in acts of war, preferably even the incidents themselves, and rejected staged war scenes as fakes, especially when they were billed as actualities.[15] I believe that this expectation of verisimilitude is deeply imbricated with the experience of cinematographic space, which differed profoundly from that offered by *tableaux vivants*. One report in Nördlingen's local newspaper wrote about films of the Boer War shown on the fairground: 'During the presentation of the Transvaal battles, one imagines oneself to be *displaced onto the battlefield*, such is the lifelike manner in which the actions are shown to the eyes of the shocked beholder'.[16] Reports such as these, describing an alignment of the point of view of the spectator to that of the camera, were in fact quite common around 1900. They betray a change in the relationship between image and viewer that cinematograph shows brought about. Whereas *tableaux vivants* promised to bring past events *to the spectator*, recreating them on a stage, in film it was rather the spectator who was transported to the place of events. Thus, both media created a specific kind of presence: the presence of the past *in* the present with *tableaux vivants*, the presence of the spectator at distant but real events with film.

Views of the fire brigade

As in the case of war veterans, *tableaux vivants* of the fire brigade presented real people posing as themselves. However, while military *tableaux vivants* brought past and distant events to the here and now, those of the fire brigade rather represented topical events. I want to look at these performances from two angles, first as 'motion pictures' and second as 'local views'. *Tableaux vivants* depicting fire rescues had been popular at least from 1890 on. They all had been 'motion pictures' in a sense because the actions they displayed were usually full of movement. However, there had always been a tension between their dynamic content and the presentation by bodies in static poses. The sequence performed in Nördlingen is certainly an extreme case. While it was common for other picture sequences to break up more complicated actions, such as the rescue of someone through an open window, into two separate images or even to show such a rescue from two different angles,[17] *The Fire Brigade's Fight* went much further than that. In twelve static pictures, displaying various parallel actions with up to twenty-seven performers simultaneously on stage, the sequence showed how members of the local fire brigade manage to put out a huge fire in a house and rescue a small girl and an old woman from the flames just in time before the roof crashes down. Each of the twelve pictures represents a specific moment of this unfolding action so that the sequence on the whole must have resembled a succession of phase images. While there is no way to be sure of how this actually looked like on stage, the manual conveys quite a good impression of it. For convenience, each of the twenty-seven characters is first given a specific number, followed by detailed descriptions of the poses that the performers have to assume for each picture. Figure 1 shows the description for the first picture called 'Alarm' with seven characters on stage. It reads:

> Nr. 1 [the house-owner] stretches out his hands from a window of the burning house, begging for help / Nr. 2 [his wife], in front of the door in a pose of running

Stellungen.

Bild 1: Alarm.

Nr. 1 streckt die Hände hilfsbedürftig aus einem Fenster des brennenden Hauses.
" 2 vor der Türe des Brandobjektes in forteilender Stellung, hält in der linken Hand ein Kleidungsstück; mit der rechten zieht sie Nr. 3 nach.
" 3 mit einem Spielzeug in der rechten Hand noch unter der Haustüre; siehe Nr. 2.
" 6 erscheint unter der Türe der zweiten Kulisse rechts mit vorgestrecktem Kopf.
" 7 schaut ängstlich zum Fenster der ersten Kulisse rechts heraus.

Bild 2: Feuer.

Nr. 1 reicht eine Wanduhr zum Fenster herab.
" 2 eilt, Nr. 3 nach sich ziehend, einige Schritte nach rechts, den Kopf nach dem Brandobjekt gewendet.
" 3 wie Nr. 2.
" 6 eilt zu Nr. 1 heran und streckt beide Hände nach der Uhr empor.
" 7 tritt an die Türe des Brandherdes und macht sie halb auf, als ob er eintreten wollte.
" 8 kommt hinter der ersten Kulisse rechts herein; die linke Hand hält das Seitengewehr, die rechte ist beruhigend erhoben.
" 9 erscheint im Lauf hinter der Seitenkulisse rechts.
" 11 läuft von links herein hinter der ersten Kulisse.
" 12 läuft von rechts herein vor der ersten Kulisse.

Bild 3: Straßengetümmel.

Nr. 1 übergibt Nr. 6 die Uhr und verschwindet vom Fenster.

Figure 1: A page from the *tableaux vivants* manual *Die Feuerwehr im Kampfe mit dem entfesselten Element* (1905).

away, holds a piece of clothes in her one hand, with the other she pulls her little son. / Nr. 3 [the son] with a toy in his hand is still in the doorway / ... / Nr. 7 [a neighbour] anxiously looks out of the window on the right side of the stage.[18]

In the second picture, the house owner is supposed to be still at the window but now he is passing a clock through the window to his neighbour, who was still in the house on the other side of the stage in picture 1. Picture 2, as becomes clear, represents the same scene as picture 1, only a few moments later. Correspondingly, the poses seem to be less modelled on classical painting or sculpture than on representations of arrested motion in media such as instantaneous photography or chronophotography. This becomes especially obvious in paradoxical phrases such as 'in a pose of running away' or when it is explicitly said that the boy must be shown at the exact moment when he is still 'in the doorway'.¹⁹ The impression that the actual poses are really slices of one continuous movement is reinforced, in contrast to standard presentations of *tableaux vivants*, by the lack of curtain fall between one picture and the next. Instead, the transformations are meant to be visible to the spectators and sometimes even contain elements relevant to the narrative. The animation of the otherwise motionless *tableaux*, the rhythmic alteration between motion and standstill, was part of the attraction of the performance. This is furthermore underlined by labelling the sequence a 'moving' or even 'moveable living picture' ('Beweglich lebendes Bild') in the manual.

I want to propose, then, that just like instantaneous photography, optical toys, chronophotography, and film, we must come to regard *tableaux vivants* as a visual medium that self-consciously, and often in playful ways, exhibited surprising images of standstill and motion by performing acts of freezing and animation. In the case of *tableaux vivants*, this has, I believe, ideological implications. While on one hand the fire rescue sequence depicts a chaotic, confusing, and potentially contingent action – in this sense mirroring the modern experience of the street and even of early film – it on the other hand arrests these actions at several points for at least one minute each so that spectators have enough time to study the pictures in detail and take them in as an orderly representation of a comprehensible causal chain. In fact, each character's action follows quite logically from the previous one. Also, within the still images, the members of the fire brigade are clearly depicted in rehearsed poses that denote control and mastery of the situation. The performance can thus be considered a display of the binding or taming of chaotic movement, of contingency and danger. After all, the purpose of the performance was to celebrate the fire brigade as a local institution.

If we take into consideration that members of the local fire brigade posed as themselves for an audience that was to a large degree comprised of locals, we can also speak of these pictures as *local views*. For Nördlingers, the voluntary fire brigade was certainly an important part of local identity. Highly visible in the town's everyday life, it often held public rehearsals and just the week before their anniversary they had to put out a real fire within the town's centre.²⁰ But Nördlingers also got to know a very different kind of local views in the itinerant cinema of Peter Leilich on the fairground. In these films, shot by Leilich himself, spectators could see themselves and people they knew attending the *Stabenfestzug*, a traditional town parade. The local newspaper wrote: 'How surprised the spectator must have been when he saw his own portrait in the kinematograph. The picture is so clear that each person can easily be recognized'.²¹

Leilich's local views were first shown in 1904 and then repeated in 1905, the same year as the fire brigade's *tableaux vivants*. These local views were more popular than any other film genre and even though they are not extant, we can assume that they were of a very different sort than the *tableaux vivants* of the fire brigade. Recent scholarship has emphasised that in many cinematographic local views, unpredictability and contingency played a vital role. As Martin Loiperdinger argues, the actual occasion of the filmed gatherings – official celebrations, parades or leavings of the church – often became less important than the uncontrolled images of the crowd itself. Audiences liked seeing acquainted people in funny or unflattering poses while they did not know in advance what they would look like on the screen themselves.[22] In relation to local views, Tom Gunning mentions the 'ability of the cinema to capture contingent happenings in all their details, seeming to sacrifice principles of selection and hierarchy found in traditional images'.[23] Hence, with their potential for unfamiliar views of the local, cinematographic local views opened up a public space that must have differed from the intended admiration and glorification of the fire brigade in their organised and rehearsed *tableaux vivants* that emphasised efficiency and discipline at work.

On several levels, then, audiences in Nördlingen could compare *tableaux vivants* and film. Both media shared certain genres or subject matters while offering rather different experiences of time, space and presence; both were performances of stillness and motion, displaying acts of freezing and animation, of binding and releasing; and both offered views of the local, rendering the seemingly known in either a highly codified and controlled manner, or in unexpected new ways.

Notes

1. Quoted from "Filmdramatik", *Kinema* 3, no. 11 (15 March 1913): 6.
2. I am indebted to the support of the municipal archive of the town of Nördlingen, especially Dr. Wilfried Sponsel.
3. Charles Musser, "A Cornucopia of Images: Comparison and Judgment across Theater, Film, and the Visual Arts during the Late Nineteenth Century", in Nancy Mowll Smith and Charles Musser (eds), *Moving Pictures: American Art and Early Film, 1880–1910* (Manchester, Vermont: Hudson Hill, 2005), 9.
4. Ibid., 5.
5. See *Nördlinger Anzeigenblatt* (16 June 1900), 595, 597. For the beginnings of cinema in Nördlingen, see also Günther Holzhey, "Neu! Zum ersten Male in Nördlingen! Der Kinematograph", in Rieser Volkshochschule Nördlingen e.V. / MUSICA MAGICA (eds), *Mach Dir ein paar schöne Stunden ... Vom Guckkasten zum Filmtheater, Nördlinger Kinogeschichte* (Nördlingen: self-published), 20–24.
6. See *Rieser Volksblatt* (10 June 1904).

7. *Nördlinger Anzeigenblatt* (7 September 1906): 1036.
8. See *Rieser Volksblatt* (21 July 1905); *Nördlinger Anzeigenblatt* (24 July 1905): 783; *Rieser Volksblatt* (31 January 1906); *Nördlinger Anzeigenblatt* (10 July 1905): 753–754; *Rieser Volksblatt* (12 July 1905).
9. J. Diehl, *Kriegs-Scenen: Darstellungen von lebenden Bildern aus dem Kriegsjahre 1870/71 mit verbindender Dichtung und Musik*, (Hamm i.W.: C. Dietrich, 2nd edn 1892). All manuals cited here are in the Berliner Staatsbibliothek.
10. Heinrich Heber, *Die Feuerwehr im Kampfe mit dem entfesselten Element: Beweglich lebendes Bild in 12 Verwandlungen nebst begleitendem Text* (Mühlhausen i.T..: G. Danner 1905).
11. See Stephen Bottomore, *Filming, faking and propaganda: The origins of the war film, 1897–1902* (Ph. D. dissertation, Universiteit Utrecht, 2007), chapter 2, 1–20.
12. Diehl, *Kriegs-Scenen*, 3. Italics are mine.
13. *Rieser Volksblatt* (31 January 1906).
14. 'Auratic' in the sense of Walter Benjamin for whom 'testimony to the history which it has experienced' is part of an object's aura. Walter Benjamin, "The Work of Art in the Age of Mechanical Reproduction", in Leo Braudy and Marshal Cohen (eds), *Film Theory and Criticism* (New York/Oxford: Oxford, 6th edn, Oxford University Press, 2004), 794.
15. See Bottomore, *Filming, faking and propaganda*, chapter 2, 1–20.
16. *Nördlinger Anzeigenblatt* (6 June 1900): 595. Italics are mine.
17. Schulze, *Freuden und Leiden des Freiwilligen Feuerwehrmannes: Lebende Bilder mit Text in Versen*, Liegnitz: Georg Gradenwitz, 1890. This manual describes a sequence of three pictures that begins with a burning house seen from the outside, followed by the house from the inside and then another picture of the outside, this time with the fire brigade at work. This, of course, resembles the shot sequence in *Fire!* (James Williamson 1901).
18. Heber, *Die Feuerwehr im Kampfe*, 9.
19. In fact, instantaneous photography was sometimes associated with *tableaux vivants*, as in a picture sequence entitled "Snapshots form the big city", a series of street scenes: Paul R. Lehnhardt, *Moment-Aufnahmen aus der Großstadt: eine Reihenfolge lebender Bilder mit erläuterndem Text* (Mühlhausen i.Th.: G. Danner, [1907]). See also "Der Moment-Photograph", in Max Schumm, *Das Wettrennen: Gesellschaftsscherz = Fastnachts-Bühne 7* (Berlin: Bloch [1890]).
20. See *Nördlinger Anzeigenblatt*, (3 July 1905): 707.
21. *Nördlinger Anzeigenblatt*, (8 June 1904): 601.
22. See Martin Loiperdinger, "Akzente des Lokalen im frühen Kino am Beispiel Trier", in Corinna Müller and Harro Segeberg (eds), *Kinoöffentlichkeit (1895–1920): Entstehung – Etablierung – Differenzierung* (Marburg: Schüren, 2008), 241–242.
23. Tom Gunning, "Pictures of Crowd Splendor: The Mitchell and Kenyon Factory Gate Films", in Vanessa Toulmin, Simon Popple and Patrick Russell (eds), *The Lost World of Mitchell and Kenyon: Edwardian Britain on Film* (London: BFI, 2004), 50.

29

Performing Painting: Projected Images as Living Pictures

Valentine Robert

Projecting painting

> How might we recover this madness, this insolent freedom that accompanied the birth of photography? In those days images travelled the world under false identities. To them there was nothing more hateful than to remain captive, self-identical, in *one* painting, *one* photograph, *one* engraving, under the aegis of *one* author. No medium, no language, no stable syntax could contain them; from birth to last resting place, they could always escape through new technologies of transposition.[1]

In this remarkable description of the dynamic that took hold of images around 1900, Michel Foucault invokes, emblematically, the 'birth of photography'. Yet it was the proliferation of all these 'new technologies of transposition', all the new media of the nineteenth century, which made possible and gave stimulus to these images' 'mad escapes'. Among these new technologies, one new 'cultural platform',[2] the screen, had a very important role.

Projection is a major means of disseminating artistic images. Stereopticon slide catalogues[3] show that the 'principal paintings in French museums',[4] the 'contemporary art' of the nineteenth century,[5] were *exhibited* on screen. These included the complete works of Raphael[6] and 'Gustave Doré's Fine Engravings'.[7] This was true not only in art history lectures. History lectures were also illustrated with 'paintings by the great masters'.[8] Lives of kings or of Joan of Arc were shown with pieces from museums.[9] Biblical stories were also 'compiled from pictures by various artists',[10] while most popular stories were re-transcribed using engravings by Cruikshank, Kaulbach or Grandville. We find the same phenomenon among the earliest projections of *moving* images: several films are advertised in the catalogues as 'inspired by paintings by the great masters',[11] as 'living reproductions' of 'familiar' painted scenes,[12] or as 'faithful recreations of famous paintings on film'.[13]

Projected images were thus part of the iconographic succession described by

Foucault. They even had a special place therein, because they did not limit themselves to reproducing these compositions: they changed the way images were perceived and received. In the present article, we will see how, in this frenzy of visual transfers, projection brought a new dimension into play by *spectacularising* the image and by transforming *established* images into *performed* images.

Fine arts spectacularisation

To demonstrate this claim, I will focus on the case of what are surely the projections richest in terms of iconographic heritage, namely religious lectures. Biblical images have a nodal position in the history of projection, both fixed and moving. While the first Domitor conference demonstrated the predominant role of the Passion Play in the earliest film entertainments,[14] depictions of Christ were just as central to fixed projections, because religious circles, more than any other, developed, theorised and documented the medium, which they saw as an ideal device for education and propaganda. Biblical depictions were thus not only unavoidable in projected images; they are also exemplary for the present discussion. For this 'apostleship through images' did not wish to break with fifteen centuries of iconography; it sought instead to 'popularise the names of the great artists' at the same time as 'Christian ideas':[15]

> Let us make an Apologetic by the Artistic. Let us leave aside the mediocre daubers and draw on the work of the great masters. . . . The people are more able to appreciate art than we think. They know how to appreciate true beauty. When a true master's painting appears on the screen they are fascinated, they are drawn in. We can explain the painting to them, they are interested in it, they fix it in their minds, they don't forget it, and neither will they forget the explanations of it given to them.[16]

Projections thus became 'reproductions of masterpieces',[17] with some lanternist priests even pursuing the ideal of 'depicting great religious subjects *solely* through paintings by the masters'.[18] The sources demonstrate the extent of the phenomenon. In an illustration of a sermon with projections given in a Paris church in 1903, Fra Bartolommeo's *Deposition* was magnified on the wall of the nave (Figure 1).[19] Many collections of preserved religious lantern slides reproduce canonical works such as Munkácsy's *Christ before Pilate*, to which an entire section of floor has been added to adapt it to the square format of the slide (Figure 2b).[20] In catalogues, most religious series are riddled with references to the great names of art history, particularly Renaissance painters.[21] Contemporary artists are also cited, illustrators in particular, as new iconographic models took hold in illustrated Bibles in the nineteenth century.[22] Tissot, Doré, Bida, Copping and Hofmann brought about changes in Biblical imagery in a manner

Figure 1: Fra Bartolommeo's *Deposition* projected in the Church of Sainte-Anne in Paris
[*Le Fascinateur* 4 (April 1903): 98].

so widespread as to be of almost graphic novel proportions, meeting with 'phenomenal worldwide success'[23] and becoming the preferred model for illustrated lectures. These biblical slides were already placed in series compiled to accompany the speaker's remarks. Several catalogues, moreover, offer monographic series reproducing almost all the engravings in a single illustrated Bible, presented as a veritable 'projected Bible'.[24] These gave concrete meaning to the adage that 'projection is to the lecture what engravings and illustrations are to books'.[25]

This comparison between illustrated Bibles and illustrated lectures, however, has a fundamental limit in that, in the case of projection, the text is *performed*. A lecture involves an orator reading a text aloud while facing the audience, live: it is a kind of performance. The reader must become an actor:

> To be alive is the lecturer's entire programme, the entire secret of his power over the audience. Eloquence is a form of drama. The lecture is a tussle. Through the strength of his conviction and the energy of his will, the orator tries to take hold of his listeners. And in this violent tension of his whole being, as he himself is greatly moved, sooner than the others, by the violent effort he expends to rouse them, oratorical passion, momentum and movement suddenly appear in his speech.[26]

And, proclaimed the First Congress of Catholic projections, 'speech is not everything': 'the speaker's physiognomy, the gestures accompanying his words, must give them more energy and expressiveness'.[27] Finally, the religious context heightened the intensity of this 'embodiment of the Word' by the actor-preacher, through his words but also through his 'voice', 'his breathing, his palpitation, his quivering':[28] 'It is no longer a voice we hear, but a living soul, stirring both speaker and audience'.[29]

Multimedia exhibition

The performance quality of the event is not limited to the lecturer: we are in the presence here of true 'multimedia' spectacles. Projections were added to pre-existing sermons, ceremonies, lectures and catechism sessions, which already had numerous rhetorical and media resources at their disposal. Projections did not take the place of these resources, but joined them in a new performative logic which provided for 'the eye and the ear'.[30] In 1909, for example, it was decided, emblematically, to incorporate projections into the traditional Catholic schools concert at Armentières, renamed 'Redemption after the Great Masters of Music *and Painting*'.[31]

In this audio-visual dynamic, preachers became veritable *performers*, one-man bands handling a thousand media at once, as this review of the Easter projections put on in Saint-Joseph that same year makes clear: 'Behind the screen and invisible to the viewers [nothing could be more impressive]: the projection device, a harmonium, a choir of 50 girls, a group of a dozen men and youngsters and, in the midst of all that, the worthy priest directing it all, running his lamp, showing his slides, keeping time, singing along'.[32] The songs could also be accompanied by media, as gatherings of this kind specialised in using the phonograph, making it possible to play airs and hymns sung by experienced singers. Most often, these 'great melodies' were paired with 'great paintings', matching famous works of art with recorded songs in a dual play of references, both musical and pictorial.[33] Sometimes the slides themselves displayed this two-fold reference by joining verbal and visual quotations, such as the Newton slide which arranged the words and music of the hymn 'O Sacred Head' around a central medallion showing Guido Reni's *Ecce Homo*.[34] These slides, a sort of karaoke *avant la lettre*, encouraged those in the audience to become a chorus, transforming the multi-media event into a *total performance* involving the spectators. This 'active role' that members of the flock should 'take on in the ceremony'[35] – praying, singing, standing up, kneeling – was, moreover, a typical performative element of these religious lectures. And recognition of (and often applause for) the masterpieces projected was an essential part of this interactivity.[36]

The final element was the intervention of another medium: the *kinematograph*. The joining of fixed and moving projected images was a specialty of these religious events, as Jacques and Marie André have noted[37] and as demonstrated by machines such as the Immortel, a projector specifically designed (and named!) by the French apostolic industry to make possible instantaneous transitions between glass slides and films. Guillaume-Michel Coissac suggested that 'perfection consists in knowing how to use fixed and moving projected images in combination',[38] and it was indeed in multimedia form – using a magic lantern, phonograph and kinematograph – that religious projection met with phenomenal success[39] and even received absolution by the pope in 1904! This play of media could go as far as pure juxtaposition, if we go by the sample programme presented at the 1910 congress, which suggested that the same story, the legend of St Nicholas, be projected *first* as fixed images by the stereopticon and *then* as moving images by the kinematograph.[40] This gives an idea of the extent to which the pleasure afforded by the performance resided in comparing the effect the new media had on the same imagery.

An exemplary case of this performative blend of fixed and moving projected images was *Jeanne d'Arc*, given by Father Fouchécour in Paris in 1903, which used slides (copied from paintings by Lenepveu in particular) for the explanatory section addressed to the viewer's 'intelligence' and film sequences for the dramatic moments to 'lead them' and make them 'more than understand': to 'see, feel and *live* the truth'.[41] These transitions occurred instantaneously and were carried out surreptitiously by trained assistants, playing on their surprise effect: '[Suddenly] the picture we were looking at was different from those that had come before it: the kinematograph had replaced the fixed-image device and we now admired a truly living spectacle before us'.[42] Film projections were more 'alive' than fixed images because the spectacle had gained a supplementary performative dimension. With films, the performance was no longer limited to the live elements in the hall: the images themselves were performed.

Model Acting

With respect to the original picture – such as this painting by Munkácsy (Figure 2a) – slides reproduced the inanimate painted or engraved forms (Figure 2b) while in film the images took shape, moving and coming alive (Figure 2c). Cinematic staging necessarily involved the scenes being acted out by flesh and blood actors who, at the moment of the film shoot, before the projection, already

29 Performing Painting: Projected Images as Living Pictures

Figure 2: (a)Mihály Munkácsy, *Christ before Pilate*, 1881 [oil-on-canvas, 417x636cm; Art Gallery of Hamilton]; (b)T.H. McAllister's lantern slide *Christ before Pilate: Munkacsy*, n.d.[gelatin-on-glass, 8.3 x 10.2cm; George Eastman House]; (c)*Vie et Passion du Christ* (Pathé, 1902). [35mm film frame; Cinémathèque suisse.]

transformed the imagery into performance. In their filmic 'escapes', masterpieces of painting and engravings in illustrated Bibles were not just reproduced; they were embodied. Acted-out interpretations of sacred iconography were, moreover, controversial, especially in the theatre, where putting Christ on stage ran up against censorship.[43] Cinematic 'embodiment' gave rise to more nuanced discussions, by virtue in particular of the sublimation made possible by the silent, two-dimensional projection, creating a painterly effect. This iconographical re-embodiment was not, moreover, exclusive to projections of moving pictures. A genre of fixed projection slides, called 'Life Models', appeared in the late nineteenth century; these were not painted or engraved images but staged photographs with real actors posing. Once again, religious circles played a key role in exploiting this technique,[44] but most of the time sacred figures were not depicted in flesh and blood, continuing rather to be *drawn* in hybrid slides that were part-photograph, part-painting. La Bonne Presse appears to have been one of the only publishers of glass slides with true embodiments of religious iconography, such as *Pastorale de Noël* (1908), *Saint Tarcisius* (1909) and *Sainte Cécile* (1910), adapted from painterly models but photographed using *living* models.

At the initiative of Honoré Le Sablais, a filmmaker-priest, La Bonne Presse went even further and produced the *same* staged event in the form of *both* fixed and moving images. I have been able to identify more than a dozen of these double-edged productions which gave rise simultaneously to both a film (or more precisely to a series of sequences which could be obtained individually) and to a series of slides. The film and photographic versions were sold under the same title, such as *La Passion de Notre Seigneur* (thirty-five slides/twenty-two sequences), *Jeanne d'Arc* (thirty-two slides/seven sequences) and *Bernadette et les Apparitions de Lourdes* (twenty-six slides/eleven sequences), to mention only the first titles released, in 1909. The publisher's advertising encouraged people to alternate between the fixed and moving image series and to use them to complement each other, announcing from the outset that the 'complete film' was 'not for every budget' and suggesting that the work be purchased 'in pieces' in a manner conducive to hybridisation.[45] Lecturer-priests could thereby allow themselves the luxury of 'selecting the most moving scenes' from the moving images version[46] without forgoing the complete and uninterrupted story, told in all the colourful slides.[47]

In the case of the films at issue here, which is to say films with an iconographic referent which cultivated an intertextual relation with still images, filmic and photographic shoots were made compatible thanks to 'living pictures' or 'tableaux vivants' (English speakers often used the French term, with its high-brow social and cultural resonances).

Living pictures have been mostly forgotten today, but in the nineteenth century one could speak of 'tableau-mania'.[48] They consisted in reproducing famous artistic compositions on stage with immobile (or almost immobile) actors, and they appeared in every kind of live performance (theatre, opera, pageants, music-hall numbers, fairground attractions, high-society entertainments), especially in religious theatre, which specialised in these 'immortalised' painterly 'embodiments'. In the iconographic interlocking that Foucault described, leading from the painted to the projected picture, the performed living picture is a true missing link: it transferred a drawn composition to a living scene and transformed an established image into a performed image in the form of a live, collective show. In this sense, it was a direct, explicit and essential model for both the Life Models and the films. Performed living pictures were the key to these 'dual' film and photographic shoots, and the key and conclusion to the present article.

Living Pictures

On all his many 'cine-photographic' shoots, Honoré Le Sablais worked with living pictures. Reviews and visual documents show that the scenes were recreated 'from paintings by the greatest masters'[49] or from widely circulating engravings, for example in François Guizot's volume *Histoire de France*.[50] Descriptions of the day remark that the actors wore 'faithfully reproduced' costumes and moved slowly, more slowly even than all the other 'religious scenes depicted in the cinema to date'[51] – which was no mean feat given the hieratic acting found in all the versions of the Passion Play[52] – whose gestures tended towards 'poses',[53] enabling them to be photographed as well as filmed.

Projected images thus became a new field for the growth of living pictures, to the point that the terminology changed and was appropriated by film and photography. At first, the expression 'tableaux vivants' was applied to the technique 'executed'[54] by the models acting in front of the still and movie cameras of La Bonne Presse, to their manner of both 'interpreting' and 'fixing' the scene, of 'embodying' a 'perfect recreation' of the 'theme'.[55] People spoke of 'photographs of tableaux vivants',[56] of tableaux vivants 'recorded and reproduced' by the still camera and the kinematograph.[57] Gradually, however, a terminological slippage led to the expression being used to describe the final product, the media performance, the slides and films projected – in other words, the re-lived picture on the screen in front of the viewers.

The expression 'tableaux vivants' became current as one of the French equivalents of the English expression 'Life Models'. On 1 January 1909 (twenty-five years after Bamforth), *Le Fascinateur* pompously announced an 'entirely new genre' of 'projection slides' under the heading 'tableaux vivants',[58] and the term became standard amongst projectionists to describe these 'series' in generic terms. The journal vaunted these 'finely coloured tableaux vivants'[59] and, in some slide catalogues, the term became a veritable category.[60] The term 'tableaux vivant' also extended to descriptions of films: '[The] operator played *La Cène*, one of the 11 films on the *Passion de Notre-Seigneur* published by la Bonne Presse. This very well-made tableau vivant made a great impression on the assembly'.[61] This use of the term 'tableau vivant' to describe moving pictures was common in French. We find the same linguistic association in English, because until the expression 'moving pictures' was stabilised, the term 'living pictures' was often used to describe films and was even more common than the French expression.[62] This terminological re-appropriation was 'officialised' in a way by the Governor General of Canada when he discovered films embodying Napoleonic iconography: 'The scenes represented may indeed justly be termed Living Pictures, actually made to live and move before our eyes'.[63] This terminological shift is thus the 'last word' in my demonstration by showing that fixed and/or moving projected images created living pictures of a new kind, in which the 'life' breathed into works of art was not solely carnal but also media-based, wherein it was no longer so much bodies performing as it was media.

Translated by Timothy Barnard

Acknowledgements: Adapted from a conference paper in French entitled "De la page à la performance, de la toile à l'écran – ou comment la nouvelle culture des médias s'approprie et transforme le tableau vivant". This text derives from research conducted for the author's doctoral dissertation (directed by François Albera and approved by the Swiss National Science Foundation [SNSF]) on the importance of the tableau vivant and the concrete *realizations* of paintings in early cinema. Many thanks to the personnel of the Médiathèque Guy-L.-Coté at Cinémathèque québécoise, of the Bibliothèque Nationale de France, and to GRAFICS collaborators who have kindly granted me access to the various documents examined in this paper.

Notes

1. Michel Foucault, "Photogenic Painting (1975)", trans. Dafydd Roberts, in Sarah Wilson (ed.) *Photogenic Painting: Deleuze, Foucault, Fromanger* (London: Black-Dog Publishing, 1999), 84. Translation modified slightly – Trans.
2. Charles Musser, "Le stéréopticon et le cinéma: forme de média ou plate-forme de médias?", in François Albera and Maria Tortajada (eds), *Ciné-dispositifs* (Lausanne: L'Age d'Homme, 2011), 136 [forthcoming in English, Amsterdam University Press].
3. Ibid., demonstrates that, rather than the term 'magic lantern' (associated with children's stories

and entertainment), the word 'stereopticon' (more serious and technical) became institutionalised for illustrated lectures.
4. *Catalogue des projections de la Bonne Presse* (Paris: La Bonne Presse, 1905), 194.
5. *L'histoire de l'art par les projections lumineuses* (Paris: Molteni, 1912), 47.
6. Ibid., 108.
7. *Marcy's Scioptican Catalogue* (Philadelphia: Moore, 1877), 36.
8. *Catalogue La Bonne Presse*, 113.
9. *Catalogue des vues sur verre pour les projections lumineuses* (Paris: J.-E. Bulloz, 1911), 6–17.
10. *The Lantern Slide Gallery: A Catalogue* (London: Newton & Co., n.d.), 18.
11. *Liste générale des vues cinématographiques Gaumont* (Paris: Gaumont, 1903), 3.
12. *Catalogue La Bonne Presse*, 262.
13. *Le Sacre de Napoléon*, Pathé KOK Advertisement 17-D [n.d.].
14. Roland Cosandey, André Gaudreault and Tom Gunning (eds), *An Invention of the Devil? Religion and Early Cinema* (Lausanne: Payot, 1992).
15. Fr. Poulin, "L'Apostolat par l'image", *Le Rayon* 7, no. 2 (February 1912): 28.
16. Fr. Jager, "L'Art en projections", *Le Rayon* 5, no. 2 (February 1910): 20.
17. Fr. Limagne, "A Montluçon", *Le Fascinateur* 28 (April 1905): 175.
18. Fr. Lemoine, "La question des projections artistiques", *Le Rayon* 5, no. 5 (May 1910): 66.
19. Fr. Clair, "Les Projections à l'Eglise", *Le Fascinateur* 4 (April 1903): 98.
20. The George Eastman House lantern slide collections are representative of this painting reproduction trend, with series by C.W. Briggs (86:0768-0770), Levy & Ses Fils (88:0401-0402), La Bonne Presse (87:0555) and T.H. McAllister (89:0377, from which is taken the illustrated slide [fig. 2b]).
21. See for example *Catalogue La Bonne Presse*, 81–83.
22. See for example *The Lantern Slide Gallery*, 15–18.
23. Philippe Kaenel, "De l'édition illustrée à la bande dessinée: réimaginer la Passion au XXe siècle", *Relief* 2, no. 3 (2008): 312.
24. The best example concerns Gustave Doré's Bible, see Valentine Robert, "Gustave Doré's Works on Screen", in Philippe Kaenel, Edouard Papet and Paul Langand (eds), *Gustave Doré (1832–1883). Master of imagination* (Paris/Ottawa: Musée d'Orsay/National Gallery of Canada, forthcoming).
25. G.-Michel Coissac (plagiarising Fouchécour), *Manuel Pratique du Conférencier-Projectionniste* (Paris: Bayard, 1908), 177.
26. Fr. Thellier-de-Poncheville quoted by G.-Michel Coissac, "La séance de cinématographie", *Le Fascinateur* 105 (September 1911): 238.
27. Fr. Fouchécour, "Organisation d'une conférence", *Le Fascinateur* 27 (March 1905): 108.
28. Fr. Thellier-de-Poncheville quoted by G.-Michel Coissac, 238.
29. Fr. Fouchécour, 108.
30. Ibid.
31. *Le Rayon* 4, no. 4 (April 1909): 49–50. My emphasis.
32. *Le Rayon* 4, no. 3 (March 1909): 36.
33. *Le Rayon* 5, no. 2 (February 1910): 19.
34. Private collection (http://janehousham123.blogspot.ch, June2011).

35. Fr. Thellier-de-Poncheville, "Les conférences dans les églises", *Le Fascinateur* 27 (March 1905): 134.
36. Karen Eifler, "Between Attraction and Instruction: Lantern shows in British poor relief", *Early Popular Visual Culture* 8, no. 4 (November 2011): 376.
37. Jacques and Marie André, "Le rôle des projections lumineuses dans la pastorale catholique française", in *An Invention of the Devil*, 46–48.
38. G.-Michel Coissac, "La séance de cinématographie", 237.
39. See the emblematic *Soldiers of the Cross* lecture (www.nfsa.gov.au/collection/documents-artefacts/soldiers-cross).
40. *Le Rayon* 5, no. 10 (October 1910): 131.
41. Fr. Fouchécour, "Instruire en amusant", *Le Fascinateur* 6 (June 1903): 163–164.
42. Ibid., 164–165.
43. See Valentine Robert, "La Sainte Face interdite de toile: Apparitions et disparitions du Christ au cinéma", in Paul-Louis Rinuy and Isabelle Saint-Martin (eds), *Visages de Dieu dans l'art contemporain* (Paris: Presses de Paris-Ouest, forthcoming).
44. Bamforth, the principal publisher of Life Models, explained that 'the main source for [his] business was to do with the religious worship of the time and the social movements associated with religion'. Quoted by Robert MacDonald, *The Illustrated Bamforth Catalogue* (London: Magic Lantern Society, 2009), 27.
45. *Le Fascinateur* 84 (February 1910): 23.
46. Paul Feron-Vrau, *Le Fascinateur* 84 (December 1909): 388.
47. The economic argument for this fixed-moving hybrid was of primary importance, as La Bonne Presse did not move to a film rental system until 1920. See Pierre Véronneau, "Le Fascinateur et la Bonne Presse: des médias catholiques", *1895 Revue d'histoire du cinéma* 40 (June 2003): 31.
48. *Athenaeum* (3 February 1849): 118.
49. "Jeanne d'Arc", *Le Fascinateur* 74 (February 1909): 43.
50. *Le Rayon* 4, no. 6 (June 1909): 85.
51. "La *Passion de Notre Seigneur*", *Le Fascinateur* 84 (December 1909): 358.
52. See Valentine Robert, "Les Passions filmées: des codes en appropriation, un cinéma en canonisation", in Peter Bianchi, Giulio Bursi and Simone Venturini (eds), *The Film Canon* (Udine: Forum, 2011), 371–379.
53. Honoré-Le-Sablais, "Le Cinématographe", *Le Fascinateur* 84 (December 1909): 387.
54. "*Pastorale de Noël*", *Le Fascinateur* 84 (December 1909): 357.
55. G.-Michel Coissac, "Quelques précisions", *Le Fascinateur* 89 (May 1910): 117.
56. *Le Rayon* 4, no. 4 (April 1909): 49.
57. G.-Michel Coissac, "L'Art de demain", *Le Fascinateur* 88 (April 1910): 84.
58. *Le Fascinateur* 73 (January 1909): 14.
59. *Le Fascinateur* 96 (December 1910): 424.
60. "Nouvelles Séries de Vues de Projection", *Le Rayon* 4, no. 7 (July 1909): 100.
61. G.-Michel Coissac, "Une séance de projection", *Le Fascinateur* 2 (February 1903): 40.
62. See Valentine Robert, "Le tableau vivant ou l'origine de l'*art* cinématographique", in Léonard Pouy and Julie Ramos (eds), *Le tableau vivant ou l'image performée* (Paris: INHA, forthcoming).
63. "Government House testimonial (22 March 1898)" quoted by Germain Lacasse, *L'Historiographe. Les débuts du spectacle cinématographique au Québec* (Montreal: Cinémathèque québécoise), 17.

30

Colour as Performance in Visual Music, Film Tinting and Digital Painting

Joshua Yumibe

At the *Scottish Film Consortium* in 2012, Lucy Brett, a representative of the British Board of Film Classification, spoke about the Board's approach to censorship.[1] One of the flags for the British censors has to do with violence against children, which *The Hunger Games* (2012) ran afoul of specifically because of the amount of realistic looking blood in the film. It was initially given a 15 rating, suitable for audiences fifteen and over, but the studio wanted a 12A rating for younger viewers, so they worked with the Board to make adjustments. This normally occurs through cuts, excising portions of scenes to bring the film in line with censorship policies. When the Board received the revised version of the film, nothing at first seemed altered as the time codes were the exact same. After a closer inspection, the Board realised that no scenes were actually cut in this initial revision; instead, the blood that had been applied was toned down, desaturated, and removed in post-production in the film's digital layers.[2] Such an approach perhaps should not come as a surprise given the film's direction by Gary Ross, whose expertise in this kind of layered, digital manipulation of colour is well known through his ground-breaking work in *Pleasantville* (1998).[3]

This structured type of colour work presents a useful example of what David Rodowick has recently discussed in terms of the palimpsestic nature of the digital image in which layers are composed atop one another. From such a perspective, he sees a film such as Alexander Sokurov's *Russian Ark* (2002) not as a film based on the long take, but rather as a montage film because the single shot that lasts the length of the film is comprised of some thirty thousand post-production edits on its digital layers.[4] Rodowick's conception of the digital image as a palimpsest is useful for theorising the nature of colour in cinema more generally, and I want to use *The Hunger Games*' layered example of blood – or rather, in

Jean-Luc Godard's formulation not blood, but red – to think through the related connections that Lev Manovich makes between what he calls digital painting effects in new media and the functions of early applied colouring in silent cinema.[5]

The digital image after all is not the only palimpsest in film history. To move from the censorship of *The Hunger Games* to early film, a related layered use of red can be found in the fragmentary elements of Segundo de Chomón's trick film, *Les Tulipes* (Pathé, 1907), as housed in the Davide Turconi Nitrate Frame Collection.[6] The film features a female conjurer who magically appears to a woman picking tulips. The conjuror goes on to performs a series of dazzling tricks: she makes coloured fountains and fireworks appear, and then calls forth a series of dancing women, which culminates in the film's apotheosis. All of the women in the film wear relatively short skirts with low cut blouses, revealing bare legs and upper chests. As occurred from time to time in early cinema, prudish censors applied red dye over the flesh of the performing women, thus using colour to produce an occluding layer of censorship rather than a digitally removed one. These examples from early film to digital cinema thus call attention to colour's ability to add and superimpose meanings onto the moving image, through analogue addition and digital removal.

Relatedly, such instances of palimpsestic colour illustrate the ways in which elements of film can act performatively: that is, how in exhibition red performs blood when projected. To these ends, it is worth developing further Philip Auslander's deconstruction of the ontological opposition between live performance and 'mediatized performance'.[7] Auslander's focus is on the traditional forms of live entertainment (theatre, opera, concerts, etc.) that have become increasingly distributed through mass media such as television, cinema theatres, and over the internet. However, the terms of his argument can also be reversed productively to examine the live, performative element of mass media, which in our context is the specific performative qualities of cinema exhibition.

To examine the performative element of cinematic colour, it is vital to take an intermedial approach by comparing colour's function in a variety of new media practices from nineteenth-century theatre and lantern slide exhibition to early film and to experimental and digital colouring effects. Across this range of material, the focus here is on three interrelated examples that illustrate colour's performativity. The first example examines the projection of abstract colour as a form of popular entertainment from the late nineteenth to the mid-twentieth centuries known as colour music and also visual music.[8] The second example then traces how such practices overlapped with other forms of colour media

30 Colour as Performance in Visual Music, Film Tinting and Digital Painting

Figure 1: *The Hunger Games* (2012, video still).

exhibition, in particular through the use of newly developed gel 'tinters' on top of lights to colour theatre and dance performances, and eventually also lantern slides and films. In each of these uses of colour filters, new technologies and techniques were developed to superimpose tints on the recorded moving image during exhibition. At the same time, the aesthetic ideals often promoted through these uses of colour resonated structurally with similar notions found within the visual-music tradition. If the first two examples deal explicitly with the live, non-recorded projection of colour, the final example of this essay looks to how these colourful performance practices are useful for thinking about colour in the recorded moving image, from the first uses of hand colouring in film to new technologies of digital painting.

To begin then with the projection of abstract colour music. This was a form of visual entertainment popular from the late nineteenth to the mid-twentieth centuries, though with longer roots in which a musical analogy was applied the visual arts: the harmonies of colour parallel and interrelate with the harmonies of sound. Grounded in the notion of synaesthesia (the cross-modal blurring of the senses, as in hearing colours and seeing sounds simultaneously), approaches to colour music can be traced, for instance, in painting from James McNeill Whistler to Wassily Kandinsky to Francis Picabia, and in performative traditions encompassing the works of Richard Wagner, Alexander Scriabin, Mary Hallock-Greenwalt, and Thomas Wilfred, amidst others.[9] In particular through performance, colour music was a mode of visual entertainment that was almost always based upon the development of new technologies of colour and light, amongst which film plays an important role, particularly in the experimental approaches developed by filmmakers such as Walter Ruttmann, Oskar Fischinger, Harry Smith, and John Whitney Sr.

As I have detailed elsewhere, this tradition of experimental film can be traced to the 1890s through the work of C. Francis Jenkins.[10] In his *Animated Pictures* from 1898, Jenkins discussed his development of a device for projecting colour music in 1895, which was integrated with his Phantoscope film projector.[11] As he delineated, he used the Phantoscope in tandem with his colour-music experiments to project tinted strips of celluloid that formed alternating, pure fields of colour. In Jenkins's words, this would, 'produce the same impression upon the senses of feeling through the medium of the eye which music does through the ear'.[12] Given the interrelated development of Jenkins's colour music experiments with his Phantoscope projector, another way of understanding his colour work is through André Gaudreault's intermedial notion of cultural series: even though he was using filmic devices to carry out this experimentation, Jenkins's initial colour work as he conceived it was not a form of cinema per se, but rather part of the cultural series of colour music.[13] In other words, he designed this aspect of the Phantoscope with the aim of performing colour music rather than what we might think of today as abstract cinema.

The kind of crossmodal mixing of colour with sound found across a variety of nineteenth and twentieth century experiments with music, coloured light, and film is inherently performative in nature, in the sense that the projected colours must be experienced as live performance if they are to function synaesthetically. Thus, in fundamental ways, synaesthetic art is performative and based experientially. Through this tradition, colour also accumulated genteel, avant-garde, and psychophysiological connotations, such as with chromotherapy in which psychologically troubled viewers could be treated by the projection of abstract colour images.[14] Relatedly, Theosophists Annie Besant and C.W. Leadbeater developed an influential, occult codification of colour: black, for example, 'means hatred and malice', whereas, 'affection expresses itself in all shades of crimson and rose'. Such colours, and their spiritual meanings, could be projected out as auras, 'capable of acting upon the astral bodies of other men as well as their minds, so that it can not only raise thought within in them, but can also stir up their feelings'.[15] At the beginning of the twentieth century, Theosophy's spiritual codification of colour was famously influential on painters and visual musicians such as Kandinsky and Scriabin.[16]

If this abstract, colour tradition emphasised the projection and experience of shifting fields of pure colour, a second example of performative colour entails the live projection of colour superimposed atop performers, images, and films through the use of gel tinters. Tinters were developed in the nineteenth century to filter lights during theatre and dance performances, something that Loïe

Fuller pioneered for her dance routines, in particular for her serpentine dances. Her multimedia performances innovatively superimposed coloured tints and also lantern slide images over her silken robes as she danced, creating richly saturated, palimpsestic images upon the stage.[17] Furthermore, in her autobiography, she discussed in detail the synaesthetic influences and meanings of colour, in ways that were akin to the concurrent Theosophical discussions: 'yellow causes enervation and that mauve engenders sleep', and through a quotation from another source, 'colour must exert some sort of influence, moral or physical, or perhaps both simultaneously'.[18] It is this confluence of performative colour with physiological and quasi-occult inflections that runs throughout the visual-music tradition of the twentieth century.

By the late nineteenth century, tinters were being used to superimpose colours atop of performers and lantern slides, and a range of colour effects was present upon the stage and screen.[19] Skilled projectionists could transform the colour scheme across a performance, adjusting the lighting from daytime to moonlit hues by shifting the tinters during the performance. In the 1890s, these types of tinter-based, transforming effects were also used over projector lenses to colour films during an exhibition as a live, performative element of the show. Francis Jenkins, for instance, proposed using his colour-music apparatus to double-project chromatic effects on top of films, in particular for films of serpentine dancers.[20] A 1903 Cecil Hepworth catalogue described the company's development of toning techniques for films. Here is found a mention of gel tinters which distinguishes their effects from toning: 'The colours are not produced by staining or dyeing the picture, and the effect is the opposite of that produced by "tinters". In our films, the image is a coloured one, while the high lights remain pure white'.[21] The performative use of tinters continued throughout early film history. D.W. Griffith, for instance, developed a gel-lighting system in 1919 for double-projecting colours onto *Broken Blossoms*.[22] Later, Harry Smith experimented with similar effects during screenings of *Heaven and Earth Magic* (1957–1962). He used elaborately designed tinters and hand-painted glass slides during live performance to colour the otherwise black-and-white collage film, which is comprised of cut-outs from nineteenth-century catalogue images.[23] Relatedly, Smith had earlier in the 1950s experimented with coloured slides to produce visual-music light shows and his colour experiments with *Heaven and Earth Magic* can be seen as a palimpsestic extension of this earlier work.[24]

In each of these instances, the filmmakers developed new, performative technologies and techniques to add colour on top of the recorded, moving image during projection. At the same time, the aesthetic ideals that these filmmakers often promoted for their new applications of colour resonated with aesthetic notions found in the visual-music tradition. Smith was a well-known occultist, steeped in the traditions of alchemy and Theosophy, and his colours were a form of magic that he layered upon the cinematic image. Relatedly, reviewers of Griffith's colouring device in *Broken Blossoms* described the effects synaesthetically as being, 'fragrantly poetic'.[25]

If in this second set of examples, colour was deployed performatively, as a non-recorded, double-projection of colour over performers and films, a final set of examples pertain to how these various colouring practices open up productive ways for theorising the performative nature of colour in the moving image. As with the connection between visual-music and gel tinters for live performance and film projection, the earliest films in which colour was physically part of the celluloid strip were hand-coloured dance films, which extended these parallels in that the films emulated Loïe Fuller's performances. Growing out of Fuller's success, a series of imitators emerged in Europe and the United States such as the Chicago and then New York based dancer, Annabelle Moore (née Whitford). Between 1894 and 1897, she performed in numerous dance films for Edison and for the American Mutoscope and Biograph Company, most famously a series of serpentine films that were frequently hand coloured.[26] She produced four in total for Edison with William Heise on camera, one in 1894, two in 1895, and one in 1897, as the films were so popular that they had to be remade because the frequent printing wore out the negatives. Moore's style and performance in these films imitated Fuller's innovations of the dance form. Wearing a draping white robe, Moore would swirl it around her body, while sometimes pirouetting around the stage of Edison's Black Maria studio. The women who coloured prints of the films for the Edison Company, such as the spouse of Edmund Kuhn (an Edison technician), used tiny brushes to apply aniline dye into the emulsion of the prints, frame-by-frame. Like the tinted colours on Loïe Fuller's costume, the abstract colours of these films shimmer and transform over the spinning robes of Moore's costume in reds, blues, greens, and yellows. As a palimpsest, these moving images also register two forms of cinematic production: that of the photographic record of the dance in the Black Maria, and of the abstract colour animation later superimposed in the emulsion on top of the silver image.

Similar, palimpsestic uses of colour can be found throughout film history. As noted earlier, the censored version of Chomón's trick film *Les Tulipes* (1907) in the Turconi Collection calls attention to the hybrid nature of colour. This occurs, however, not just through the censor's use of red, but Pathé's stencil colours in the film also add their own form of coded meaning onto the image. The light stencil blue of the female conjuror's skirt, for instance, provides a sense of pictorial realism, just as do the greens used in the film to colour the grass vegetation of the mise-en-scène. Beyond realism, the stencil colours also factor into the magic of the film: with the fireworks and water fountains called forth by the conjuror, the applied dyes on top of these – bright reds, oranges, blues, and yellows – explode forth in a riot of colour, providing a saturated layer of fantasia to the film.

Such palimpsestic effects occur also in natural-colour systems of film. Even with Technicolor across its various additive and subtractive systems developed between 1916 and 1932, colour is produced through a process of layering – separating out and then recombining the two-colour and three-colour values to produce a composite image on the screen. To an extent the natural-colour process removed the colourist's hand from painting directly onto the positive filmstrip, but this distinction is more a matter of degree than absolute difference. Throughout Technicolor's processes, the company was able to control the saturation levels of its colour separations to produce a wide range of aesthetic effects and meanings. Working with Douglas Fairbanks in 1925 on *The Black Pirate*, Technicolor strove to achieve Fairbanks's vision of recreating the look and colour palette of Howard Pyle's pirate illustrations for the novels of Robert Louis Stevenson. As Herbert Kalmus, one of the founders of Technicolor, recounted, 'There was great discussion as to the colour key in which this picture would be pitched. We made test prints for Mr. Fairbanks at six different colour levels, from a level with slightly more colour than black and white, to the most garish rendering of which the Technicolor process was then capable'.[27] Colour is thus always, in varying degrees, the product of aesthetic intervention. Similarly, as Scott Higgins has thoroughly traced, it is this question of controlling the colour layers and their attendant meanings that drove Technicolor's stylistic and technical development of its three-strip process in the 1930s.[28]

Through the question of layering, the palimpsestic nature of the chromatic image comes to the fore. Colour, rather than being natural, is always coded through discourse to create a variety of meanings – from realistic transparency to sensuous tactility to occult harmony – that become superimposed onto the filmic image. In aesthetic theory, colour has often been analysed, and denigrated, for the surplus of meaning that it can produce. Typically, this takes the form of distinguishing between the function of line from colour in aesthetic works, and in this binary, theorists praise the masculine, black-and-white virtues of line (or formal design, or with film the indexical image) and warn against the feminine, ornamental wiles of colour, which are charming and like make-up can make the image look pretty.[29] This binary is part of the discourse and aesthetic history of colour that cinema inherited at its inception, but what is of interest here is how an emphasis on colour's layered performativity, on and in the image, might shift the oppositional terms of this relationship. By focusing on layering, all cinematic images become in a sense palimpsests comprised of signs and codes that perform a series of overlapping meanings, as is apparent from the very beginnings of film history.

Given the intermedial context of Loïe Fuller and also of visual music, the earliest use of hand-colouring in cinema was a technical means of superimposing tints upon the image during projection without having to double-project colour and image separately. By looking backwards at these colours in relation to the cultural series of visual music from which they emerged, the aesthetic meanings that colour was thought to evoke can be traced in relation to the nineteenth-century interest in the sensual, emotional, and occult effects of colour on the spectator. Colour thus codes the palimpsestic image historically and intermedially. In this way, the colour layers of the contemporary digital image are nothing new. Digital painting, as Lev Manovich discusses returns the contemporary image to a hybridised mode: one in which red can animate and perform (or be erased and not perform) blood with relative ease in the palimpsestic layers of the moving image. As *The Hunger Games* demonstrates, colour presents certain types of coded, culturally determined meanings. What is objectionable, overly sensual and dangerous for British censors is not necessarily the same red as it is in the United States, where the film was passed uncut with a PG-13 rating.[30]

Across such palimpsestic examples, specific colour meanings may vary, but the ways in which they are analysed still remain structured in interpretive approaches that are embedded culturally and intermedially in occult-inflected, aesthetic understandings of colour. Sergei Eisenstein has also made this point in his writings on vertical montage, where he turned to the legacies of Symbolism and the occult in his exploration of the cinematic correspondence between colour and music.[31] For Eisenstein, each individual work performs meaning in a unique way, determining its own codes and sensualities across its interweaving layers. If the particulars of a work are unique, the performative structure through which they operate are enabled dialectically by intermedial legacies. As such, with the intermedial palimpsest – from visual music to early film to digital painting – montage is performed in the colour layers of the shot.

Notes

1. Lucy Brett, "The BBFC Centenary Debate", *Scottish Film Consortium* (Dunkeld, Scotland: 8 June 2012).
2. See the BBFC records, accessed 2 April 2013, http://www.bbfc.co.uk/CFF284121/. Eventually, on a second round of edits, four seconds were revised and replaced, and three seconds completely cut. For a detailed analysis, see "*The Hunger Games*", accessed April 2, 2013, http://www.movie-censorship.com/report.php?ID=488119.
3. On *Pleasantville*, see John Belton, "Painting by the Numbers: The Digital Intermediate", *Film Quarterly* 61, no. 3 (Spring 2008): 58–65.
4. D.N. Rodowick, *The Virtual Life of Film* (Cambridge, Mass.: Harvard University Press, 2007), 169, 173.
5. Lev Manovich, *The Language of New Media* (Cambridge, Mass.: The MIT Press, 2001), 304.
6. See '*Les Tulipes*', accessed April 2, 2013, http://www.cinetecadelfriuli.org/progettoturconi/title.php?TITLE_NUMBER=747.
7. Philip Auslander, *Liveness: Performance in a Mediatized Culture*, 2nd edn (New York: Routledge, 2008), 4.
8. See for example Kerry Brougher, Jeremy Strick, Ari Wiseman, and Judith Zilczer, (ed.), *Visual Music: Synaesthesia in Art and Music since 1900* (New York: Thames and Hudson, 2005); and William Moritz, "The Dream of Color Music, and Machines that Made It Possible", *Animation World Magazine* 2, no.1 (April 1997): 69–84.
9. Judith Zilczer, "'Color Music': Synaesthesia and Nineteenth-Century Sources for Abstract Art", *Artibus et Historiae* 8, no.16 (1987), 101–126.
10. Joshua Yumibe, *Moving Color: Early Film, Mass Culture, Modernism* (New Brunswick, N.J.: Rutgers University Press, 2012), 137–141.
11. See "C. Francis Jenkins", *Evening Item* (November 14, 1895): 1.
12. C. Francis Jenkins, *Animated Pictures* (Washington, D.C.: H.L. McQueen, 1898), 92–93.
13. André Gaudreault, *Film and Attraction: From Kinematography to Cinema*, trans. Timothy Barnard (Urbana: University of Illinois Press, 2011), 64–65.
14. J. Leonard Corning, "The Uses of Musical Vibrations Before and During Sleep", *Medical Record* 55 (1899): 79–86.
15. Annie Besant and C.W. Leadbeater, *Thought-Forms* (Wheaton, Ill.: Theosophical Publishing House, 1999), 22–25.
16. See Sixten Ringbom, *The Sounding Cosmos: A Study in the Spiritualism of Kandinsky and the Genesis of Abstract Painting* (Âbo, Finland: Âbo Akademi, 1970).
17. Yumibe, *Moving Color*, 52–54.
18. Loïe Fuller, *Fifteen Years of a Dancer's Life* (New York: Dance Horizons, 1976), 114, 117.
19. For further discussions of gel tinters, see Yumibe, *Moving Color*, 98.
20. C. Francis Jenkins, "The Jenkins Phantoscope, 26 April 1896", in *Motion Picture Catalogs by American Producers and Distributors, 1894–1908: A Microfilm Edition*, ed. Charles Musser (Frederick, Md.: University Publications of America, 1984–1985), C-009; and Charles Francis Jenkins and Oscar B. Depue, *Handbook for Motion Picture and Stereopticon Operators* (Washington, D.C.: Knega Company, Inc., 1908), 83. Also see Yumibe, *Moving Color*, 139.
21. Hepworth and Co., "A Selected Catalogue of the Best and Most Interesting 'Hepwix' Films (1903)", in *Early Rare Filmmakers' Catalogues: 1896–1913*, collected by British Film Institute, reel 2 (London: World Microfilms Publications, 1983).
22. "D.W. Griffith Patents Apparatus for Picture Projection with Color Effects", *Moving Picture World* 4.3 (April 17, 1920): 388.

23. Paola Igliori, ed., *American Magus Harry Smith: A Modern Alchemist* (New York: Inanout Press, 1996), 80.
24. Harry Everett Smith, *Think of the Self Speaking: Harry Smith, Selected Interviews*, ed. Rani Singh (Seattle: Elbow/Cityful Press, 1999), 107.
25. Quoted in Lillian Gish with Ann Pinchot, *Lillian Gish: The Movies, Mr Griffith, and Me* (Englewood Cliffs, N.J.: Prentice Hall, 1969), 222.
26. Yumibe, *Moving Color*, 49–50.
27. Herbert T. Kalmus, "Technicolor Adventures in Cinemaland", *Journal of the Society of Motion Picture Engineers* 31.6 (December 1938): 570.
28. Scott Higgins, *Harnessing the Technicolor Rainbow: Color Design in the 1930s* (Austin: University of Texas Press, 2007).
29. See for instance Immanuel Kant's critique of colour, in favour of design, found in *The Critique of Judgment*, trans. James Creed Meredith (Oxford: Clarendon Press, 1978), 67. For a recent discussion of this binary in relation to film and film theory, see Rosalind Galt, *Pretty: Film and the Decorative Image* (New York: Columbia University Press, 2011), 3–6.
30. "*The Hunger Games*", accessed April 2, 2013, http://www.filmratings.com/search.html?filmTitle=hunger+games&x=0&y=0.
31. Sergei Eisenstein, "Vertical Montage", trans. Michael Glenny, in *Selected Works: Towards a Theory of Montage*, vol. 2, ed. Michael Glenny and Richard Taylor (London: British Film Institute, 1991), 349–370.

Coda

Early Cinema Today and its 'Digital Performance': The Re-discovery of *The Soldier's Courtship* (1896)

Franziska Heller

Introduction

The Domitor Conference 2012 proposed a new research focus on the performative aspects of Early Cinema. In this paper I would like to extend this perspective by considering how the performative character of Early Cinema is transferred to the present through digital dispositifs. How do digital technologies help make Early Cinema visible in today's media environment? DVDs and the web are ubiquitously accessible and are therefore the 'mass' media for engaging with early films today.[1] Through these means, the question is: what kind of image is thus constructed of Early Cinema and how does this serve as an introduction to film history? In other words, how is Early Cinema performed today?

My notion of 'today', the present, means the distinct historic situation marked by digital media technology. Frank Kessler's understanding of this moment is very relevant: 'Even though, once again, the "death of cinema" is being proclaimed as digital images conquer our media environment, animated photographies from the years around 1900 can work their magic in many and sometimes unexpected ways'.[2]

I will specify these 'magical and unexpected ways' within the context of digital technology. The questions revolve around and refer to the two main ideas on which I am working on in a broader research project at the Institute of Cinema Studies at the University of Zurich entitled *Film History Remastered*. They are:
  i. How are processes of digitisation shaping our perception and experience of early film history?
  ii. How is 'cinema' history being written and exploited in order to shape our idea of digital technologies?

Firstly, I will specify certain terms and methodological aspects that are important for my approach to a particular set of historiographical dynamics. Then I will present a film restoration case study which was published and promoted in 2011 and focuses on the (digital) re-discovery of *The Soldier's Courtship*.[3] In my conclusion I will reflect more generally on the attraction(s) of Early Cinema in its digitised form.

Terms and methodological specifications

This research is shaped by the concept of the dispositif; in particular Kessler's understanding of it as a mode of address rather than a mode of representation.[4] He describes, 'the cinema of attractions as *dispositif*', and offers this valuable definition: 'The aim of such studies (…) is to understand the complex interaction between texts, viewers and viewing situation (including also aspects of technology and institutional framings) in a given *historical* context'.[5] I want to push this perspective even further by understanding the film historic concept of 'the cinema of attractions as dispositif' in the context of the reissue of early films through digital technology and the corresponding reshaping of the idea of 'the cinema of attractions' and its historicity.

These ideas require a methodological specification in terms of how we understand historiographical dynamics in view of digital technologies and the activity of re-mediating media. The model I will use is that of a *cluster*. The concept of a cluster structure is to think of several layers that coexist and intertwine with each other. The cluster in question here is imbued by the two main research questions above. It is the analysis of the dialectics between the viewing situation of Early Cinema today as a digital dispositif[6] and the historic situation of circa 1900 that is either quoted or simulated by the new dispositif. As a result, I understand my specific case as the study of a cluster where particular historiographical motives and narratives as well as a film's content and aesthetic form interact with today's viewing situations and perceptional modes. To explain this concept further, I will focus on two keywords that within the cluster have an ambivalent relationship with each other: *Performance* and *Attraction(s)*.

Performance means not only the performative act of making Early Cinema accessible in digital media today, but also the idea of the 'digital' as a construct that is culturally and socially produced through performative acts, which affect our impression or feeling of presence and immediacy in specific ways. Furthermore, from the point of view of the computer industry, the term has very particular connotations in terms of a machine's speed and quality. To measure its 'efficiency' is paramount to the realisation of the 'digital'.

In a more general sense, performance stands for a concrete action within a temporal dimension (as found in different disciplines associated with acts of communication and social interaction).[7] So with these concepts in mind, one can think of the label 'digital' as well as 'historicity' as the result of cultural, discursive and communicative processes that are deeply linked to a given historical situation in which new conditions for historiography are shaped.

Attraction is the second term I use within this cluster-like perspective. I understand the term 'attraction' in a very broad and general sense because I want to employ its ambivalent and transhistorical implications. As Kessler and Gunning have done, one can understand 'attraction' as a mode of address in relation to a film's content and specific historical situations. The attractions can be reinforced by the dispositifs in which these moving images are shown, e.g. the nature of the venue, programme, audience, musical accompaniment and lecturer.

For an audience today the alien-ness[8] of the aesthetic of an early film text can become an element of attractions (such as the first-time surprise of these visual stimuli).[9] This alien-ness constitutes the historical dimension because of its obvious deviation from what moving images are today. The aesthetic difference can signify a document of the past through a particular patina or aura.[10] These mechanisms have been introduced throughout film and media history every time Early Cinema is encountered through film screenings and the related dispositifs. But what happens today in view of digital technologies? The attraction of the digital dispositif is a very specific presentation mode. The digital framework brings crucial changes to our perception of cinema history.

Giovanna Fossati has theorised archival and restoration practices in the digital age and her work provides a very fruitful basis for the theoretical conceptualisation of digital film.[11] In contrast to her, I focus more on film-historiographical mechanisms, such as the selection and presentational modes of the restoration process. In other words, how does a possible (mass) audience get to know about film preservation and restoration? The second difference is a methodological one. I suggest that when talking about film restoration and digital dispositifs, one must not forget to take the film text into account because through it an audience (both expert and non-expert) literally see, feel and experience the value of historical film.[12] So the actual question for the following case study will be: how do the aesthetics and the historicity of Early Cinema reinforce the narrative of digital technologies?

The (digital) re-discovery of *The Soldier's Courtship*

There was a significant re-discovery event at the *Giornate del Cinema Muto* in Pordenone 2011: 'Most sensational is the reappearance, after some 115 years, of one of Britain's (and one of the world's) first fiction films, Robert Paul's *The Soldier's Courtship (1896)*. Known till now only from a few surviving frames and a "flip-book" extract, the film was found in the Cineteca Nazionale of Rome, and will be unveiled, almost complete and painstakingly restored, in the Giornate'.[13] The film *The Soldier's Courtship* premiered at the festival in its restored version on 3 October 2011. It was placed as the first film in a two-hour long programme of early films entitled *Rediscoveries*. [This was one of the few occasions (out of three in total, the others being in Rome in December 2011 and Belgrade in June 2013) when the film was projected from a film print on a theatre's large screen and as part of a programme of early films.]

The quote above is from the introductory part of the Pordenone catalogue. In the same publication, the historian Ian Christie and curator Irela Núñez of Cineteca Nazionale co-authored the catalogue's entry on the film. In it Christie underlined the film's historical and historiographical importance: 'Newly discovered in the Cineteca Nazionale of Rome, after long being considered definitively lost, *The Soldier's Courtship* restores a vital missing link in the early history of "animated photography"'.[14] Núñez detailed the restoration process. Through different narratives, they described the importance of the film. Being one of the first fiction films, Robert Paul's role as a technological pioneer (which helped identify the material) and the film's popularity in 1896 are presented as the reasons for this film's selection for restoration. The catalogue's entry positions the film within a very particular discourse of Early Cinema as it is defined as a first film by a first filmmaker.

This historiographic process is also deeply influenced by the interests and conditions of the present as it was framed in terms of seeing a 115 year old film for the first time in living memory, a realisation of digital technology's potential and the processes associated with digital restoration. Karen F. Gracy has described in her book *Competing Definitions of Value, Use, and Practice* how the often assumed (cultural) value of historic films affects film preservation practices. Gracy emphasises in particular the higher value placed on fiction films.[15] Dealing with the case of the restoration of *The Soldier's Courtship*, it becomes important for the argument to know that the print found in Rome and used for the digital restoration had been manually retouched as early as 1900 because of its extensive use. Furthermore, interestingly enough the success of the film is illustrated in the catalogue through the description of the performative qualities of the film presentation in which the aesthetics of film were highlighted by corporeal as well as slapstick elements: 'According to the film historian Amandino Videira Santos (...) contemporary screenings of the film were accompanied with the sound of kisses and of someone being brusquely thrown to the ground'.[16]

After its identification and selection as a valuable object, the concrete problems of digitising the film began. The Cineteca Nazionale and the postproduction company Omnimago, the restoration team, became aware that the print had narrative and image gaps (literally missing sections). The film was also in a poor state:

> The film's condition made duplication difficult: besides brittleness and the unusually small size of the perforations, the film base was laterally shrunken by 3–4% and very warped which prevented uniform focus and risk-free transportation. Added to this was detachment of the emulsion, which finally determined that the restoration had to be out digitally, without any prior chemical treatment, to prevent further damage to the film.[17]

Giovanna Fossati believes that it is crucial to always take into account the frameworks and goals when a restoration is executed. In the case of *The Soldier's Courtship* Irela Núñez says that they were, 'determined as far as possible to restore the film to its original state …'.[18]

The process of selection of this film for restoration is fundamentally linked to the measurement of value. If this value is determined above all by its exceptional cultural and entertainment value, then this determines not only the choice taken to restore the film but also the nature of the restoration process itself. To the audience today the value is communicated through the entries in the catalogue. On a conceptual level one can summarise that the assessment of the film's historical performative presentation and perceptual situation in 1896 became intertwined with the restoration practices and decisions as well as with the promotion of the restoration itself in 2011. The distinction that it was the 'first' fiction film represents the outstanding value of being one of the supposed starting points in film history. Within a cluster-like structure – a dispositif – that spans the past and the present, the glamour of being a 'first' is interwoven into a state-of-the-art of digital restoration. The proven performative qualities and values of 1896 are translated in the future into another performative presentation of the film: the restoration becomes the performance.

The restoration as a spectacle[19]

So far the film has been presented mostly within a particular digital restoration framework. The Cineteca Nazionale di Roma made the first thirty seconds accessible on their website (see Figure 1, Screenshot F.H.).[20]

The accompanying text is focused on the restoration, providing both contextu-

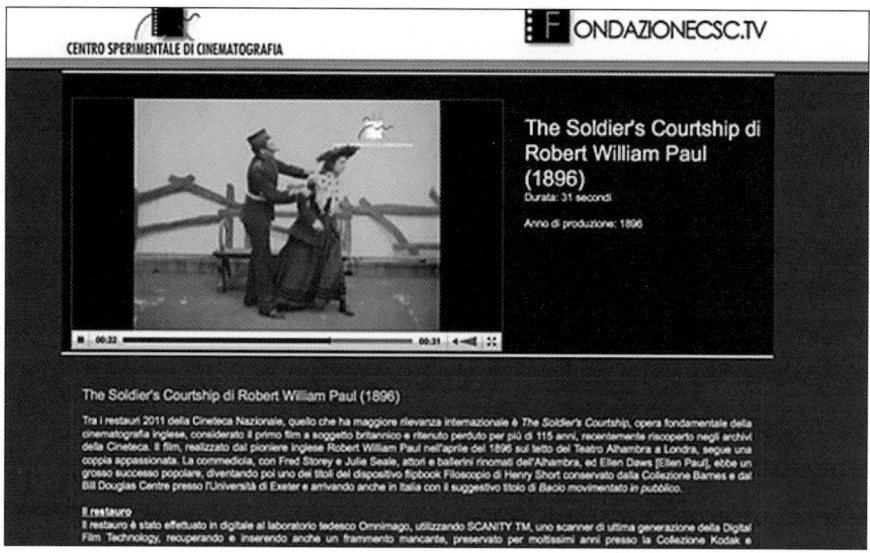

Figure 1: "Tra i restauri....."; "Through the restoration…".

alisation and valorisation for this project. One can watch the film via the link called 'web-TV'. This connotes another media dispositif with various aspects. The film content is now visible on the small screen (only as a 'teaser' compared to its original length, form and format). The term 'TV' stands for a window to a different world, to appropriate something far away into your own private space of home or wherever you might watch it and is linked to the viewer / user's choice of what to view. The 'web' stands for participation, interactivity and access: the user-centered pull-model of curatorship.[21] Broeren might call this a 'digital dispositif' in the context of his work on YouTube.[22] I would argue, what you find here is a combination of the pull and push model because the user chooses to see the film (the pull) and receives a teaser of thirty seconds framed by a curated contextualisation dedicated to the restoration process and the outstanding performance of the scanner (the push).

This focus on the technological state-of-the-art framework, as Giovanna Fossati identified it in the restoration discourse, was amplified by the Collegium Dialogue at Pordenone, one day after the screening. The session carried the congruent title: *Restoration: State of the Art*. Irela Núñez introduced the extensive scientific and historic research surrounding the film while Hendrik Teltau presented the technical workflow and the advantages of their special scanner, the SCANITY at Omnimago.[23] In this context, during this presentation, *The Soldier's Courtship* was shown again but this time as a Quicktime file from a computer.

The project subsequently has been presented at a number of international events and each time the film is shown it has been accompanied by a presentation on the digital restoration workflow (such as on 10 October 2011 in London at the archiving symposium *Large Scale Digitization of Cultural Heritage*, at the World Day of Audiovisual Heritage, on 27 October 2011 in Wiesbaden at the F.W. Murnau Foundation and in the context of a film festival: Cinefest 2011, the VIII International Festival of the German Film Heritage in Hamburg, 12–20 November 2011). What becomes obvious is that the film (text) itself is not autonomous as a transhistorical work of film history. The film text, with its own history, has become part of a new performance where it is re-narrated and repurposed from the viewpoint of the technological present.

Conclusion: The attraction(s) of Early Cinema in its digitised form

The case of *The Soldier's Courtship* is interesting because its current visibility and accessibility are closely connected to the presentation of its restoration which is defined by the use of digital state-of-the-art technology. I would like to call this *dispositif* – 'digital re-discovery'. My thesis is that this dispositif plays an important role in composing the attraction(s) of Early Cinema today.

The 'digital re-discovery' dispositif consists of the dialectical interaction of film historic narratives, especially those that deal with 'firsts', and technological innovations and their authors, often called pioneers. Here the historic technological breakthroughs are parallelised with the narrative of the restoration and the state-of-the-art of the equipment used. The categories 'novelty' and 'new' are important concepts in the theory of media historiography as Thorburn and Jenkins have pointed out.[24] In the case of *The Soldier's Courtship* it becomes obvious that its public 'screening' is closely linked to, framed and even motivated by the performative presentation of its digital restoration.

One interesting aspect concerning digital tools and technologies is that one really needs to have a very particular discursive framing to be able to perceive the 'digital performance' of the restoration process. If one doesn't have a very well-trained eye, it will not be possible to identify the digitally interpolated parts of the image. One might realise that the image has been stabilised to a certain extent but the main point of the digital restoration is that the work on the image is supposed to remain invisible by simulating (remediating) photochemical aesthetics and characteristics. In the *Soldier* case the impression of authenticity is maintained as many of the print's original imperfections were left in view and therefore not 'corrected' by the restoration.

The 'invisible' result of the use of digital tools works to give a faithful illusion of the historic original[25] – and especially, in the presented case, it enables an undisturbed aesthetic and entertaining experience of the content. On the other hand, without the digital intervention the film wouldn't be visible or accessible. The current attraction of the film is drawn from the restoration process and its content: a slapstick sketch whose humour still works today because it plays with timeless moral categories like the public versus the private spheres. We witness an 'animated kiss in public'.

To explore the dispositif 'digital re-discovery' one could expand on Kessler's conceptualisation of performing Early Cinema today: "Bridging the gap, marking the difference".[26] The alien-ness (and often astonishing aesthetics) of Early Cinema establishes such a historic distance (on numerous levels) that it reinforces the efficiency of the current digital narrative. This narrative consists of the idea of interaction, participation and accessibility and through this dialectic the film is drawn to the present or at least the (non-expert mass) public gets the impression of immediacy. Are these the 'magical and unexpected ways'[27] of experience of things that have never been seen before?

These thoughts lead back to the remediation concept developed by Bolter and Grusin in 1999.[28] In one chapter of their famous study, they discuss their key concept of immediacy and hypermediacy within the cinema of attractions. They sum up, 'In all these cases, the amazement (...) requires awareness of the medium. If the medium really disappeared, as is the apparent goal of the logic of transparency, the viewer would not be amazed because she would not know of the medium's presence'.[29] The amazement of Early Cinema in digital dispositifs is the complex experience of re-discovery: the old becomes new again! Early Cinema with its aesthetics plays a major part because it is the farthest away from our understanding of 'film' and 'cinema' today. Thus the awareness of the medium is constructed through a very particular historical dimension. The promises made by the new media – early film *and* digital technologies – are quite similar. But while in Early Cinema you could directly experience the new ways of perception, in the digital realm with digital images, it happens – paradoxically – through the historical images themselves and their discursive and institutional framing.

At the same time, the restoration narratives use the film's content to illustrate and mediate the attraction. In watching and enjoying the film, one appreciates the efficiency of the restoration process. The film becomes the performance of the digital restoration. It is a dialectical interplay between difference, repetition and assimilation. 'Historicity' becomes a central category but has to be discussed much further than I could do here as a discursive and perceptual effect.

Notes

1. For watching film history at home: Barbara Klinger, *Beyond the Multiplex* (Berkeley/Los Angeles: University of California Press, 2006), esp. chapter 3.
2. Frank Kessler, "Programming and Performing Early Cinema Today: Strategies and *Dispositifs*", in Martin Loiperdinger, (ed.), *Early Cinema Today: The Art of Programming and Live Performance*, KINtop 1/2011 (New Barnet: John Libbey Publishing, 2011), 145.
3. Many thanks to Hendrik Teltau (Omnimago, Wiesbaden, Germany), Irela Núñez (Cineteca Nazionale – Centro Sperimentale di Cinematografia, Roma, Italy).
4. Wanda Strauven, "Introduction to an Attractive Concept", in Wanda Strauven (ed.), *The Cinema of Attraction Reloaded* (Amsterdam: Amsterdam AUP, 2006), 21. Cf. also Frank Kessler, "The Cinema of Attractions as Dispositif", in ibid., 57–69.
5. Kessler, "Programming and Performing", 139, my emphasis.
6. Joost Broeren, "Digital Attractions: Reloading Early Cinema in Online Video Collections", in Pelle Snickars and Patrick Vonderau (eds), *The YouTube Reader* (Stockholm: National Library of Sweden, 2009), 164.
7. Such as Linguistics (Austin 1962/1972, Searle 1979/1982, resp. Butler 1998) and Sociology (Habermas 1981).
8. Originally: 'extranéité' Gaudreault/Simard quoted by Kessler, "Programming and Performing", 138.
9. Andrea Haller and Martin Loiperdinger, "Stimulating the Audience: Early Cinema's Short Film Programme Format 1906 to 1912", in *Early Cinema Today*, 11ff.
10. "Von Transparenz und Intransparenz. Über die Atmosphäre historischen Filmmaterials", in Phillipp Brunner, Jörg Schweinitz and Margrit Tröhler (eds), *Filmische Atmosphären* (Marburg: Schüren 2012), 39–52.
11. Giovanna Fossati, *From Grain to Pixel* (Amsterdam: AUP, 2009).
12. Annette Kuhn has criticised the dualism in Film Studies that leads to the opposition between film analysis and the study of socio-cultural conditions and framings. Annette Kuhn, *Dreaming of Fred and Ginger: Cinema and Cultural Memory* (New York: N.Y. UP, 2002), 4.
13. David Robinson and Livio Jacob, "Introduction" *Catalogue. Le Giornate del Cinema Muto 1–8. October, Pordenone* (2011): 4.
14. Ian Christie, "The Soldier's Courtship", *Catalogue* (2011): 137.
15. Karen F. Gracy, *Filmpreservation*. (Chicago: The Society of American Archivists, 2007), esp. 90ff.
16. Irela Núñez, "The Soldier's Courtship. The Restoration", in *Catalogue* (2011): 138–139.
17. Ibid.
18. Ibid.
19. Cf. "Restoration as a spectacle" in Marco Pescetelli, *The Art of Not Forgetting: Towards a Practical Hermeneutics of Film Restoration*. Ph.D. Thesis (London: University College, 2010), 117ff http://discovery.ucl.ac.uk/1302399/ (05.04.2013).
20. http://www.fondazionecsc.tv/webtv_video.jsp?id_video=920 (01.04.2013).
21. Giovanna Fossati and Nanna Verhoeff, "Beyond Distribution: Some Thoughts on the Future of Archival Films," in Frank Kessler and Nanna Verhoeff (eds), *Networks of Entertainment* (Eastleigh: John Libbey Publishing, 2007), 333f.
22. Broeren, "Digital Attractions".
23. For further technical details on the restoration process please contact Hendrik Teltau and Irela Núñez.

24. David Thorburn and Henry Jenkins (eds), *Rethinking Media Change. The Aesthetics of Transition* (Cambridge: MIT Press, 2004), 1–16.
25. The term 'original' is very difficult. Hediger identifies the concept of the originial as a 'set of practices'. Vinzenz Hediger, "The Original is Always Lost" in Malte Hagener and Marijke De Valck (eds), *Cinephilia* (Amsterdam: AUP, 2005) 133–147.
26. Kessler, "Programming", 137f.
27. Ibid. 145.
28. Jay David Bolter and Richard Grusin, *Remediation* (Cambridge, MA: MIT Press, 1999).
29. Ibid., 158.

Editors and Contributors

Kaveh Askari is an associate professor in the English department at Western Washington University. His recent work includes articles on the magic lantern, on early cinema and art education, and on imported cinema in Iran.

Canan Balan is an assistant professor in the Department of Cinema and Television at Istanbul Sehir University. She received her PhD from the University of St Andrews with a dissertation on the early cinema spectatorship in Istanbul. She has published articles on early cinema, shadow-play and the cinematic representations of Istanbul. Her research interests also include female spectatorship, cinema and literature and Alevi identities in cinema.

Ivo Blom is a lecturer in Comparative Arts and Media Studies at VU University, Amsterdam. He specializes in film and visual arts, film distribution, Italian cinema and silent cinema. Recent publications include a contribution to *Italian Silent Cinema: A Reader* (2013), edited by Giorgio Bertellini.

Alain Boillat is a full professor at the Film Department of the University of Lausanne (UNIL), director of the Centre d'études cinématographiques (CEC) and president of the Reseau Cinéma CH. He published among others the books *Du bonimenteur à la voix over* (2007) and *Cinema, machine à mondes* (2014).

Ian Christie teaches film and media history at Birkbeck College, London, and is mentoring a project, 'Representing the Past', at the Palacky University, Olomouc, in the Czech Republic. He has published and broadcast widely on early film, Russian and Soviet cinema, Powell and Pressburger, Scorsese and digital media, and is currently working on a book about Robert Paul and the beginnings of the British film industry (http://www.ianchristie.org/).

Denis Condon lectures on film at the School of English, Media and Theatre Studies, National University of Ireland Maynooth. His research interest lies in the area of early cinema, and his publications on this subject include the book *Early Irish Cinema, 1895-1921* (2008), and articles in such journals as *Early Popular Visual Culture, Screening the Past* and *Field Day Review*.

Malcolm Cook was recently awarded a PhD at Birkbeck, University of London. His research addresses early British animated cartoons prior to the advent of sound cinema, with a particular focus on the relationship between the moving image and the graphic arts and other pre-cinematic entertainments, as well as the neurological processes involved in the perception of these forms. He holds a BA in Film and Literature from the University of Warwick and an MA in History of Art, Film and Visual Media from Birkbeck.

Scott Curtis is an associate professor of Radio/Television/Film at Northwestern University in Evanston, Illinois. He is currently President of Domitor, the international society for the study of early cinema.

Marina Dahlquist is an associated professor in Cinema Studies at the Department of Media Studies at Stockholm University. She has published articles on cinema and civic education, health discourses and colonial structures. Recent publications include the edited volume: *Exporting Perilous Pauline: Pearl White and the Serial Film Craze* (2013).

Sarah Dellmann is a PhD candidate in the NWO project 'The Nation and Its Other' at Utrecht University, The Netherlands. In her dissertation she investigates the role of visual media in the creation of supposed common knowledge about the Dutch in the late nineteenth century with special regards to magic lantern slide sets and early cinema.

Franziska Heller is a post-doctoral researcher and lecturer at the Institute of Cinema Studies at the University of Zurich. As of June 2013, she is also a researcher in the two-year CTI research project DIASTOR: Bridging the gap between analog film history and digital technology (www.diastor.ch).

Gunnar Iversen is professor of Film Studies in the Department of Art and Media Studies at the Norwegian University of Science and Technology. His writings have appeared in *Early Popular Visual Culture*, *Film History*, *The Journal of Scandinavian Cinema*, and many Scandinavian-language journals.

Frank Kessler is a professor of Media History at Utrecht University and currently the Director of Utrecht University's Research Institute for Cultural Inquiry (ICON). His main research interests lie in the field of early cinema and the history of film theory. He is a co-founder and co-editor of *KINtop. Jahrbuch zur Erforschung des frühen Films* and the *KINtop-Schriften* series. From 2003 to 2007 he was the president of DOMITOR.

Kristina Köhler is a research assistant and lecturer at the Department of Cinema Studies at the University of Zurich. Her dissertation *Moving Bodies, Dancing Images. Dance Analogies in Film and Film Theory between Corporeality and Abstraction* focuses on the intersections between cinema and dance culture in the early twentieth century.

Sabine Lenk is a film archivist, and affiliated researcher at Utrecht University. She is a co-founder of *KINtop. Jahrbuch zur Erforschung des frühen Films*, *KINtop Schriften* and *KINtop. Studies in Early Cinema* and has published widely on film archiving, cinema museology and early cinema. Her most recent book is *Vom Tanzsaal zum Filmtheater. Eine Kinogeschichte Düsseldorfs* (2009).

Thierry Lecointe est chercheur indépendant. On lui doit des articles édités dans des ouvrages collectifs et dans la revue *1895*. Il a publié *Le Cinématographe Lumière dans les arènes*, Montpellier, UBTF, 2007.

Martin Loiperdinger is a professor of Media Studies at the University of Trier. He co-edited *KINtop*, the German yearbook of early cinema, and now, *KINtop – Studies in Early Cinema*. Recently, he co-edited *Importing Asta Nielsen. The International Film Star in the Making 1910-1914*, and the DVD *Screening the Poor 1888-1914*.

Editors and Contributors

Leslie Midkiff DeBauche teaches at the University of Wisconsin-Stevens Point. She is the author of *Reel Patriotism, the Movies and World War I,* and she is currently at work on a study of the American Girl character in films of the 1910s and of the real American teenagers who consumed those movies.

Christopher Natzén, holds a position at the Research Department, National Library of Sweden. He is currently work package leader in the three year EU funded EUscreenXL 2013-2016 as well as a researcher in the Swedish Foundation for Humanities and Social Sciences (RJ) funded project for the development of the Swedish film site filmarkivet.se.

Charles O'Brien teaches Film Studies at Carleton University in Canada. He is the author of *Cinema's Conversion to Sound* and various articles and book chapters on topics in early cinema history.

Chris O'Rourke is a research associate at University College London in the Centre for Humanities Interdisciplinary Research Projects (CHIRP). He is currently researching the history of cinema and cinemagoing in interwar London.

Louis Pelletier is a SSHRC postdoctoral fellow at Université de Montréal and Concordia University, where he is research coordinator of the Canadian Educational, Sponsored and Industrial Film Archive project. He has published on film exhibition, silent cinema and industrial films in *Living Pictures, Cinémas, Film History* and *The Moving Image.*

Jennifer Peterson is an associate professor in the Film Studies Program at the University of Colorado Boulder. She is the author of numerous articles and a book entitled *Education in the in the School of Dreams: Travelogues and Early Nonfiction Film* (2013).

Valentine Robert is a lecturer at the University of Lausanne in Switzerland, where she is completing a PhD on *tableaux vivants* in early cinema (directed by François Albera, approved by the Swiss National Science Foundation and affiliated to the GRAFICS). She specializes in the interplay between painting and cinema, still and moving pictures and has contributed essays about cinematic *realizations* of paintings such as the work of Gustave Doré, Leonardo DaVinci's *Last Supper* and the Passion iconography.

Shelley Stamp is the author of *Movie-Struck Girls: Women and Motion Picture Culture after the Nickelodeon, Lois Weber in Early Hollywood* and co-editor with Charlie Keil of *American Cinema's Transitional Era: Audiences, Institutions, Practices.* She is a professor of Film and Digital Media at the University of California, Santa Cruz.

Frédéric Tabet est docteur de l'Université Paris-Est et chercheur associé au LISAA (EA 4120); ses champs de recherches portent sur le spectaculaire dans les arts de la scène et la circulations des effets entre anciens et nouveaux médias. Il co-dirige actuellement l'organisation d'un colloque qui sera consacréaux effets magiques des technologies.

Ansje van Beusekom is an assistant professor Film History at Media and Culture studies at Utrecht University. Her publications focus on early and silent cinema and the ideas on film as art.

María Antonia Vélez-Serna is a post-doctoral researcher in the Early Cinema for the Scotland project at the University of Glasgow. Her work on the emergence of regional film distribution, early exhibition practice, and the use of geo-databases for historical research has been presented at international conferences including NECS, SCMS, Screen, and Domitor, and she has published on Scottish and Colombian cinema history and audiences in *Post-Script* and *Particip@tions*.

Ludwig M. Vogl-Bienek is senior researcher of the Screen1900 research group at the University of Trier, and a founding member of the magic lantern ensemble *illuminago* which performs lantern shows internationally. He publishes widely on the art of projection and on screen culture in the nineteenth century.

Gregory A. Waller, the editor of *Film History*, is a professor of Film and Media Studies at Indiana University. His current research focuses on the history of nontheatrical cinema in the 1910s.

Peter Walsh recently completed his doctorate on early cinema at the University of Sheffield, and now works as a data editor at the IMDb in Bristol. Alongside improving the quality of information held on the database, he continues his research into early British networks of cinema, and is active in fostering wider public interest in silent and early cinema through the Bristol Silents screening group.

Gwendolyn Waltz is an independent scholar and theatre historian whose research focus is in film-and-theatre multi-media stage performance. Her publications include "'Half Real-Half Reel': Alternation Format Stage-and-Screen Hybrids" in *A Companion to Early Cinema* (2012) and "Filmed Scenery on the Live Stage" (*Theatre Journal*, December 2006), as well as Domitor and other conference publications and an article-length review of *The Griffith Project* (*Nineteenth Century Theatre and Film*, Summer 2010).

Daniel Wiegand is a PhD candidate in Film Studies at the University of Zurich, Switzerland. In his dissertation, he examines how early cinema related to the culture of *tableaux vivants* around 1900, focusing on variety theatres and small-town associations.

Tami Williams is an associate professor of Film Studies and English at the University of Wisconsin-Milwaukee, co-secretary of Domitor, and author of *Germaine Dulac: A Cinema of Sensations* (forthcoming 2014). She has published numerous articles on silent cinema, edited *Germaine Dulac: Au dela des impressions* (2006), and curated film programs for Musée d'Orsay, Cinema Ritrovato, and the National Gallery of Art. She is currently co-editing a volume on contemporary global cinema.

Artemis Willis is a PhD candidate in the department of Cinema and Media Studies at the University of Chicago, a curator of media arts and a nonfiction filmmaker. Her dissertation focuses on the intersections between the magic lantern and cinema.

Joshua Yumibe holds a joint appointment as director and assistant professor of Film Studies at Michigan State University and as lecturer in Film Studies at the University of St Andrews. He is the co-director of the Davide Turconi Project, and is also working on the Leverhulme Trust funded project, Colour in the 1920s: Cinema and Its Intermedial Contexts.

Index of Films

A

A Corner in Wheat (1909)	42–43
A Japanese Idyll (1912)	13, 16, 18–19
A Modern Magdalen (1915)	193, 200
A Trip to the Moon (see *Le Voyage dans la Lune*)	
Adventure of a French Gentleman Without Trousers, The (1905)	115
Affaire Dreyfus, L' (1899)	270
Ah Ah die Oscar (1905)	120
Al-Sa'alik (1967)	260
Animated Cotton (1909)	54
Avaries, Les (1914)	177

B

Barbe-Bleue (1901)	119
Bernadette et les apparitions de Lourdes	288
Bican Efendi (1917–1922)	8, 254–262
Bican Efendi Seeking Money (1918)	254
Bican Efendi the Cautious (1917)	254
Bican Efendi the New Rich Man (1918)	254
Bican Efendi the Steward (1922)	254–262
Bican Efendi the Teacher (1921)	254
Binnaz (1919)	261n10
Black Pirate, The (1926)	299
Bous-Bous-mee, La (1909)	208
Broken Blossoms (1919)	297–298
Burgos (1918)	188

C

Cabinet des Dr. Caligari, Das (1919)	77
Cartes vivantes, Les (1905)	147
Cendrillon (1899)	119, 270
Cène, La	290
Charlie's Reform (1912)	175
Comedy Cartoons (1907)	54
Comin' Thro' the Rye (1923)	71

Course de taureaux à Roubaix	270
Courses de taureaux	269

D

Dances of Today (1914)	206–207
Death in Antarctic Blizzards (1915)	6, 154–159
Dream of Bican Efendi, The (1921)	254

E

Éclipse de soleil en pleine lune, L' (1907)	247
Electrical Engineer, The	60
Epidemic, The (1914)	208

F

Faust aux enfers (1903)	119
Feeding the Snakes (1911)	187–188
Fine Feathers (1912)	13, 16, 17, 18, 19
Finest Police, The	181
Fire Fighters, The	181
Fire! (1901)	281n17
Fireman, The (1916)	257

G

Gauntlet, The	72
Gavroche et la valse obsédante (1913)	208
Gertie the Dinosaur (1914)	93

H

Hand of the Artist, The (1906)	54
He Danced Himself to Death (1914)	208
Heaven and Earth Magic (1957–1962)	297
Her First Long Dress (1910)	190
Heroine of '76, The (1911)	13
His Golden Hour (1916)	111
Hope, a Red Cross Seal Story (1912)	175
How Bill Adams Won the Battle of Waterloo	233

Hunger Games, The (2012)   293–295, 300, 301n2

I
I Tronens Skygge (1914)   199

J
Jeanne d'Arc   288
John Dough and the Cherub (1910)   144

K
Kri Kri balla (1915)   209–210
Kri-Kri e il tango (1913)   208, 210

L
Land of Oz, The   144
Légende de Rip van Winkle, La (1905)   119
Lieutenant Daring (1911)   69
Life of an American Fireman (1903)   233
Livre magique, Le (1900)   147
Locked Door, The   181

M
Ma l'amour mio non muore (1913)   26, 27, 31, 32
Making a Good Citizen   181
Martin Luther, his Life and Times   88
Mesavontures van een Fransch heertje zonder pantalon (see *The Adventure of a French Gentleman Without Trousers*)   120
Moving Picture Dance Lessons (1913)   206–207
Musketeers of Pig Alley, The (1912)   45

N
Neptune's Daughter (1914)   199
New York, Past and Present   181

O
Oz the Great and Powerful (2013)   142, 147, 148n6

P
Passion du Christ   269
Passion Play of Oberammergau, The (1898)   126
Passion, La   270
Passion de notre Seigneur, La   288
Pawnshop, The (1916)   257
Peinture a l'envers (1898)   52
Phonoscènes   77, 79, 84n19, 84n28
Playhouse, The (1921)   251
Pleasantville (1998)   293, 301n3
Public and Private Care of Infants, The (1912)   175

R
Ramona (1910)   44
Rough Sea at Dover (1896)   53
Russian Ark (2002)   293

S
Sherlock Jr. (1924)   251–252
Shipbuilding in Toulon, France   189
Shrimps   189–190
Soldier's Courtship, The (1896)   9, 305–314
Souls of New York, The (1916)   199
Squirrel, The (1913)   188–189
Suspense (1913)   13

T
Tango Craze, The (1914)   208
Teddy Bears, The (1907)   144
Toss of a Coin, The (1911)   38
Tulipes, Les (1907)   294, 298, 301n6
Turkey Trot Town, The (1914)   208
Two Clowns (c. 1906)   10n3
Two Portraits of Washington, The   72
Tzar en France Cortège impérial à Paris, Le   271n31

U
Unchanging Sea, The (1910)   44

V
Victimes de l'alcoolisme, Les (1902)   127
Vie et Passion du Christ (1903)   287
Voyage à l'imaginaire, Le   119
Voyage dans la Lune, Le   119

W
Wizard of Oz, The (1933)   147
Wizard of Oz, The (1939)   147
Wonderful Wizard of Oz, The (1910)   143

Z
Zeppelin, The   120
Zoological Gardens in Antwerp   189

Index of Names

A

Acres, Birt	52
Albera, François	228, 290
Albers, Rommy	115
Alexandra of Denmark, Princess	79
Allen, Robert C.	106, 112
Altenloh, Emilie	91
Altman, Rick	57, 78, 81–82, 135–136, 144, 230
Amisani, Giuseppe	30
Amundsen, Roald	150, 152
Anderson, Benedict	128
André, Jacques	286
André, Marie	286
Arbuckle, Roscoe 'Fatty'	251
Arvidson, Linda	44
Åslund, Protus	133
Auslander, Philip	50, 73, 294
Austin, Edgar (William Edgar Piercey)	48–50, 55, 56n12
Avenarius, Ferdinand	169
Aylott, Dave	75n18

B

Babalo, Azig	50
Bachmann, Anne	182
Baer, Nicholas W.	212n1
Baggot, King	40n4
Bakker, Gerben	105–106
Balan, Canan	8
Balázs, Béla	211
Baldini, Ettore	23
Bamforth, James	290, 292n44
Barker, Jennifer	211
Barnard, Timothy	290
Barnes, Hattie Delaro	248, 250
Barnes, John	53
Bartolommeo, Fra	283–284
Bataille, Henry	28
Batchelor, David	186–187
Baum, Frank Joslyn	146
Baum, L. Frank	6, 141–149
Baxandall, Michael	31
Bazin, André	143
Ben-Ali, Mohammed	232
Benjamin, Walter	281n14
Bennett, Carl	80
Bennett, Colin	107
Bergson, Henri	204
Bernardini, Aldo	57, 60
Bertemes, Claude	92–93
Berton, Pierre Samuel	30
Besant, Annie	296
Bessy, Maurice	267
Beynon, George W.	190
Bida, Alexandre	283
Bienek, Franziska	226
Billig, Michael	128–129
Bitzer, Gottfried Wilhelm 'Billy'	250
Blaché, Herbert	77
Blackton, J. Stuart	42, 48
Blaisdell, George	14
Blom, Ivo	5, 20n2, 24, 88, 209
Boggs, Francis	144
Boillat, Alain	7
Boldini, Giovanni	27
Bolter, Jay David	22, 312
Bonnaud, Dominique	264
Booth, Elmer	45
Booth, Walter	53–55
Borelli, Lyda	5, 20n2, 22–33
Börner, Wilhelm	163
Bottomore, Stephen	10n1, 276
Bowser, Eileen	14
Brett, Lucy	293
Brieux, Eugène	177
Briggs, C.W.	291n20

Bromhead, Colonel A.C.	96–99, 102	De Forest, Lee	148n2
Bruère, Henry	179	de Neuville, Lemercier	264, 267
Brunel, Georges	264	deCordova, Richard	68
Brunner, Karl	164, 171n2	Dellmann, Sarah	8
Bryan, Jane	68	Desmet, Jean	115–116, 121
Burrows	69, 74n7	Devant, David	53
Bushman, Francis X.	178	Dickens, Charles	10n3
		Dickson, William Kennedy Laurie	76
C		Diederichs, Helmut H.	164
Calò, Romano	28	Dilthey, William	170
Carloni Talli, Ida	28	Dinnie, George	100–101
Carney, Kate	69	Dittmar, Siegismund Gottfried	219
Carolus-Duran (Charles Auguste Émile Durand)	27	Dockstader, Lew	249–250
Carrá, Carlo	27	Donnadieu, A.L.	264
Carter, Lincoln J.	147–148	Doré, Gustave	282–283, 291n24
Caserini, Mario	27, 31	Dranem (Charles Armand Ménard)	84n19
Castelli, Giannina	26	Dreams, Lydia Miss (Walter Lambert)	51
Caughie, John	112	Duca, Lo	267
Cavalieri, Lina	23, 27, 30	Durand, Charles Auguste Émile (*see* Carolus-Duran)	
Chaplin, Charles	256–258	Duse, Eleonora	28
Châteauvert, Jean	232	Dvořák, Anton	137, 190
Chemartin, Pierre	113n6		
Christie, Ian	5, 10n1, 308	**E**	
Clayton, Ethel	68	Edel, Harold	207
Clerici, Fabrizio	26	Edison, Thomas	52, 72, 76–79, 81, 97, 100, 245, 247–250, 298
Cochrane, Tom D.	34, 37		
Coissac, Guillaume-Michel	229–230, 234n5, 286	Edwards, Gus	245
Colagreco, Luiggi	57	Effendi, Bertrand Victor	264
Condon, Denis	6–7	Eisenstein, Sergei	189, 191, 300
Conklin, Chester	251	Elsaesser, Thomas	81–82, 210
Conradt, Walther	163–164	Elsberg, Nathaniel A.	35
Cook, Joe	250	Erskine, Little	49
Cook, Malcolm	5	Eshbaugh, Ted	147
Cooper, Mark Garrett	16		
Copping, Harold	283	**F**	
Corot, Jean-Baptiste-Camille	265	Fairbanks, Douglas	299
Costello, Maurice	42	Fessenden, Reginald	148n2
Crafton, Donald	48, 135–136, 147	Feuillade, Louis	208
Cruikshank, George	10n3, 282	Fevrell, Walter	182
Curtis, Scott	10n1	Fielding, Raymond	203
		Fischinger, Oskar	191, 295
D		Flaherty, Robert	153
d'Ache, Caran	265	Foalkes, William 'Fatty'	99
d'Alcy, Jehanne	267	Foersterling, Hermann O.	125
D'Annunzio, Gabriele	28, 31	Fossati, Giovanna	307, 309–310
Dahlen, Nicole	92–93	Foucault, Michel	9, 282–283, 289
Dahlgren, B.E.	184n25	Fouchécour, Father	286
Dahlquist, Marina	6	Fourtier, H.	264
Daly, William Robert	40n4	Francis, David	10n3, 218, 224
de Chomón, Segundo	294, 298	Fregoli, Leopoldo	5, 57–66

Index of Names

Friese-Greene, William — 2
Fuller, Loïe — 141, 296–298, 300
Fusella, Signor — 132

G

Gastine, Louis — 264
Gaudig, Hugo — 170
Gaudreault, André — 3, 22, 113n6, 122, 228, 265, 296
Gaumont, Leon — 78–79, 84n19, 117, 152, 175, 270
Gaupp, Robert — 164, 168
Gauthier, Philippe — 265
Giesekam, Greg — 67
Gilbert, W.S. — 79
Ginex, Giovanna — 22, 29
Ginsberg, Terry — 259
Gish, Lillian — 45
Godard, Jean–Luc — 294
Goethe, Johann Wolfgang — 218–219
Goldin, Horace — 252n8
Gooes, Anton — 136
Gooes, Gustaw — 136
Gordigiani, Michele — 27
Gordon, Rae Beth — 204, 212n7
Götze, Carl — 170
Gounod, Charles — 79
Gracy, Karen F. — 308
Gramatica, Irma — 28
Grandis, Suzanne — 111
Grandon, Frank J. — 38, 40n4
Grandville, Jean Ignace Isidore Gérard — 282
Gray, Frank — 10n1, 10n3
Griffith, D.W. — 5, 37, 39, 41–47, 84n30, 297–298
Griffiths, Alison — 244
Griffiths, Trevor — 106
Grusin, Richard — 22, 312
Güçbilmez, Beliz — 260
Guizot, François — 289
Gunning, Tom — 42, 46, 127, 145–146, 194, 203, 280, 307
Guy-Blaché, Alice — 76–77, 208

H

Häfker, Hermann — 164–173
Hahn, Wilhelm — 165
Hallock-Greenwalt, Mary — 295
Hals, Frans — 27
Hammond, Michael — 108
Hansen, Miriam — 144, 210
Hanssen, Eirik Frisvold — 187
Hardy, Oliver — 251, 260
Harris, Neil — 183
Haugan, Trond E. — 125
Havez, Jean C. — 250–251, 253n19
Hearn, Michael Patrick — 145
Hearst, William Randolph — 175
Hediger, Vinzenz — 314n25
Hégé, A. — 264
Heise, William — 298
Held, Anna — 245–246, 248
Heller, Franziska — 9
Hellwig, Robert — 164
Hepworth, Cecil — 71, 297
Herbart, Johann Friedrich — 169
Hickmont, Debbie — 10n1
Higgins, Scott — 299
Hinton, Luther — 87
Hodges, Seymour — 72
Hofmann, Ernst Theodor Amadeus — 283
Hogenkamp, Bert — 88, 115
Holmes, E. Burton — 147, 150
Holmes, Fred — 95, 98–99
Hommerson, Willem — 116
Honri, Percy — 247
Horne, Stephen — 10n3
Hubbard Flaherty, Francis — 153–154, 156
Hurley, Frank — 152

I

Ince, Thomas — 38, 40n4
Iversen, Gunnar — 6

J

James, William — 166–167
Jameson, James T. — 198
Jasset, Victorin-Hippolyte — 268
Jeapes, William Cecil 'Billy' — 77
Jenkins, C. Francis — 296–297
Jenkins, Henry — 311
Johnson, Arthur — 44
Jones, Richard — 201

K

Kalmus, Herbert — 299
Kalulu — 50
Kandinsky, Wassily — 295–296
Kant, Immanuel — 302n29
Karagözoğlu, Şadi — 257

323

Karenne, Diana	30	Lichtwark, Alfred	169
Kaulbach, Hermann	282	Liesegang, Franz Paul	222–224
Keaton, Buster	245, 251	Lindau, Paul	273
Keedick, Lee	152–153	Linder, Max	46, 47n12
Keil, Charlie	13, 14	Lippard, Chris	259
Keith, B.F.	81	Lloyd, Harold	251
Kellum, Orlando	82	Loiperdinger, Martin	5, 10n1, 81–82, 280
Kember, Joe	101, 109	Lorraine, Harry	75n18
Kerschensteiner, Georg	170	Low, Rachael	71, 77–78, 82
Kessler, Frank	6, 9, 77, 237, 305, 307, 312	Lowell, Judge	39
Key, Ellen	170	Lumière, Auguste	78, 97–98
King Haakon	126	Lumière, Louis	58, 78, 97–98, 267–270
Kipp, Rudolf	169	Lützen, Jens	88
Kirby, Lynn	207		
Kirkwood, James	42	**M**	
Klee, Paul	82	Ma'luk, Yusuf	260
Kleine, George	245–246, 249	MacDonald, Farrell	40n4
Klimt, Gustav	26, 27	Mack, Hayward S.	40n4
Klippel, Heike	166, 168	Magnusson, Charles	134
Ko-Ko	50	Makowska, Elena	30
Köhler, Kristina	6–7	Maloney, Paul	106
Köpke, Carl	6, 124–130	Maltby, Richard	157
Köpke, Curt	126	Malthête-Méliès, Madeleine	267
Köpke, Erik	126	Mann, Nathanial D.	144
Köpke, Gertrud	126	Mannoni, Laurent	235n11
Kracauer, Siegfried	148	Manovich, Lev	294, 300
Krämer, Sybille	22	Marey, Étienne-Jules	204
Kräusslich, Paul	6, 124–130	Margherita, Queen (Margherita of Savoy)	26, 27
Kuhn, Annette	313n12	Marinetti, Filippo Tommaso	194–195, 197
Kuhn, Edmund	298	Marion, Frances	22
		Marishio	50
L		Marks, Laura U.	211
Lacasse, Germain	227	Marle, Clifford	69
Laemmle, Carl	38, 46	Marsh, Joss	10n3
Lange, Konrad	164, 169–170	Martin, Clyde	189
Larkin, Jim	194–195, 199	Marzen, Peter	89
Larkin, William	193–195, 198–201	Massay, A.C.	70
Larroumet, Gustave	228	Mathewson, Ernest	200–201
Lauder, Harry	79–82	Matthews, Shaller	203
Laurel, Stan	251, 260	Maud, Queen of Norway	126
Lavery, Philip	201	Maudsley, Henry	167
Lawrence, Florence	34, 68	Maurice, Clement	76
Layton, George	253	Mawson, Sir Douglas	6, 151–159
Le Sablais, Honoré	288–289	May, Edna	248
Leadbeater, C.W.	296	Mayer, David	67
Lecointe, Thierry	8	Mayol, Félix	84n19
Leilich, Peter	279	Mazar-Spyropoulos, Farida	145
Lemke, Hermann	164	McAllister, T.H.	291n20
Lenk, Sabine	6, 77	McCay, Winsor	48, 93, 147, 250–251
LeSaint, Edward J.	40n4	McDermott, Marc	72–73

Index of Names

McMahon, Alison	76–77
Mecham, William (see Tom Merry)	
Meertz, Xavier	151, 154
Mefoto	50
Méliès, Georges	42, 48, 119, 121–122, 147, 247, 267–270, 271n31
Ménard, Charles Armand (see Dranem)	
Mendel, Georges	271n31
Merry, Tom (William Mecham)	48–50, 52–55, 56n22
Messager, André	79
Meumann, Ernst	168
Michaels, Dan	80
Midkiff DeBauche, Leslie	5, 20n2, 46
Millen, Charles	201
Miller, Walter	45
Miner, Edward	248
Molteni, Alfred	227
Mongo, Abbé	219
Monks, Victoria	80
Monteverdi, Claudio Giovanni Antonio	27
Moore, Annabelle (née Whitford)	298
Moore, Owen	34, 38–39
Moran, D.P.	196–198
Moran, Percy	69–70, 75n18
Morrison, Jack	251
Moss, Robert	201
Mullens, Bernard Albert	115, 120–123
Mullens, Willem (Willy)	115, 119–123
Müller, Georg Elias	168
Munkácsy, Mihály	283, 286–287
Murch, Walter	76
Murnau, F.W.	311
Murphy, A.	201
Musser, Charles	104–105, 190, 226, 249, 274

N

Nadar, Paul	267
Natzén, Christopher	6
Neill, John	144
Nesbitt, Miriam	72–73
Newby, J.	106
Nicodemi, Giorgio	30
Nilsson, H.	135
Ninnis, Lt. Belgrave	151, 154
Nöggerath, Franz	120
Norton, Frederick	247
Núñez, Irela	308–310, 313n3, 313n23
Nuri, İbn-ür Refik Ahmet	255

O

O'Brien, Charles	5, 37
O'Brien, Judge	36
O'Rourke, Chris	5
Ohnet, Georges	28
Olsen, John Sigvard 'Ole'	127
Örzön, Nijat	256–257

P

Parchomenko, Laure	235n17
Paul, Robert	9, 52, 54, 78, 308
Pearson, Roberta	42, 46, 47n7
Perlmann, Emil	164
Perrault	231–232
Perrot, Victor	271n31
Perry, Clarence A.	175
Peterson, James	40n2
Peterson, Jennifer	6–7
Peterson, Numa	134
Pharoah, Mark	157
Picabia, Francis	295
Pickford, Lottie (Charlotte Smith)	39
Pickford, Mary (Gladys Smith)	5, 20n2, 34–40
Piercey, William Edgar (see Edgar Austin)	
Pike, Oliver	189
Polin	84n19
Pollock, Channing	250
Pope, Alvin E.	176, 181
Porter, Edwin S.	13, 14, 42, 144–145, 249–250
Powers, Tom	68
Praz, Mario	29
Price, Gertrude	14
Pyle, Howard	299

Q

Quinn, Michael	110

R

Rabinovitz, Lauren	203
Rajewsky, Irina	22
Randall, Bill	10n3
Rapée, Erno	189–190
Raphael, Sanzio da Urbino	282
Rauer, Philip	181
Read, A.J.	177
Redfern, Jasper	5, 95–103
Redi, Riccardo	57
Reni, Guido	285
Richardson, F.H.	68
Riche, Daniel	261n2

325

Ricketts, Tom	177	Smith, G.A.	2, 10n3
Ring, Blanche	80	Smith, Gladys (*see* Mary Pickford)	
Rivière, Henri	265	Smith, Harry B.	245, 295, 297–298
Robert, Valentine	8	Smith, Jacob	57
Robinson, David	83n4	Smith, Rachel	201
Rodowick, David	293	Snow, Marguerite	178
Rolf, Ernst	136	Sobchack, Vivian	211
Röntgen, Wilhelm Conrad	97	Solomon, Matthew	57, 252n8
Roosevelt, Theodore	249	Solter, H.L.	34
Rosenthal, Alfred	165	Sommariva, Emilio	22, 23–26, 28–32
Ross, Gary	293	Sparling, Frederick Arthur	193, 200–201
Rossell, Deac	96–97, 102	Spehr, Paul	3
Ruggeri, Ruggero	28	Sponsel, Wilfried	280
Russell, James	75n18	Stamp, Shelley	4
Ruttmann, Walter	295	Stern, Julius	40n4
Rydell, Robert W.	183	Stevens, Alfred	27
		Stevenson, Robert Louis	299
S		Sukurov, Alexander	293
Saarikko, Katie	157	Sullivan, Arthur	79
Sadoul, Georges	57, 269	Sylvani, Gladys	71
Sage, Russell	175		
Sainati, Augusto	57, 63	**T**	
Salis, Rodolphe	263–264, 266	Tabet, Frédéric	5
Salmon, W.	100–101	Tallone, Cesare	22, 23–32
Salt, Barry	42, 46	Tallone, Gigliola	26
Sandes, Daisy	200–201	Teltau, Hendrick	310, 313n3, 313n23
Santos, Amandino Videira	308	Tennyson, Alfred J.	106
Sapelli, Luigi (Caramba)	28, 32	Thomas, Frank D.	247, 253n17
Sardou, Victorien	28	Thorburn, David	311
Sargent, John Singer	27	Thornbury, Professor	48
Schmitt, Thomas	78, 84n28	Thorne, George	79
Schoenberg, Arnold	82	Tierney, Peter	201
Schröter, Jens	22, 32	Tissot, James	283
Schultze, Ernst	163–164, 169	Titian (Tiziano Vecelli)	27
Scognomillo, Giovanni	256, 261n11	Todd, Frank Morton	176–177, 179, 181, 183
Scriabin, Alexander	295–296	Toulmin, Vanessa	92, 102–103
Sebus, Gwen	238–239, 243	Touttain, Pierre-André	28
Selig, William Nicholas	149n9	Trewey, Félicien	267
Seligsberg, Walter	38	Trutat, Eugène	227–229, 264
Sellmann, Adolf	164, 168, 170	Tsivian, Yuri	204
Shackleton, Ernest	152	Turconi, Davide	294, 298
Shafik, Viola	260	Turner, Otis	144
Shail, Andrew	68	Turnour, Quentin	154, 157
Shay, William E.	40n4		
Simon, Charles	30	**U**	
Singer, Ben	110	Urban, Charles	54
Sirois Trahan, Jean-Pierre	46		
Slieker, Christian	120	**V**	
Smalley, Phillips	13, 14, 16, 17	Vaërting, Mathilde	168
Smith, Charlotte (*see* Lottie Pickford)		van Beusekom, Ansje	6, 88

Index of Names

van Dooren, Ine	88
Vasey, Ruth	157
Vecelli, Tiziano (*see* Titian)	
Velázquez, Diego	27
Vélez-Serna, María Antonia	5
Verdi, Giuseppe	79
Verdo, Hal	49
Verma, Neil	148n2
Veronese, Paolo	27
Vertov, Dziga	211
Victoria, Queen of England	98
Vogl-Bienek, Ludwig	7, 10n1
von Bismarck, Otto	56n22
von Kaulbach, Wilhelm	282
von Sybel, Alfred	168

W

Wagenaar, William	220
Wagner, Richard	148, 295
Wales, Prince of	79
Wales, Princess of	79
Waller, Gregory	6, 21n24, 147, 178, 184n11
Walsh, P.J.	201
Walsh, Peter	5
Walthall, Henry	45
Waltz, Gwendolyn	8, 67, 73, 148
Ward, Monte	36
Warren, Low	74
Warstatt, Willy	164
Washinton, George	13
Watson, Harry	246
Weber, Lois	4–5, 13–21
Weinberg, Sigmund	261n9
West, Alfred	71
Whistler, James McNeill	295
White, Chrissie	71
White, Pearl	68
Whitney Sr., John	295
Wiegand, Daniel	8
Wierzbicki, James	77, 82
Wilde, Oscar	26, 28, 32
Willat, Carl A.	35, 37, 40n4
Williamson, James	2, 10n3, 281n17
Williamson, W.A.	107
Willis, Artemis	6
Winthrop Sargent, Epes	15
Wolgast, Heinrich	163, 169, 171n2
Wood, Frank	37-38
Wunsch, A. David	148n2
Wynn, Ed	250

Y

Youngston, W.C.	250
Yumibe, Joshua	8-9, 112, 146, 187-188, 191

Z

Zecca, Ferdinand	127
Ziegfeld, Florenz	245, 247, 250-251
Zink, Adolph	247-248, 250, 252n8
Zobu, Vasfi Riza	261n1
Zumthor, Paul	234

327